Field Guide to Project Management

DAVID I. CLELAND, Editor

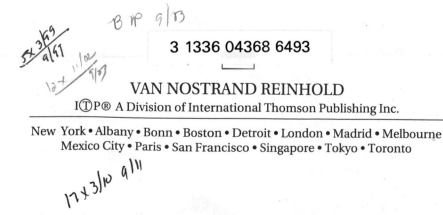

VAN NOSTRAND REINHOLD

I(T)P® A Division of International Thomson Publishing Inc.

New York • Albany • Bonn • Boston • Detroit • London • Madrid • Melbourne
Mexico City • Paris • San Francisco • Singapore • Tokyo • Toronto

I(T)P ® International Thomson Publishing Company.
The ITP logo is a registered trademark used herein under
license.

The ideas presented in this book are generic and strategic. Their specific application to a particular company must be the responsibility of the management of that company, based on management's understanding of their company's procedures, culture, resources, and competitive
situation.

Printed in the United States of America.

Visit us on the Web   www.vnr.com

For more information contact:

Van Nostrand Reinhold
115 Fifth Avenue
New York, NY 10003

Chapman & Hall GmbH
Pappalallcc 3
69469 Weinham
Germany

Chapman & Hall
2-6 Boundary Row
London SEI 8HN
United Kingdom

International Thomson Publishing Asia
60 Albert Street #15-01
Albert Complex
Singapore 189969

Thomas Nelson Australia
102 Dodds Street
South Melbourne 3205
Victoria, Australia

International Thomson Publishing Japan
Hirakawa-cho Kyowa Building, 3F
2-2-1 Hirakawa-cho, Chiyoda-ku
Tokyo 102 Japan

Nelson Canada
1120 Birchmount Road
Scarbourough, Ontario
MIK 5G4, Canada 11560

International Thomson Editores
Senncca, 53
Colonia Polanco
Mexico D.F. Mexico

1 2 3 4 5 6 7 8 9 10 QUEBP 01 00 99 98 97

Library of Congress Cataloging-in-Publication Data

Field guide to project management / David I. Cleland, editor.
        p.   cm.
    Includes bibliographical references and index.
    ISBN 0-442-02345-6 (flexibind)
        1. Industrial project management.   I. Cleland, David I.
    HD69.P75F54   1997   97-14585
    658.4'08—dc21   CIP

Contents

Acknowledgments

This book, like any literary initiative, required the cooperative effort of many people. The authors who provided the chapters are the real contributors: an assemblage of experts in the discipline of project management. Their contributions reflect a wide expanse of competency and viewpoints on this growing field of management. I thank and am deeply indebted to these chapter authors.

I thank my students and my consulting clients who provided both the motivation and the preliminary strategy for this field guide. These people all contributed in some way to the design, development, and publication of this "first of its kind" practical field guidebook.

I continue to be deeply indebted to Claire Zubritzky, who managed the overall development and administration of this guidebook. Her professionalism and dedication played a major role in the successful creation of this guidebook.

Special thanks to Dr. Harvey W. Wolfe, Chairman of the Industrial Engineering Department, and Dr. Gerald D. Holder, Dean of the School of Engineering of the University of Pittsburgh, who provided the resources and the environment to pursue the successful creation of this guidebook.

My thanks to my wife and children, who again tolerated my absences from family gatherings while I worked on another book.

Finally, I hope that the people who use this guidebook will find it a useful and timely source for the enhancement of their knowledge, skills, and attitudes in managing projects in their respective competitive worlds.

Dr. David I. Cleland
Ernest E. Roth Professor and
Professor of Engineering Management
Pittsburgh, Pennsylvania

Project Management

Strategic Planning

David I. Cleland

Biographical Sketch. . . | **David I. Cleland, Ph.D.,** is currently the Ernest E. Roth Professor and Professor of Engineering Management in the School of Engineering at the University of Pittsburgh. He is the author/editor of twenty-six books in the fields of project management, engineering management, and manufacturing management. He has served as a consultant for both national and foreign companies and has been honored for his original and continuing contributions to his disciplines.

Projects are the building blocks in the design and execution of strategies for an enterprise. Projects provide an organizational focus for conceptualizing, designing, and creating new or improved products and services. Failure to create and maintain a portfolio of projects in the strategic management of an enterprise means the decline and ultimate failure of that enterprise. The successful enterprise maintains a portfolio of projects centered around improved and new products and services.

The changes enterprises face today have no precedent. Companies must keep up with legal, social, economic, and technological changes as well as changes brought about by competitors' advances and new needs of customers. The enterprise must offer extraordinary modifications in products and services to ensure survival in the competitive marketplace.

Senior managers, who have the most direct responsibility for the future of the enterprise, must develop the ability to assess opportunities, evaluate risk and uncertainty, and make informed decisions concerning which strategies and projects best prepare the enterprise for its future.

In a successful enterprise, the portfolio of projects is under constant change. Some projects are preliminary ideas, some are under development, and some are nearing completion to join the inventory of products and services maintained by the enterprise as well as to provide supporting organizational processes such as manufacturing, engineering, and marketing. As the preliminary project ideas are evaluated, some will survive and undergo development; others will fall by the wayside.

Why Projects Fail

A project may fail for reasons such as the following.

- The enterprise lacked suitable resources to support the project.
- Development costs are too high.
- Development falls too far behind what competitors are offering.
- The market changes too quickly.
- Technology needed to support the project is not developed.
- The project does not fit with the strategic direction of the enterprise.

Senior managers must maintain surveillance over the portfolio of projects, develop insight into the probable success or failure of individual projects, and determine whether projects support the strategic purposes of the enterprise.

Project Evaluation Checklist

As senior managers maintain surveillance over the project portfolio, answers to the following questions need to be sought:

- Are the project results innovative and effective?
- Do the project results reflect state-of-the-art technology?
- Does the cost of the resources used on the project permit the company to competitively price the results?
- Are there customers for the expected project results?
- How do the project results compare with identified customer needs?
- What unique customer attributes and benefits will the project results provide?
- How do these unique attributes and benefits compare to what the competitor is likely to provide?
- What distinct advantage will the project results provide to the customer?
- Do the project results reflect the unique strengths and capabilities of the enterprise?
- What specific need in the enterprise will the project results satisfy?
- Does the enterprise have the resources—both human and nonhuman—to develop, produce, and market the project results?
- What is the probability that the project results can be successfully achieved in time to support organizational strategic purposes?
- Will the project results provide a suitable return on investment for the enterprise?
- Will the project results have a strategic fit in the future purposes of the enterprise?

Senior managers can use this checklist to gather data that will sharpen their insight into which projects are the most promising, which are likely to survive, and which projects might best be terminated. As senior managers conduct their regular review of the ongoing projects and deal with the issues likely to arise in seeking answers to questions in the checklist, an important message will be sent throughout the enterprise: Projects are important in the design and execution of competitive strategies in this organization.

Performance Standards

An organization can employ performance standards to determine how its resources are being used.[1] (Key strategic performance standards are listed in Figure 1-1.)

Vision: A Picture of the Future

A vision for the enterprise sets the stage for performance standards and all that follows. A vision, according to Jonathan Swift, is the art of seeing things that are invisible to others. Senior managers with foresight, competence, and

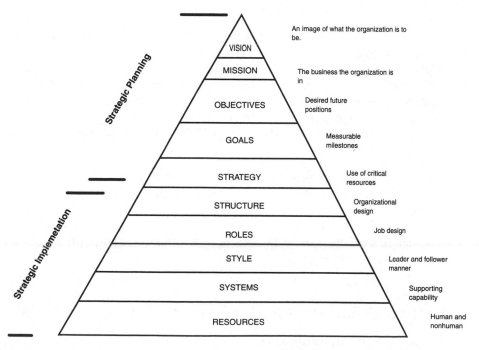

Figure 1-1   The strategic context of organizational planning

discernment have the opportunity to develop a vision for the strategic direction of the enterprise along with its supporting projects.

A vision is in a sense a dream of what the future should be for the enterprise—the general direction in which the enterprise should travel to be what the organizational leaders want it to be. The expressions of vision by senior managers at the organizations below offers insight into how such visions provide a dream of what the future of those organizations should be:

- "A corporation that will look gigantic but have the dynamics of little teams" (Motorola, Inc.).
- "PP&L will be the energy supplier of choice" (Pennsylvania Power & Light Company).
- "A vision for growth based on critical mass in large product categories, geographic diversity, brand leadership, and marketing innovation" (H. J. Heinz Company).

How important is it for an organization to have a vision? One study that benchmarked the performance of business teams found compelling evidence on the importance of a vision for high-performance project teams. Team members stated that it was the most important factor for high performance.[2]

Mission: A Strategic Purpose

The mission statement declares what business the organization is in. It is a broad declaration of the overall strategic purpose toward which all organizational resources are directed and committed (see Figure 1–1). An organization's mission is the final strategic performance standard for the enterprise. All organizational activities have to be judged on how well individual activities ultimately contribute to the mission.

Some examples of mission statements by contemporary organizations include the following:

- "To be the number one aerospace company in the world and among the premier industrial concerns in terms of quality, profitability, and growth" (The Boeing Company).
- "Our mission is to develop, manufacture, market, and sell and distribute a broad line of high quality generic drug products at competitive prices" (Marsam Pharmaceuticals Inc.).

Objectives: What Must Be Achieved

Organizational objectives pinpoint what must be achieved to ensure the accomplishment of the mission. These objectives are usually stated in quantitative or qualitative terms, or in a combination of both. Examples of objectives are the following:

- "Providing customers with quality goods, and making the goods available when and where customers want them" (Wal-Mart).
- "Meeting or exceeding the state-of-the-art of competitors in machining capability" (Machine tool builder).

Attaining objectives provides strong evidence that progress is being made toward accomplishing the organizational mission. An organization's goals provide milestones for evaluating whether that organization reached its objectives.

Goals: Measurable Milestones

Goals are milestones in meeting organizational objectives. Projects are the building blocks for accomplishing those goals. For example, an auto-parts manufacturer established a goal for the enterprise to "conceptualize, design, build, and put in operation an automated factory on a green-field site by December 31, 1995." Another example of a goal, by an electronics company, includes, "attaining financial performance capability of fifteen percent return on investment by the end of 1992."

An example of how a project team attained a goal is provided by Fiat in Italy. In the agricultural region of Basilicata in southern Italy, the auto maker used project teams to design, build, and open a $2.9 billion plant designed to eliminate traditional, inefficient work practices. A major $64 million program was launched to train workers and engineers to operate in independent, multiskilled project teams. Factory workers and office staff worked together under the same roof. Top-down decision-making was eliminated so that problems and opportunities were explored by teams actually working on specific problems in areas such as manufacturing, purchasing, marketing, or customer service.[3]

In the strategic management of an enterprise, executives find the concept of objectives easy to accept. However, when dealing with a time-sensitive goal, many executives are uncomfortable making a commitment. Failure to reach a goal could be the basis for criticism or an unfavorable performance rating. Nevertheless, goals can provide effective criteria to measure progress in the strategic management of an enterprise. Goals attainment also tests whether the strategy for the organization is working.

If a project lags behind schedule, accumulates overrun costs, or is unlikely to attain its expected results, then the goal of the enterprise will be impaired.

Strategy: Use of Critical Resources

A strategy uses critical resources to reach goals and to accomplish the mission. The following are used in the design and execution of strategies: plans, policies, procedures, resource-allocation schemas, organizational design, motivational techniques, leadership processes, evaluation and control systems, and project teams. To implement strategies, teams use benchmarks, new product and service development, facilities and equipment construction, procurement techniques, recapitalization, and information systems.

Some examples of strategies used by organizations include the following:

- "Concentrating on improved earnings from Kodak's core photography business and building a future with digital technologies such as all-electronic cameras, thermal printers, and image-storage devices" (Kodak Company). The CEO of Kodak, George Fisher, has formed ten project teams to examine such strategic issues in the company as research and development productivity, and cycle-time improvement.
- "Develop an interlocking computer/information support system augmented by a private satellite-communication system to video link connecting all stores, distribution centers, truck fleets, and corporate headquarters" (Wal-Mart).

Structure and Organizational Design: The Best Use of People

Survival and growth must be deliberate and planned, not serendipitous. How human resources are aligned is critical.

Corporate America is implementing many changes that affect the use of human resources. These changes include reduction of staff, new boundaries for individual jobs, employee empowerment, closer relationships with suppliers and customers, improved information systems, better telecommunications capabilities, new organizational structures, and globalization of products and services.

Another innovation, organizing around project teams, has had a noted impact on the success of companies. For example, *Fortune* magazine reports, "The ability to organize employees in innovative and flexible ways and the enthusiasm with which so many American companies have deployed self-managing teams is why U.S. industry is looking so competitive."[4]

As project teams evaluate new technologies and resources, they gain insight into the need for making changes. Projects provide a central point where new knowledge, skills, and attitudes can be developed.

Project Defined

A project is any undertaking that has a defined objective, a cost parameter, and a time element for its development. Sometimes a project is defined as a cluster of activities that are pulled together to deliver something of value to a customer. The use of a project to define the cluster of activities needed to develop a new product or service has particular appeal, because a key characteristic of a project is the creation of something that does not currently exist but is needed to create something of value for the enterprise—a new product, service, or organizational process.

A project is a miniature of the complete organization composed of team members from different disciplines of the enterprise, including customer representatives and suppliers. In some cases, representatives from unions, the local community, and other interested and relevant stakeholders may be team members. Project teams provide for the integration of the disciplines, technologies, and resources needed to take a project from concept through to delivery of the results to the customer. Through the workings of the project team, an ongoing test of the use of resources, management systems, strategies, and values of the whole enterprise are studied and pulled together.

Why Projects Benefit Organizational Design

Some of the advantages projects provide in preparing the enterprise for its future include the following:

- An organizational and stakeholder focal point for integrating the resources required to bring to pass something for the enterprise that does not currently exist.
- A strategic pathway element for the commitment of people and resources dedicated to creating value in future products and processes.
- A learning opportunity for the development of knowledge, skills, and attitudes needed to support future enterprise purposes.
- A model through which progress can be measured in positioning the enterprise for its future.

Teams can reduce the number of management layers. In some situations, an organization can be rebuilt around tasks. This reorganization makes information available on a much broader scale than under traditional organizational designs. Traditional management levels, according to Peter Drucker, manage nothing. Instead, they merely amplify faint signals coming from the top and the bottom of the infrastructure. Drucker points out that every relay doubles the noise and cuts the message in half. According to Drucker, most management levels neither manage nor make decisions—they serve only as relays. In the future, Drucker believes that few businesses will have more than two or three layers.[5]

Roles: Job Design

No longer can individuals perform their work without giving thought to how they are expected to work with other people, many of whom can be outside of their local organizational environment. Organizations fail or succeed because members of the organization fail or succeed in their work. If people are unclear about what is expected of them, the chances for difficulties or even failure exist. In cases where employees have control, authority, and responsibility to do their jobs, employees' roles must be specific. People will do a good job if they know what is expected of them and receive feedback on how well they are doing their jobs.

Management Style

The most important variable in the strategic management of an enterprise is the leadership, which develops a vision, marshals resources, and provides direction for the organization. Style has to do with the overall excellence, appearance, skill, and grace in performing the leadership role. A manager's style can be autocratic, dictatorial, democratic, participative, empathetic, caustic, friendly, or abusive. Followers tend to unknowingly emulate the manager's style. Some examples of leadership style today follow:

- "People at Goodyear headquarters say that CEO Stanley Gault's presence 'permeates' the corporate headquarters. . . . He is perceived as seldom giving orders, but everyone knows what he wants done. . . . He runs the company based on trust."[6]
- At Siemens Company in Germany, "the management style is tailored to Germany's consensus-style corporate culture. . . . Rigid hierarchy is out and an entrepreneurial drive is in."[7]
- At the Levi Strauss Company, efforts are underway to have all employees feel as if they are an integral part of the making and selling of blue jeans. Strategies to develop an "Aspiration Statement" will help create a company culture in which employee empowerment becomes a reality and a competitive tool. Employees are evaluated by their superiors, subordinates, and peers. This evaluation process is not always pleasant. The use of project teams to help solve production problems and to assume responsibility for the complete assembly of products has reduced cycle time from seven days to three. Under the team system at the company, a worker's incentive pay is tied to team performance.[8]

Systems and Resources: Project Support

The systems and resources that support the organization, such as software, hardware, accounting, information, marketing, production, and design, also support ongoing projects. The technology offered by computer and information systems has changed the traditional role of managers and other employees. Technicians are becoming core employees. According to the Bureau of Labor Statistics forecasts, one of every four new jobs is going to a technical worker. Technicians are gaining new importance because of increasingly powerful, versatile, and user-friendly technologies. As companies become more dependent on these technicians, cultural support is required to keep them productive and satisfied with their work environment.

Key Elements of Project Management

Several important elements are found in the project-management system. They include the following:

- *Matrix.* A matrix organization establishes the formal authority and responsibility patterns and reporting relationships among the general managers, the project manager, the project team members, the functional managers, and other key stakeholders of the project. In Chapter 14, the matrix organization is presented in detail.
- *Project planning.* This begins with a work-breakdown structure (WBS) that shows how the total project is broken down into its component parts. In Chapter 7 the development of a WBS is presented, and in Chapter 6 project life-cycle planning techniques and processes are described.
- *Information systems.* These systems may be informal or may involve the use of formal retrieval programs to determine the status of the project. Information provides those involved with a project the ability to plan, organize, and control the use of resources on the project. Project managers—and other key stakeholders—need information to determine the status of the project and to make informed decisions on how to plan and implement the use of resources on the project. Chapter 23 describes a project-management information system.
- *Project-control system.* The most basic standards include project cost, schedule, and technical performance. By comparing planned progress with actual performance, project managers can determine the need for corrective action. Because projects are linked to the goals of the enterprise, knowing the status of projects gives extraordinary insight into how well or how poorly progress is being made to attain enterprise goals. Project monitoring, evaluation, and control means are described in Chapter 24.
- *Cultural ambience.* The emotional patterns of the social groups, their perceptions, attitudes, prejudices, assumptions, experiences, and values, all go to develop the project and cultural ambience of the enterprise. This ambiance influences how people act and react, how they think and feel, and what they say and do concerning the project and the enterprise. There are no organizations without people—and project organizations are no exception. This field guide stresses the need to be aware of people issues when managing projects. In particular, chapters in Section III Project Leadership and in Section V (Team Management) emphasize people issues.

Throughout this book, the key topics involved in the management of projects will be identified and described to provide guidance to those people associated with the use of projects in the enterprise. These topics are presented in the spirit of practical guides for those stakeholders associated with the management of projects in the enterprise's strategy.

ENDNOTES

1 Material on the strategic performance standards is stated in a somewhat different context in my book, *Project Management—Strategic Design and Implementation*, New York: McGraw-Hill Book Company, 1994. In addition, I have drawn additional material from my book, *The Strategic Management of Teams*, New York: John Wiley & Sons, 1996

2 Carl Larson and Frank LaFasto. *What Must Go Right/What Can Go Wrong*, Newbury Park, CA: Sage, 1989

3 Jane A. Sasseen, Robert Neff, Shekar Hattangadi, Silvia Sansoni, and bureau reports. The winds of change blow everywhere. *Business Week*, Special Report, October 17, 1994, p. 92

4 Rahul Jacob. Corporate reputations. *Fortune*, March 6, 1995, pp. 54–64

5 Peter Drucker. Infoliteracy. *Forbes ASAP*, August 29, 1994, pp. 105–109

6 Peter Nulty. The bounce is back at Goodyear. *Fortune*, June 29, 1992, pp. 76–79

7 Gail E. Schares, et al. The new generation at Siemens. *Business Week*, March 9, 1992, pp. 34–39

8 Russell Mitchell and Michael O'Neal. Managing by values. *Business Week*, August 1, 1994, pp. 46–52

BIBLIOGRAPHY

Archibald, R. D. Projects: Vehicles for strategic growth. *Project Management Journal* September 1988, pp. 31–34

Cleland, David I. Defining a project management system. *Project Management Quarterly* 10:37–40, 1977

Cleland, David I. *Project Management: Strategic Design and Implementation*, 2nd Edition. New York: McGraw-Hill Inc., 1994

Freeman, R. E. *Strategic Management—A Stakeholder Approach*. Boston: Pitman, 1984

Gulliver, Frank R. Post-project appraisals pay. *Harvard Business Review* March–April 1987, pp. 128–132

Thamhain, Hans J. *Engineering Program Management*. New York: John Wiley & Sons, Inc., 1984

Chapter

2

The Elements of Project Success*

Jeffrey K. Pinto

Biographical Sketch . . .

Jeffrey K. Pinto, Ph.D., is Associate Professor of Management in the School of Business Administration at Pennsylvania State University, Erie. For the past six years, Dr. Pinto has served as Editor of the *Project Management Journal*, the scholarly journal of the Project Management Institute, the largest professional project-management organization in the world. He has published five books and over seventy-five research articles on a variety of topics, including project management, information-systems introduction, innovation and change, leadership, and learning theory. His most recent book, *What Made Gertie Gallop? Lessons From Project Failures* was published in 1996 by Van Nostrand Reinhold.

The process of developing a method for analyzing and predicting the likelihood of success or failure of an ongoing project is by no means a simple one. There are a number of reasons why this process presents a challenge: One obvious reason is that words like "success" and "failure," like beauty, are often in the eye of the beholder. Put another way, until we can establish a set of criteria that have some generally accepted basis for assessing projects, then at best we run the risk of mislabeling as failures projects that may, in fact, be successes. A second problem with accurately predicting project outcomes lies in the often incomplete nature of the data itself. Many times a project's development is surrounded by a great deal of ambiguous and even contradictory data that makes midstream assessments problematic. Project assessment may be influenced by individuals having biases for or against the project. The subjective nature of project assessment makes it difficult to

---

*Portions of this chapter were adapted from *Successful Information System Implementation: The Human Side*, by Jeffrey K. Pinto, PMI Publications (1994) and *Successful Project Managers*, by Jeffrey K. Pinto and O.P. Kharbanda, Van Nostrand Reinhold (1995).

develop objective measures that offer a reasonably reliable method for judging project outcomes. To address some of these issues, this chapter provides a field reference for project managers to use in tracking the status of their projects.

The Unique Setting of Project Management

Almost all innovative new products developed within companies are created by using project-management techniques. Because projects play such an increasingly significant role in organizational profitability, it is vital to have an understanding of their unique properties.

Project managers' careers often hinge on their ability to deliver the goods in the form of successfully completed projects. Consequently, in the absence of disaster (e.g., structural collapse in construction or banned or abandoned pharmaceutical development), it seems that for every detractor of a specific completed project there is often a champion singing its praises.

Project success is not always as clear-cut as we would sometimes believe. Any one of a number of confounding issues can cloud our ability to view a project's outcome in an objective light. For example, the point in time when a project is evaluated can make a very real difference in its evaluation. Likewise, egos and personal agendas of top managers in a company can serve to obscure the true outcome of a project, because these powerful individuals seek to protect themselves and their turf from the side effects of bumpy projects.

It is often the case that while successful projects are trumpeted throughout the organization and publicized externally, the majority of project failures are quietly swept under the carpet. People naturally tend to promote the positive. If this is not possible, they adopt a simple philosophy: out of sight, out of mind. The irony, of course, is that all organizations experience project failure far more often than rousing success. Consider, for example, the results of a recent study by Peat Marwick of 300 large companies attempting to implement computer software development projects. Fully sixty-five percent of the organizations reported experiences where their projects were grossly over budget, far behind schedule, or the technology was nonperforming. In some cases, the companies experienced all these factors. Perhaps more impressively, over half of these firms considered this state as "normal" or "of no concern."

A working definition of project success may help to clear up the confusion about what success is. In the old days, project managers commonly made use of a concept known as the "triple constraint" to evaluate a project at completion. This triple constraint offered a three-legged stool as a metaphor for a project's viability. The three constraints were:

1. *Time:*   The project had to come in on or under its initially scheduled time frame.
2. *Money:*   The project had to be completed within its budget limits.
3. *Performance:*   The end result had to perform in the manner that was intended.

Seen in this light, it was relatively easy to make some initial value judgments about a project. Project control consisted of tracking these milestones of any particular project. One had only to consult the project's timeline to assess schedule constancy, review the cost accountant's report to determine budget adherence, and see if the project worked.

Although simple, the triple constraint does not work in the modern business world. In an era of tremendous competition and enhanced concern for customers, the triple constraint has become a dangerously out-of-date convention. In considering the three components of the triple constraint, it is clear that the primary thrust of each of these measures is internal; that is, each measure is intended to satisfy some interest group internal to the organization rather than in the outside environment. For example, satisfying time and budget considerations is often the concern of cost accountants who must keep costs down. Likewise, the performance criterion has often been seen as primarily an engineering concern for making a product that works.

Historically, what was lost in the confusion was any real concern for the customer, that is, the desire to satisfy the concerns of the client for whom the project was intended. Within many companies, a fundamental conceit emerged in the assumption that once a project was completed, the public would be offered a fait accompli that they would naturally buy or use. The underlying theme of this position seemed to be an arrogant assertion: *Don't tell us what you need. Trust us to know what you want.* The result of such attitudes was predictable: Customers went increasingly to companies whose projects and products reflected a concern for the customer, as illustrated by the phenomenal success of the Ford Taurus.

The new rules governing global business require that project management adopt a new standard by which future success will be measured: the so-called quadruple constraint. The additional feature of the quadruple constraint requires us to include *customer satisfaction* as one of the pillars of project success. Customer satisfaction refers to the idea that a project is only successful to the extent that it satisfies the needs of its intended user. This addition has tremendous implications for the way companies manage projects and the manner in which the success or failure of both past and future projects will be assessed. With the inclusion of customer satisfaction as a fourth constraint, project managers must now devote additional time and attention to maintaining close ties with and satisfying the demands of external clients.

In effect, project managers must now become not only managers of project activities, but sales representatives for the company to the client base. The product they have to sell is their project. Therefore, if they are to facilitate acceptance of the project and, hence, its success, they have to learn how to engage in these marketing duties effectively.

Assessing Success over Time

One of the truly difficult tasks confronting any project manager lies in making reasonable and accurate assessments of a project's viability early in its development. Part of the problem lies in the fact that many projects do not proceed in a perfectly linear fashion from start to finish. In other words, it is an error to assume that a project's progress can be tracked according to a well-understood path, particularly if that project represents a unique technical challenge or employs features that company has never dealt with before. The perfect world follows a linear development path; that is, when fifty percent of the project's resources are expended, one expects the project to be fifty percent completed and so on.

The true project activity line often follows a far different path. For example, it is not atypical to find that far into the project (from an expense and time point of view), little actual progress has been made. In fact, when fifty percent of the resources have been spent or the schedule has elapsed, it is not uncommon to find less than twenty percent of the activities completed. Such a progress sequence presents a true test of nerves and savvy for many project managers. The natural response to such a state is either to panic and find scapegoats who can be removed from the team, or to throw additional resources at the project in the hope of "buying" progress. Either approach, though understandable, is almost always counterproductive.

In his landmark book, *The Mythical Man-Month*, Frederick Brooks[1] describes the sequence of events leading to the development of IBM's 360 operating system in the mid-1960s, a project for which he was responsible. He discovered a fascinating effect caused by belatedly adding additional resources to ongoing, late activities. Additional personnel simply caused the project to slip further behind schedule. Rather than make up for lost time, the net effect was to delay the project even more.

According to Brooks, all project activities are subject to delays caused by the learning curve. The rapid ramp-up in progress that occurs near the activity's completion date is a result of the initial learning that had to take place prior to adequately performing the necessary tasks. Assume that the team has just completed this activity, using the learning-curve model. If the same personnel were then asked to immediately replicate the process with a new project, in all likelihood their progress line would much more closely match the linear, perfect-world path. Why? Because they have now charted this activity sequence and learned the appropriate lessons. Hence, any new activities would simply involve replicating the old sequence, with the learning curve completed.

The underlying point that project managers need to understand is that projects, which usually involve new or untried technologies or development processes, require a natural learning curve as part of the implementation process. As a result, when attempting to assess the viability of a project and make a reasonably accurate determination of the likelihood of its successful completion, project managers must first acknowledge that they are operating in uncharted territory filled with misleading and even contradictory indicators. This point should be kept in mind when facing the decision of whether to terminate a project that is over budget or behind schedule.

The decision of whether to terminate a project is never easy. We may be making such decisions on the basis of misleading indicators. A recent study of research and development (R&D) projects sheds some important light on the termination decision, arguing that many times the seeds of future disaster are sown early in the project's development. The difficulties do not typically stem from technical problems, but from decisions and assumptions of the top-management team. The study measured a number of factors that, it could be argued, help or hinder a project's development, including the priority assigned to the project, the viability of its commercial objectives, and the authority given to team members and the project manager. The study findings are intriguing: Within the first six months of an R&D project's existence, there are often clear signs that the project may be a good candidate for termination. For example, the research suggests that terminated projects "were seen by their team members to have a low probability of achieving commercial objectives, did not have team members with sufficient authority, were targeted at fairly stable markets, were given low priority by R&D management, but were managed efficiently and were receiving valuable information from a business gatekeeper."[2]

The final two points are particularly important: Unsuccessful projects may end up that way regardless of the efficiency with which the actual development process is managed. The best management in the world cannot obviate the other determinants of project success or failure. Likewise, even having someone in top management consistently providing valuable information is not, in itself, sufficient to ensure that a project will succeed.

Another frequent error many organizations slip into when assessing the performance of their project development is to make inadequate allowances for the impact of time on a project's viability.

EXAMPLE.   A company was determining the success of a recently completed hardware computer-development project. Based on internal cost-accounting data, the project looked good: It had come in on time and only slightly over budget. Further, the hardware performed as it was intended to perform. As a result, the project manager was given a performance bonus and a reassignment as a reward for a job well done. Unfortunately, the story does not end there. The project, although internally efficient, was a disaster in the marketplace from its first introduction. The technology that the company had assumed would be adequate turned out to be so user-unfriendly that the product was withdrawn within nine months.

This story illustrates a number of the problems faced in making judgments about projects as either successes or failures. First, it was clear that from the company's point of view, this project was not seen as a failure at all; in fact, just the opposite was the case. The second problem had to do with the incomplete picture of project expectations that top management painted. Obviously, client satisfaction was never held up as a concern of the project manager, who naturally devoted his time to the measures that *did* matter for his performance appraisal: schedule, budget, and performance. Third, the story demonstrates a subtler point: It is important, in the absence of full information, to refrain from assuming that a project is a success or failure too early in its life, before the final returns have had an opportunity to come in.

This conclusion suggests that many projects deemed successes are, in fact, failures. The reverse, however, is also true: Many projects that give every evidence of being instant failures may actually demonstrate themselves to be long-term successes.

EXAMPLE. One example that comes immediately to mind is the well-known English Channel tunnel project, known simply as the Eurotunnel, or "Chunnel." Opening in 1994, nearly eighteen months behind schedule, the Chunnel project was originally budgeted for £7.5 billion. The final bill, at £15 billion, was twice the initial projection. From an internal auditing perspective, the Chunnel represented a financial nightmare, particularly in light of news that it defaulted on the bond financing made by the initial investors in the venture. Nevertheless, looking at the project's long-term potential, one must admit that its contribution to society may be significant. In effect, the judgment of project success or failure is in the hands of future generations.

This case illustrates the importance of balancing immediate assessment against long-term project viability. Clearly, there are definite benefits involved in waiting until after the project has been completed and is introduced to its intended clients before assessing the success and impact of the system. On the other hand, one must be careful in not prolonging a project that probably won't be a success in the market.

Almost every researcher who has studied the impact of internal and external factors on project outcomes has concluded that it is the human, rather than the technical, factors that are the primary determinant of whether a project will succeed.[3] Although no one will deny that computers, scheduling, and budget models are important elements in controlling a project, the research suggests that the larger, *managerial* issues are typically the key determinants of a project's likelihood of success. Project management has always been, and remains, a people-management challenge first and foremost.

A Ten-Factor Success Model

A study of critical success factors (CSFs) in the project implementation process looked at over 400 projects varying greatly in terms of the basic characteristics.[4] A wide range of representative samples included R&D projects, construction projects, and information-system projects. Their study validated the following model of CSFs for project implementation.

PROJECT MISSION
Most people intuitively understand the importance of conducting a feasibility study prior to project kickoff. Further, it is vital that project managers answer some fundamental questions not only at the start of a new project, but throughout its development. The following are two key questions: Are the goals clear to me and the rest of the organization? Are the goals of the project in line with the general goals of the organization?

TOP-MANAGEMENT SUPPORT

Management support is extremely important for the success of any new project. Project managers not only depend on top management for direction and authority in running their projects, they rely on them as a safety valve as well. That is, when the project is undergoing difficulties, it is vital that top management be aware of the problems and be willing to offer necessary additional aid or resources for the project manager and team. Top management's support of the project may also consist of the project manager's confidence in their support in the event of crisis.

PROJECT PLANS AND SCHEDULES

Project planning refers to the importance of creating a detailed outline of the required stages in the implementation process, including work breakdown, resource scheduling, and activity sequencing. Scheduling, on the other hand, is generally understood to refer to the tasks of creating specific time and task interdependent structures, such as Critical Path and Gantt charts. The schedule should include a satisfactory measurement system as a way of judging actual performance against budget and time allowances. Project managers need to identify the important personnel skills required for successful project completion and make contingency plans in case the project is off schedule.

CLIENT CONSULTATION

The client is anyone who will ultimately use the final project, as either a customer outside the company or a department within the organization. The degree to which clients are personally involved in the implementation process will cause great variation in their support for that project. It is, therefore, important to determine whether clients for the project have been identified. Once project managers are aware of the major clients, they are better able to determine accurately if their needs are being met.

PERSONNEL

In many situations, personnel for the project team are chosen with less-than-full regard for the skills necessary to actively contribute to implementation success. Project managers need to recruit, select, and train members of the project team so they have the requisite skills and commitment to perform their functions. Team members need to be committed to the project's success and understand the lines of authority.

TECHNICAL TASKS

Companies have to ask themselves if they have the necessary technology and training to support project development. The decision to initiate a new project must be predicated on the organization's ability to staff the team with competent individuals and to provide the technical means for the project to succeed.

CLIENT ACCEPTANCE

This refers to the final stage in the implementation process, at which time the overall efficacy of the project is to be determined. Too often project managers make the mistake of believing that if they handle the other stages of the implementation process well, the client will simply accept the resulting system. In fact, client acceptance is a stage in project implementation that must be managed like any other. Project managers must be prepared to sell the project to clients.

MONITORING AND FEEDBACK

At each stage of project implementation, key personnel should receive feedback on how the project is comparing to initial projections. Within many organizations experienced in running projects, there is little general agreement on how to track projects, what features to track, and how to report this data. However, making allowances for adequate monitoring and feedback mechanisms gives the project manager the ability to anticipate problems, oversee corrective measures, and ensure that no deficiencies are overlooked.

COMMUNICATION

The need for adequate communication channels is extremely important in creating an atmosphere for successful system implementation. Communication is essential within the project team, between the team and the rest of the organization, and with the clients. Typical communication involves issues such as the project's capabilities, the goals of the implementation process, changes in policies and procedures, and status reports.

TROUBLESHOOTING

Problem areas exist in almost every project-implementation effort. The measure of a successful project-implementation effort is not how well problems are avoided, but knowing the correct steps to take once problems develop. Regardless of how carefully the implementation effort is initially planned, it is impossible to foresee every problem that could possibly arise. As a result, it is important that the project manager make adequate initial arrangements for troubleshooting mechanisms to be included in the implementation plan. Such mechanisms would make it easier to react to problems and forestall potential problem areas in the implementation process. Project managers should spend a part of each day looking for problems that have just begun or that have the potential to begin.

Finding a Balance

The client is the ultimate arbiter of successful project implementation, not the project manager. However, overemphasis on client concerns and sacrificing internal constraints such as budgets, schedules, and performance, is not the answer either. What is required is a balance that allows one to correctly prioritize activities while ensuring that the project is not done in by a factor that could have been controlled but was not addressed. If such a balance is achieved, it will go far toward creating an atmosphere in which project priorities are well-understood and serve as guideposts to reduce the manageable reasons for projects to fail.

ENDNOTES

1 Brooks, F. P. *The Mythical Man-Month: Essays in Software Engineering*, Third Edition. Reading, MA: Addison-Wesley, 1995

2 Green, S. G. Green, M. A. Welsh, and G.E. Dehler. Red flags at dawn, or predicting R&D project termination at start-up. *Research-Technology Management* 36(3):10–12, 1993

3 Baker, B. N., P. C. Murphy, and D. Fisher. Factors affecting project success. In *Project Management Handbook*, Second Edition (D.I. Cleland and W.R. King, eds.), pp. 902–919. New York: Van Nostrand Reinhold, 1988

4 Pinto, J. K. and D. P. Slevin. Critical factors in successful project implementation. *IEEE Transactions on Engineering Management*, EM-34:22–27, 1987

Why Project Management?

Curtis R. Cook and
Carl L. Pritchard

Biographical Sketch . . .

Curtis R. Cook, Ph.D., is a Vice President of the Educational Services Institute. He has twenty-five years of experience in managing high technology projects and contracts and has taught project management and contracting courses to practicing professionals around the world. Before joining ESI, Dr. Cook headed the Department of System Acquisition Management at the Air Force Institute of Technology, the graduate school for the United States Air Force. Dr. Cook has a Ph.D. in Business Administration (Logistics, Operations, and Materials Management) from George Washington University and an M.B.A. from the University of Utah. He is a Certified Project Management Professional, and a Certified Professional Contracts Manager.

Carl L. Pritchard is Curriculum Director for Management Programs for Educational Services Institute. He has written numerous project management programs, including *Scheduling and Cost Control, Project Management Applications, Innovation Project Management, Writing and Presenting to Win, Project Planning Analysis and Control, Risk Management,* and *Strategic Project Management.* A former major-market news director, he has considerable experience in research and analysis. Mr. Pritchard is active in professional project management associations and is a Certified Project Management Professional.

The answer to that question drives to the heart of doing business. Yet getting beyond it is a major barrier in many organizations worldwide. Project management has value from a variety of perspectives, but until organizations recognize that value, it can be difficult to sell. So why discuss or use it?

- It is a proven practice.
- It is a time-saver.

- It is a money-saver.
- It optimizes organizational efficiency.
- It meets customer needs.

Over time, numerous organizations have recognized these qualities, but have been reluctant to implement modern project management because of the perceived challenges and barriers associated with putting it to work.

Project Management Is a Proven Practice

Project management has been in practice for anywhere from fifty to 5,000 years. As a modern management practice, project management evolved out of World War II and U.S. Department of Defense projects.[1] These projects required organizations to break the existing functional boundaries and find new ways to accomplish complex work. Resources from a variety of skill areas had to be drawn together toward a common goal. Objectives were carefully outlined, including performance criteria, schedules, and budgets. The foundations were set for modern project management.

During the past fifty years, more public and private organizations have embraced project management. The construction industry was among the earliest to take on the trappings of modern project management with network diagrams, work-breakdown structures (WBS), and Gantt charts. Other major sectors of commerce also came in the first wave, including the aerospace and pharmaceuticals industries. As the technologies for project management became more refined, other types of business joined in the practice, ranging from technology firms to the telecommunications industry. With the ongoing refinement of project-management tools, few business sectors are untouched by project management.

What makes project management progressively more attractive to such a broad industrial and commercial base? In addition to claims that project-management practice saves time, money, and organizational efficiencies, project management is rapidly being recognized as a value-added profession from the customer perspective. Customers recognize and want project management to support their projects. Several organizations have taken the lead in promoting project management around the world.

PROFESSIONAL ASSOCIATIONS

In the United States, the foremost organization is the Project Management Institute (PMI). PMI was founded in 1969 to draw the industry together.[2] PMI faced a unique challenge in building its professional association because members came from a variety of practices. Approaches to project management varied widely, and industries were not ready to change those approaches readily. In 1981, PMI's Ethics, Standards and Accreditation (ESA) group took a major step forward, making an effort to create an umbrella of practices that would lead to professional accreditation. By 1984, the first certified Project Management Professionals (PMPs) were recognized. Since that time, the PMP certification has become a standard, particularly in the United States. PMI cites that the number of PMPs worldwide crested past the 5,000 mark in the mid-1990s.

Just as project-management professionalism was evolving in the United States, project managers in the United Kingdom had similar aspirations. The Association of Project Managers (APM) was founded in 1972 to promote project management in the United Kingdom. Today, APM boasts over 4,000 members and 140 corporate members. As with PMI, the APM is also promoting certification through its Certified Project Manager program.

The International Project Management Association (IPMA) was founded in 1965 and is based in Denmark. With a membership of 9,500, the organization provides leadership for national project-management associations in twenty-one countries.

These professional associations add value to organizations as they allow them to speak a common project-management language with their customers, whether their customers are internal or external. Such common understanding encourages intelligent dialogue and improves overall customer relations. By providing some measures of professional consistency, the various associations encourage project managers to carry similar skill sets and a consistent lexicon. With those parallels across organizations and industries, project managers enable and encourage clear communication and more effective overall management.

PROJECT MANAGEMENT TODAY

Project management today is a far cry from where it was in the 1960s when only the best-financed organizations could afford to integrate project information into software applications. Only massive projects could be evaluated against heuristic measures. Only organizations supporting massive capital-spending efforts could afford full-time project managers dedicated solely to the advancement of projects. Project management was the preserve of a small cadre of individuals who alone possessed the dark secrets of network diagrams, Monte Carlo analysis, and earned-value interpretation.

As the tools and practices slowly migrated away from huge capital projects, project-management software products became progressively more affordable. Organizations began to test project management to see how well it could function. Today, organizations of virtually every description practice project management, and they are taking full advantage of certified professional project managers. Project-management professionals, who were once locked into their respective areas of expertise, are now branching out and becoming more skilled as generalists.

Project Management

One of the major reasons that project management has become increasingly popular is its role as an organizational time-saver. In many modern projects, time is a consideration equal to, or more important than, money. However, with the attention to detail required by project management, it can also cost time for an organization. A 1994 study[3] of electrical-utilities projects showed that even with professional project management, schedule targets were more consistently exceeded than not—from about twenty percent under the projected duration to about a hundred percent over. Although the study concluded that companies were less sensitive to schedule targets, the analysis may also be a tribute to organizations' general optimism in setting schedules.

Project managers need to be able to establish realistic schedules. In many (if not most) organizations, however, project managers don't even participate in the negotiation process when it comes to establishing budgets and schedules. Instead, project managers are assigned to projects only after the initial time and cost budgets have been clearly established.

EXAMPLE.   A project manager at a Regional Bell Operating Company tells of her dismay at being assigned to a project with an unrealistic schedule. Undaunted, she went to her management, diligently reporting that the project would take two weeks longer than the schedule allowed, unless significant additional resources were provided. Management expressed confidence in her capabilities, but refused to grant the additional time or resources. They told her that they were sure she would "figure out a way." At project completion, the project was four days late, based on the original schedule. As the project manager, she was ecstatic. She had been able to trim six days off a very tight schedule. Management did not reward her, however, preferring to acknowledge only the fact that the customer's schedule expectation had been exceeded. Based on a realistic schedule, the project manager had saved the organization time. Based on a preordained schedule, the project manager—and the application of project management—looked less than effective.

EARLY INTERVENTION

Project management saves time most effectively when it is used from the beginning of the project. In the Swiss-Swedish power-generation firm ABB, the corporate project-management policy[4] calls for the project manager to always be assigned during the proposal phase of the project. Policy also cites ABB's creed: "Time is the highest priority." In an organization where projects may stretch for over a decade, they are committed to meeting deadlines. They see project management (from the very beginning) as a key to meeting those deadlines.

Project managers need to be brought in at the very beginning of projects because project managers are supposed to *plan* the projects on which they work. They're supposed to outline the work to be done and then work to that plan. For project managers to save time on projects, they must have some measure of control at the outset.

AUTHORITY AND CONTROL

Control is a critical issue in developing project management as a time-saving practice. The project manager who is simply assigned to monitor tasks and oversee personnel performance will not have the opportunity to maximize the project schedule. If the project manager is granted some measure of control early in the process, and allowed to monitor it over time, the odds for success increase greatly. In many cases, it is the project manager who first identifies impending schedule delays, as well as the causes for those delays. Many are not the fault of the project manager or the project, but instead rest with the organization, which dilutes the resource pool or modifies the project approach midstream.[5] Chapter 13 covers legal reasons for giving project managers authority and control in contract agreements.

ORGANIZATIONAL SUPPORT

Project management as a time-saving practice involves a variety of organizational support functions. In the proposal-analysis phase, the project manager has the opportunity to contribute to the project approach, the promotional methodology, and the technical solution. In developing the schedule, the project manager has the opportunity to establish what time-saving workarounds will function, and which time-saving approaches are overly optimistic. Historically, many of these tasks have been taken on by functional specialists or by proposal writers, neither of whom may understand the intricacies of the work involved. The project manager can both inject realism and facilitate their efforts.

As the project evolves, the project manager saves time for the organization by tracking which activities are ahead of or behind schedule. Although that sounds like a simple task on the surface, it is the nuts and bolts of project management. Project managers must take it upon themselves to review failures and successes, taking home the lessons learned from each. Prior to the evolution of project management, such activities were the province of the functional managers. These activities, however, detracted from what they perceived as their "real" jobs.

Project managers save time for upper management as well, serving as buffers between the executive suite and members of the project team. In any organization, team members sometimes feel the need to address issues with the upper echelons of the organization. Although project managers cannot universally resolve such concerns, they can shield upper management from some of the day-to-day issues raised by the team members. Conversely, project managers may also serve as shields for team members against executive intervention. Some higher-level managers like to intervene in team-member activities, providing insight and guidance. Although such guidance may be helpful, it can also detract from team-member performance (and from the project manager's authority). Project managers save team members' time by serving as communications conduits.

EXAMPLE.   The classic proof of project management as a time-saver came in 1992 in San Diego, California. There, the local Building Industry Association set out to prove its effectiveness by constructing a home in world-record time. Prior to the San Diego construction, the world record for conventional home construction was just over four hours. After six months of extensive project planning and analysis, the implementation phase was ready to begin. For the San Diego project, the actual construction (including pouring concrete, frame construction, roof-truss construction, heating, plumbing, wiring, wall placement, and landscaping) lasted less than three hours.[6] Three-hundred-fifty team members on site were perfectly coordinated. With each project phase detailed to the minute, the project ran almost flawlessly. Project management can save time. But, as this example points out, investments have to be made in planning and providing resources for the project to ensure that schedules can be met.

Project Management

Project management saves time. *Time is money.*[7] In addition, project management saves money in other ways. Project management saves money in planning, resource deployment, tracking, use of reserves, and project close-out. If the project manager is allowed to pursue these basic practices, project management can be a money-saver. By doing a project right the first time, an organization can avoid rework and warranty service that can prove prohibitive.

PLANNING

Planning costs are historically the lowest costs an organization faces during the project life cycle. Virtually all project cost models begin with a low, smooth, slow gradient during the planning phase (see Figure 3–1). Costs are low because most of the costs in this phase are personnel, rather than material.

Careful and extensive planning allows for intelligent use of resources later on. It also allows for more thorough reviews of the project.

The project plan must be made early, but it must also be based on sound business judgment.[8] If the business plan is weak, it will lose integrity, because the project will be evaluated against a false model throughout its life cycle. If the plan isn't realistic, it can not be used as a barometer for project success. A good business plan is not a guarantor of success. But if the plan is sound and maps to reasoned business judgment, the chances of success improve significantly.

Without a clear, well-defined plan, there can be no honest baseline. Without an honest baseline there can be no objective evaluation of project

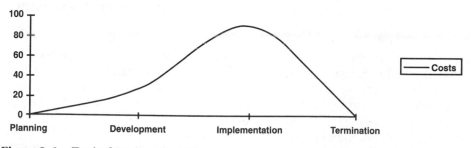

Figure 3–1   Typical Project Cost Curve

success. Without an objective evaluation of what constitutes project success, success (or failure, for that matter) can never be achieved. Before project management became an accepted practice, functional managers were, in large part, responsible for establishing the baselines. Although they proved highly skilled in their own areas, they lacked the cross-functional frame of reference essential to building a valid baseline for the project as a whole. Project management affords organizations that frame of reference.

RESOURCE DEPLOYMENT

Project management also saves organizations money by deploying resources more effectively. In an era of downsizing and corporate efficiency, each individual must be encouraged to broaden his or her skills and knowledge by participating in a broader portfolio of projects. Although training and on-the-job development are still broadly applied, the project manager often takes on the responsibility of a mentor to foster personnel development. Functional managers have the knowledge and skills to build insight within their functional areas, but project managers encourage greater cross-functional understanding and capability.

The importance of the project manager's role in resource deployment can be seen in the range of commercially available software. Virtually every project-management software package is built, in large part, around resource loading. One package[9] has even gone so far as to make the responsibility matrix the first view to appear on the screen every time the software is loaded. With this level of attention given to employees' tasks and responsibilities, the organization is assured that individual team members are being fully deployed. Project management allows for greater tracking and understanding of employees' roles and responsibilities both in the project as well as in the organization as a whole.

TRACKING

Project managers save money by tracking the project's progress. "That which is not tracked does not exist" is a maxim long supported by project managers. Early identification is often touted as the key to effective risk management, as well as effective cost management. Since project problems often turn into small-scale projects on their own, early identification of those problems allows for greater planning. Better planning means lower overall costs for implementation. Tracking also encourages increased accountability from all project participants.

USE OF RESERVES

One way in which project management can save money is through the deployment of reserves. Project managers in the field rarely get access to a management reserve or contingency account, even though such practice is acknowledged time and again in project-management literature.[10] Reserves allow project managers to reduce or eliminate the tendency to build padding into the project budget at the work-package or cost-account level.[11] Reserves allow project managers to manage problems by applying funds as appropriate. Organizations that establish reserves provide project managers with a valuable tool to identify specific problem areas and respond accordingly.

PROJECT CLOSE-OUT

One other way project managers save organizations money is by ensuring a thorough, effective close-out. Project termination is a key role for the project manager, and ensures that all parties involved are aware that the project has drawn to a close. As simple as that may sound, it is actually a process that is forgotten or lost on some projects, prompting them to linger beyond their time and drain an organization's resources.

In September 1993, a cost-effectiveness initiative was instituted for the Idaho Chemical Processing Plant (ICPP).[12] Clear criteria were established for project cost targets and tracking methodologies. In one department alone, cost savings of over $500,000 have been realized.

Project Management Optimizes Organizational Efficiency

Project management drives organizational efficiency. As far back as 1959, project managers were lauded for their ability to corral organizational resources from a task-oriented (rather than a function-oriented) perspective.[13] Project managers enable cross-functionality, team development, and employee growth while maximizing use of employees' time.

CROSS-FUNCTIONALITY

Project management evolved out of a need to draw upon the resources and insights of the entire organization. Throughout the early 1900s, the need for functional organizations evolved, affording businesses a structure to bring together the individuals capable of performing a single mission and doing it effectively. Functional organizations allowed individuals to develop within their areas of expertise, and encouraged upward mobility through the ranks. As the mid-twentieth century arrived, it brought with it new diversity, challenges, and possibilities. To achieve these possibilities, it was essential to draw on the capabilities of individuals from a variety of functions. Customers were demanding more from their product providers. They began to expect service as well. Integration became a buzzword.

Modern project management is an outgrowth of precisely those issues. For any integration effort, it is essential that there be a focal point of responsibility, insight, and oversight. Project management took the pressures of cross-functionality off the backs of functional managers. Project managers became responsible as second bosses for many of the employees they oversaw. In this role, project managers have become both a blessing and a curse to functional managers. No longer do functional managers need to learn the business of the other line organizations. However, they do have to learn to cope with project managers who make demands for resources and support.

As a result, project managers become versed in the policies, politics, and practices of each organization with which they deal. They become conduits for both information and corporate attitude. They serve as the bellwethers of conflict or calm between the factions within an organizational hierarchy.

TEAM DEVELOPMENT

On a much smaller scale, project managers also provide organizations with opportunities for extensive employee development. In the functional organization, employees might spend their entire careers wed to a single function. With promotions built on a blend of politics, longevity, and capabilities, long-term stability within an organization bodes well for the individual hoping for the executive suite. In today's organizations, however, that is changing. Careers are built in a series of organizations, rather than a single employer. Organizations grow and shrink rapidly. Today's opportunity may become tomorrow's reengineering project.

The project manager is compelled to create temporary organizations, and encourage team members to function as effectively as groups that have worked together for years.[14] In the video, *Four-Hour House*,[15] the narrator makes reference to the fact that this massive team was brought together for one purpose but "they're working together like they've been doing this for years." It is evident that the clear sense of direction, the well-defined objective, and the potential for significant accomplishment all worked together to motivate the 350 people to function as a team. These lessons can be learned and applied outside this context. Project managers have the opportunity to build teams using the same approaches. The team members must have a clear understanding of the project objective, a sense of responsibility, and a role in the process. Each time the project manager succeeds in drawing together a team and making it function effectively, a significant stride is taken toward making the entire organization completely cross-functional.

EMPLOYEE GROWTH

Project managers take on a great deal of responsibility when it comes to their team members. In addition to accounting for their time, the project manager must prove that something has been accomplished through an individual's participation in the project. Without such proof, it will be far more difficult to garner resources for the next project. But optimization goes beyond whether the organization is being served. The individual team member must be served as well. Team members must have a sense that they contribute to and participate in the success (or failure) of the project.

To accomplish this, the project manager must ensure that the team members are working in the same direction, that they have contributions to make, and that they're implementing against those goals. Working in the same direction is an issue that relates closely to cross-functionality. In many organizations, team members must serve two or more bosses. As such, the project manager's direction may be at odds with the functional manager's direction.

Unifying that direction is the joint responsibility of the project and functional manager, but in many cases, it falls to the project manager to implement. Similarly, the project manager must ensure that all team members have contributions to make to the project. Although functional managers may determine which team members are assigned to the project, the project manager must validate those determinations both before and during implementation.

During implementation, the lines of authority must be clear, and anything the organization can do to support the project manager will serve both the project and the organization well. Granting project managers tools of influence, such as performance reviews, opens the door for project managers to exercise increased authority during the project. This role is crucial to the organization that hopes to evolve with the times and enhance its capability to meet customer needs.

Eastman Chemical is a model for implementing what the organization calls "innovation project management." Because many of its products are based on cutting-edge research and development, the company has adopted what it calls an *interlocking team structure*.[16] The structure encourages cross-functionality and the development of project teams. This type of approach clearly breeds success; the organization has won the Malcolm Baldrige National Quality Award (1993), the Texas Quality Award (1994), and the Tennessee Quality Awards Governor's Award (1993). The company's use of project management also breeds financial success; its 1994 earnings statement showed significant improvements in every category and more than a fifty percent jump in earnings per share between 1993 and 1994. Project management optimizes organizational efficiency.

Project Management Meets Customer Needs

Customer expectations are established from the very first contact. Every meeting, every connection between the organization and the customer helps to further establish those expectations.

EXAMPLE.   A project manager walked into the client site wearing khaki slacks and a polo shirt. Because the company had a dress code of "business casual," no one said a word or thought anything of it. However, several months later, a new project manager took over. This project manager arrived in a suit and tie. The new project manager was quickly assaulted with questions about his attire and whether it represented a shift in the relationship with the project organization.

Every word, every appearance, every element of presentation works together to generate expectations. Customers have expectations, but in many ways, the project organization is responsible for establishing them. If the first project manager had always worn a suit and tie, no one would have said anything to the second. Similarly, had the second project manager come to work dressed casually, there would have been no questions asked.

PROJECT MANAGER BUILDS CUSTOMER LOYALTY

Although sales and marketing teams are paid specifically to set the customer expectations, many of the real-world, day-to-day expectations are established by the project management and the project-manager team. And it goes well beyond attire. If a project manager shows a willingness to introduce minor changes at no cost, that becomes a customer expectation. If a project manager directs project-team members to always leave the client facility at 5:00 P.M., that becomes an expectation as well. The project manager establishes major tenets of the relationship, and it's up to the project manager to ensure that that information is communicated across the organization.

Those expectations will serve, in many ways, to determine the success or failure of the project organization. If the customer sees consistency in the way expectations are managed, both organizations benefit. The project team pursues a unified vision, while the customer benefits by knowing what will and will not work in dealing with the project team.

An empirical study examined what made technology transfer projects successful and what didn't.[17] The conclusions drawn pointed to the somewhat subjective issues of establishing customer expectations and customer relationships early. The project manager becomes a shared resource between the project and customer organizations. The more clearly (and the earlier) the project manager's relationship with the customer can begin, the more effective the project manager can be. (See Chapter 26, Total Customer Satisfaction.) While the project manager is assigned to a particular customer, he or she becomes the organization's representative. A customer's favorable response to a project organization is, in many ways, a direct function of how well the customer representatives like the project organization representatives. Specifically, the project manager is in the lead. The project manager is responsible for ensuring customer satisfaction, so it is critical that the project manager be as highly ranked and as highly visible as possible.[18]

Needs are not static. Project managers have the responsibility to constantly identify and reassess customer needs in the most current context. Project managers must be willing to challenge the customer's perception of need to ensure that the deliverables at the end of the project will afford true customer satisfaction. As part of this process, project managers must become intimate with all project stakeholders in an effort to understand the drivers behind the customer needs and the organizational challenges that the project will help resolve.

A project manager at AT&T was retiring. As he announced his retirement to the customer, the customer representative blurted out, "You *can't* go, you *are* AT&T!" Project management is crucial in building customer satisfaction.

Project management makes cross-functional organizations effective from time, cost, and quality perspectives. With effective resource development, project managers can open doors for organizations that might otherwise be closed.

ENDNOTES

1 J. Davidson Frame. *Managing Projects in Organizations*. San Francisco: Jossey Bass, 1987, p. 2

2 Project Management Institute. *Guide to the Project Management Body of Knowledge* (PMBOK). 1996, p. 139

3 Walter Brunner, Doug McLeod, and Kerry J. LaLiberte. *Benchmarking Provides Insights on How to Improve Project Management Performance*. PMI Proceedings, 1995 Symposium, New Orleans, LA

4 *Project Policy and Handling Guidelines*, ABB, 1994

5 Chris Comber. *Project Portfolio Communication Incorporating Continuous Estimating*, PMI Proceedings, 1995 Symposium, New Orleans, LA

6 San Diego Building Industry Association. *The Four-Hour House*, Video. San Diego Buildng Industry Association. 1992

7 Benjamin Franklin. *Advise to a Young Tradesman*. 1748

8 Patrick Barwise, Paul Marsh, and Robin Wensley. Must finance and strategy clash? *Harvard Business Review*, September–October 1989

9 *Cascade*, © 1995, Mantix Corporation

10 Frame, pp. 179–180

11 PMBOK, p. 120

12 Michael Wilberg, and Wayne Simpson. *Did You Pave the Road to Project Completion with Gold, Asphalt, or Mud?* PMI Proceedings, 1995 Symposium, New Orleans, LA

13 Paul O. Gaddis. The project manager. *Harvard Business Review*, May–June 1959

14 Tony Allen, Mike Companik, Bob Harvey, Harry Doo. *Partnering and Program Planning as Communication Tools*, PMI Proceedings, 1995 Symposium, New Orleans, LA

15 *The Four-Hour House*, Video, San Diego Building Industry Association, 1992

16 *Eastman Chemical Profile*. Eastman Chemical Company, 1995

17 Raykun Tan. Success criteria and success factors for external technology transfer projects. *Project Management Journal*, June 1996, p. 55

18 Ibid., p. 55

Project Planning Techniques

Practical Tools for Project Selection

Christopher A. Chung and
Abu Md. A. Huda

Biographical Sketch . . .

Dr. Chung is an assistant professor in the Department of Industrial Engineering at the University of Houston. His areas of interest are engineering management and manufacturing systems. He has a B.A. from Johns Hopkins University and an M.A. and Ph.D. from the University of Pittsburgh. Dr. Chung has management experience as the commanding officer of a U.S. Army bomb-disposal unit and industrial experience as a manufacturing-quality project engineer for Michelin Tire Corporation.

Abu Md. A. Huda is a graduate master's student in the Industrial Engineering Department at the University of Houston. He is working as a research assistant for the Industrial Engineering Department. He holds a B.S. degree in mechanical engineering from the Bangladesh University of Engineering and Technology. His research interests include simulation, manufacturing, and management. He is involved in developing a simulation model for a local coffee company as part of his master's thesis. Mr. Huda is also a member of the IIE.

The selection of appropriate projects is critical to the execution of organizational strategies. Because of this strategic importance and the significant resources that may be dedicated to a project, project managers should insure that all potential projects undergo a formal evaluation process. This evaluation process should identify promising projects and reject those that are inferior with respect to the organization's mission, objectives, goals, and strategies.

Projects are a primary means of executing organizational strategies. (See Chapter 1.) For this reason, project management practitioners should have a working knowledge of practical project-selection techniques. This knowledge should include how to identify individual project-selection factors, choose among a variety of project-selection models, and implement the chosen model.

Project-Selection Factors

The first step in the project-selection process is to identify a set of factors against which the project manager must evaluate potential projects. These factors will differ according to each organization's mission, objective, goals, and strategies. Though selection factors are unique to each organization, the following list of factors may serve as a preliminary starting point.[1]

- Alignment with core business
- Top-management support
- Positive impact on various stakeholders
- Stage of technology development
- Adequate organizational knowledge of technology
- Existing facility and equipment
- Availability of raw materials
- Potential market for output
- Probability of adequate share of potential market
- Ability to reach market in a timely manner
- Adequate return on investment
- Adequate payback period

Although these project-selection factors may serve as a starting point, project-management practitioners should direct significant effort toward identifying an organization-specific set of factors. Though many methods are available to identify these factors, brainstorming is the simplest and most effective.

BRAINSTORMING

Brainstorming is the process of generating new ideas by a group of people in an organization. In a brainstorming session, five to twelve qualified people gather together to discuss alternative ways of handling a situation or solving a problem. The idea is to generate a spontaneous expression of new ideas regardless of evaluation. The process requires that there be no criticism or evaluation of any suggestion during the initial phases of the session. There should be no limit on the number of ideas generated, and participants may suggest new ideas based on other participants' ideas. A brainstorming session generally consists of the following three-step procedure.

   Step 1—Problem statement. The process of brainstorming starts with the statement and a small introduction of the problem. For the purpose of this chapter, the problem would be the identification of project selection factors for a particular organization.

   Step 2—Brainstorm. In this stage, participants are asked to submit their own suggestions for the selection factors. Participants offer suggestions in a sequential manner. All the suggestions are recorded on an overhead or chart. Being able to view the growing list of selection factors may help the participants generate new ideas of selection factors. Ideas are recorded until all participants "pass." After all participants pass, there can be free discussion and clarification of the recorded ideas. Once this discussion is completed, the nominal group technique can be used to retain the most important ideas for project-selection factors.

Step 3—Nominal group technique. In this stage, each participant is given a certain number of votes to cast in favor of the listed ideas. The votes in favor of each idea are totaled and a certain number of the most popular ideas are retained as project-selection factors.

Project-Selection Models

The next step in the project-selection process is to choose one or more project-selection models. The choice of model is dependent on the amount of information and time available to the project-management practitioner. The two basic categories of project-selection models are nonnumeric and numeric methods.

NONNUMERIC METHODS

Nonnumeric methods are generally used when there is only a limited amount of information available on each project or when the selection process must be completed quickly. These methods are characterized by the use of expert opinion, graphical, and "go–no go" means to select projects. Nonnumeric methods include comparative benefit, Q-sort, decision tree, and profile models.

Comparative-Benefit Model

Project-management practitioners can use the comparative-benefit model when a number of dissimilar projects are under consideration. This allows a ranking to be obtained, even though it may not be possible to evaluate the projects against each and every individual project-selection factor. One variation of the comparative-benefit model utilizes the Q-Sort technique.

Q-Sort

Q-sorting is used in rank-ordering projects in the process of project selection.[2] The process can be carried out by an individual or by a committee of people. It involves the evaluators sorting a deck of cards containing the project titles from the most preferred to the least preferred projects. The sorting is based on an overall subjective evaluation of the projects based on a set of predefined guidelines. These guidelines may include one or more of the organization's project-selection factors. The steps in Q-sorting are as follows:

Step 1. Each participant is given a set of cards bearing the name or title of a project.
Step 2. The participant is asked to sort the cards into two categories, one of high priority and the other of low priority, according to an

overall knowledge of the selection guidelines. There is no requirement that there be an equal number of cards in each category.

Step 3. Both the high- and the low-priority cards are sorted again to identify medium-priority projects. These projects are extracted and
placed in a new pile. There should now be high-, medium-, and
low-priority piles.

Step 4. The high-priority pile is sorted into two groups, one group of high-
priority projects and a second group of very-high-priority projects.
Similarly, the low-priority pile is sorted to form a new low-priority
group of projects and a very-low-priority group of projects.

Step 5. There should now be very-high-, high-, medium-, low-, and very-
low-priority piles of projects. The selections should now be further
surveyed by the individuals to adjust any card that seems to be out
of place.

After the completion of the Q-sorting, the individual decisions are tallied for
presentation to the entire committee. This tally shows the degree of agreement within the group. The group then discusses the result to modify it or
reach a general consensus. The projects in the very-high-priority category, for
example, would be further considered for funding.

Decision-Tree Model

The decision-tree model uses a series of branches to determine which projects
best meet the needs of the organization.[3] In simple decision-tree models, the
project is evaluated on a "go–no go" basis at each branch, according to the
requirements of the selection factors. Projects that meet the requirements
proceed to the next branch. Projects that fail any requirements are considered
as having zero value to the organization and are removed from further consideration.

EXAMPLE. For the decision-tree method and all other subsequent techniques, we will utilize two projects, A and B, as examples to illustrate the application of various project-selection models. The following paragraphs
summarize these projects with respect to the starting-point project-selection
factors previously identified.

Project A will produce a product that is aligned with the core business of
the organization. The project has the support of top management and is
favorably viewed by the organization's stockholders. However, it is early in the
stage of technology development, the organization does not have a great deal
of specific technological knowledge about the manufacturing process and
does not possess facilities to manufacture the product. If the organization
decides to go ahead with the project, raw materials are readily available. The
organization believes there is a potential market, the company can reach the
market in a timely manner, and the company can gain a share of the market.
Unfortunately, the investment in the manufacturing process is not likely to
provide an initial adequate return on investment. Similarly, the project may
entail a longer than acceptable payback period.

Project B will produce a product that is not specifically associated with other products the organization has manufactured in the past. The project is well received by top management, but the organization's stockholders are concerned about entering a market that is already close to saturation. Because the organization has not previously been in this business, little technological know-how is present in the company. However, the technology required to manufacture the product is well developed and the organization can easily modify existing facilities and equipment to manufacture the product with readily available raw materials. The market already exists and the organization can rapidly enter the market. However, there is some question about the probability of gaining a significant market share. Because little research and development is necessary, the organization is confident that there would be an adequate return on investment and a reasonable payback period.

Application of the decision-tree model to project A would be as follows. At the first branch, project A would be evaluated for its alignment with the organization's core business. Since this requirement is met, it would then be evaluated for top-management support. Because there is top-management support, project A is next evaluated for its impact on various stakeholders, including the organization's stockholders. Project stakeholders view the project favorably, so the evaluation process proceeds. At this point project A has successfully negotiated the first three project-selection-factor branches. However, it is discarded at the fourth factor, because the technology is in an early stage of development. Project B is discarded at the start of the decision-tree process because it is poorly aligned with the organization's core business. Thus, it would appear that neither project A nor project B supports the needs of the organization.

An advantage of the decision-tree model is its ability to graphically depict the evaluation process. Project managers and teams can quickly identify the limitations of individual projects. Unfortunately, the decision-tree model possesses a number of disadvantages. One disadvantage is that the project either meets or does not meet the project-selection-factor requirements. Thus, the project manager and team is forced to make go–no go decisions at any point. Only those projects that meet all of the needs will successfully negotiate the decision-tree model. This may cause projects that are strong in many respects and weak in only one or two respects to be discarded. Particularly rigorous decision trees may not yield any suitable projects.

Profile Model

The primary use of the profile model is in situations where an organization has limited information about the potential contribution of each project. The profile model may use the set of organizational project-selection factors. For each factor, the project evaluators make a binary decision. That is, they decide either yes or no about whether the project meets the requirements of a given selection factor. After evaluating all of the factors, the project manager totals the number of factors the project fulfills. The project manager and team can then select either all projects that meet a minimum number of the requirements or a certain number of the projects that meet the most requirements.

EXAMPLE.   An examination of projects A and B with respect to the preliminary project-selection factors would yield the results shown in Table 4–1. According to the profile model, project A meets seven requirements while project B meets eight requirements. It would appear that project B is a slightly better choice for the organization to pursue than project A.

Although the profile model is simple and easy to use, it suffers from a number of limitations. The most serious of these is that the project manager/team must decide that the project either meets or does not meet each of the selection requirements. There is no mechanism to account for varying degrees to which a project meets the selection requirements. A second limitation is that this model assumes that each selection requirement is of equal importance to the organization. Thus, a selection factor that may actually have significantly less value to the organization will have the same mathematical impact on the final rating as a more critical selection factor.

NUMERIC METHODS
Numeric methods are normally used when more information is available about the potential projects and a sufficient amount of time is available to conduct a more rigorous evaluation. Most of these models may be easily implemented using spreadsheet software such as Microsoft Excel or Lotus 1, 2, 3. Two general categories of numeric methods are scoring and accounting.

Scoring Models
Scoring models are more complex versions of the basic profile model. Where the basic profile model required a simple yes or no response to each selection factor, scoring models require a numeric assessment of the degree to which

Table 4–1. Preliminary Project Selection Factors

Selection Factor	Meets Requirements	
	Project A	Project B
Alignment with core business	Yes	No
Top management support	Yes	Yes
Positive impact on various stakeholders	Yes	No
Stage of technology development	No	Yes
Organizational knowledge of technology	No	No
Existing facility and equipment	No	Yes
Availability of raw materials	Yes	Yes
Potential market for output	Yes	Yes
Probability of share of potential market	Yes	No
Ability to reach market in a timely manner	Yes	Yes
Adequate return on investment	No	Yes
Adequate payback period	No	Yes
Total requirements met	7	8

the project contributes to the factor. Scoring models include unweighted- and weighted-factor models.

Unweighted-Factor Model

The unweighted-factor model consists of assigning a numeric score for each selection factor for each project. This model assumes that each selection factor is of equal importance. Typically, each project is rated as very high, high, medium, low, or very low with respect to each selection factor. A numeric value is associated with each rating. A project rated very high for a particular factor would receive a value of five. Conversely, a project rated very low may receive a value of one. After assessing the numeric score for each selection factor, the values for all of the selection factors are totaled. The total score for each project is compared with other competing projects. The projects with the highest scores are presumed to offer a better fit with the strategic and tactical needs of the organization.

EXAMPLE.   With additional information, a reevaluation of projects A and B with the unweighted-factor model could yield the results seen in Table 4–2. Using the unweighted-factor model, both project A and B receive a rating of 41 points. Although project B was rated higher using the profile model, the increased sensitivity of the unweighted-factor model indicates that the projects are approximately equal in opportunity for the organization. As with the profile model, the unweighted-factor model is limited by its inability to take into account selection factors that are more important to the organization.

Weighted-Factor Model

The limitations of the unweighted-factor model are taken into account in the weighted-factor model. With this model, there is the addition of a weight associated with each project-selection factor. This allows selection factors deemed as more important to the organization to apply greater influence on the final

Table 4–2. Reevaluation with the Unweighted-Factor Model

Selection Factor	Project A	Project B
Alignment with core business	4	4
Top management support	4	4
Positive impact on various stakeholders	5	2
Stage of technology development	1	4
Organizational knowledge of technology	2	2
Existing facility and equipment	1	3
Availability of raw materials	5	5
Potential market for output	5	5
Probability of share of potential market	5	1
Ability to reach market in a timely manner	5	3
Adequate return on investment	2	3
Adequate payback period	2	5
Total unweighted score	41	41

scoring of individual projects. One difficulty inherent in the weighted-factor model is determining the individual weights for each of the factors. The Delphi method is one way to determine the individual weights.

The Delphi method utilizes a panel of members to make subjective judgments on the relative importance of each project selection factor.[4] Judgments are collected in an anonymous manner so that the participants are free of undue influence or inhibition in expressing their opinion. The responses are aggregated in a statistical format by an administrator and are fed back to the panel. The panel individually deliberates judgment based on the feedback. After a number of iterations, a final judgment is made and documented. The implementation of the Delphi method to determine project-selection factors can be summarized by the following steps.

1. *Group forming.* The administrator forms a group of experienced individuals to participate in the Delphi process.

2. *Opinion gathering and feedback.* Individuals in the group rate the relative importance of each selection factor on a zero to ten scale. This data is collected and statistically summarized. The statistical summary is distributed to the participants to enable them to compare their individual responses with the anonymous views of the others.

3. *Iterative balloting.* Members of the panel revise their opinion of the relative importance of the selection factors based on the statistical analysis.

4. *Consensus.* The iterative process may include anonymous written explanations of the correctness or incorrectness of any response. The process continues until a certain percentage (for example, 70 percent) of the members has reached consensus. Otherwise the final statistical analysis is displayed with a note that consensus could not be reached. This statistical analysis results in the raw weights for each of the project-selection factors.

After determining the relative importance of the selection factors by the Delphi method, it is necessary to normalize the factors. The values for all of the factors are totaled and then the relative importance of each factor is divided by the total. This yields a weight between zero and one for each project-selection factor (see Table 4–3).

EXAMPLE.   The score for each project is calculated in a similar manner as the unweighted model. However, the value for each selection factor is multiplied by the project-selection factor weight.

With the weighted-factor model, project A shows clear superiority over project B. These results were obtained even though project A is rated lower than project B with the unweighted-factor model. The additional effect of the weighting for each selection factor is directly responsible for this differentiation.

Accounting Models
Accounting models can be used by project managers and teams either in isolation or in conjunction with some of the previously discussed models. When

Table 4–3. Normalized Project Scores

Selection Factor	Raw Weight	Normalized Weight
Alignment with core business	8	8/95 = 0.084
Top management support	10	10/95 = 0.105
Positive impact on various stakeholders	10	10/95 = 0.105
Stage of technology development	6	6/95 = 0.063
Organizational knowledge of technology	7	7/95 = 0.074
Existing facility and equipment	4	4/95 = 0.042
Availability of raw materials	9	9/95 = 0.095
Potential market for output	10	10/95 = 0.105
Probability of share of potential market	10	10/95 = 0.105
Ability to reach market in a timely manner	8	8/95 = 0.084
Adequate return on investment	8	8/95 = 0.084
Adequate pay back period	5	5/95 = 0.053
Total Weights	95	

used in isolation, models fail to take into account the impact of any other factors that are not specifically financially related. In contrast, when used in conjunction with the weighted-factor model, an approach results where accounting issues are considered, but not used to dominate the evaluation. The following describes the accounting models called payback period and return on investment.

Payback Period
This method is used to determine the length of time required for a project's accumulated cash flow to equal the amount of capital that was originally

Table 4– 4. Weighted Project Scores

	Selection Factor	
	Project A	Project B
Alignment with core business	$4 \times 0.084 = 0.336$	$4 \times 0.084 = 0.336$
Top management support	$4 \times 0.105 = 0.420$	$4 \times 0.105 = 0.420$
Positive impact on various stakeholders	$5 \times 0.105 = 0.525$	$2 \times 0.105 = 0.210$
Stage of technology development	$1 \times 0.063 = 0.063$	$4 \times 0.063 = 0.252$
Organizational knowledge of technology	$2 \times 0.074 = 0.148$	$2 \times 0.074 = 0.148$
Existing facility and equipment	$1 \times 0.042 = 0.042$	$3 \times 0.042 = 0.126$
Availability of raw materials	$5 \times 0.095 = 0.475$	$5 \times 0.095 = 0.475$
Potential market for output	$5 \times 0.105 = 0.525$	$5 \times 0.105 = 0.525$
Probability of share of potential market	$5 \times 0.105 = 0.525$	$1 \times 0.105 = 0.105$
Ability to reach market in a timely manner	$5 \times 0.084 = 0.420$	$3 \times 0.084 = 0.252$
Adequate return on investment	$2 \times 0.084 = 0.168$	$3 \times 0.084 = 0.252$
Adequate pay back period	$2 \times 0.053 = 0.105$	$5 \times 0.053 = 0.265$
Total Weighted Score	3.366	

invested in the project. In the most simple case, if one assumes that the net cash flow will be equal year-to-year, the number of years to pay back the project investment is:

Payback period in years = Total project investment/Net annual cash flow

Generally speaking, a payback period of one year or less is considered excellent, while most organizations will require a payback period of less than three years.

EXAMPLE.   Project A has a total investment of $200,000. Operating expenses, including direct labor and maintenance, are anticipated to be $30,000 per year. Expected revenues as a result of the project will be $75,000 per year. The net cash flow is $75,000 – $30,000 = $45,000. The payback period is $200,000/$45,000 = 4.44 years.

Project B has a total investment of $100,000. Operating expenses, including direct labor and maintenance, are anticipated to be $20,000 per year. Expected revenues as a result of the project will be $83,000 per year. The net cash flow is $83,000 – $20,000 = $63,000. The payback period is $100,000/$63,000 = 1.59 years. Thus, in isolation, it would appear from the payback period analysis that Project B would be more advantageous to the organization.

Return on Investment

Many organizations require that investment in a project meet a minimum rate of return. Typical minimum rates of return are between 20% and 50%. Rates of return may be calculated with the following equation:

Total project investment × (A/P, Rate of Return, Service Life) =
Net annual cash flow A/P, Rate of Return, and Service Life.
Can be found in an Engineering Economy table of interest factors.

EXAMPLE.   If the expected service life for Project A was eight years, we would have the following equation:

$$200,000 \times (A/P, \text{Rate of Return, 8 years}) = 45,000$$
$$(A/P, \text{Rate of Return, 10}) = 0.225$$

Using an Engineering Economy table of interest factors, 0.225 corresponds to a Rate of Return of approximately 15%.

If the expected service life for Project B was three years, we would have the following equation:

$$100,000 \times (A/P, \text{Rate of Return, 3 years}) = 63,000$$
$$(A/P, \text{Rate of Return, 3}) = 0.63$$

Using an Engineering Economy table of interest factors, 0.63 corresponds to a Rate of Return of approximately 40%. Thus, if the minimum return on investment for the company was 30%, Project B with a Rate of Return of 40% would be far more attractive than Project A with a Rate of Return of 15%.

Appropriate project-selection factors can be identified using a preliminary list and then modifying the list through brainstorming sessions. The choice of project-selection model depends on the amount of information available on individual potential projects and the amount of time available for the evaluation. Some project-management practitioners may find it beneficial to use the simpler nonnumeric models to screen out the most promising projects and then use the more complex numeric models to assist in the final decisions.

ENDNOTES

1 Merrifield, Bruce. Industrial project selection and management. *Industrial Marketing Management*, 7(5): 324–330, 1978; Meredith, Jack R. and Mantel, Samuel J. Jr. *Project Management: A Managerial Approach*, Third Edition. New York: John Wiley & Sons, Inc., 1995

2 Souder, William E. and Tomislav Mandakovic. R & D project selection models. *Research Management*, 24:4, July–August

3 Hess, Sidney W. Swinging on the branch of a tree: Project selection applications. *Interfaces*, 23:6, Nov.–Dec. 1993

4 Delbecq, Andre L., Van de Ven, Andrew H., and Gustafson, David H.. *Group Techniques for Program Planning*. Glenview, IL: Scott, Foresman, 1975

A Project-Management Model

John R. Adams and
Miguel E. Caldentey

Biographical Sketch. . .   **John R. Adams, Ph.D.,** a past President and Chair of the Project Management Institute (PMI), is currently a Professor of Project Management and Director of the Master of Project Management Degree Program at Western Carolina University in Cullowhee, North Carolina. He has extensive experience as a practicing project manager, and as a consultant. He is a champion of the project management profession and a frequent contributor to its literature.

Miguel E. Caldentey, a resident of Caracas, Venezuela, completed his system engineering degree and worked for several years with Andersen Consulting Company in its Caracas offices, participating in reengineering and system installation projects. He recently completed his M.B.A degree and Project Management Certificate at Western Carolina University, where he also served as a teaching and research assistant in the College of Business.

Although many expert project managers have developed different models for managing projects, no one model has been accepted as the standard for describing the processes a project must go through to move an idea from a concept to a finished product. Each model variation has strengths and weaknesses. The traditional model that is most widely accepted within the project-management profession is termed the project life cycle (see Figure 5–1). This is a useful model for explaining what must be accomplished to complete a project, but it is not entirely realistic in describing how that should be accomplished.

The Project Management Institute's *Guide to the Project Management Body of Knowledge* (PMBOK) has attempted to develop a model of the process a project must go through from conception to completion. The model leaves much to be desired in explaining the progress of managing a project through

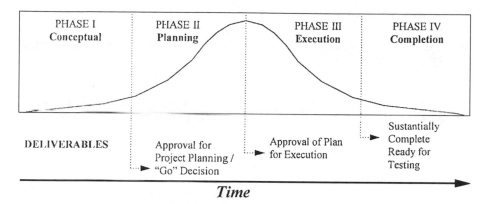

Figure 5–1   A Typical Project Life Cycle Model

its life cycle because it fails to recognize the need to use knowledge acquired during the project to modify decisions made in earlier phases.

This chapter presents a model that builds on both the traditional life-cycle concept and the work presented in the PMBOK to produce a more comprehensive model of project management. Unlike the other two models, the model presented in this chapter uses feedback of newly developed information gathered during later phases of the life cycle to change the project's plans and modify decisions that are made early in the project life cycle.

Toward a Realistic Model

A model is a simplification of reality, constructed for the purpose of explaining, illustrating, and emphasizing some of the main characteristics of that reality. If a model tried to incorporate all of the real world's complexity, it would be as complex and difficult to understand as the real world. For this reason, a model should be designed to highlight the most important attributes of the real-world situation being modeled, the attributes that, when understood, provide an overall explanation of what occurs in the actual situation examined. In this case, the situation to be examined is the generic process of managing a project. It is a complex process, one that appears on the surface to vary significantly in detail from one organization to another, yet one that also demonstrates high levels of similarity regardless of the project being considered. The challenge here is to model the commonalities that cut across projects and organizations while recognizing and allowing for the fact that the details of implementing this process will vary greatly from project to project and from organization to organization.

Traditional Project Life Cycle

Most models of the project management process are based on the concept of the project life cycle in which the project is broken into phases based upon the type of work being performed in that phase and the type of individuals needed to perform the work. One example of a typical project life-cycle is shown in Figure 5–1. In this model the project's life cycle is divided into four phases with clearly defined deliverables or goals marking the transition from one phase to another. The project life cycle is traditionally explained as follows:

Phase I: Conceptual. Management above the level of the project manager conceives of a project, evaluates it with respect to other possible projects, and commits to proceeding with this project. This commitment is generally associated with the appointment of the project manager, and marks both the deliverable of this phase and entry into the planning phase of the project.

Phase II: Planning. This phase involves the development of the detailed project plan and the project's managerial team. Formal acceptance and approval of the plan by the project's sponsor or owner marks the transition to Phase III and the initiation of physical work to accomplish the project.

Phase III: Execution. This phase may involve subcontractors, construction workers, programmers, medical personnel, or other skilled personnel necessary for accomplishing the particular project. The actual work of progressing on and completing the project is accomplished in this phase.

Phase IV: Completion. The transition to the completion phase traditionally occurs when the product being produced by the project is ready for testing or some form of demonstration to confirm that the product is complete and ready to be accepted by the sponsor or owner. The project ends with the formal acceptance by the sponsor or owner of a product, or with the project's early termination if it is determined that the project should be abandoned.

Deliverables

The phases of the project life cycle typically deal with the product being produced by the project, rather than the process of managing the project. The model of project management presented by the PMBOK attempts to relate the project's phases to the *processes* being implemented to accomplish that work. According to the PMBOK:

> Each project phase is marked by completion of one or more *deliverables*. A deliverable is a tangible, verifiable work product such as a feasibility study, a detail [sic] design, or a working prototype. The deliverables, and hence the phases, are part of a generally sequential logic designed to insure proper definition of the product of the project.[1]

The term *project* could be substituted for the term *project phase* in the first line of this quotation, and the statement would be just as valid. Thus the project itself could be considered a "phase" in a larger, ongoing work effort of the organization—such as developing or implementing a strategic plan. In fact, this quoted statement applies equally well to a project, a phase of a project, a subproject, a task within a project, an activity, or a work package. The only difference would be the scope of the work being discussed.

Processes

The PMBOK attempts to relate the processes involved in managing a project to the phases of the project's life cycle. A "process" is defined as "a series of actions bringing about a result,"[2] a concept that can also be interpreted at several different levels of detail within the project context. This general concept is used in the PMBOK to classify a variety of management processes into different process groups depending on the nature of the action that is being accomplished, such as initiating, planning, executing, controlling, and closing.[3]

In the real world, project managers will grant the value of identifying project phases, defining the activities that should occur in each phase, and identifying management review points for making a transition from one phase to another. This is a useful technique for describing to others what needs to be accomplished when and by what groups. However, no project manager will propose that the project is actually conducted in this manner, and a model of the project-management process needs to explain how the project is actually conducted. The problem with the project life cycle is its implication that a project progresses in a continual flow through its life cycle. For example, the project life cycle implies that planning is completed, reviewed, and approved in detail during the planning phase of the project, and the project is then implemented only according to the approved plan during the execution phase. Real-world experience clearly demonstrates that information obtained during the execution phase of the project is consistently and regularly fed back to the project plan and used to revise that plan based upon actual occurrences in the field over which the project manager may or may not exercise control. The same issue exists with other phases. That is, feedback of occurrences in the field that result in improved knowledge of what the project will actually require or accomplish is regularly used to modify the decisions made earlier in the life cycle. Because a comprehensive model of project management deals with the *process* of managing a project, the model must provide for information feedback needed to modify the schedule, the budget, the work flow, and even the basic project objectives. The feedback reflects what is actually happening when managing projects in the field.

EXAMPLE.   Several years ago the U.S. Air Force was working on an approved and funded project to develop a replacement aircraft for the B-52 bomber. The B-52 was the most recent in a long line of aircraft that included the famous B-17 Flying Fortress; the B-24 Liberator and the B-29 Super Fortress of World War II fame; the B-36 Stratofortress developed immediately after World War II; and the first jet-powered long-range bomber, the B-47. These aircraft were specifically designed to carry large bomb loads over long distances and drop them on enemy targets from very high altitudes. For accurate bombing, they had to fly straight and level for a period of time immediately before dropping the weapons so that the bombardier could take accurate aim on the targets. The aircraft were essentially large, slow, multi-engined cargo carriers with very little maneuverability and limited defensive capability. For the new aircraft, the original project specifications called for implementing new technology to create a new weapon system of similar design but capable of carrying larger bomb loads at higher speeds over longer distances. The new aircraft would need to operate at higher altitudes with an increased capability for survival in a combat environment.

Several years into the project, studies and analyses of potential enemies and their future defensive capabilities demonstrated clearly that ground- and air-launched guided missiles and radar-detection equipment were being deployed that would soon make it impossible for a large, relatively slow, high-altitude bomber to survive long enough to reach its target, much less return from enemy airspace. It was clear that an entirely new approach to long-distance bombing was required and that the basic project objectives would have to be modified if a useful, effective, and survivable weapon system was to be developed.

The existing project objectives, of course, had been approved and funded by the Congress of the United States. Any significant modification to the basic weapon-system design would have a significant impact on the approved schedule, budget, design specifications, and capabilities of the new weapon system. Neither the project manager nor any other military personnel had the authority to make such changes without the specific approval of both the U.S. Congress and the military Commander-in-Chief, the President of the United States.

The project manager prepared documentation making the argument for a significantly different weapon-system design. The documentation included the impact such changes would have on the schedule and budget for the project. The project manager took the proposal through the military chain of command, to the Secretary of Defense, and finally to a joint session of the House and Senate Armed Services Committees. The Committees voted to endorse the proposal. The committee members encouraged Congress to approve the proposed adjustments to the project's schedule, budget, and specifications. The Committees also encouraged Congress to authorize new research projects aimed at developing the specialized electronic equipment needed by the new bomber. Congress and the President approved the proposed changes, and the project plan was totally revised to reflect the new requirements. The final result of the project was a weapon system designed to penetrate enemy defenses by flying well below the potential enemies' radar detection system using a terrain-following airborne radar developed specifically for this aircraft.

During the execution phase of the project, the project manager discovered that it was necessary to change basic decisions that had been made and approved during the conceptual phase of the project. From the modeling point of view, information developed during the project was provided as feedback to the sponsor and owners of the project so that appropriate decisions could be made. The result was a complete redesign of the project plan that had been developed and approved during the planning phase of the project.

This rather extreme example is intended to show that feedback across a project's phases is an absolutely essential part of the processes used to manage projects. This feedback process is used regularly in large and small projects to make both major and minor adjustments to the previously defined project plan. An acceptable model of project management must therefore provide for the feedback of information about events that occur during the life cycle of the project.

Core Processes and Facilitating Processes

The PMBOK introduces a classification scheme for defining more detailed processes that occur in managing projects. These processes are called *core processes* and *facilitating processes*. The PMBOK identifies core processes as those that "have clear dependencies that require them to be performed in essentially the same order on most projects."[4] Facilitating processes are those that are "more dependent on the nature of the project." That is, they "are performed intermittently and as needed during"[5] the project.

The core processes include those activities that must be accomplished uniquely for each project as the detailed project plan is developed. The core processes include developing the specific work-breakdown structure (WBS), the logic flow and schedule of activities to be conducted, and the budget that will be used to manage and control the project. Also called *project-management knowledge areas*, core processes cover the following:

- The scope of the work to be accomplished
- The time available to complete the project
- The money or resources senior management is willing to commit to the project
- The integration of the scope, time, and money necessary to complete the project.

The facilitating processes include those activities that are frequently provided as a service to the project on an as-needed basis depending on the specific characteristics of the product being developed. In organizations that lack some of the required support, or in stand-alone projects, facilitating processes must be developed or provided by the project itself. For example, projects that subcontract much or all of the work involved may require a high level of procurement management services and skills for the entire project's duration. Other projects may need procurement skills only for a limited number of large-scale purchases of material or equipment. Facilitating processes include human-resources management, risk management, communication management, and quality management.

Project-Management Process Model

The following project-management process model is specifically designed to incorporate five process groups defined in the PMBOK (i.e., initiating, planning, executing, controlling, and closing). The model also demonstrates the complex interactions that occur among these process groups as the project progresses. The basic model is shown in Figure 5–2. Notice that the facilitating processes as defined in the PMBOK are shown outside the flow of the core processes, indicating that they can be integrated into the project's work flow as needed based on the particular characteristics of the project. The core processes—those that must be conducted in approximately the same sequence on any project—are shown as providing the feedback necessary to modify the project's plan, and even the project's objectives, during the conduct of the project. The model can be interpreted at any level of detail appropriate to the project, including the phase, task, activity, and work-package levels of detail, but for the sake of clarity the discussion begins at the project level. The typical phases of a project's life cycle referred to in Figure 5–1 can be directly associated with four of the five process groups shown in this model.

INITIATING-PROCESS GROUP
Work on a project begins with the initiating-process group. Senior management defines the basic requirements of the project and requests that a project be initiated. Senior management consists of the people to whom the project manager looks for guidance and direction concerning the project's objectives. Senior management could include managers above the project manager in an organization, the sponsors of the project, the future owners of the product resulting from the project, or any combination of these. The goals of the project are defined in terms of the following:

- The scope of the work to be accomplished
- The time available to complete it
- The money or resources senior management is willing to commit to the project

These are three of four project-management knowledge areas defined by the PMBOK as contributing to core processes. (The fourth project-management knowledge area is described later.) Before moving to the next phase, called the planning process group (or planning phase), a project manager is appointed and a project objective is established.

PLANNING-PROCESS GROUP
Planning takes place at two different levels within the planning process group. The project manager interacts with senior management to define the project objective in more detail; to specify the priorities among the scope, time, and budget aspects of the project; and to determine the appropriate levels of decision-making authority within the project. In particular, the project manager must develop at least a general understanding of the following:

- What decisions are within his or her prerogative
- When senior management wishes to be involved in making decisions relevant to conducting the project

The project team then develops an integrated project plan, to include the project's action plan or work flow, the schedule, the budget, and the interac-

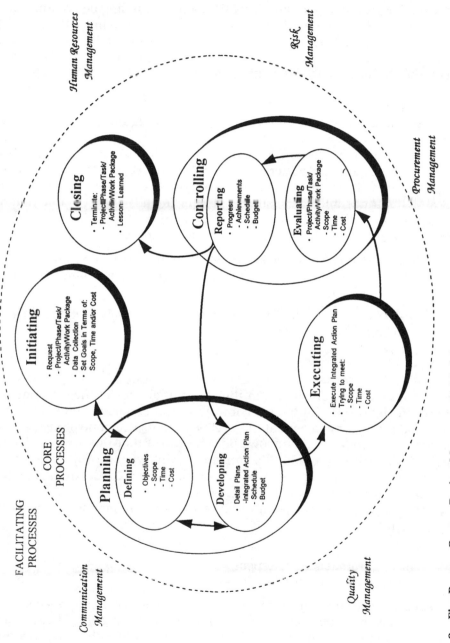

Figure 5-2 Five Process Groups Project Management Model

tions among them. This is where the fourth core process defined in the PMBOK and drawn from the "project integration management" knowledge area is brought into the model. More specifically, the project-management process requires that planning, executing, and controlling be accomplished as an integration of the project scope, time, and cost-management knowledge areas. The feedback arrows in the model indicate that the project manager gets senior-management approval for the integrated project plan before the project proceeds to the executing phase.

EXECUTING-PROCESS GROUP

The executing-process group involves implementing the planned activities according to the approved schedule and budget. This is where the work of the project is actually performed and consumes both resources and time. One must recognize that, no matter how carefully and well developed the project plan, it is actually based on a complex structure of estimates or guesses concerning durations and costs, and no project manager will assume that all these guesses will prove to be correct. Instead, the project manager must implement a series of checks and balances designed to:

- Identify when the project is deviating from the approved plan
- Provide the information needed to take action concerning any significant deviations(s)

This series of checks and balances are defined collectively in the PMBOK as the controlling-process group.

CONTROLLING-PROCESS GROUP

The controlling-process group, unlike the other four process groups, does not have an equivalent phase in the traditional project life-cycle model shown in Figure 5–1. Rather, the control process is the area that is missing from the project-management life-cycle concept. The controlling process provides the feedback that allows (and requires) that the project plan be revised. Failure to include this concept in the typical project life-cycle model is what makes the life cycle inappropriate as a model of the project-management process.

Periodically, project personnel must evaluate and document progress in the following areas:

- The time that has been consumed
- The money that has been spent
- The work that has actually been accomplished

On small projects, this may be a very informal process. On large projects, however, it tends to become a very formal process consuming considerable time and effort. The current project status must be compared with the current project plan to determine how progress varies from what was planned. Progress must be reported in terms of specific activities, and the status of each activity must be documented. When a given activity is completed, the work associated with that activity proceeds to the closing-process group so the activity can be terminated. In all other cases, variances from the plan should be used as a basis for revising the project plan to provide the best opportunity possible under the existing conditions for accomplishing the overall objectives of the project.

The closed loop from the planning-process group through the executing-process group and the controlling-process group back to the planning-process group is the key to demonstrating how feedback is used in managing projects to revise both the integrated project plan and the basic objectives of the project.

Projects are completed activity by activity. Schedules and resources may need to be revised any time an activity's actual accomplishments vary from what was planned. Controlling processes identify these variances and report them so that the necessary adjustments can be made in the project plan. As an example, if an activity is accomplished late, other activities may have to be delayed and resources reallocated to minimize the impact of the delayed activity on the project as a whole.

If the impact is small, or if the impact can be managed by a minor adjustment in schedule, budget, or resource allocation, then the adjustments to the plan can usually be accomplished within the project. If the impact is large, however, or if a significant opportunity develops that had not been considered when defining the project's scope, the project manager may need to prepare documentation and make proposals that could modify the overall objectives of the project—that is, the time, budget, and/or scope of work assigned to the project. In such a case, the project manager must consult with senior management to determine the appropriate course of action that would best serve those for whom the project is being conducted. This latter situation is reflected by the double-headed arrows leading back from planning to the initiating-process group.

CLOSING-PROCESS GROUP
The project is completed when the objectives (as revised during the project to include the possibility of simply terminating the project completely) have been met. In the closing-process group, termination processes such as closing out contracts, paying contractors, reassigning responsibilities for the project's product and personnel, and documenting lessons learned are implemented.

A Hierarchy of Projects

It is important to note that projects are made up of projects, that are made up of projects, that are made up of projects. The model depicted in Figure 5–2 is equally applicable to a project, a phase of a project, a task within a phase, an activity within a task, a work package, or to any other subdivision of work within a project that has a specified *deliverable*. The only difference would be the scope of the work being performed, or, in other words, the scope of the project. The model is therefore applicable at all levels of detail associated with a program or project. It basically emphasizes the repetitive nature of the process groups at all levels of detail within the project and documents the continuous interaction among them as the project progresses over time toward completion. Figure 5–3 demonstrates that the model can be applied at any level of detail within the project.

At the highest level, the project must follow the behavior explained by the model as shown in Figure 5–2. At this level, as the project is examined from the perspective of the project manager, four of the process groups can be considered phases of the project, integrated together by the processes incorporated within the control-process group. All activities of the project must be initiated, planned, executed, controlled, and closed, with all the required interaction taking place among these processes.

However, subprojects may be initiated that must also be implemented through a project-management process. Examining the subproject from the perspective of the subproject manager, the full model should be implemented through the initiating, planning, executing, controlling, and closing-process groups of the subproject. From the perspective of the overall project manager, however, the subproject is being executed as part of the overall project. Figure 5–3 is intended to demonstrate this concept, showing that, although subprojects or tasks may require the full project-management process, they are all part of the subordinate activities for the manager overseeing the total project effort.

Procurement management, a facilitating process, provides an example for how a subproject can be carried out. The following are the phases for a procurement subproject:

- *Initiating:* In this process group the general contracting strategy is determined, including whether the project is to be conducted primarily in-house, by contract, or somewhere in between. If it is to be a mixed project with some work conducted in-house and some contracted outside the project, the individual who will determine what work is to be contracted outside should be identified as part of this process group.
- *Planning:* In this process group there are the following two main subprocesses:
  - *Defining:* Clear objectives should be defined that guide the decisions about whether to procure, what to procure, when to procure, and who is responsible for the procurement decisions.
  - *Developing:* The detailed procurement plan is developed and integrated into the overall project plan.
- *Executing:* In this process group the contracts are developed, solicitation is performed, and the contracts are awarded and executed on a schedule designed to support the integrated project plan.
- *Controlling:* In this process group there are two main subprocess groups:
  - *Evaluating:* Here the contracted work is tracked to determine what work has actually been performed at any specific point in time.

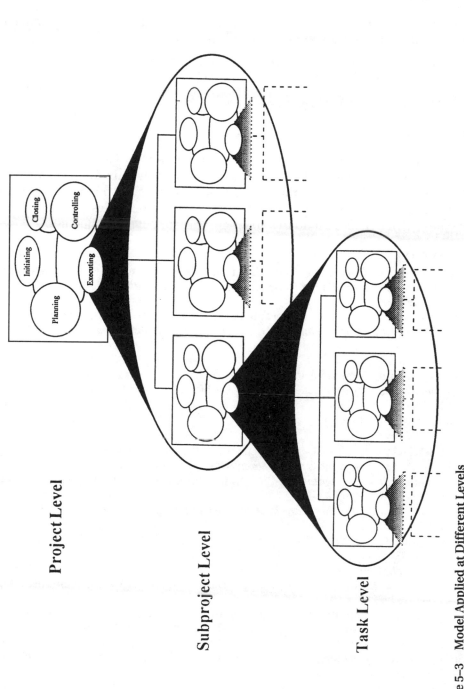

Project Level

Closing
Controlling
Initiating
Executing
Planning

Subproject Level

Task Level

Figure 5–3   Model Applied at Different Levels

59

— *Reporting:* The contracted work actually completed is compared to what was scheduled to be completed in the project plan. Any significant variances are documented and reported to the project team so that needed adjustments can be made to the integrated project plan.

- *Closing:* In this process group completed contractual work is paid for and the contract is closed out.

Conclusion

Having a comprehensive process model is an important issue for a growing profession. One of the basic tenets of professionalism is that one can define and describe the knowledge that an individual needs in order to participate in the profession. That definition can be used to teach the basics of what a professional in the field must do to implement the work of the profession.

ENDNOTES

1 PMI Standards Committee. The project management context. In *A Guide to the Project Management Body of Knowledge.* Upper Darby, PA: Project Management Institute, 1996
2 PMI Standards Committee. Project management processes. In *A Guide to the Project Management Body of Knowledge.* Upper Darby, PA: Project Management Institute, p. 27, 1996
3 Ibid, p. 28.
4 PMI Standards Committee. Project management processes. In *A Guide to the Project Management Body of Knowledge.* Upper Darby, PA: Project Management Institute, 1996, pp 30–32
5 Ibid.

BIBLIOGRAPHY

Cleland, David I. The project management process. In *Project Management, Strategic Design and Implementation.* Blue Ridge Summit, PA: TAB Professional and Reference Books, pp. 21–35
Dinsmore, Paul C. *The AMA Handbook of Project Management.* New York: AMACOM, 1993
Lewis, James P. *The Project Manager's Desk Reference.* Chicago: PROBUS Publishing Co., 1993
PMI Standards Committee. The project management context. In *A Guide to the Project Management Body of Knowledge.* Upper Darby, PA: Project Management Institute, 1996, pp 11–26
PMI Standards Committee. Project management processes. In *A Guide to the Project Management Body of Knowledge.* Upper Darby, PA: Project Management Institute, 1996, pp 27–35
Steward, Tomas A. Planning a career in a world without managers. *Fortune,* March 20, 1995, pp 72–80
Steward, Tomas A. The corporate jungle spawns a new species: The project manager, *Fortune,* July 10, 1995, pp 179–180

Chapter

6

Choosing a Project Life Cycle

Thomas C. Belanger

Biographical Sketch . . .

Mr. Belanger is the President of The Sterling Planning Group in Massachusetts. He has provided project management services to clients in aerospace, consumer products, financial services, high technology, education, and insurance. He is the author of *Successful Project Management, The Complete Planning Guide for Microsoft Project*, and over twenty-five articles on project management. The Sterling Planning Group published *How to Plan Any Project*, Second Edition, in 1995. He is currently a member of the World Future Society and the Project Management Institute.

There are many benefits to providing structure in the form of a life cycle to the project planning and management process. This structure can improve communication in the organization by reinforcing common terminology and practices. Also, the structure is one element in the standardization of project-management practices that includes guidelines for preparing a project plan, ensuring quality, assessing and managing risk, and clarifying roles of team members. By standardizing project-management practices and terminology, one can accomplish the following:

- Improve quality
- Meet or exceed customer requirements
- Reduce project-planning time
- Reduce costs
- Reduce duplication of work
- Reduce duplication of effort
- Improve the quality of communication among employees, partners, and customers

Life-cycle models can be customized to plan and manage a variety of projects, such as those in new-product development, management-information systems, reengineering programs, and capital projects. Because most projects that are carried out within these environments have many similarities, integrated product teams and other project teams benefit by starting their planning with a basic outline or skeleton plan that is made up of phases or stages, and states the project's deliverables or objectives.

Life-Cycle Stages

Standards vary according to the particular product or service. The project life cycle for a construction project is very different from the life cycle for software development. Though very different in most ways, similarities also exist because the project basically develops with the following phases:

- General concept
- Definition
- Detailed planning
- Development and construction
- Implementation and operation
- Closeout or retirement

The Final Outcome Is Known

For many projects, the desired outcome is known from the start. For example, if one plans to convert three offices to one large training room, the team can confidently plan the entire project during the planning phase. For this type of project, specifications and drawings provide precise information about what is to be done and standard phases provide a general structure and flow. Though minor changes and refinements to the project are likely to occur, the team can still plan the details of the project with a high confidence level. As the project is monitored, readjustments and modifications are made as needed. At the end of the project life cycle, the renovation will be complete, contractors paid, and in all probability, the new training room will open for business.

A MODEL USED BY ALLMERICA FINANCIAL

The following description of a life-cycle model provides a structured process for project planning and managing a wide variety of projects. It can be applied to projects that have known outcomes and to those that have unknown outcomes. The purpose of the following phases is to assist project managers and project teams in planning, monitoring, and controlling an automation project.

Phase I: Work Request Initiation
Phase II: Requirements Definition and Alternative Assessment
Phase III: Design
Phase IV: Construction and Testing
Phase V: Implementation
Phase VI: Postimplementation Review

Phase I: Work Request Initiation

The project manager may or may not be named at this stage of the project. If an individual is assigned, he or she has a supportive role to the project sponsor who must conceptualize what is needed by the business unit. During Phase I, the project manager and the project sponsor hold several informal meetings. As a result of these discussions and the information gathered, a decision is made to continue with the development of the project or to cancel it.

The purposes of the informal meetings are to accomplish the following:

- Allow the project manager to gain a high level of understanding of the project scope, objectives, constraints, and expectations. The project manager is responsible for communicating this information to the project team.
- Discuss the preliminary plan and schedule until both the project manager and sponsor are comfortable with the purpose, approach, and expectations of the project.
- Understand the preferences of the sponsor for communication methods and frequency throughout the life of the project. Status information can be communicated through meetings or reports. The level of detailed information required is also a decision the sponsor must make.

The project manager may assist the project sponsor in defining and documenting the feasibility study and the project's scope, objectives, and constraints. It is imperative for the project manager to build a relationship with the project sponsor from the start of the project so that a strong communication link is maintained throughout the life of the project. During this phase, the project manager and team members create a preliminary plan and schedule. They typically need to gather and assemble information necessary to have the project approved.

Phase II: Requirements Definition and Alternative Assessment

The project manager is heavily involved in phase II of the project, and should develop a detailed understanding of it. After team members have been chosen, a notice is sent out informing each one that they have been selected as a team member for a particular project. The notice should include:

- Agenda for the kickoff meeting
- The team composition, with roles and responsibilities of each team member
- Documentation on purpose, scope, objectives, constraints, and approach
- Preliminary plan
- Preliminary schedule
- Possible meeting schedule (work meetings, status meetings, sponsor meetings, steering-committee meetings, and other meetings)
- Special instructions, documentation, and requests (including background information, equipment, supply requirements, and other project-related information)

At this point, a software tool is used to help build the work-breakdown structure (WBS) and project schedule. The project manager is responsible for coordinating, monitoring, and ensuring the completion of all phase-II activities. During this phase the project manager is also responsible for:

- Communicating the status of all activities and costs to the appropriate stakeholders
- Requesting assistance from the sponsor(s) to gain cross-company commitment as needed
- Defining the project approach
- Choosing tools and techniques to be used
- Identifying the training needs of the team and working through the appropriate channels to fulfill training requirements

Phase II includes "project kickoff." A meeting is held with the entire project team and project sponsor to discuss key information. It is within the kickoff meeting that project details are confirmed, challenged, and agreed upon by the entire team and sponsor before the project is activated. Key pieces of information that need to be communicated are the budget, the preliminary plan, the scope, the objectives, the approach, all roles and responsibilities, and administrative items. Administrative items include meeting times, cost tracking, reporting issues, and communication standards. These items are documented and distributed in an agenda. Other factors may come into account based on knowledge base, experience, and corporate culture.

Phase III: Design

During the design phase, the project manager must gain an understanding of the functional and technical designs and must be kept informed of potential issues or changes that would disrupt the project plan. The project manager must work with the team members to refine estimates and the project plan.

In this phase, the project manager must facilitate communication between business and technical affiliates. The project manager is heavily involved in this phase by ensuring that the design will fulfill the business need and coordinate the work of those involved with database administration, system schedules, training, security, auditing, quality assurance, operations, and systems programming.

During this phase, the team decides appropriate intervals for checkpoints and walk-throughs. Formal checkpoints, sign-offs, and walk-throughs are required when a traditional waterfall approach is taken. (See "The Waterfall Life-Cycle Model" later in this chapter.) When using an iterative or evolutionary approach, the customer and developer collaborate closely, reducing the need for formal checkpoints.

Phase IV: Construction and Testing

The project manager is again involved from an administrative and coordination perspective in this phase. Depending on the type of project and the customer requirements, technical personnel such as programmers, operations workers, and security administrators may be added to the team, or, if they are already team members, they may become more actively involved.

During this phase, the project manager acts as a liaison between the team and customer to ensure that requirements are clearly understood by the team. The project manager must also work with the team to clarify the system or application to be constructed and how it will be tested. The project manager must stay close to the details during this phase. In this phase, the project manager is also responsible for the following:

- Ensuring that construction of the solution is proceeding according to plan
- Working with the team to refine the project plan
- Creating test plans
- Addressing the training needs of the user community
- Tracking, monitoring, and reporting costs
- Responding appropriately to problems identified during testing
- Coordinating the transition of the project into the production environment

For projects in which the final outcome is not known, this phase may be made up of several segments or iterations, depending on the life-cycle model chosen. This will be discussed later.

Phase V: Implementation

The project manager's level of involvement may appear low during this phase of the project. However, the project manager must recognize that during this phase the stress level of team members is likely to be high. She must be alert and sensitive to the signs of stress, providing encouragement, positive reinforcement, and recognition to help keep motivation and morale high. During this phase, the project manager is also responsible for the following:

- Ensuring that all areas have coordinated their roles during installation
- Coordinating procedures, training, and the new environment
- Facilitating discussion of minor details

During the implementation phase, careful attention must be paid to maintaining parallel operations. The client organization must be able to serve customers and run its operations in such a way that all or most business functions can be performed with minimal disruption. The project manager must work closely with the team to coordinate the transition from the old system to the new system.

Phase VI: Postimplementation Review

Approximately six months after installation is complete, the project manager assembles the team for a postimplementation review. At this review, the team identifies key learning from the project. They list the project successes and failures (process) and the system (product). The project manager will document the review so that the company can derive lessons that are then incorporated into revisions of the process. The project manager must extract key pieces of documentation from the project work papers such as the original estimated benefit studies, cost-tracking reports, schedules, and other data as appropriate.

THE WATERFALL LIFE-CYCLE MODEL

The most common life-cycle model, the waterfall model, is sometimes known as the traditional model. This model is made up of a number of sequential phases. It employs what is sometimes known as serial engineering, which means that project phases are performed sequentially. In a pure waterfall life-cycle model, phase II does not begin until phase I has been completed. Figure 6–1 displays a Gantt chart or bar graph with the phases in a series. Of course, there are limitations to the waterfall model. If applied rigidly, project work can come to a complete stop while team members decide whether to pull the plug or let the project live. In most projects some of the objectives and activities in a phase can be started or completed while the previous phase is accomplished.

In organizations where project-management practices have been standardized, project templates are available to plan and manage similar efforts such as those needed for system conversions, new-product development projects, or capital projects. In these environments, standard project templates and standard life cycles are often used as a starting point for project planning. When standard templates or standard life cycles are used, members of the project team typically begin project planning by customizing or "scaling" the standard model. Customizing or scaling a model consists of eliminating tasks, combining tasks, and adding new tasks. If an organization does not use standard templates or life cycles, but many projects are very similar, it may be worthwhile to consider developing one or more standard templates. By using a standard template to assist in project planning, managers are likely to prevent many different teams from reinventing the wheel. An obvious but major drawback to the waterfall model where it is applied rigidly, is that often a successor phase cannot begin until *all* work in the predecessor phase is complete. This has translated to costly delays in new product introduction.

PARALLEL-WORK LIFE-CYCLE MODEL

Until international competition intensified, traditional new-product development was largely a serial process, using a waterfall model. When one design group finished its work, the work was thrown over the wall to the next group. Products were designed, and systems developed in an assembly-line fashion. To shorten the time it takes to finish a project and eliminate delays inherent in the waterfall model, many organizations have overlapped the phases. Overlapping phases is often called concurrent or parallel engineering. Figure 6–2 shows how the parallel-work life-cycle model can reduce the time it takes to implement a new system.

The concept of concurrent engineering applies to all functions, not just engineering. Professionals in information management, marketing, and manufacturing can and do apply the concept. With the waterfall model, the

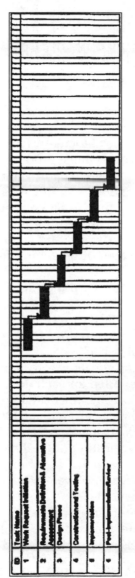

Figure 6–1 Waterfall Life Cycle Model

67

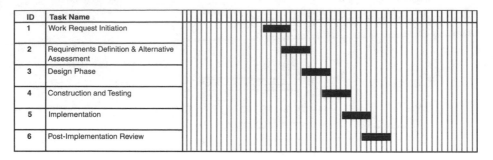

ID	Task Name
1	Work Request Initiation
2	Requirements Definition & Alternative Assessment
3	Design Phase
4	Construction and Testing
5	Implementation
6	Post-Implementation Review

Figure 6–2   Parallel Work

focus of each function tends to be parochial so that the goal is to produce the best product or system design or the most producible design. Companies that rigidly adhere to the waterfall model when concurrent engineering is more appropriate can be, in effect, indulging in high-stakes gambling. Concurrent engineering requires that cross-functional communication be planned and coordinated, beginning with the work-request initiation, continuing throughout the execution of all project work, and ending with implementation. Requirements are available in their original form for inspection and problem analysis.

Engineering specialists in new-product development provide requirements to the designer, and results are reviewed continuously for conformity to established requirements. In the best systems, fully developed design alternatives are studied to create true alternative solutions that optimize all design requirements. Creativity is unleashed.

With concurrent engineering, the team is responsible for defining the categories of analysis data to be reported for each design structure item as appropriate. Each engineer is responsible for designated parts of the design. As analysis proceeds and as estimates are replaced by verified facts, goals and responsibilities are reallocated. Team progress is monitored by collecting metrics on the completion and verification of the final design structure. Process flexibility is increased by adding the capability to incorporate changes throughout the design cycle. System-level and detail-level requirements are promptly and thoroughly analyzed. This interactive system results in better informed decisions at both the engineering and management levels. The need for simulation activity or prototype testing required for decisions is defined promptly. All told, better decisions equal reduced cycle time and improved design quality.

To reengineer waterfall or serial engineering processes and move to a concurrent engineering process, a major revision in mindset and methods is necessary. State-of-the-art technology that includes three-dimensional computer-aided design and manufacturing, rapid prototyping and manufacturing, as well as real-time interactive communication between different team members at different locations are the keys to shortening product-development time.

The Final Outcome Is Not Known

Just as human life cycles can vary widely from person to person, so too can project life cycles vary from project to project. In the design phase of an organization-wide system-development project, a complete vision of the final project output may not exist for many reasons. Process reengineering, process mapping, and the resulting new processes will need to be integrated. This type of project may make it necessary to develop customer requirements in several increments over a span of a year or more. The way that business functions will be performed and the ultimate end product of the project may be fuzzy at best when the project begins. A different type of life cycle is needed in which detailed planning is delayed until enough information can be obtained.

EVOLUTIONARY LIFE-CYCLE MODEL

This life-cycle model provides a flexible structure in which the design of the outcome changes as feedback is received from the client, users, system, and software engineers. Unlike the previous life-cycle models, the evolutionary life-cycle model can be used for projects where many of the requirements are not known at the outset. Born in the software development and system development environments, its basic concepts can also be applied to other project environments.

Using this model, the team often develops a number of functioning systems in segments. With each succeeding segment, more business functions or enhancements such as graphics are added. Requirements for performing business functions are first defined in Phase I of the Allmerica financial model work-request initiation. The techniques used to clarify customer requirements are formal and informal interviews, process-flow models (e.g., the flow of an order from a customer to order fulfillment), and quality-function deployment (QFD), a method of converting customer needs to engineering choices. For example, stock-trader information requirements can be converted to the design of a screen that meets those information requirements. Although requirements are defined early in the project, they evolve and are redefined as the project unfolds.

Using the evolutionary life-cycle model, a project team works closely with a customer or client to develop and install a computing system in small steps often known as process kernels, segments, or increments. The team collaborates closely with the customer or client throughout the project life cycle.

The model consists of the same six phases shown earlier in the waterfall life-cycle model. The construction and testing phase is made up of a number of increments or segments that can easily change or be augmented later in the project. Detailed planning of these segments is delayed until its predecessor segment is nearly complete or totally complete. Each phase is made up of objectives, activities, and tasks. Larger system-development projects are more likely to include lower levels of breakdown. The accomplishment of activities and tasks results in outputs or deliverables. Figure 6–3 displays a

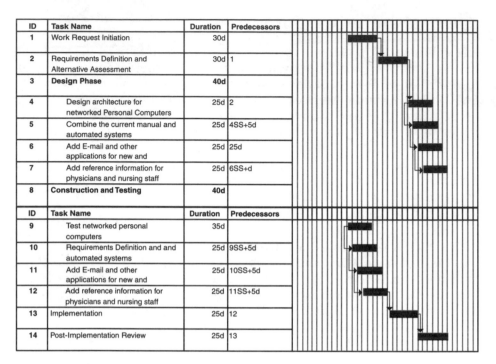

ID	Task Name	Duration	Predecessors
1	Work Request Initiation	30d	
2	Requirements Definition and Alternative Assessment	30d	1
3	**Design Phase**	**40d**	
4	Design architecture for networked Personal Computers	25d	2
5	Combine the current manual and automated systems	25d	4SS+5d
6	Add E-mail and other applications for new and	25d	25d
7	Add reference information for physicians and nursing staff	25d	6SS+d
8	**Construction and Testing**	**40d**	

ID	Task Name	Duration	Predecessors
9	Test networked personal computers	35d	
10	Requirements Definition and and automated systems	25d	9SS+5d
11	Add E-mail and other applications for new and	25d	10SS+5d
12	Add reference information for physicians and nursing staff	25d	11SS+5d
13	Implementation	25d	12
14	Post-Implementation Review	25d	13

Figure 6–3   Evolutionary Life Cycle Model

bar chart showing the timing of each phase. The construction and testing phase could change significantly as the project unfolds and as customer requirements change to include new functions. Because all project work has not been identified, time estimates may bear little resemblance to reality at this point.

Design, Construction, and Testing

The success of a project that uses an evolutionary life-cycle model rests largely on the dynamic strategy that drives the project. The strategy lays out a broad vision and general flow of the project, and breaks both phase III (design) and phase IV (construction and testing) into segments. As the project team learns more about the customer's requirements, more segments may be added—but only with the customer's full knowledge and concurrence.

A key element of the strategy is choosing an appropriate segmentation of the design phase and the construction and testing phase.

EXAMPLE.   In setting up a computer network for a Health Maintenance Organization (HMO), you could segment or partition both phases into four segments such as the following:

- Configuring and installing networked personal computers and work-stations

- Combining the current manual maintenance of patient records and automated appointment-scheduling systems into a fully functioning automated system
- Adding electronic mail and project-management software for new and existing users
- Adding an interactive database of reference information to be used by physicians and the nursing staff.

With the evolutionary life-cycle model you can normally choose more than one way to sequence the segments. You may want to start with the segment or kernel with which the team has the most experience and therefore the lowest risk. You may want to begin where the customer hurts most to "stop the bleeding." You may also want to start with a segment that will win over the client or customer. A key benefit of this model is that significant changes can be made at or near the end of each segment. The same model can be applied to a marketing project in which strategy and tactics are modified after test marketing a new product.

The way that you partition and sequence the project lays the groundwork for communication between the project team and the user or owner organization. This groundwork establishes general expectations where specific expectations cannot be set, and demands close coordination between customers and the project team.

Before developing segments, it is essential to devise assessment tactics at the beginning of the project that will help the project team to fully understand user functions and system characteristics. By ensuring complete understanding during the early phases, the team will be better able to choose the segments and their sequence that will help to ensure project success. Within this structure, the inevitable changes and enhancements will be easier to define and manage.

The design phase and the construction and testing phase are the heart and soul of the evolutionary life-cycle model. These phases represent the primary distinguishing features of the model. They are dynamic phases during which the principles of evolutionary development are activated. Essential to both phases is ongoing collaboration with the client. Beginning with one or more segments or kernels, the team collaborates with the customer or client to do the following:

- Refine the vision of the system
- Refine the customer requirements and alternatives
- Plan the segments
- Develop all segments
- Integrate new segments with the results of previous segments

During these phases, detailed planning takes place one segment at a time. Resource assignments, training, time estimating, installation, constraints, risks, cost estimating, and the impact on customer business functions are planned in earnest. When necessary, the segment is broken into pieces, where detailed planning occurs. Because several activities such as tests, may be identical, one must ensure that each activity has a unique WBS number and name. (See Chapter 7, How to Use the Work-Breakdown Structure.) In parallel with regular customer meetings, the project manager and team meet weekly, with additional communication occurring on an as-needed basis.

During the design phase, the scope statement and customer requirements are refined. The computing environment for the target system, system architecture, quality metrics, and acceptance criteria are revisited together with unresolved issues. User involvement and feedback are actively sought as the team works to define, construct, test, and install the new system as seamlessly as possible.

The Implementation Phase

During this phase, the customer or client is supported in the process of finalizing the transition to the new system and its functions. The sponsor, customer, or client officially accepts the system, and the project results are archived for future use. During this phase, the project sponsor, project manager, team, and users all contribute feedback. As each segment is implemented, subsequent segments are considered, and decisions about future segments are made. At this point, it may be necessary to do the following:

- Identify a new segment
- Change the user functions in upcoming segments
- Redefine the system environment and characteristics
- Resequence the segments
- Make changes in deliverables or outputs

After each segment is implemented, an engineering review takes place. The review is intended to evaluate the segment to ensure that all activities are complete and performed within development constraints. If it is possible that the engineering team will violate the constraints, anomalies will be identified and acted upon.

The Postimplementation Review Phase

The postimplementation review is the ritual used to evaluate the project. The evolutionary strategy, team competencies, tools, and techniques are all reexamined for future use. In addition, the recyclability of system components is examined, and reusable components are catalogued.

The Value of a Life-Cycle Model

Large organizations such as AT&T, Digital, and Rubbermaid all have standardized project-management methodology available for their respective project teams. Other organizations in financial services, pharmaceuticals, construction, and insurance are also moving toward standardization. The standards employed commonly include life cycles, planning, and management methodology, guidelines, techniques, and templates. When project-management practices are standardized, the project experience gained from all projects can be archived. When archived, this experience can chart a path through the wilderness by providing road signs and markers for future teams. By not planning in sufficient detail, project managers choose a reactive life for their projects. In these situations, project managers are pushed, pulled, and manipulated by events and by people who may be at cross purposes with the project. The result can be a tortured project life and an untimely end.

To standardize project-management practices in an organization, an essential component is a flexible life-cycle model. This chapter has presented a discussion of the waterfall life-cycle model, concurrent engineering, and the evolutionary life-cycle model, using a standard set of phases contributed by Allmerica Financial. Though the life cycle presented is used in a system design and installation environment, the same concepts can be adapted to many other environments.

Customizing or tailoring a life-cycle model consists of deleting nonapplicable activities and tasks and adding unique activities and tasks. By examining these concepts, you can develop a flexible life-cycle model for your organization that will increase the proportion of successful projects.

BIBLIOGRAPHY

Arthur, L. J. *Software Evolution.* New York: John Wiley & Sons, Inc., 1988

Arthur, L. J. *Rapid Evolutionary Development: Requirements, Prototyping and Software.* New York: John Wiley & Sons, Inc., 1992

Basili, V.R. and Rombach, H. D. Tailoring the software process to project goals and environments. *In Proceedings of the IEEE 9th International Conference on Software Engineering.* Washington, DC: Computer Society Press, 1987

Belanger, Thomas C. *How to Plan Any Project: A Guide for Teams (and Individuals).* Second Edition, Sterling, MA: The Sterling Planning Group, 1995

DeGrace, P. and Stahl, L. H. *A Catalogue of Modern Software Engineering Paradigms.* Englewood Cliffs, NJ: Yourdon Press, 1991

Filteau, M. C., Kassicieh, S. K., and Tripp, R. S. Evolutionary database design and development in very large scale MIS. *Information & Management,* November 1988

Hager, J. A. Developing maintainable systems: A full life-cycle approach. In *Proceedings of the IEEE Conference on Software Maintenance.* Washington, DC: Computer Society Press; 1989

Hughes, J. R. Evolving from the waterfall cycle. *CIPS Review,* November/December 1988

ISO/IEC 12207, *Information Technology Software Life Cycle Processes,* 1995

Lorenz, M. *Software Development: A Practical Guide.* Englewood Cliffs, NJ: Prentice-Hall, 1993

Martin, J. *Rapid Application Development.* New York: Macmillan Publishing Co., 1991

Martin, J., *User-Centered Requirements Analysis.* Englewood Cliffs, NJ: Prentice Hall, 1988

Tate, G. and Verner, J., Case study of risk management, incremental development and evolutionary prototyping. *Information & Software Technology,* Apr 1990

Tran, P. and Galka, R. On incremental delivery with functionality. *IEEE Software,* May 1991.

How to Use the Work-Breakdown Structure

Paul Warner

Biographical Sketch . . .

Paul Warner is currently working toward his Ph.D. in industrial engineering at the University of Pittsburgh. He is the plant manager of the University of Pittsburgh's Manufacturing Assistance Center (MAC). The MAC is a working/teaching factory, equipped with the latest CNC machine tools and CAD/CAM software, with a mission to integrate state-of-the-art manufacturing technology into local western Pennsylvania companies. He is on an academic leave from the Allison Engine Company in Indianapolis, Indiana.

"The greatest improvement in the productive powers of labour, and the greater part of the skill, dexterity, and judgment with which it is any where directed, or applied, seem to have been the effects of the division of labour."
—from Adam Smith's *The Wealth of Nations*

The project's work-breakdown structure (WBS) is a visual model generated and utilized by the project team, which breaks down project requirements (end items, tasks, and resources) into manageable work units. A WBS divides the overall project deliverables into distinct work elements that are assigned to functional areas within the organization or to outside contractors. It defines a project's scope in a manner that ensures that all components are included and that their relations to each other are identified.

Standard WBS definitions only generally explain the WBS. Although these definitions encourage project teams to use a WBS, many team members lack the specifics of how a WBS helps achieve project goals.

Not a New Subject

Though formalized in this century, WBS and project management have been used throughout history. Since the beginning of time, people have recognized that to complete a major job, they would have to break it down into manageable tasks. Many are well aware of the saying "A thousand mile journey begins with the first step." In this Biblical story of creation, God divided the monumental assignment of building the world into six manageable days. (One might even conjecture that there was a planned open day—day seven—for project overruns.) The monoliths at Stonehenge, the building of the Egyptian pyramids, and the Roman aqueducts were all built to fulfill a purpose and were planned from an initial scope of the work required.

Regardless of the size of the project, its costs, or the intricacy of its deliverables, the foremost issue is that the project team not overlook any components or steps required to deliver the end results. As the complexity of today's projects grows, it becomes necessary for a project team to use a disciplined, systematic methodology to organize the job and prevent any accidental oversights of necessary steps and resources.

The WBS for a Wedding

In his book *The Goal*, Goldratt used two examples to support his methodology, the rebuilding of a failing company and the rebuilding of a failing marriage.[1] The beauty of this is Goldratt's proposition that common sense, applicable in private affairs, is just as applicable in business. A WBS is common sense. People have recognized the need for it for years. There are many examples of industrial use of the WBS in literature today. Though one does not usually get married every day, every year, or even more than once, the following can demonstrate the use of WBS in everyday affairs.

EXAMPLE. Recently, the author became involved with the project that started a new organization: the wedding.

As the close to this project draws near, I now recall with a bit of envy the assignment many of my male friends were given for their wedding project: Just show up at the ceremony on time. My project leader (the future Mrs. Warner and also a fellow doctoral classmate of mine) did not afford me such a simple role on this project (in all fairness, her project). Apparently she had versed herself on team management and contemporary motivational techniques of involving all of the team members in the planning and execution of the project. Without me even asking, she allowed me to be an equal partner in the venture. However, though she has never married before, the project leader clearly had superior technical competence to me in this venture.

Just a sampling of the assignments I participated in include:

- Scoped out what was required to fulfill the project mission
- Secured funds and planned extra consulting work to make up any deficiencies

- Secured a church, a priest, a reception hall, the dinner menu and bar items, and a place for the rehearsal dinner
- Interviewed and secured a photographer, a videographer, a singer, organist, limousine drivers, and disc-jockeys
- Selected, ordered, and obtained tuxedos, flowers, invitations, thank-you cards, table favors, napkins, matchbooks, and little candies that are wrapped in netting and secured with a bow
- Designed, generated, and assembled wedding programs
- Selected wedding songs for the happy couple, bridal dance, and parental dances
- Negotiated and determined the invitation list (not an easy assignment), amassed current addresses, assembled invitations, procured stamps for mailing the invitations and for the envelope for the response card
- Wrote up directions to the church, reception hall, and the rehearsal dinner location
- Planned for the location, security, and transportation of wedding presents
- Secured a honeymoon location and provided funds
- Paid for the reception
- Showed up to the wedding on time!

This is just a portion of the total necessary work required for a wedding.

To help determine what needed to be done to pull off the wedding in a successful manner, we simply broke the job down into manageable tasks through a work-breakdown structure (see Figure 7–1). We utilized the WBS to set a budget, prioritize and make sure we didn't overlook any details, and schedule tasks. The honeymoon is included in the WBS because we needed to coordinate it with the wedding. Our WBS does not include any engagement tasks, selecting items for the bridal registry, attending wedding classes, plus a host of other things that needed to be done. It is simply for the big day.

Our WBS had four levels:

1. The Wedding
2. Major components (single digit 1–9)
3. Key categories of activity to attain each component (single digit 1–9)
4. Components of activity required (double digit 01–99)

Level three stemmed from our observations that each component involved materials (sometimes expensive), facilities (most always expensive), people, and communication tasks. Often, a WBS is matched against an organizational chart to involve the necessary people, but ours included them. Since we are a start-up organization, most of the people resources came from the outside.

Too many couples who planned their weddings ended up with horror stories. Many warned of things that do not go as planned, people and items whom they overlooked, and the incredible stress that prevailed. All went well with our wedding. Through basic project-management techniques, namely a WBS, we saved a lot of trouble.

The Wedding

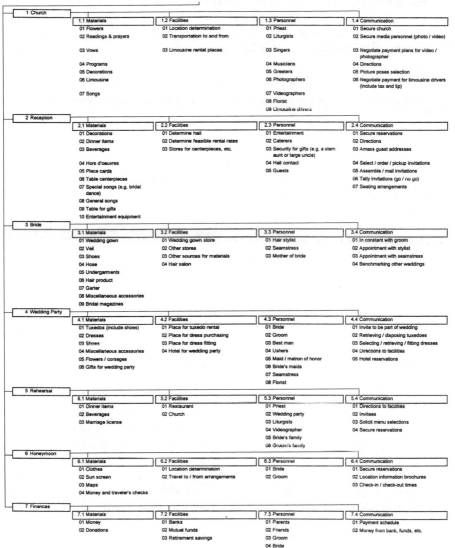

Figure 7-1   Wedding Work-Breakdown Structure

Creating a WBS

How is a WBS formed and who should be involved in its creation? What is derived from a WBS and how can the team best use one? The focus of this chapter is to address these and many more questions that project teams may have regarding a WBS.

THE NATURE OF PROJECTS VERSUS OPERATIONS

Running a project is very different from running the day-to-day operational activities of an organization. Though both require decisions to be made in complex environments and the allotment of resources to meet specified goals, there are differences that teams need to keep in mind when planning, organizing, executing, managing and controlling projects. Operational activities deal with familiar, continual work, supported by work methods and job definitions that have been engineered over a relatively long period of time. There is a legacy of performance history and data to guide managers thus reducing the risk of decisions. Projects are an ad-hoc effort, dealing with unique, often cutting-edge work. Many projects are a first attempt at a technology. Projects rely heavily on estimates and because of the scarcity of solid, supporting data for these estimates, are often conducted in an environment of much risk.

Teams must approach a project with an understanding of the high risk environment surrounding it. This will guide them in the way they break down the work required, the deliverables and goals they will set, and the flexibility designed for the processes they will undergo to meet them.

CONSISTENCY IN AN ENVIRONMENT OF RAPID CHANGE

The world has changed a lot over the past twelve years. In 1985, how many ten-year projects included the Internet, foresaw the Persian Gulf War, or anticipated the opening up of the Soviet-bloc nations? No one expects any slowdown in the pace of change into the next century.

Project teams must be able to deal with change. The involvement of various stakeholders combined with the ever-growing complexity in today's technological requirements and rapidly changing world has heightened the need for fluid communication within projects. All members in the project must have access to a mutual information source. The WBS provides a mechanism to define tasks required to meet project targets. But more important, the WBS allows team members to track and evaluate performance of defined tasks from one common information source on a regular basis and make necessary adjustments to changing conditions.

JUSTIFYING THE END THROUGH THE MEANS

To depict the sometimes insurmountable odds that project teams face, comedic scheduling charts connect the resources of a project to its end deliverables with the phrase "And then a miracle occurs." Unfortunately, project teams cannot rely on such serendipity. Instead, most use a WBS to generate this miracle (see Figure 7–2).

A project has two major parts: what is to be accomplished at its completion— the *end items*—and the *means* by which they are to be attained. In an environment of uncertainty, the end and the means must be thoroughly defined and easily communicated. The WBS serves dual functions. It includes all the deliverables—end items, such as equipment, facilities, services—and the major tasks—

Requirements   Deliverables

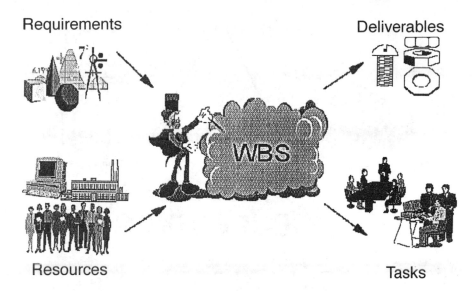

Resources   Tasks

Figure 7–2   Building a Miracle with a WBS

the means, which are essential for the conception, design, creation, operation, test, and disposal of these end items.

THE ROAD MAP TO GOOD, FAST, AND CHEAP
Common in many businesses are signs that facetiously offer:
   You can have service one of the following ways:

* *Good* and *Cheap*—but it won't be *Fast*
* *Cheap* and *Fast*—but it won't be *Good*
* *Fast* and *Good*—but it won't be *Cheap*

The purpose of all projects is to organize various human and material resources in an ad hoc manner to meet technical performance parameters through a detailed schedule under a specified cost budget (see Figure 7–3).

Essentially, the purpose of projects is to meet the universal metrics: good (products and services that meet or exceed technical performance parameters), fast (within the time horizon), and cheap (utilizing a specified budget).

The fact that good, fast, and cheap often compete with each other has never stopped the end users of the project deliverables from demanding all three. To meet project objectives and satisfy customers, the project teams need a road map to allow them to attain good, fast, and cheap. By breaking down project requirements into specific tasks and assigning them to a resource(s) to fulfill them, the WBS paves the way.

WHAT THE WBS PROVIDES
The WBS provides a model of the resources required to meet a project's deliverables. The model becomes the means by which to manage the project. The

Figure 7–3   Project Objectives

WBS enables project members and various management groups (project, functional, and general) to envision the aggregate of all products and services comprising the project.

In general, the development of the WBS provides the means for:[2]

- Summarizing all the deliverables, resources, and activities of a project.
- Relating work elements to each other and to the total project.
- Building the matrix organization for the project by cross referencing the work elements to the organizational resources responsible for their completion.
- Addressing all contracted resources required for the project.
- Estimating costs, simulating project scenarios, and conducting risk analysis.
- Providing information to define, budget, schedule, perform, and control work packages.

Functions

The WBS accomplishes four major tasks:

1. It converts project requirements into manageable tasks.
2. It translates tasks into specific work packages for the project team members.
3. It communicates the objectives of the project to all project stakeholders.
4. It forms the foundation for planning and scheduling.

CONVERTING REQUIREMENTS INTO MANAGEABLE TASKS

The WBS converts requirements into manageable tasks. A project's WBS should identify all tasks to be accomplished to fulfill the deliverable end-item obligations. Thus, managers developing the WBS must have a clear understanding and definitive statement of the objectives of the work to be performed. However, the developers face two competing objectives with regard to the WBS: manageability and comprehensiveness. If comprehensiveness dominates, a team can quickly break down a project into a very large number of steps, adding to the challenge of managing the project. For instance, the author has been involved in many projects regarding the conversion of production facilities from job shops to cellular manufacturing. One of the tasks is the relocation of machinery. This may involve functions such as relocation of equipment, and functional area duties, such as plant engineering (location of power, air, and water lines; location of waste removal); industrial engineering (plant layout, ergonomics/work-station design, machine-capacity management); manufacturing engineering (machine capabilities, reprocessing and rerouting parts); safety engineering (identification and removal of health hazards—e.g., barriers for robots); and production shop (worker input and understanding).

Clearly, relocating equipment is more than just physically moving it. As each task is broken down into its subtasks, it becomes evident that the implementation of manufacturing cells requires a significant amount of effort and many organizational resources.

To ensure both manageability and comprehensiveness, the team can reasonably document many of the low-level tasks without listing them directly on the WBS through statements of work. These describe the actual effort to be performed on the project. As Cleland states, this effort, when combined with the specifications, usually forms the basis for a contractual agreement on the project. It describes what is going to be accomplished, a description of the tasks, the deliverable end products from the work, plus necessary references to specifications or standards.[3]

TRANSLATING TASKS TO SPECIFIC WORK PACKAGES

Through the WBS, the project is broken down into *work packages*, process steps by which the deliverables are attained, that are assignable, and for which responsibility can be expected. Each work package then becomes a performance-control element assigned to a work-package manager. This individual is responsible for a measurable, specific objective, detailed task descriptions, specifications, schedules, and budgets.[4]

Russell Archibald points out that the product-development process strongly effects the definition of work packages at the lowest level of the WBS. The process of developing the WBS is to determine the scheme for dividing the project into major groups, groups into tasks, and tasks into subtasks. When an acceptable level of detail is obtained, the tasks and subtasks are matched against the organizational structure and task definitions are further refined.[5] Forming the WBS in a product-oriented manner ensures that each of the proper functional areas are involved in the execution of the project (see Figure 7–4).

COMMUNICATING PROJECT OBJECTIVES TO PROJECT STAKEHOLDERS
In projects, both human and material resources are brought together from a variety of areas. Each area may represent a system that must be integrated into the project. Engineers, production, lawyers, contractors, human resource personnel, and so on, must not only understand their roles in the project, but also what systems they must integrate into the project and how the others' functions and systems fit into the overall project mission.

Each stakeholder must be aware of the status of the project throughout its life. Gary Lavold describes the WBS as the project information link.[6] The project-control systems are the key to warning of any imminent problems

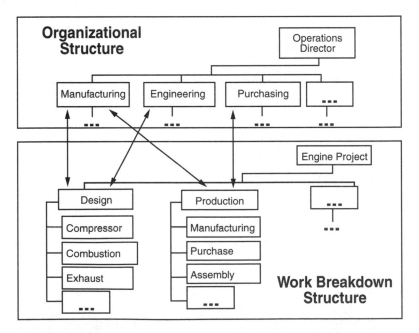

Figure 7–4   Translating Project Tasks to Functional Work Packages

early enough so that the team can make decisions and solve them or, better yet, avoid them altogether. Control systems, such as scheduling, cost and performance measurement, personnel, equipment, and material tracking must be understood by all stakeholders. Lavold also points out that the team must be cognizant of the project-accounting systems such as accounts receivable, accounts payable, capital assets, and a project-cost ledger. The WBS is a mechanism to provide this.

Adding to the communication challenge is that many projects are conducted over a variety of sites. This challenge is met through a well-designed WBS. For example, terrain and weather conditions may differ widely from area to area. In these situations, the importance of effectiveness in communication provided by the WBS becomes even more evident.

FORMING THE FOUNDATION FOR PLANNING AND SCHEDULING

The WBS lays the foundation from which planning and scheduling can be conducted. The process of creating a WBS, or even conducting a project in general, is basically the same regardless of its scope. However, as Rastelli notes, a project team's trepidation (and especially that of the project leader) tends to be a function of the amount of money at stake in a project.[7] He asserts that if a team properly exercises the methodologies of project management, the magnitude of the cost of a project should be of no concern to any of the team members. The WBS provides a systematic approach to define all the work packages along with their interrelationships from the scope of the project. Through this process, a team can break down a large project into smaller, controllable, and more "comfortable" work packages. The road map to a successful project is built from the combination of the results of the WBS, tested planning tools such as PERT and CPM, and the collective analytical effort of the team.

Elements

The WBS coding philosophy and methodology is paramount to ensuring that all parties understand the entire scope of the project and their role within that scope. There are three basic elements of the WBS:

1. Displaying (reporting)
2. Structuring
3. Coding (the dictionary)

DISPLAYING (REPORTING)

Difficulty in controlling projects grows with the complexity of the project deliverables, the process used to achieve them, and with the inclusion of every new team member and/or stakeholder. It is important that the WBS designers have an understanding of what the users of the WBS will want reported to control the project. Once reporting requirements are understood, the developers can select the proper structure and code for the WBS.

Different stakeholders of the project will need to know varying degrees of project details, depending on their level of responsibility, authority, and accountability. When designing the WBS, all levels of reporting should be reviewed. This will range from high-level senior management down to the person inputting project data. The WBS reporting capability must encompass all user requirements. For example, a project engineer may want to bill hours against a job order for a project component; a project group leader may want to know the total hours billed against that job order by week; and a project manager may want to know the total costs summed-to-date of the component to compare against an estimate. These various levels of details will dictate the structure and coding of the WBS.

In generating reports, flexibility and speed are of utmost importance. Reports from the WBS must be easy to produce without requiring complicated computer programs or manual collection of data. Designers of the WBS must ensure that both the WBS and the reports generated from it clearly convey what is required, what work has been done toward it, and what is expected by the user of the report.

STRUCTURING

GIGO is an acronym for "garbage in—garbage out." It is often related to computer systems. GIGO reminds designers and users that no matter how good a reporting system is, if the data it is compiling is corrupt (garbage), the information gained from it is useless (garbage).

Lavold describes the WBS is the device by which all project information is gathered and dispersed.[8] He stresses that the structure design of the WBS is the key to an effective working project. The designers must carefully structure the WBS considering both the data collection needs of the project and the reporting needs. It is important that each level serves a purpose and renders meaning to its users. The lowest levels provide the information to plan, manage, and control the project. Each higher level will be a summary point of all the activities of the levels directly beneath it.

Designers have many examples to benchmark to determine the number of WBS levels that will optimize effectiveness. For example, designers should remember the last time they used an automated answering service. Many can remember the frustration they experienced going through seemingly 100 levels of options to find out, for example, a balance in a checking account. The designers must not include too many levels into the structure of the WBS to maintain manageability. Four to six levels is sufficient for most large projects.

CODING (DICTIONARY)

Large projects will have many diverse team members, often from various parts of the organization and sometimes from outside the organization, Regardless of position or background, the WBS code should be easily understood by all members. By using systemic procedures early, the team can reduce or eliminate costly assumptions regarding the coding and ensure better integrity in the use of the WBS.

WBS codes are related to the structure design, for each level of the structure adds a segment to the code. The code for each work element is the combination of the number or letter coded work levels preceding it plus its own identifier. For example, in the aforementioned WBS for a wedding (see Figure 7–1), 3 represents the bride element of the wedding, 3.1 represents materials for the bride, and 3.1.01 represents the bride's gown (since this project was not incorporated into any other project, the top level (the wedding) was not coded).

The project team uses the code to label and identify work packages, thus the combination of segments comprising each code must be unique. By including the preceding levels related to the work element, the coding system enables the summary of the costs and activities of lower level work packages along the correct path of higher level work elements in the WBS. This helps establish the WBS as the device to be used by the project control systems.[9] Utilizing the WBS code for entering and summarizing all project data and information enables the team to compare progress to a baseline.

Continuing with the wedding example, the team originally provided an aggregate budget for all of the materials for the bride. When a project member entered performance data into a project tracking system, the person inputted the data under the code from the WBS (e.g., on March 21, 1995, the bride-to-be entered the cost of her gown next to the work element 3.1.01 in the project information system). Thus, at any time during the project, when the team summed up the total costs associated with 3.1, all of the recorded bride-material element expenditures were included. The team could then compare actual total costs of materials for the bride against the original budget. Through effective WBS coding, the costs of other unrelated work elements were not included in this summary (e.g., 2.3.02 the cost of the caterers).

Proper coding enables the WBS to build the project dictionary. The WBS will be the source where all project work elements and their associated scope, resources, personnel, budgets, and estimates are defined and documented. A good coding scheme that is understood by the team will facilitate the use of the WBS.

Software

It is unclear whether it is the growing complexity of projects that has spurred the integration of the computer into project management or whether it is the power of the computer that allows organizations to even attempt complex projects (see Chapters 24 and 25). In either case, the use of project-management computer software in organizations has exploded over the past decade.

Computers rapidly process large amounts of data to generate meaningful information (assuming the data is not garbage). With the correct project-management software, a team can quickly integrate project data, generate performance reports, conduct risk analyses, and simulate multiple scenarios to estimate the effects of any proposed changes.

In selecting a project-management software package, organizations should give a high priority to those that can be customized to meet specific project needs. Organizations must also remember that they will rely heavily on data provided by the project team. Therefore, when selecting project management software, organizations have to consider the structure, coding, and displaying requirements of the WBS. These include:[10]

- What types of information must be stored and what types are optional
- How much space is required to store that information (e.g., whether the item is a one- or two-digit number, such as in the example above, or a paragraph, such as a daily log)
- What sorts of report layouts the software can provide

Putting Together a WBS

The author of this chapter is the plant manager of the University of Pittsburgh's Manufacturing Assistance Center (MAC), a working and teaching factory for manufacturers in southwestern Pennsylvania. The MAC team is putting together a comprehensive training curriculum to train individuals to meet local manufacturers' needs. The team is in the process of developing a WBS. It is not complete, however; thus, only a partial WBS is available for this chapter (see Figure 7–5).

The creation of the WBS needs to be a manageable team effort. The process used in a project is a series of tasks and activities that are necessary to create the final end items or deliverables of the project. Because the WBS ultimately determines who is to be included on the team, the designers are usually a group of people experienced in project management who are knowledgeable about the project end items and the availability of necessary inside (organizational) and outside (contractor) resources required to produce them. In the training program project, the designers are the MAC's plant manager and training coordinator.

When creating a WBS, the designers first look at the project as a whole: the end items and the means to attain them. For the MAC project, the designers need to determine what they want students of the class to leave the MAC knowing and understanding, their employment possibilities and marketability, and how the MAC can cost-effectively provide them this opportunity. The WBS designers should first engage in brainstorming what they believe are the major components of the project. They start at the top-level (e.g., training program), then break this down by the major elements of the project at the next level down (e.g., area of manufacturing to train, location for training, resources, instructors, funding, area manufacturers, etc.). The designers then divide each of these elements into its subcomponent.

Through this process, the designers may venture into areas beyond their expertise. Thus, they should not immediately bog themselves down with all the details. The group should begin with a simple structure, outlining the project with two to three levels. Initially, the structure should be clear, with

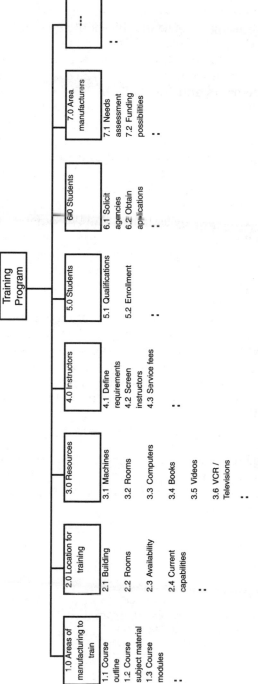

Figure 7–5 Partial WBS for Developing a Training Curriculum

the code open to further refinement after the structure has been finalized by the team. This is where the project currently resides.

Once the structure and code are prepared, the designers should generate a few sample reports using the WBS and distribute them to various team members (e.g., the MAC's general management and technical trainers) and major stakeholders (e.g., local-area manufacturers who will hire the students, government funding agencies, etc.) for review. The designers should solicit input from the team members and stakeholders who will be using it. The team should then test the initial WBS with data to ensure that the team can retrieve the type of information they will need. This may require a few iterations.

The team continues this level-by-level breakdown, clarifying the project's scope, until the proper *practical* level of end-item definition and cost are reached. This process allows the team to break down the project elements into the major work packages required to produce the final project deliverables. Thus, complex project elements and tasks become manageable units and the responsibility of each is clearly assigned. The WBS enables the team to begin planning, estimating, budgeting, scheduling, executing, and controlling the work required to meet the project's purpose.[11]

After the final design of the structure, code, and reports, the WBS is presented by the designers and explained to the team and stakeholders, including the dictionary of each WBS element.

The process of generating a WBS has important benefits. It forces the team to think through all elements of the project. This way, they do not overlook any important items and clearly specify the scope of work assigned to each project member. The WBS provides a visualization of the entire project in a meaningful way with insight to all the team interrelationships.[12] Below is an example of a framework adapted from Archibold for the creation, use, and control of the WBS.[13]

CREATION
- Develop the WBS in a top-down manner involving the project manager, planner, and key project members.
- Solicit the team for input, be open to suggestions, and make revisions until an accord is reached.
- Identify for each work element and work package (task) required to meet project objectives

    —Resources required, both internal to the organization and contracted outside.
    —Methods of procuring resources (e.g., purchase orders, cost account number (task level only), work order number).
    —Authority and responsibility for its completion.
    —Product specifications.
    —Estimates and budgets.
    —Milestone events and scheduled dates.

- Test the WBS with data to ensure reporting requirements are met.

USE
- Input project data (e.g., accomplishments, expenditures, etc.) for each work element under its WBS code.
- As a project control device, periodically total this information up the levels of the WBS and compare actual performance against budgets and estimates.
- Use these comparisons to identify problems and initiate corrective action.
- Adjust work element budgets, schedules, and scope of work accordingly.

CONTROL
Enact policies and require signatures for changes, additions, and deletions to the WBS document to control WBS and maintain it as a valid communication tool.

Conclusion

A WBS is a highly useful and invaluable management tool. It is a disciplined, systematic methodology to organize the job ahead of project teams to prevent any accidental oversights of necessary steps and resources. It adds clarity to the venture by providing a visual communication tool for all project stakeholders that details the end items of the venture along with the processes by which they will be attained.

ENDNOTES
1 Goldratt, Eliyahu, M., and Cox, Jeff. *The Goal: A Process of Ongoing Improvement. Second Edition, Revised*, Great Barrington, MA: North River Press, Inc., 1992
2 Cleland, David I. *Project Management: Strategic Design and Implementation. Second Edition*, New York: McGraw-Hill, 1994, p. 252
3 *Ibid.*, p. 256
4 *Ibid.*, p. 250
5 Archibald, Russell D. *Managing High-Technology Programs and Projects.* Second Edition (pp. 193–208), New York: John Wiley & Sons, Inc., 1992
6 Lavold, Gary D. Developing using the work breakdown structure, *Project Management Handbook.* Second Edition (pp. 302–323), Edited by David I. Cleland and William R. King, New York: Van Nostrand Reinhold, 1988
7 Rastelli, Gary W. Back to the basics of planning and scheduling, *Cost Engineering* 35:6, 13–14, 1993
8 Lavold, Gary D. Developing and using the work breakdown structure, *Project Management Handbook. Second Edition* (pp. 302–323). Edited by David I. Cleland and William R. King, New York: Van Nostrand Reinhold, 1988
9 *Ibid.*, pp. 302–323
10 Jensen, Christian A. Effective project planning techniques, *Civil Engineering* 64(2), 66–67, 1994
11 Archibald, Russell D. *Managing High-Technology Programs and Projects,* Second Edition (pp. 193–208), New York: John Wiley & Sons, Inc., 1992
12 *Ibid.*, pp. 193–208
13 *Ibid.*, pp. 193–208

Tools to Achieve On-Time Performance

J. Davidson Frame

Biographical Sketch . . .   **J. Davidson Frame** is Professor of Management
Science at the George Washington University, where
he also heads GWU's International Center for Project
Management Excellence. He was the Project Management Institute's Director of Certification from 1990
to 1996. He currently serves as PMI's Director of
Educational Services. He has published two book on
project management: *Managing Projects in Organizations*, Second Edition, and *The New Project Management.* He is currently writing a new book titled *Project
Management Competence: Assessing the Core Capabilities of Individuals, Teams, and Organizations.*

T he capacity to schedule projects effectively is one of the most significant
competencies a project professional should master. This has always
been true in project management, but today it is more important than
ever, because in this brutally competitive world, speed of product development and service delivery provides organizations with an edge that enables
them to beat their competitors.

This chapter examines the basic issues of project scheduling. First, it
reviews the process of estimating the duration of project activities. If realistic
estimates can serve as the basis of project planning and implementation, the
likelihood of conducting a project successfully grows dramatically. Then the
chapter examines four dominant techniques of project scheduling: Gantt
charts, milestone charts, PERT/CPM networks, and earned value.

Time Management

What most distinguishes effective project professionals from professionals
working in other areas is their focus on the management of time. Project professionals are expected to be experts in the art and science of scheduling pro-

ject efforts. They should be good at estimating how long it takes to carry out specific activities, identifying when key milestones can be achieved; at developing alternative scheduling scenarios, tracking schedule progress, and offering guidance on how schedules can be accelerated.

Moreover, the need to supply customers with goods and services quickly has created serious problems for many project teams. It has led to a situation in which unrealistic promises are being made as to when goods and services can be delivered. If these promises are not kept, then customer disaffection arises.

Ongoing research conducted by the author suggests that among the well-known triple constraints of time, budget, and specifications, project teams are having their greatest difficulty working within the time constraint. For example, in one recent survey of fifty-five project professionals working in forty-two organizations, I found that, although 31.5% stated they were facing budget problems and 20.4% stated they were having trouble meeting the specifications, 70.9% reported facing schedule slippage. Clearly, schedule-related problems are the key problems facing this group of respondents and other project teams.

DEVELOPING PROJECT SCHEDULES

Effective project scheduling rests heavily on developing accurate estimates of the duration of individual activities. The ability to create accurate estimates depends largely on the estimating organization's prior experience in doing the activities. If the project team is carrying out a set of activities for the first time, then it is likely that the estimates will be rough. For example, researchers carrying out a project to identify the causes of a newly discovered disease are treading new ground and have only the vaguest sense of how long it will take them to do the job. On the other hand, if the team has carried out a set of activities many times before, then the estimates can be quite precise.

Organizations are beginning to implement procedures to capture their experiences systematically by having staff maintain accurate records of their activities. Thus, software testers keep track of how long it takes to test certain software modules, and equipment installers track the duration of standard hook-ups.

Distinguishing Between Working Time and Elapsed Time

In developing project schedules, it is important to recognize that the passage of time can be viewed from different perspectives. For example, there is a fundamental difference in computing the time spent by a painter in painting a chair and the time it takes for the paint to dry on the chair. If while the painter is painting the chair she is interrupted with a phone call, then work on the chair temporarily stops. Similarly, during the time the painter takes a lunch break, work on the chair stops. This concept of time is called *working time*. For workers who work eight hours a day for five days a week, their working-time effort is forty hours per week.

In contrast, phone interruptions have no bearing on whether paint dries on the chair. The paint will dry no matter what. This concept of time is called *elapsed time*. Elapsed time activities are common in projects that entail physical activities, such as construction and facilities-management projects. On such projects, freshly poured concrete must be given time to cure, paint must be given time to dry, and glue must be given time to set. Even more conceptual projects in, say, the software arena may encounter elapsed-time situations: For example, mainframe computers operate twenty-four hours a day, seven days a week. They do not take lunch breaks or shut down on holidays. Thus a software-testing job may be sitting in a queue until 2:30 on a Sunday morning, at which time it is finally enabled to execute.

Failure to recognize the difference between working-time and elapsed-time activities may lead to incorrect schedule estimates. For example, Marvin finishes painting a chair at 5:00 on a Friday afternoon. Immediately upon finishing the chair, he goes home and has a relaxing weekend with his family until he returns to work at 8:00 on Monday morning. This is a clear illustration of working time.

Meanwhile, the paint on the chair begins drying at 5:00 p.m. on Friday. If it takes two days for paint to dry, then the paint-drying effort will be completed at 5:00 p.m. Sunday. This illustrates an elapsed-time effort. However, if in entering data into the computerized scheduling software the project scheduler treats the paint-drying activity as a working-time effort, the computer will calculate that the paint will begin drying at 8:00 Monday morning and will be completely dry by 5:00 p.m. Tuesday—an incorrect conclusion.

Use of the Beta Distribution to Estimate Durations

Experienced project estimators know that whatever duration they estimate for a task, their estimate will not be 100 percent correct. An estimator might predict that a particular task will take two days to undertake. When carried out, the task might actually take 2.2 days. Had project conditions been a little different, it might have taken 1.9 days. The point is that the exact duration of a task will almost certainly vary from the estimated duration.

Often, the variability of estimates assumes what statisticians call a *Beta distribution*. An example of a Beta distribution is pictured in Figure 8–1. Assume that this particular distribution shows how many hours it can take for the paint on freshly painted chairs to dry. The distribution suggests that the quickest time for paint to dry is three hours. The slowest is seven hours. Most frequently, paint dries on chairs in four hours. A number of factors contribute to the variability of paint-drying times: humidity, ambient temperature, and thickness of the paint are three significant factors. As these factors vary from job to job, so will the time it takes for the paint to dry.

The Beta distribution mirrors what frequently happens on projects: The very best time a job can be done in (three hours in our example) is not that much better than what happens most typically (four hours). However, when things go wrong, durations can stretch out (up to seven hours in our example). It should be noted that what happens most frequently is not a good estimator

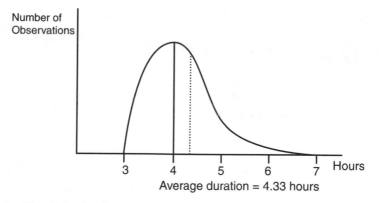

Figure 8-1   Beta Distribution

of how long it takes for a task to be carried out. A good estimator is the *average* time spent on a task. If the pessimistic estimate of duration is substantial, then the average time spent on a task will be longer than what happens most frequently because the worst-case situations cause the average value to grow in size.

Calculating the average value of a Beta distribution is nontrivial because this distribution is fairly complex mathematically. However, statisticians have developed a simple formula to estimate the average with a fair degree of accuracy. The formula is:

$$\text{Average duration} = (a + 4b + c)/6$$

where a = optimistic duration, b = most typical duration, and c = pessimistic duration. In the paint-drying example, average duration is (3 + 4 × 4 + 7)/6, or 4.33 hours. This means that if we were to track the drying times of, say, a thousand painted chairs, we would find that they took an average of 4.33 hours to dry.

Even here, we know that it will not take exactly 4.33 hours for the paint to dry. The actual result will be something greater or less than this. The level of precision of the estimate can be roughly identified by using the following formula (in statistics, this level of precision is called the *standard deviation*):

$$\text{Standard deviation} = (c \times a)/6$$

where c = pessimistic duration and a = optimistic duration. In the numerical example, the standard deviation is (7 × 3)/6, or 0.67 hours. Thus, in reporting the estimate for how much time it takes for paint to dry on chairs, we would make the following statement:

"We are quite confident that it will take 4.33 hours, plus or minus two-thirds of an hour, for paint to dry on most chairs. That is, the paint can dry in as little as 3.67 hours or as long as 5.00 hours."

Of course, the actual values can lie outside this range. On a particularly hot, dry day, the paint may dry very quickly—say, in 3.25 hours. Or on a cool, humid day it may dry slowly—say, in 6.1 hours. The key point here is that by computing the average and the standard deviation, we have a good sense of the range of time it will take for most cases.

The Need for Independent Verification

No amount of sophisticated statistical treatment will produce accurate estimates if the numbers that go into the formulas are off-target. Unfortunately, this is fairly common today. For example, sales people face substantial pressure to sell an organization's goods and services to clients because their incomes are often tied—through the use of sales commissions—to the volume of revenue they can generate. To make the sale, they may promise customers that projects can be carried out according to dates that are unrealistic. If the project team cannot make these promise dates, the customer is dissatisfied.

To avoid this kind of problem, it is a good idea to have schedule-promise dates independently verified. This verification can occur by using outside parties to cross-check promise dates (this is the preferred mode of operation of the U.S. Department of Defense) or by employing internal resources. The important point is that the promise dates should be reviewed from both a technical perspective (e.g., whether it is technically possible to do the work as quickly as promised) and from a broad managerial perspective (e.g., whether the qualified resources are available to carry out the work as planned).

If the assessment of the independent verification is that the promise dates cannot be met, then the project should not be carried out unless the promise dates are renegotiated.

Monte Carlo Simulation: Avoid Gambling with Project Schedules

Project planners have recently begun employing Monte Carlo simulations to obtain better estimates of project schedules. This technique was developed in the 1940s, but it has only gained widespread usage in the 1990s with the advent of user-friendly software that runs the simulations on personal computers. The technique allows planners to factor uncertainty into their estimates of schedules, budgets, and resource requirements.

Here's how the Monte Carlo simulation works. Assume that we are working on a very simple project consisting of only three phases. The first phase involves designing a widget, the second entails building it, and the third involves testing it before turning it over to the customer. Records show that on similar projects, the design effort most typically takes four days, the building effort twelve days, and the testing effort four days. If we were simply to add these numbers together, we would deduce that this project should take twenty days to complete.

However, let us assume that we carry out a Monte Carlo simulation to estimate project duration and that we have the data shown in Table 8–1 to help us with our estimate. With Monte Carlo simulation, we instruct the computer to employ a random-number generator to allow our estimated values to fluctuate according to whatever distribution we specify (say a normal distribution or a Beta distribution or a triangular distribution).

Table 8–1. Estimated Time to Carry Out the Widget Project

Task	Best Case	Most Typical	Worst Case
Design	3 Days	4 Days	7 Days
Build	10 Days	12 Days	16 Days
Test	3 Days	4 Days	6 Days

Using the random-number generator, the computer may specify that the design effort takes 4.2 days, the building effort 10.9 days, and the testing effort 4.5 days. In total, 19.6 days will have been spent on the project. Then the computer has the random-number generator change the values for design, build, and test and computes the total duration a second time. This process is repeated many times. On each occasion, the computer keeps track of the total estimated time. What is happening here is that the computer is simulating the vagaries of carrying out a project under many different circumstances.

Table 8–2 shows the results of a Monte Carlo simulation when the random-number generator is instructed to employ a triangular distribution to generate values for the design, build, and test phases. It did this for 10,000 iterations. The results show that if this project were carried out many times, the average duration for doing the work would be 21.6 days, 1.6 days longer than our original estimate of twenty days. Furthermore, the Monte Carlo simulation can give us probabilities for different scenarios. For example, the simulation described here found that 25 percent of the time, one can expect the project duration to be 20.5 days or shorter, and 25 percent of the time one can expect the duration to be 22.7 days or longer. Most significantly, the simulation suggests that it is highly unlikely that we could do the work in twenty or fewer days as initially estimated (the probability of this eventuality is only 17 percent).

At present, software exists that permits project planners to carry out Monte Carlo simulations on their computer-based PERT/CPM schedule networks (the PERT/CPM methodology is discussed later in this chapter). The duration of each task in the PERT/CPM chart is allowed to fluctuate according to whatever distribution the planner specifies. The computer can be instructed to go through hundreds of iterations, where durations are allowed to fluctuate randomly for all tasks. The simulation tracks the results of all these runs to identify a broad range of project outcomes. As a consequence, planners can create reasonably realistic scheduling models.

Table 8–2. Results of Monte Carlo Simulation, Using 10,000 Iterations

Average Duration	Standard Deviation	Minimum Duration	Maximum Duration	25% Likely That Duration Is Less Than:	25% Likely That Duration Is More Than:
21.6 days	1.6 days	16.9 days	27.5 days	20.5 days	22.7 days

SCHEDULING TECHNIQUES: FROM SIMPLE TO COMPLEX

Presently, three basic scheduling techniques dominate project-management practice: Gantt charts, milestone charts, and PERT/CPM networks. In addition, a forth approach that focuses on integrated cost/schedule control is gaining currency. Each of these techniques will be discussed in turn.

Gantt Charts: No Training Required

The Gantt chart is the most commonly employed project-management scheduling tool. Its simplicity is its strength. Project staff, customers, and upper-level managers can interpret Gantt charts without training. Project workers can begin constructing them immediately. Overall schedule status can be determined at a glance.

Gantt charts come in a number of variants. The most common variant—the bar chart—is shown in Figure 8–2. This simple Gantt chart pictures a project to build a birdhouse. The project is being carried out by Susan and her young son, Randy. In this variant, bars are used to display the interval of time in which an activity is supposed to be carried out.

The Gantt chart contains data on when tasks begin and when they end. Given this information, we can determine the length of the tasks. For example, the task "Obtain kit" starts at 9:00 a.m. and ends at 10:00 a.m. Thus it consumes one hour of effort. Similarly, "Gather tools" starts at 10:00 a.m. and finishes at 10:30 a.m., consuming one-half hour of effort.

By inspecting the chart, we can also identify the proposed sequencing of activities. For example, while the task "Assemble birdhouse" is being carried out, first "Emplace pole" and then "Help assemble" are being implemented.

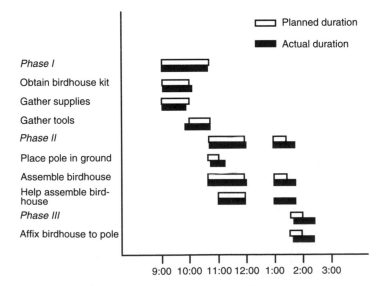

Figure 8–2   Gantt Chart

Gantt charts are the most effective way of portraying schedule status to customers, staff, and management. That's because they allow actual effort to be juxtaposed directly against scheduled effort. In Figure 8–2, planned effort is pictured with empty boxes and actual effort is pictured with the solid black boxes. A review of the "actuals" data suggests that work was achieved according to the schedule for the first three tasks (phase I), but that slippage occurred in phase II. Specifically, "Assemble birdhouse" began a little late and ended late, and "Help assemble" began late and took longer to carry out than planned.

Milestone Charts: Markers Along the Highway

Gantt charts are a simple way to picture how tasks are scheduled to occur. In contrast, milestone charts focus on the desired results of activity. In a sense, they provide targets at which the project team aims its efforts. In addition, like the milestones travelers encounter along highways, they are markers indicating where individuals are in regard to their starting point as well as their destination.

Figure 8–3—a milestone chart—lays out the birdhouse project according to a number of key milestones. It should be noted that the milestones contained in the chart reflect anticipated results, not tasks per se.

When milestone charts are employed with a measure of creativity, they can provide the project team with valuable insights. For example, they can be employed to enable the project team to estimate the amount of work they have carried out. To see this, consider a 2,500-person-hour project in which the scheduler has carefully identified five milestones, each of which represents an estimated 500 person-hours of work. Once the work associated with the first milestone has been accomplished, the project team can state that it has

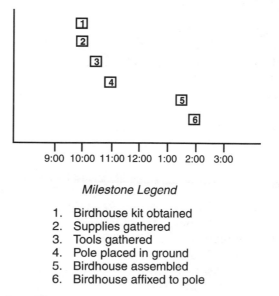

Milestone Legend

1. Birdhouse kit obtained
2. Supplies gathered
3. Tools gathered
4. Pole placed in ground
5. Birdhouse assembled
6. Birdhouse affixed to pole

Figure 8–3   Milestone Chart

achieved 20 percent of its targeted effort. When the work associated with the second milestone has been accomplished, the team can state that it has achieved 40 percent of its target effort, and so on.

Milestone charts have valuable applications. For example, they can highlight political milestones (e.g., "It is politically wise to finish phase I by August 13 so that the CEO can announce project progress at the stockholder meeting on August 15"), budgetary milestones (e.g., "To obtain project funding for the next fiscal year, we must have our budget request form submitted to the finance office by June 30"), and bureaucratic milestones (e.g., "Our next quarterly progress report is due on October 15").

PERT/CPM Networks for Complex Projects

PERT (Program Evaluation and Review Technique) and CPM (Critical Path Method) were developed in the 1950s to allow more effective scheduling of large, complex projects. These methodologies employ network diagrams that are roughly equivalent to flow charts. As we have seen, Gantt charts lay out when different tasks will be implemented and milestone charts focus on the achievement of key results. In contrast, PERT/CPM networks show how the different tasks are connected to each other, enabling the project team to view the project as a system comprised of interrelated parts. Virtually all the new software approaches PERT/CPM by using what is called the Precedence Diagram Method (PDM). With this approach, tasks are pictured as boxes, and interdependencies as lines.

FUNCTIONING OF PERT/CPM: THE BASICS.   Figure 8–4 shows a PERT/CPM network for the birdhouse project. This network contains two paths. The tasks along one path are carried out by Susan and the tasks along the other path are carried out by Randy.

In phase I, Susan will drive to the hardware store to pick up a birdhouse kit. This will consume one hour. Meanwhile, Randy will gather supplies (one-hour effort) and tools (one-half-hour effort) from around the house. In all, Randy will devote 1.5 hours to phase I and Susan will devote 1.0 hours. The duration of phase I will be defined by the longest path (Randy's). Thus, phase I will last 1.5 hours. In PERT/CPM, the longest path is given the name *critical path*. Susan's path is noncritical. In fact, because she is scheduled to carry out only one hour's worth of effort, she has a half hour of flexibility in implementing her task. This flexibility is called *slack* or *float*, two terms that are used interchangeably.

Because she has one half-hour of slack built into her schedule, Susan has a measure of flexibility in when she begins her task to obtain a birdhouse kit. She can begin as soon as the project begins at 9:00 a.m. (this is called earliest start, or S_E), or she can begin it as late as 9:30 a.m. (this is called latest start, or S_L). Slack is $S_L - S_E$, or 9:30–9:00, or thirty minutes.

This same kind of reasoning can be extended to phases II and III. The double-lined path indicates the critical path for the whole project. This path enables the project team to calculate the estimated duration for the entire

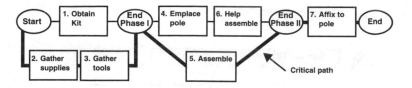

Legend

1. Obtain kit, early = 9:00 am, late = 9:30 am
   slack = 30 minutes, duration = 1 hour
2. Gather supplies, early = 9:00 am, late = 9:00 am
   slack = 0, duration = 1 hour
3. Gather tools, early = 10:00 am, late = 10:00 am
   slack = 0, duration = 30 minutes
4. Emplace pole, early = 10:30 am, late = 11:00 am
   slack = 30 minutes, duration = 30 minutes
5. Assemble birdhouse, early = 10:30 am, late = 10:30 am
   slack = 0, duration = 2 hours
6. Help assemble, early = 11:00 am, late = 11:30 am\
   slack = 30 minutes, duration = 1 hour
7. Affix to pole, early = 1:30 pm, late = 1:30 pm
   slack = 0, duration = 30 minutes

Figure 8–4   PERT/CPM Chart (Precedence Diagram)

project, which is four hours (the sum of the durations for the tasks that lie on the critical path). If one hour is added to the project duration to take into account an hour lunch break at noon, then the end time for the work is 2:00 p.m.

The example offered here has been kept simple to explain some key characteristics of PERT/CPM logic. This same logic can be extended to cover large, highly complex projects. In fact, PERT was invented in 1957 to deal with precisely this category of project. It was created in order to give U.S. Navy personnel and government contractors guidance on how to schedule activities for the Polaris missile project.

LOGICAL VERSUS RESOURCE-DRIVEN LINKS.   The trick to creating effective PERT/CPM network diagrams is to know how to link tasks together. Two ways of linking tasks are: (1) recognizing the difference between logical links (sometimes called *hard logic*) and resource-driven links (sometimes called *soft logic*), and (2) understanding the use of start-finish, start-start, finish-finish, and finish-start links.

The difference between logical and resource-driven links is illustrated in Figure 8–5, which shows a number of tasks that George and Martha will carry out in order to prepare lunch for a picnic. George and Martha have decided to split the workload as equitably as possible. Thus, while George is preparing sandwiches (ten minutes), Martha is preparing lemonade (four minutes) and gathering food for snacks (five minutes). Once the sandwiches, lemonade, and snacks are ready, they will be put into a picnic basket. The links connecting "Prepare sandwiches" and "Prepare lemonade" with "Pack picnic basket" are *logical links:* What the PERT/CPM network suggests is that the picnic basket cannot be packed until the food is prepared.

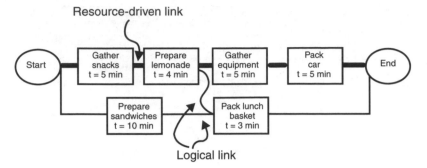

Figure 8–5   Logical and Resource-driven Links

Note, however, that the link connecting snacks to lemonade is a *resource-driven link*. There is no logical reason why "Gather snacks" must lie on the same path as "Prepare lemonade", or why, for that matter, it should precede "Prepare lemonade." It could just as easily have followed "Prepare lemonade" without affecting the quality of the lunch. In fact, if there were a third person to help with the project, he could have worked in parallel with George and Martha, preparing the lemonade while George worked on the sandwiches and Martha gathered the snacks, in which case the PERT/CPM network would have three paths rather than just two.

The principal point here is that with logical links, schedulers do not have much flexibility in connecting tasks to each other. Logically, these tasks *must* be linked together in a prescribed order. On the other hand, with resource-driven links, there is a good measure of flexibility in connecting tasks. For example, the more resources there are, the more possible it is to carry out tasks in parallel.

DIFFERENT TYPES OF LINKS.   All the links described so far in the examples that have been offered are finish-start links. That is to say, the successor task cannot be started until the predecessor task is finished. Thus, in the picnic example, Martha will not begin gathering food for snacks until she has first completed preparation of the lemonade. Today's software makes it easy to build lags into the links, so it is possible to create a PERT/CPM network that indicates that Martha should finish preparing the lemonade, wait one minute (a one-minute lag), and then begin gathering food for snacks.

Another link that can be created is a start-start link. For example, Painter A may begin applying a coat of quick-drying paint to the walls of a large house. Painter B is instructed to start applying a second coat of paint two hours after Painter A begins his work. This is a start-start link with a two-hour lag.

A third link is the finish-finish link. Three writers might be instructed to finish writing their sections of a technical report by a specific date. Although they may have begun their work at different times, the key point is to finish together. This is a finish-finish link with zero lag.

The final link is a start-finish link. Assume that Mary's task is to edit a number of chapters of a long, technical report. She instructs Ralph that he should complete work on his chapter two days after she begins her editing chore so that she can work directly on editing his piece at that time. This is a finish-start link with a two-day lag.

The great majority of precedence links employed by project schedulers are finish-start links. The other types of links are available, however, to enable schedulers to portray their schedules more realistically under appropriate circumstances.

Chief Value of PERT/CPM

A major value of PERT/CPM networks is that they serve as mathematical models projects. For example, by creating a PERT/CPM network, project planners can estimate the duration of the overall project, and possess knowledge of the latest and earliest start times for individual tasks.

Beyond this, today's PERT/CPM-based project-management software provides planners with an integrated view of schedules, costs, and resource requirements. Consequently, project planners can conduct various "what-if" analyses to see the impact of different situations on schedules, budgets, and resource requirements.

GRAPHICAL INTEGRATED COST/SCHEDULE CONTROL

Control is the process of comparing planned activity against what is actually happening. By itself, looking at planned versus actual schedule performance is only marginally useful. It is more useful to engage in integrated cost and schedule control. To learn that a project is two weeks ahead of schedule may be small consolation if it turns out that it is also facing a 25 percent cost overrun. On the other hand, a two-week schedule slippage may be easier to take if it turns out that the project is experiencing a 25 percent cost savings.

Integrated cost/schedule control can be carried out easily by reviewing schedule and cost performance graphically. This is illustrated in Figure 8–6, in which Gantt charts represent schedule performance, and cumulative cost curves (also called S-curves) picture cost performance. Figure 8–6a shows a situation in which the project is being carried out faster than planned. However, it is encountering a serious cost overrun. Figure 8–6b pictures a situation in which the project is encountering schedule slippage and a cost overrun. Finally, Figure 8–6c illustrates a project that is being carried out on time and within budget.

Integrated Cost/Schedule Control with Earned Value

One of the most significant innovations in project management methodology was the creation in the 1960s of what is called the cost/schedule control system (C/SCS). This methodology is a cost accounting approach to reviewing schedule and budget performance simultaneously.

At the heart of C/SCS is a measure of work performance, called *earned value*, which provides information on how much work has actually been performed. This work performance is measured in monetary terms. For example, the computation of earned value for a project may show that $3,500 worth of work has actually been accomplished. Cost variance becomes a matter of comparing how much money has been spent against how much work has

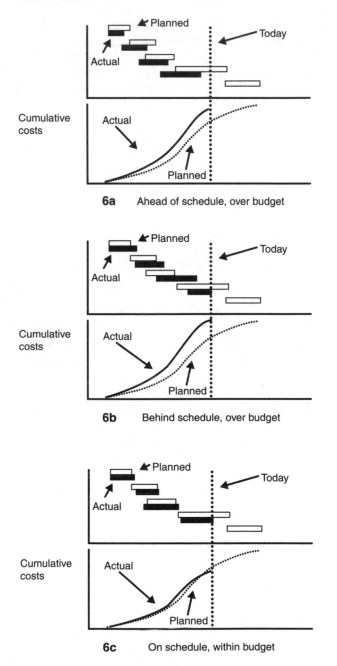

6a   Ahead of schedule, over budget

6b   Behind schedule, over budget

6c   On schedule, within budget

Figure 8–6   Integrated Cost/Schedule Control

been done. If actual expenditures are $3,700, the project is experiencing a $200 cost overrun, since $3,700 has been spent to do $3,500 worth of work.

Schedule variance is computed by comparing how much work has been done against what was planned to have been accomplished. If $4,000 of work was planned to have been achieved, but only $3,500 worth of work was actually carried out, then the project is behind schedule, because less work was done than planned.

The key to employing the C/SCS methodology is being able to compute earned value. Here are three options: (1) using the fifty-fifty rule, (2) computing earned value based on historical experience, and (3) making best-guess estimates.

THE FIFTY-FIFTY RULE.   Say that a particular project is comprised of four tasks. In creating the work breakdown structure (WBS) for the project, we devise each task to be roughly of equal size. Since with C/SCS we are employing a cost-accounting approach, size is measured in monetary terms. Thus, in our example, each task is a $100 task. If budgetary data are not available, one can employ person-hours of effort (or person-days) as a substitute—for example, each of my four tasks is scheduled to consume eighty person hours of effort.

Our goal is to measure work performance. To do this, we assume that the moment a task begins, we have done half the value of planned work. Thus when a $100 task begins, we say, for accounting purposes, that we have done $50 worth of work. Only when the task is actually finished do we say that we have done the remaining half of the work. When a $100 task is completed, we can then state that we have achieved our $100 planned effort.

Let us say that in our hypothetical example we have completed work on three of the tasks and have begun work on the fourth. Using the fifty-fifty rule, we estimate that we have accomplished $350 worth of work: our earned value.

It should be noted that the fifty-fifty rule provides the project team with an *estimate* of earned value, not the real figure. Project staff who are concerned that the estimate may be too optimistic can employ a more conservative approach to calculating earned value: the 0–100 rule. As its name implies, the value of work associated with a task is not recorded until after the task is complete. In the four-task example, earned value is $300 when the 0–100 rule is employed.

HISTORICAL EXPERIENCE.   A more accurate way to calculate earned value is to base the estimate on historical experience. Let us say that we are trying to compute earned value to track roofing work on twenty houses. Historical experience may suggest that when a roof has been framed out, it is 20 percent complete. When plywood panels have been laid down on the framework, creating a "solid" roof, the roof is forty percent complete. When tar paper has been placed over the plywood panels, the roof is 50 percent complete. When shingles have been laid on one side of the roof, it is 70 percent complete, and when they have been laid on both sides, the roof is 90 percent complete. Finally, after finish work has been carried out, the roof is 100 percent complete.

To compute earned value, a technician can be sent to the houses to tabulate progress. If she sees fifteen houses whose roofs have only been framed out, she notes that fifteen houses are at the 20 percent mark. If she also identifies three houses where plywood panels have been laid down on the framework, then she notes that three houses are at the 40 percent mark. She determines that two houses have tar paper laid down on the plywood panels, indicating that they are at the 50 percent mark. By taking a weighted average of the progress of the twenty houses ([15 × 0.2 + 3 × 0.4 + 2 × 0.5]/20), she determines that the roofing effort is 26 percent complete. If the planned cost of the roofing effort for all twenty houses is $200,000, then earned value is $52,000 (26% of $200,000).

BEST-GUESS ESTIMATES.   It may be that, owing to a lack of project data, the only available way of calculating earned value is to make a best-guess estimate of how much work has been done. This probably reflects the practice of most organizations in their attempts to measure work performance. An expert may review progress on a module of project work and guess that the module is 70 percent complete.

The problem with this approach is that it tends to lead to optimistic assessments of project performance. When projects start out, it often looks as if they are making tremendous progress, so best-guess estimates of earned value may inflate the true figure. Thus, the team may report that the project is at the 90 percent mark quite early in the life cycle. However, as projects are being wrapped up, it seems to take forever to tie up loose ends. We even quip that the last 10 percent of a project often takes 50 percent of the work effort. Consequently, the project is reported to be 90 percent complete for each of the last several months of its existence. This phenomenon occurs so frequently that we have even given it a name: the 90 percent hang-up.

Using Earned Value to Report Project Progress

Project progress can be tracked quite clearly when project staff employ the C/SCS methodology. Consider tracking schedule performance. This is done in two ways. First, schedule variance is computed by contrasting the work that has been done (earned value) with the work that was supposed to be done (measured as planned cost). In the C/SCS approach, earned value and planned costs are given special "labels": Earned value is called BCWP (budgeted cost of work performed) and planned cost is called BCWS (budgeted cost of work scheduled). Using these new labels, schedule variance is defined as:

$$SV = BCWP \times BCWS \quad (minus)$$

Thus, if BCWP is $350 and BCWS is $400, this indicates a schedule variance of −$50. That is, this effort has achieved $50 less work than it should have.

A related way to examine schedule performance is to create a schedule performance index (SPI), which is defined as:

$$SPI = BCWP/BCWS$$

What the SPI measures is how much work has been done (BCWP) as a fraction of how much was supposed to be done (BCWS). If BCWP is $350 and BCWS is $400, SPI is 0.875, which indicates that the project has achieved 87.5% of what it was supposed to achieve.

To track cost performance, earned value (BCWP) is compared to actual costs, which is called ACWP (actual cost of work performed). The data for ACWP come from the accounting department and reflect money spent on salaries, purchases of materials, purchases of services, and so on. Cost variance is defined as:

$$CV = BCWP \times ACWP \quad (minus)$$

If BCWP is $350 and ACWP is $450, cost variance is –$100. That is, for the work that has been achieved (BCWP), the project team spent $100 too much.

A related way to examine cost performance is to create a cost performance index (CPI), which is defined as:

$$CPI = BCWP/ACWP$$

What CPI measures is the efficiency with which project funds are being expended. If BCWP is $350 and ACWP is $450, then CPI is 0.778, which indicates that the project is achieving 77.8 cents of work for every dollar spent. This project clearly will run out of funds if it continues to operate at this level of efficiency.

An important function of CPI is that it lets the project team estimate what the final cost of the project will be. This estimate of final cost is called estimate at completion, or EAC. It is computed using the following formula:

$$EAC = (Total\ project\ budget)/CPI$$

If the total project budget is $1 million and the CPI is 0.778, the EAC is $1,285,714. This means that if the project continues to generate 77.8 cents of work for every dollar spent, it will have a $285,714 shortfall unless major adjustments are made (e.g., work can be cut back, budgets can be increased).

Together, the C/SCS tools we have just examined provide project teams with the capacity to carry out solid analyses of cost and schedule performance. These analyses can be carried out at whatever level of detail the team chooses. They can focus on aggregate data for the project as a whole, or they can concentrate on reviewing performance at the task and phase levels.

Conclusion

The pressure to deliver goods and service faster and faster has created a situation in which organizations often promise delivery dates that are unrealistic. If scheduled delivery dates are not met, then this certainly leads to customer disaffection.

Consequently, effective schedule management requires that project professionals develop accurate estimates of how much time it will take to do the job, create schedules that offer project teams good guidance on how they should carry out their work, track performance to determine whether the project will achieve its performance targets, and adjust schedules to accommodate the new realities that arise as the project is being executed.

Keeping the Lid on Project Costs

Kim LaScola Needy and
Kimberly L. Petri

Biographical Sketch. . .   **Kim LaScola Needy** is an Assistant Professor of Industrial Engineering at the University of Pittsburgh. She received her B.S. and M.S. degrees in industrial engineering from the University of Pittsburgh and her Ph.D. in industrial engineering from Wichita State University. She has accumulated nine years of industrial experience while working at PPG Industries and The Boeing Company. Her research interests include activity based costing, TQM, integrated resource management, and engineering management. She is a licensed professional engineer in Kansas.

Kimberly L. Petri received her B.S. in mathematics from Allegheny College and her M.S. in industrial engineering from the University of Pittsburgh. She is currently a Ph.D. candidate in the Department of Industrial Engineering at the University of Pittsburgh. Her research interests include applying neural networks, fuzzy logic, and artificial intelligence techniques to problems in manufacturing.

Changes in the marketplace—such as heightened global competition, rapid advances in technology leading to shorter project life cycles, and a strong emphasis on quality and customer satisfaction—have led to an increased focus on project costs. In many cases, project work has evolved from an unstructured activity with loose cost guidelines to a highly structured activity with well-defined procedures for estimating, controlling, and collecting data on costs. For example, contract work for the military must now adhere to a set of Cost/Schedule Control Systems Criteria outlined by the Department of Defense (DoD Instrumentation No. 7000.2). Customers expect high quality and on-time delivery from all project bidders and often use the cost estimate in deciding between potential contractors.

Impact of Cost on Schedule and Technical Performance

Cost affects schedule and technical performance measures. Cost, schedule, and technical performance measures can be thought of as a triangle where changes to one measure necessitate changes to the other two. For example, expediting the project schedule while maintaining the level of technical performance will increase costs. A common Japanese approach to managing the interactions among these measures is to use target costing. In this approach, a target cost is set for a project, and technical performance parameters and the project schedule are adjusted to meet the target cost.

A project costing system should yield accurate and timely cost information at the required level of detail. It should allow the project manager to evaluate the trade-offs when making decisions on issues affecting schedule and performance. Striking a balance between these three competing measures requires teamwork. The use of cross-functional teams with representatives from areas such as accounting, sales, service, and manufacturing is an effective means of promoting consensus in the event that all measures cannot simultaneously be met and of ensuring that one measure is not "optimized" at the expense of another.

Cost and the Project Life Cycle

Costs must be closely managed throughout the entire project life cycle. The project life cycle consists of a conceptual phase, a definition phase, a production/construction phase, an operational phase, and a divestment phase. The conceptual phase establishes the feasibility of the project, develops a basic budget and schedule, and leads to the formation of the project team. The project's cost, schedule, technical performance objectives, and design are established in the definition phase. The production/construction phase entails procuring project materials, producing/constructing the desired system, and verifying its performance. The operational phase involves installing the resulting system in the environment for which it was developed. Lastly, the divestment phase involves training personnel and transfering materials and responsibility for the system to the end user.[1] Chapters 5 and 6 discuss the project life cycle and how to manage it in greater detail.

At the start of a project, it is difficult to estimate with certainty the final cost. As the project nears its end, many of the expenses have already been incurred, leaving a smaller portion of the total expense to estimate. A large portion of project costs are typically expended in the production/construction and operational phases of the project, but the definition phase sets project's cost, schedule, and technical performance standards as well as the resource requirements and the work-breakdown structure (WBS).

Decisions made in the definition phase of the life cycle affect project costs far more than any cost-control measures adopted during the production/construction and operational phases. In fact, approximately 75 to 90 percent of project costs are determined during the definition phase of the project.[2] Design practices that can aid in the development of realistic cost, schedule, and technical performance measures include the use of computer aided design/computer aided engineering (CAD/CAE), Design for "X," concurrent design, simplification, robust design, and designed experiments.[3]

Costs Keep Corporate Strategy in Sight

An effective cost estimating and control system sets performance measures and requires the selection of a cost management system that complements the company's corporate culture and strategic objectives. Note that the set of relevant performance measures often changes in different phases of the project life cycle. A good cost management strategy should not merely be a way to track exactly where costs were expended, it should encourage employees to support the company's strategies and cost reduction measures.

The Many Ways to Examine Cost

Costs can be examined with respect to type (direct or indirect); frequency of occurrence (recurring or nonrecurring); opportunity to be adjusted (fixed or variable); and schedule (normal or expedited).

DIRECT VERSUS INDIRECT COSTS

As the name suggests, direct costs can be traced directly to the project that generated the cost. The most common examples of direct costs include labor and materials. For example, consider the construction of a bridge. All of the labor costs associated with the workers involved with the actual construction process can be traced directly to the project. Note that this would not necessarily include nondedicated resources such as project management and accounting personnel who may be concurrently overseeing multiple projects.

In the case of a manufacturing setting, workers may clock in to a particular production work order via a labor collection system. Labor can then be accumulated for the work order (which is generally associated with a particular product) by type and quantity. Direct labor rates can subsequently be applied to the labor hours to derive the total direct labor cost. Although fringe benefits can be built into the worker's direct labor rate, they are generally placed into an indirect cost category. Like direct labor costs, material costs are readily traced directly to a specific project. For example, purchase orders may be issued to procure the needed materials to complete the project. In a production environment, the bill of material (BOM) will identify the type and quantity of all materials needed to manufacture the product.

Typically, anything that cannot be classified as a direct cost gets placed into an indirect cost category. Indirect costs are generally placed into one of two categories: overhead, or selling and general administration. Examples of overhead costs include indirect materials, utilities, property taxes, insurance, depreciation on equipment, repairs, maintenance, and, in general, all costs associated with operations. Costs that fall into the category of selling and general administration include advertising, shipping, executive salaries, sales and secretarial support, sales travel, sales commissions, and the like.

The process of tracing indirect costs to specific projects is not straightforward. Most organizations choose instead to use some method of allocation. In the past, when the ratio of indirect to direct costs was very low and when computer sophistication was crude, there was little concern with an allocation approach. In the wake of the computer age and as the ratio of indirect to direct costs rises sharply, more attention is being paid to how to equitably trace indirect costs to the projects responsible for driving the costs. If care is not taken, there is a potential to grossly misstate the true project costs. Activity-based costing (which will be discussed in the final section of this chapter) has evolved to address this shortcoming.

RECURRING VERSUS NONRECURRING COSTS
Costs can also be examined with respect to their frequency of occurrence (recurring or nonrecurring). Typically, nonrecurring costs occur at the beginning and end of the project life cycle, whereas the recurring costs occur in the middle of the project life cycle. Examples of nonrecurring costs include preliminary design, market assessment, capital investment, training, divestment, and so on. Recurring costs are those that occur most frequently in the production/construction and operational phases of the project. Examples of recurring costs include material, direct labor, distribution, transportation, packaging, and sales.

To help ensure profitability, cost-reduction efforts should focus on both recurring and nonrecurring costs.

FIXED VERSUS VARIABLE COSTS
Costs also can be classified as fixed or variable. Fixed costs do not vary with respect to usage. For example, the leasing cost for a piece of equipment will not vary with the rate. The cost will be fixed regardless of whether the piece of equipment is fully utilized or sits idle. Similarly, the hardware associated with the running of a computer system is fixed regardless of the number of transactions processed through the system.

In contrast, variable costs vary in direct proportion to the usage level. Variable costs will rise as the usage level rises and fall as the usage level falls. Material cost is an example of a variable cost. The material cost to manufacture 100 units will be 100 times as great as the material cost to produce just one unit.

NORMAL VERSUS EXPEDITED COSTS
Normal costs include the costs to complete the project according to the planned schedule agreed upon by the parties at the onset of the project. Note that the planned schedule may be aggressive and include the use of overtime

to meet the completion date. In this case, overtime expenditures are considered to be normal. Expedited costs refer to those costs that are unplanned. They are additional costs incurred as a result of accelerating the schedule or staying on schedule when the project has fallen behind. Examples of these types of costs include the cost associated with temporarily increasing human resource capacity through overtime pay, hiring temporary workers, or subcontracting work to outside entities; and premium transportation costs for overnight shipment of products or overnight receipt of materials or supplies.

CLASSIFYING COSTS

Because of the particular characteristics unique to each project, the same cost will not always fall into the same category. Rather, classification of costs will be project specific. A good example of this would be direct labor. For a project using permanent, full-time employees, direct labor is considered to be fixed, at least in the short term. But for a project that uses all temporary, part-time employees, direct labor is variable. In this case, workers are only paid (and direct labor cost is only incurred) for work actually completed.

Table 9–1 illustrates several examples of costs and classifications. For example, consider the building lease cost. The building lease cost is an indirect type of expense. For a company that concurrently develops multiple projects, it is difficult to precisely trace how each project will consume the resources associated with the building expense. Common approaches used to make this approximation would be to allocate the expense to the project based upon the amount of square footage occupied by the project. Although in theory this approach appears to have merit, in practice it is difficult to implement because the same space is often shared by resources that support multiple projects.

The building lease expense is considered to be recurring. This expense will be incurred each period, not simply at the start of the project or as the project draws to a conclusion. For this reason, this cost is easy to predict across the project life cycle. The building lease cost is also fixed; in other words, the charge will remain constant regardless of the rate of production. This assumes

Table 9–1. Cost Classifications

Costs	Type		Frequency		Adjustment		Schedule	
	Direct	Indirect	Recurring	Non-Recurring	Fixed	Variable	Normal	Expedited
Direct Labor	X		X		X		X	
Building Lease		X	X		X		X	
Expedite Costs	X			X		X		X
Material	X		X			X	X	

of course that the project has not exceeded the capacity constraints associated with the building. Building expense is also considered to be a normal cost with respect to schedule. To accelerate the schedule or to pull the project back onto schedule would generally not require additional building lease expenses.

Elements of a Successful Cost Management System

In "Strategic Manufacturing Cost Management," G.J. Miller defines cost management as taking:

> financial-report numbers down to a more finite level of accountability by product, organization, project, cost element, etc. and correlating meaningful nonfinancial data with it to provide relevance. It is the means of interpreting information between operating and general management of an organization.[4]

A cost management system includes data collection, cost accounting, and cost control. Figure 9–1 shows the relationship of these functions to one another and depicts how they form the building blocks of a cost management system. At the lowest stage, data collection involves collecting data on the appropriate cost measures. At the next highest stage, cost accounting compiles and presents cost data in order to allow for cost control. Cost control involves determining, explaining, and correcting cost variances.

In order to be effective, a cost management system needs to support the strategic business objectives of the firm and provide accurate information at the right level of detail and in a timely manner. The cost management system should be independent of the accounting system used for reporting external

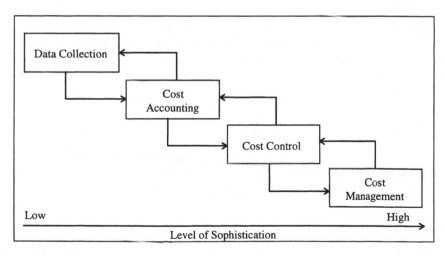

Figure 9–1   The Stages of Cost Management

Source: Miller, G. J. & Louk, P. Strategic manufacturing cost management. In *APICS 31st International Conference Proceedings*, 1988, pp. 542–547.

financial measures and should explicitly evaluate the trade-offs between satisfying cost, schedule, and technical performance objectives. Lastly, it should motivate workers to focus on project priorities.

BUILDING A COST MANAGEMENT SYSTEM

In order to be effective, a cost management system should provide the following:[5]

- *A link to the business strategy and strategic objectives.* The cost management system should provide feedback on how well the business strategies are being executed and on whether these strategies are financially successful. In addition, the business strategy helps define which operational measures are most important (e.g., reliability of a system, on-time delivery, unit production cost of a product, etc.).
- *Accurate information in a timely manner.* This is perhaps the most important element of a successful cost management system. Relevant, accurate information is valuable only if it is generated in time for management to initiate corrective action. Timely information allows cost management systems to be proactive rather than reactive.
- *Information at the correct level of aggregation.* Managers need aggregated, macro-level data in order to make strategic decisions. Information on a host of extraneous performance measures becomes overwhelming and counterproductive. At the same time, workers at the departmental level need detailed information on their performance with respect to measures that relate specifically to their work so that they can see how their work contributes to the success or failure of the project. For example, providing a machine operator with data on ROI hardly serves as a motivational factor to reduce setup times and increase throughput.
- *Data independent of the accounting system used for reporting external financial measures.* Cost data should be relevant to decision making rather than focused on external reporting measures. It should be useful for effective operational control so that cost variances can be traced back to their cause.
- *A focus on trade-offs between satisfying cost, schedule, and technical performance.* If the cost management system emphasizes only costs, then workers will focus strictly on costs, and downplay schedule and technical performance.
- *Motivation for workers to focus on the right things.* The cost management system should be used to promote teamwork within and between departments rather than competition.

SOURCES OF DATA

Data for the cost management system can be collected from existing production and process control systems and from databases used for engineering design, sales, and marketing. The use of technology such as automated data collection (barcoding, radio frequency identification, magnetic stripe, etc.)

has greatly facilitated the collection of a wide array of data. Data from existing production systems should be used whenever possible in order to avoid the inaccuracies and wasted time associated with redundant data entry into the costing system.

TECHNIQUES FOR COST ESTIMATING

A cost estimate is a forecast of expected costs based on a specified set of assumptions or conditions. The most common methods for cost estimating are expert opinion, analogy, regression, and bottom-up estimating.[6]

Although often considered a last resort, estimating costs via expert opinion is sometimes the only option available. Expert opinion should be based on fully documented assumptions. Estimates based on expert opinion are subject to bias. Generally, the quality of the estimates diminishes as the complexity of the task increases. In addition, the resulting estimate cannot be quantified in terms of uncertainty. Techniques such as Delphi can be used to quantify uncertainty when a group of experts is involved in decision making. Resources such as the *Cost Estimator's Reference Manual* (Stewart and Wyska, 1987) can be used to help substantiate expert opinion cost estimates.

Estimating cost through analogy involves analyzing the costs of a similar project (assuming that one exists) and then estimating the costs associated with the differences between the two projects. The technique typically relies on expert opinion and is therefore subject to the disadvantages discussed above.

Regression analysis to estimate costs is similar to the analogy approach. Data on cost and variables associated with a similar project are collected. A predictive model is then built and used to predict costs for the current project.

Bottom-up estimating compiles detailed estimates of the costs of all the work packages in a project. It can provide extremely accurate cost estimates when detailed information is available; however, it is not always possible to obtain such information.

THE COST FACTOR IN PROJECT SELECTION

Cost is a key factor in evaluating the relative merits of multiple alternatives and selecting the best project (see Chapter 5). When comparing the costs associated with multiple projects, consider the time value of money. That is, certain nonrecurring costs may occur in the present, whereas others may not occur until some point in the future. Recurring costs will occur periodically over a specific time horizon. Therefore, all costs should be converted to the same point in time so that they can be compared equitably. It is customary to convert all costs to the present. This type of analysis is termed a *net present value analysis*.

Another adjustment may be required with respect to the project life cycle. Projects will typically have different life cycle lengths. Thus, it will also be necessary to compare the projects over the same time horizon. By considering the time value of money and by comparing the projects over equal time horizons, the comparison of multiple alternatives will be more equitable. Techniques that focus on analyzing the trade-offs among alternatives include Simple

Multi-Attribute Rating Technique (SMART), Analytic Hierarchy Process (AHP), Monte Carlo simulation, and decision trees.

Simple Multi-Attribute Rating Technique (SMART)

SMART involves the identification of a set of attributes that are important to a decision-making problem and weighting these attributes to reflect their relative importance. Each alternative is then given a value that reflects how well it performs with respect to each attribute. The weighted average of these values shows the overall performance of each alternative.

Cost can be used as an attribute in SMART, or it can be kept separate and used to perform a cost/benefit analysis. Figure 9–2 shows an example of how SMART scores can be compared against cost to make decisions among alternatives. In this example, alternative 1 can be eliminated completely from consideration because alternative 2 provides a higher benefit score at a lower cost. Of the remaining alternatives, alternative 3 provides the lowest benefit but at a correspondingly low cost. Alternative 4 has the highest benefit score but also has by far the highest cost. The decision makers would evaluate how much they are willing to pay for an increased benefit score in order to arrive at a decision between alternatives 2, 3, and 4.

The Analytic Hierarchy Process (AHP)

AHP is another multi-attribute decision-making tool. In this method, weights of attributes are determined by developing a pairwise comparison matrix in which the relative importance of each attribute is evaluated with respect to all other attributes. As with SMART, cost can be included as an attribute, or a cost/benefit analysis can be performed.

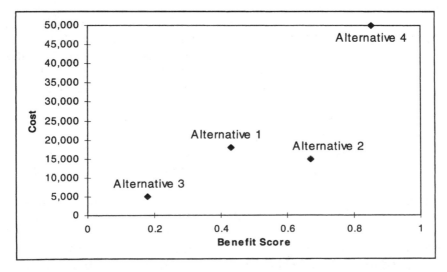

Figure 9–2   SMART Cost/Benefit Analysis Example

Monte Carlo Simulation

Both SMART and AHP are used to evaluate a set of alternatives whose performance can be explicitly measured against a set of attributes. *Monte Carlo simulation* is a technique that can be used when the performance of the alternatives is uncertain. See Chapter 4 for more detail.

Decision Trees

This decision-making technique is useful for multistage problems in which the selection of a particular option or alternative at one stage can lead to other decisions to be made at later stages. Suppose that a company wishes to manufacture a new type of product. The company needs to develop a design for the product that meets both cost requirements and specific reliability standards.

The company has two alternatives: (1) use its own experience to develop such a design, or (2) subcontract the design work to a design engineering firm. Although the probability of a successful design being developed in the second alternative increases, the expected cost of developing the design also increases. A third option is to simply not produce the new product. Figure 9–3 shows a decision tree for this problem.

The next step is to assess the probability of the design being successful or unsuccessful for each scenario. An estimated monetary gain or loss is assigned to each potential outcome. The optimal policy or set of decisions for the problem is determined through a procedure called the rollback method. The rollback method essentially determines which policy has the highest expected monetary return.

TRENDS IN COST MANAGEMENT

The heightened level of importance and awareness of cost management throughout the entire project life cycle has helped to foster the development of several new tools and methodologies that are gaining widespread use in industry. These include total quality management (TQM), concurrent enginering (see Chapter 32), design for manufacturability and assembly (DFMA), and activity-based costing (ABC).

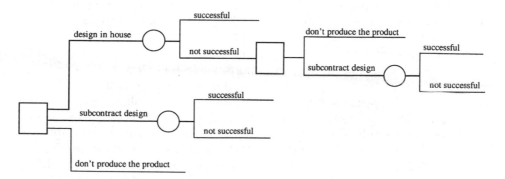

Figure 9–3   A Typical Decision Tree Structure

Total Quality Management (TQM)

Total quality management (TQM) as defined at the 1992 Total Quality Forum is:

> . . . a people-focused management system that aims at continual increase in customer satisfaction at continually lower real cost. It is a total system approach (not a separate area or program), and an integral part of high-level strategy. It works horizontally across functions and departments, involving all employees, top to bottom, and extends backwards and forwards to include the supply chain and the customer chain . . .[7]

The critical part of this definition as it relates to project costing is ". . . increase in customer satisfaction at continually lower real cost. . . ." The notion that in order to achieve higher levels of quality more money needs to be spent has been replaced with the idea that higher quality will actually result in lower costs.[8]

Quality costs have been steadily rising and can amount to a significant portion of total costs. Pioneers in the area of TQM who have looked at costs include W. Edwards Deming and Joseph M. Juran. Deming believed that a quality cost analysis should not be performed. Rather, the money should be spent upfront to do the right things the first time.

Conversely, Juran places quality costs into four categories: internal failure, external failure, appraisal, and prevention. He has examined the issue from an economic perspective and has developed a model that minimizes the total quality costs. He contends that total quality costs will be minimized at the point where failure costs (the sum of internal and external failure costs) are equal to the sum of appraisal and prevention costs (Juran and Gryna, 1988). This defines the point of enough quality.

Design for Manufacturability and Assembly

Design for manufacturability and assembly (DFMA) is an analysis technique used in a production setting. It is aimed at reducing the cost of a product (while maintaining the same functions and features), through simplification of its design. Although the actual cost to manufacture a product will be driven by the material, labor, and overhead costs, studies have shown that as much as 90 percent of the product's cost is determined in the preproduction phases of the project life cycle.[9] This represents the largest opportunity for cost and productivity improvement.

DFMA is accomplished through part simplification, usage of common parts, and part reduction. For example, fewer parts will result in lower direct material costs, fewer purchase orders placed, less component inventory held, and fewer operations performed. Assembly time will also be reduced, allowing companies to carry less finished goods inventory. This can lead to a faster response time to customers and a reduction in labor. Success stories describing the improvements resulting from implementing DFMA are impressive. For example, the April 30, 1990 issue of *Business Week* reported that U.S. manufacturers applying DFMA principles reduced product development time by 30 percent to 70 percent. Boothroyd, et al. (1994) provide a comprehensive discussion of DFMA.

Activity-Based Costing

Indirect costs are rising for U.S. manufacturers. These manufacturers are concerned that the existing traditional cost accounting systems used for costing are inadequate, particularly when the indirect cost must be traced to multiple products, systems, or projects.[10]

Activity-based costing (ABC) has recently emerged as an approach to deal with the shortcomings associated with traditional cost accounting methods, namely, their handling of the allocation of indirect costs (primarily focusing on overhead allocation). With the 1987 publication of the book *Relevance Lost: The Rise and Fall of Management Accounting*, Johnson and Kaplan describe the demise of the arbitrary methods utilized in traditional cost accounting methods for the allocation of indirect costs using volume-based measures such as direct labor. They argue that this method has lost relevance in the wake of an increasing indirect cost base and a shrinking direct labor cost base. ABC addresses this deficiency by tracing indirect cost components directly to the source. It assumes that activities consume resources and projects consume activities. Activities that drive costs and are associated with the project can thereby be identified and traced directly to the project.

ABC is closely linked with TQM. Both methodologies are concerned with analyzing activities to determine whether they add value. TQM focuses more on the identification of the non-value-added activities whereas ABC concentrates on developing meaningful costs associated with the activities. Furthermore, an ABC approach can enhance efforts in determining the cost of quality, thereby identifying improvement areas.

Summary

Cost is a critical element within project management and must be given as much attention as schedule and technical performance. Contractors and other project-based firms can incur stiff penalties for cost overruns. This chapter has described the growing importance of cost, outlined ways in which costs can be examined or reduced, described the components of a fully integrated cost-management system, and described some of the important trends in the field.

BIBLIOGRAPHY

Beheiry, M. F. New Thoughts on an old concept: The cost of quality. *CMA Magazine*, June 1991

Berliner, C. and Brimson, J. A. *Cost Management for Today's Advanced Manufacturing.* Boston: Harvard Business School, 1988

Boothroyd, G., Dewhurst, P., and Knight, W. *Product Design for Manufacture and Assembly.* New York: Marcel Dekker, 1994

Bounds, G., Yorks, L., Adams, M., and Ranney, G. *Beyond Total Quality Management: Toward the Emerging Paradigm.* New York: McGraw-Hill, 1994

Box, G. E. P., Hunter, W. G., and Hunter, J. S. *Statistics for Experimenters: An Introduction to Design, Data Analysis, and Model Building.* New York: John Wiley & Sons, Inc., 1978

Cleland, D. I. *Project Management: Strategic Design and Implementation.* New York: McGraw-Hill, 1990

Cooper, R. The rise of activity-based costing, part one: What is an activity-based cost system? *Journal of Cost Management,* Summer 1988

Cooper, R. The rise of activity-based costing, part two: When do I need an activity-based cost system? *Journal of Cost Management,* Fall 1988

Cooper, R. The rise of activity-based costing, part three: How many cost drivers do you need, and how do you select them? *Journal of Cost Management,* Winter 1989

Cooper, R. The rise of activity-based costing, part four: What do activity-based cost systems look like? *Journal of Cost Management,* Spring 1989

Cooper, R. and Kaplan, R. S. How cost accounting distorts product costs. *Management Accounting,* April 1988

Cooper, R. and Kaplan, R. S. Measure costs right: Make the right decisions. *Harvard Business Review,* September–October 1988

Crosby, P. B. *Quality Is Free: The Art of Making Quality Certain,* New York: Mentor, 1979

Cross, K. and Lynch, R. Accounting for competitive performance. In *Emerging Practices in Cost Management.* Edited by Brinker, B.J. Boston: Warren, Gorham, and Lamont, 1990

DeGarmo, E. P., Sullivan, W. G., and Canada, J. R. *Engineering Economy, Seventh Edition.* New York: Macmillan, 1984

Deming, W. E. *Out of the Crisis.* Cambridge, MA: Masachusetts Institute of Technology, 1986

Department of Defense. *Performance Measurement for Selected Acquisitions.* DoD Instrumentation No. 7000.2

Design to the rescue. *Business Week,* April 30, 1990

Discenza, R. and Gurney, B. New considerations for evaluating capital equipment purchases. *Production and Inventory Management Journal,* Second Quarter 1990

Drury, C. Activity-based costing. *Management Accounting (UK),* September 1989

Edwards, W. Social utilities. *Engineering Economist,* Summer Symposium Series 1971

Fabrycky, W. J. Design for the life-cycle. *Mechanical Engineering,* January 1987

Farmer, J. R. Activity-based accounting and performance measurement. *APICS 34th International Conference Proceedings,* 1991

Flentov, P. and Shuman, E. L. Putting ABC through its paces. *CFO: The Magazine for Senior Financial Executives,* April 1991

Golden, B. L., Wasil, E. A., and Harker, P. T. (eds.). *The Analytic Hierarchy Process: Applications and Studies.* New York: Springer-Verlag, 1989

Hiromoto, T. Another hidden edge: Japanese management accounting. *Harvard Business Review,* July–August 1988

Howard, R. A. Decision analysis: Practice and promise. *Management Science,* 34(6), 1988

Johnson, H. T. and Kaplan, R. S. *Relevance Lost: The Rise and Fall of Management Accounting.* Boston: Harvard Business School Press, 1987

Jones, J. M. Decision analysis using spreadsheets. *European Journal of Operational Research* Vol. 26 (1985)

Juran, J. M. and Gryna, F. M. *Quality Planning and Analysis, Third Edition.* New York: McGraw-Hill, 1993

Kaplan, R. S. New systems for measurement and control. *The Engineering Economist,* Spring 1991

Kaplan, R. S. Yesterday's accounting undermines production. *Harvard Business Review,* July–August 1984

Kato, Y., Büer, G., and Chow, C. W. Target costing: an integrative management process. *Cost Management*, Spring 1995

Keys, L. K. System life cycle engineering and DF "X", *IEEE Transactions on Components, Hybrids, and Manufacturing Technology*, March 1990

Kleijnen, J. P. C. *Statistical Techniques in Simulation.* New York: Marcel Dekker, 1974

Linstone, H. A. and Turoff, M. (eds.). *The Delphi Method: Techniques and Applications.* Reading, MA: Addison-Wesley, Advanced Book Program, 1975

McFadden, F. R. Six-sigma quality programs. *Quality Progress*, June 1993

Michaels, J. V. and Wood, W. P. *Design to Cost.* New York: John Wiley & Sons, Inc., 1989

Miller, G. J. and Louk, P. Strategic manufacturing cost management. In *APICS 31st International Conference Proceedings*, Falls Church, VA: APICS, 1988

Miller, J. G. and Vollmann, T. E. The hidden factory. *Harvard Business Review*, September–October 1985

Myers, R. H. *Classical and Modern Regression with Applications, Second Edition.* Boston: PWS-KENT Publishing Company, 1990

National Research Council. *Improving Engineering Design: Designing for Competitive Advantage.* Washington, DC: National Academy Press, 1991

O'Guin, M. C. Activity-based costing: unlocking our competitive edge. *Manufacturing Systems*, December 1990

O'Guin, M. C. *The Complete Guide to Activity-Based Costing.* Englewood Cliffs, NJ: Prentice Hall, 1991

Parente, F. J. and Anderson-Parente, J. K. Delphi inquiry systems. In *Judgmental Forecasting*, Edited by Wright, G. and Ayton, P. Chichester, England: John Wiley & Sons, Inc., 1987

Rampey, J. and Roberts, H. Perspectives on total quality. In *Proceedings of Total Quality Forum IV.* Cincinnati, OH: November 1992

Rubinstein, R. Y. *Simulation and the Monte Carlo Method.* New York: John Wiley & Sons, Inc., 1981

Saaty, T. L. *Decision Making for Leaders: The Analytic Hierarchy Process for Decisions in a Complex World.* Pittsburgh, PA: RWS Publications, 1990

Saaty, T. L. and Vargas, L. G. *Prediction, Projection, and Forecasting: Applications of the Analytic Hierarchy Process in Economics, Finance, Politics, Games, and Sports.* Boston: Kluwer Academic Publishers, 1991

Sackman, H. *Delphi Critique, Expert Opinion, Forecasting, and Group Process.* Lexington, MA: Lexington Books, 1975

Sakurai, M. Target costing and how to use it. In *Emerging Practices in Cost Management.* Edited by Brinker, B. J. Boston: Warren, Gorham, and Lamont, 1990

Steimer, T. E. Activity-based accounting for total quality. *Management Accounting*, October 1990

Stewart, R. D. and Wyska, R.M. *Cost Estimator's Reference Manual*, New York: John Wiley & Sons, Inc., 1987

Watson, S. R. and Buede, D. M. *Decision Synthesis*, Cambridge, England: Cambridge University Press, 1987

Worthy, F. S. Japan's smart secret weapon. *Fortune*, August 12, 1991

Yakowitz, S. J. *Computational Probability and Simulation.* Reading, MA: Addison-Wesley, Advanced Book Program, 1977

ENDNOTES

1 Cleland, David I. *Project Management: Strategic Design and Implementation.* New York: McGraw Hill, 1990

2 Fabrycky, W. J. Design for the life-cycle. *Mechanical Engineering,* January 1987, pp. 72–74; Keys, L. K. System life-cycle engineering and DF "X," *IEE Transactions on Components, Hybrids, and Manufacturing Technology,* 1990

3 National Research Council. *Improving Engineering Design: Designing for Competitive Advantage.* Washington, DC: National Academy Press, 1991

4 Miller, G. J., and Louk, P. Strategic manufacturing cost management. In *APICS 31st International Conference Proceedings.* Falls Church, VA, 1988, p. 542

5 Croos, K. and Lynch, R. Accounting for competitive performance. In *Emerging Practices in Cost Management.* Edited by Brinker, B. J. Boston: Warren, Gorham, and Lamont, 1990, pp. 411–419; Kaplan, R. S. New systems for measurement and control. *The Engineering Economist,* Spring 1991, pp. 201–218; Miller, G. J., and Louk, P. Strategic manufacturing cost management. In *APICS 31st International Conference Proceedings.* Falls Church, VA: 1988, pp. 542–547

6 Michaels, J. V. and Wood, W. P. *Design to Cost.* New York: John Wiley and Sons, Inc., 1989

7 Bounds, G., Yorks L., Adams, M., and Ranney, G. *Beyond Total Quality Management Toward the Emerging Paradigm.* New York: McGraw-Hill, 1994, p. 4

8 Crosby, P. B. *Quality Is Free—The Art of Making Quality Certain,* New York: Mentor, 1979; McFadden, F. R. Six-sigma quality programs. *Quality Progress,* June 1993, pp. 37–42

9 Berliner, C., and Brimson, J. A. *Cost Management for Today's Advanced Manufacturing,* Boston: Harvard Business School, 1988

10 Drury, C. Activity-based costing. *Management Accounting* (UK), September 1989, pp. 60–63; Farmer, J. R. Activity-based accounting and performance management. In *APICS 34th International Conference Proceedings,* 1991, pp. 156–160; Flentov, P., and Schuman, E. L. Putting ABC through its paces. *CFO: The Magazine for Senior Financial Executives* April 1991, pp. 46–50; Miller, J. G., and Vollmann, T. E. The hidden factory. *Harvard Business Review,* September 1985, pp. 142–150; O'Guin, M.C. Activity-based costing: Unlocking our competitive edge. *Manufacturing Systems,* December 1990, pp. 35–40

Calculating Costs and Keeping Records for Project Contracts

James J. O'Brien

Biographical Sketch . . . **James J. O'Brien** is Vice Chairman of O'Brien-Kreitzberg Inc., a national professional construction and project-management firm. He has a degree in civil engineering from Cornell University. He is a registered professional engineer in six states. He is a Fellow of the American Society of Civil Engineers and has served as New Jersey State section president. He is a member of the Society of American Value Engineers and is a certified value specialist. He has served as chairman of the board of Project Management Institute, is certified as a project-management professional, and is a PMI Fellow.

Many managers consider pricing an art. Estimates for contract bids must be well-thought-out decisions based on the best available information. Pricing should begin before proposal development. Project managers need to understand customer requirements, make estimates of cost targets, and establish a cost baseline. Effective cost estimates early-on permit management the opportunity to redirect or terminate the project before submitting a proposal or expending excess resources on an unsuccessful project.

Request for Proposal

The organization seeking proposals may provide requests for proposals (RFPs) to anyone responding to its announcement or advertisement about an upcoming project. A more usual approach is to use a two-step process. First, the customer uses a statement of qualifications (SOQ) to create a list of firms the customer believes are qualified to respond. Second, the customer sends RFPs to this relatively small list. Typically, SOQs are easier to review and evaluate than the more detailed proposals. The two-step process saves both time and effort.

In addition to RFPs and SOQs, a government agency may invite letters of interest (LOI). The government agency may also ask the bidding companies to submit a form SF 254, which provides general information about the company. In addition, the responding company may be required to submit form SF 255, which asks the company to address its capabilities in regard to a specific project. (Figures 10–1 and 10–2 show samples of forms SF 254 and SF 255.)

The RFP usually contains the following:

- A description of the services sought
- Guidelines for performing the work
- Format for and outline of the proposal
- Factors that will be used to evaluate the proposals and weights for different factors
- A sample of the contract form to be entered into
- Notice of any proposal meeting and the due date of the proposal

The cost part of a proposal is usually prepared in a prescribed format (see Figure 10–3). That format shows the following:

- Labor hours and rates by individual or category
- Multiplier for overhead
- Direct expenses (per allowable items), such as the cost of air or rail travel, living expenses, car rental, tolls, parking, and gas
- Fee or profit (often limited to a maximum of 10 percent)

The outline prescribed for the proposal usually calls for the proposer to provide the following in the technical part of the proposal:

- Qualifications for performing the work
- Demonstration of an understanding of the work
- Description of the plan or approach to the project
- Description of the team that would be assigned, including a staffing plan
- Description of the specific experience of team members, including resumés

How Customers Select a Bidder

Customers review and score technical proposals. A short list of three to five companies are usually invited to introduce their key team members, present their approaches, and answer questions. Customers have several options to select who gets on the short list. One is to identify which teams are qualified and select the one with the lowest cost proposal. Another is to identify the most qualified and negotiate to find a mutually acceptable scope and cost. If negotiations fail, the customer goes to the second best on the list. Another approach is to arrive at a score combining cost and qualifications.

(text continues on page 130)

STANDARD FORM (SF) **254** Architect-Engineer and Related Services Questionnaire	1. Firm Name/Business Address O'Brien-Kreitzberg & Associates Inc. 1515 Broadway New York, NY 10036	ACASS# 014208 FEIN# 94-3213883	2. Year Present Firm Established: 1972	3. Date Prepared: February 5, 1996
	1a. Submittal is for Parent Company Branch of Subsidiary Office		4. Specify type of ownership *and* check below, if applicable Corporation A. Small Business B. Small Disadvantaged Business C. Woman-owned Business	

5. Name of Parent Company, if any:
Dames and Moore, Inc.

5a. Former Parent Company Name(s), if any, and Year(s) Established:
O'Brien-Kreitzberg & Associates, Inc., 1972
James J. O'Brien, P.E., 1968

6. Names of not more than Two Principals to Contact: Title/Telephone
1) P. Cay Baldwin / Senior Vice President / (212) 921-9898
2) D. Clarke Pile / Senior Vice President / (212) 921-9898

7. Present Offices: City/State/Telephone/No. Personnel Each Office

				7a. Total Personnel 693		
Atlanta, GA	(404) 524-5505	20	Koln, Germany	011 (4922) 152-7082	3	
Baton Rouge, LA	(504) 358-4240	4	Kuala Lumpur, Mala.	011 (603) 232-7416	1	
Boston, MA	(617) 357-9800	48	London, UK	011 (44 171) 331-8900	3	
Buffalo, NY	(716) 634-9482	9	Los Angeles, CA	(818) 907-6666	108	
Chicago, IL	(312) 263-0959	10	New York, NY	(212) 921-9898	146	
Cleveland, OH	(216) 425-3193	3	North Sydney, Austl.	011 (612) 955-7772	1	
Dallas, TX	(214) 720-4445	21	Oakland, CA	(510) 839-5491	38	
Denver, CO	(303) 534-7202	14	Oklahoma City, OK	(405) 525-1066	1	
Honolulu, HI	(808) 593-9039	3	Orlando, F. _	(407) 481-8933	5	
Houston, TX	(713) 688-7880	3	Pennsauken, NJ	(609) 665-2000	56	
			Phoenix, Az	(602) 861-7426	3	
			Pitsburgh, PA	(412) 394-6388	20	
			Portland, OR	(503) 239-2210	15	
			Sacramento, CA	(916) 383-8125	4	
			San Diego, CA	(619) 514-7550	8	
			San Francisco, CA	(415) 777-0188	107	
			San Jose, CA	(408) 451-1120	20	
			Seattle, WA	(206) 628-0883	16	
			Toronto, Canada	(416) 393-3511	3	

8. Personnel by Discipline: *(List each person only once, by primary function.)*

181	Administrative	80	Cost/Scheduling Engineers	5	Industrial Engineers	7	QA/QC Managers
26	Architects	6	Draftsmer/Graphic Designers	15	Mechanical Engineers	3	Sanitary Engineers
13	Attorneys/Claims Analysts	2	Ecologists	2	Mining/Tunnel Engineers	3	Soils Engineers
4	Chemical Engineers	13	Economis s/Financial Analysts	17	MIS Analysts/Computer Tech.	4	Structural Engineers
57	Civil Engineers	12	Electrical Engineers	0	Oceanographers	16	Transportation Engineers
59	Construction Inspectors	16	Engineering Technicians	3	Planners: Urban/Regional	4	Value Engineers
68	Construction Managers	17	Estimators	23	Program Managers		
33	Contract Administrators	1	Geologists	3	Public Information Managers		

9. Summary of Professional Services Fees
Received: (Insert index number)
Last 5 Years (most recent year first)

	995	1994	1993	1992	1991
Direct Federal contract work, including overseas	6	5	6	6	6
All other domestic work	8	3	8	8	8
All other foreign work*	8	5	6	6	—

*Firms interested in foreign work, but without such experience, check here: o

Ranges of Professional Services Fees
INDEX
1 Less than $100,000
2 $100,000 to $250,000
3 $250,000 to $500,000
4 $500,000 to $1 million
5 $1 million to $2 million
6 $2 million to $5 million
7 $5million to $10 million
8 $10 million or greater

FIGURE 10–1

123

10. Profile of Firm's Project Experience, Last 5 Years

Profile Code	Number of Projects	Total Gross Fees (in thousands)	Profile Code	Number of Projects	Total Gross Fees (in Thousands)	Profile Code	Number of Projects	Total Gross Fees (in thousands)
1) 021	163	172,950	11)			21)		
2) 112	16	12,850	12)			22)		
3) 201	65	25,700	13)			23)		
4) 202	323	29,550	14)			24)		
5) 203	21	4,000	15)			25)		
6) 204	9	17,950	16)			26)		
7)			17)			27)		
8)			18)			28)		
9)			19)			29)		
10)			20)			30)		

11. Project Examples, Last 5 Years

Profile Code	P,C, JV or IE	Project Name and Location	Owner Name and Address	Cost of Work (in thousands)	Completion (Actual or Estimated)
029 019 / 021 201	P	Hudson Valley Community College, Troy, New York	Director Physical Plant, Hudson Valley Community College, 80 Vandenburg Ave., Troy, NY 12180	$14,000	1995
029 019 / 021 201	P	The West Campus Project, Pottstown, Pennsylvania	Chief Business Officer, Montgomery County Community College, 340 DeKalb Pike, Blue Bell, PA 19422	$14,000	1996
015 023 / 027 039	P	Dining Hall Rrenovation and ADA Upgrades, East Stroudsberg, PA	East Stroudsburg University, Assistant Director Facilities Management, 200 Prospect Street, East Stroudsburg, PA 18301	$8,000	1995
019 043 / 029 069 / 021	P	Columbia University Summer Construction Program, New York, NY	Department of Design and Construction, Columbia University, B-230, Central Mail Room, New York, NY 10027	$50,000	1995
029 023 089 / 021 112 039 / 201 106 060	JV	Cleveland State University 17th-18th Street Block Campus Extension, Cleveland, Ohio	Cleveland State University, Euclid at 24th Street, Cleveland, OH 44115	$70,000	1996
029 021 / 019 106 / 058 201	P	Ulster Community College Expansion and Rehabilitation Project, Stone Ridge, New York	Ulster County Community College, Cottlekill Road, Stone Ridge, New York 12484	$9,800	1993
027 047 095 / 050 201 / 089 021	P	Stanford University Student Housing and Dining Services Capital Improvements Program, Stanford, California	Stanford University, Contract Office, 855 Serra Street, 2nd Floor, Stanford, CA 94305-6114	$2,000	1994

FIGURE 10–1 Continued

019 021 029 201 023	P	Cabrillo College Learning Resource Center Aptos, California	Vice President Business Services 6500 Soquel Drive Aptos, CA 95003	$9,000	1996
204 029 201 023 015	P	New York City School Construction Authority Capital Improvement Program New York, New York	New York City School Construction Authority 30-30 Thomson Avenue Long Island City, NY 11101	$7,500,000	1993
029 201 021 106 089 043 032	P	White Plains Elementary Schools White Plains, New York	White Plains City School District White Plains Board of Education House Five Homeside Lane White Plains, NY 10605	$50,000	1992
029 201 021 112 023	P	Marshall Elementary School Marshall Township, PA	North Allegheny School District 200 Hillvue Lane Pittsburgh, PA 15237-5391	$11,000	1992
029 043 089 023 112 021	P	Bradford Woods Elementary School Bradford Woods Borough, Pennsylvania	North Allegheny School District 200 Hillvue Lane Pittsburgh, PA 15237-5391	$6,400	1992
029 043 089 023 021 112	P	Mars Area School District Mars, Pennsylvania	Mars Area School District R.D. 2, Box 150 Mars, PA 16046	$15,000	1993
029 021 106 089 204 023 112 201	P	Leechburg Area Schools Leechburg, Pennsylvania	Leechburg School District 2000 Siberian Avenue Leechburg, PA 15656	$10,000	1956
029 201 089 112 021 023	P	Fort Cherry Junior/Senior High School Renovation and Addition McDonald, Pennsylvania	Fort Cherry School District R.D. #4, Box 145 McDonald, PA 15057-0409	$10,000	1994
112 201 021 089 023 029	P	North Allegheny School District Facilities Bradford Woods and Marshall Township, PA	North Allegheny School District 200 Hillvue Lane Pittsburgh, PA 15237-5391	$40,000	1993
021 201 029 023 112	P	Marshall Middle School Marshall Township, PA	North Allegheny School District 200 Hillvue Lane Pittsburgh, PA 15237-5391	$16,000	1993

12. The foregoing is a statement of facts.

Signature: _____   Name/Title: _D. Clarke Pile, Senior Vice President_

Date:
February 15, 1996

FIGURE 10–1 Continued

125

STANDARD FORM (SF) **255**	1. Project Name/Location for which Firm is Filing: **Indefinite Delivery Contract For Architect-Engineer Design Services In Support of Military, Civil Works and Work For Others**	2. *Commerce Business Daily* Announcement Date, if any: **March 13, 1995**	2a. Agency Identification Number, if any:

Architect-Engineer and Related Services Questionnaire for Specific Project

3. Firm (or Joint- Venture) Name & Address

O'Brien-Kreitzberg, Inc.
4350 Haddonfield Road, Suite 300
Pennsauken, NJ 08109

3a. Name, Title & Telephone Number of Principal to Contact

Wesley F. Mikes., Senior Vice President (609) 665-2000

3b. Address of office to perform work, if different from Item 3

4. Personnel by Discipline: (List each person only once, by primary function.) Enter proposed consultant personnel to be utilized on this project on line (A) and In-house personnel on line (B).

(A) 1 (B) 226 Administrative	(A) 2 (B) 19 Electrical Engineers	(A) (B) 1 Oceanographers	(A) 6 (B) 55 Cost/Scheduling Engineers
(A) 3 (B) 36 Architects	(A) 4 (B) 21 Estimators	(A) 2 (B) 2 Planners: Urban/Regional	(A) 2 (B) 17 Attorneys/Claims Technicians
(A) 1 (B) 4 Chemical Engineers	(A) (B) Geologists	(A) 5 (B) Sanitary Engineers	(A) 2 (B) 25 MIS Analysts/Computer Technicians
(A) 7 (B) 89 Civil Engineers	(A) (B) Hydrologists	(A) (B) Soils Engineers	(A) (B) 17 Contract Administrators
(A) 7 (B) 78 Construction Inspectors	(A) (B) Interior Designers	(A) (B) Specification Writers	(A) (B) 13 Engineering Technicians
(A) 1 (B) 4 Draftspersons	(A) (B) 1 Landscape Architects	(A) 2 (B) 6 Structural Engineers	(A) 2 (B) 62 Construction Managers
(A) 1 (B) Ecologists	(A) 1 (B) 31 Mechanical Engineers	(A) (B) 2 Surveyors	(A) (B) 14 Industrial Engineers
(A) (B) 4 Economists	(A) (B) 1 Mining Engineers	(A) (B) 23 Transportation Engineers	(A) 41 (B) 755 **Total Personnel**

5. If submittal is by JOINT-VENTURE, list participating firms and outline specific areas of responsibility (including administrative, technical and financial) for each firm: (Attach SF 254 for each if not on file with procuring Office.)

5a. Has this Joint-Venture previously worked together? ☐ Yes ☐ No

FIGURE 10–2

126

7. Brief resume of key persons, specialists, and individual consultants anticipated for this project.

a. Name and Title: Wesley F. Mikes Senior Vice President	■ Bridgeport Oil & Rental Service Site, NJ ■ Helen Kramer Landfill, Mantua, NJ ■ Saline Groundwater Intrusion Study on C & D Canal
b. Project Assignment: **Principal-in-Charge**	**Fort Drum Claim - Phase I - Watertown, NY ($552 Million)** OK Principal-in-Charge on an assignment to provide Construction Claims Evaluation and Litigation Support to the U.S. Army Corps of Engineers, New York District. OK evaluated RFIs and modifications in order to determine whether drawings and specifications were defective. The claims team reviewed contractor's bid, government audits, schedules as-built data management plans, correspondence, submittals, and other and other relevant project documentation to identify, quantify and allocate responsibility for project delays and cost overruns. OK findings helped the COE negotiate a settlement with the contractor for $15 million ($68 million less than contractor's original claim).
c. Name of Firm with which associated: O'Brien-Kreitzberg	
d. Years experience: With This Firm **22** With Other Firms **14**	**Trout Run Wastewater Treatment Plant Expansion, King of Prussia, PA** ($11 million) Principal-in-charge for upgrade and expansion of the Trout Run Wastewater Treatment Plant for the Upper Merion Municipal Utility Authority. The upgrade and expansion program, which will increase the plant's capacity from 5.5 mgd to 6.5 mgd, is being completed using multiple prime contractors.
e. Education: Degree(s) / Year / Specialization Certificate/Architectural Design and Building Construction Technology/ 1958	**Cinnaminson Wastewater Treatment Facility, NJ ($5 million)** As Principal-in-Charge, oversaw the OK team on the upgrade and expansion. The project involved the installation and addition of a new flow equalization tank, influent wet well system, mechanical control building, two new primary settling tanks, and two new final settling tanks.
f. Active Registration: Year First Registered / Discipline	**Moorestown Wastewater Treatment Facility, NJ ($14 million)** As Principal-in-Charge, oversaw the OK team managing the upgrade and expansion of the 2.5 mgd wastewater treatment plant to 3.5 mgd. The plant expansion and upgrade involved adding two 65-foot-diameter secondary clarifiers, new aeration tanks, and the conversion of an existing chlorine disinfection system to ultra-violet disinfection.
g. Other Experience and Qualifications relevant to the proposed project: Wesley F. Mikes has been involved with the design, planning, and implementation of construction projects for over 35 years, with extensive experience in project management, claims analysis, scheduling, value engineering, and presenting expert testimony. He has served as Principal-in-Charge on several major projects, supervising management staff, engineers, architects, estimators, schedulers, and technicians performing all aspects of construction management. He currently heads OK's Mid-Atlantic Region, headquartered in Pennsauken, New Jersey. **Indefinite Delivery Contract for A-E Services in Support of Corps of Engineers (Philadelphia Dist.) Projects** Principal-in-Charge on Support Services Delivery Order Contract with the Philadelphia District with the responsibility to staff and negotiate individual delivery orders and monitor and assure quality of performance by OK project team. Directed OK and subconsultant professional staff (including separate project managers) on 15 delivery orders under COE Contract No. DACW61-91-D-0014. The individual delivery orders included: ■ South Jetty Project, Barnagett, NJ ■ Lipari Landfill Superfund Site, Pitman, NJ	**United States Postal Service (USPS) Headquarters, Washington, DC** As Principal-in-Charge of contract construction management support services contract, provides training for USPS Project Managers that includes classes in claims analysis, project administration and inspection, cost and pricing, and critical path method (CPM) scheduling. Prepared training manuals and conducts 10-hour workshops. Also served on more than a dozen individual USPS projects nationwide.

FIGURE 10-2 Continued

127

8. Work by firm or joint venture members that best illustrates current qualifications relevant to this project (list not more than 10 projects).

a. Project Name & Location	b. Nature of Firm's Responsibility	c. Project Owner's Name & Address	d. Completion Date (actual or estimated)	e. Estimated Cost (in thousands)	
				Entire Project	Work for which Firm was/is Responsible
Underground Storage Tank Program New York, NY	Design Management and Construction Management	Reza Zeynali NYC Dept. of General Services One Centre Street, Room 2100 New York, NY 10007 (212) 669-4842	1994	9,900	9,900

The New York City Department of General Services (DGS) has undertaken a comprehensive underground fuel storage tank (UST) program to bring the city's tanks into compliance with all state, local, and federal regulations. DGS retained OK to manage the upgrades of petroleum product USTs at approximately 25 sites administered by the Office of Fleet Administration for various New York City agencies.

OK has overall responsibility for the design of tank upgrades and replacements, preparation of construction documents and bid packages, and execution and management of construction contracts. The program will result in UST systems for motor fuels that are protective of the environment and comply with all UST regulations through installation of vapor recovery, leak detection, cathodic protection, and spill prevention systems or by abandoning the existing facilities and installing new ones, in addition, any spills of petroleum motor fuel will be remediated to bring each site into regulatory compliance.

FIGURE 10–2 Continued

10. Use this space to provide any additional information or description of resources (including any computer design capabilities) supporting your firm's qualifications for the proposed project.

The **Principal-in-Charge**, Jim O'Brien, will be accountable to the Corps of Engineers for the overall provision of services, both contractually and administratively. He is a senior member of the firm and is capable of making decisions and recommendations that are recognized as authoritative. Mr. O'Brien will be responsible for overseeing the **quality** of OK's work from a **contractual** point of view and is available to the **COE** should problems or circumstances arise that cannot be resolved at another level. He will be available as an expert witness and brings first-hand experience on negotiating claims and changes with many local and national contractors who are on your projects.

The **Project Director**, Wesley F. Mikes, will have day-to-day control of the team and is the principal point of contact for the COE. With the assistance of the rest of the team and the **COE**. With the assistance of Mr. O'Brien, he can assign resources from throughout the company to expedite the solution to events as they are presented. Mr. Mikes is responsible for overseeing the **performance** of OK's work from a **technical point** of view. He will assign specific tasks to the team and will assist in coordinating the assembly of reports, charts, oral presentations, schedules, and related documents. The Project Director will be responsible for the administration of this assignment and will be instrumental in the preparation of OK's progress reports to the **COE**.

The **Project Managers**, reporting to Mr. Mikes, will be responsible for the execution of document retrieval and management, strategy, discovery requirements, preparation of final reports, studies, CPM schedule analysis, settlement negotiations and trial support, quality assurance inspection, design analysis, hazard analysis, analysis of health and safety programs and procedures, and will serve as the day-to-day contact on all issues pertaining to an assignment. With the assistance of the Project Engineers and other resources, the bulk of the work will be accomplished by the Project Managers.

The **Project Engineers**, reporting to the Project Director and working closely with the project managers, will be responsible for the execution of claims analysis and support services with respect to this project. The Project Engineers will play a role in the preliminary evaluation, technical analysis and report preparation, site investigations, schedule work, estimates, and other support services. At times, the Project Engineers may be called upon during trial and post-trial activities. Additional support will be provided by Claims Technicians, Document Control Specialists and others on an as-needed basis.

On all major projects, OK assigns senior staff members to serve in a role of **Technical Advisors**. Since our growth and success are based solely on the job we perform for our clients, we always practice aggressive oversight of our technical assignments. The Technical Advisors will serve as a sounding board for the Project Director and Project Managers in defining the approaches OK will use to address technical issues. The Technical Advisors will be kept abreast of the status of the project throughout its life and will periodically participate in technical sessions with OK's staff and possibly the COE. We believe that the breadth and experience of the Technical Advisors will be most valuable to the project.

Subconsultants Pennoni Associates, Inc. and Spotts Stevens and McCoy will provide specialized support in environmental engineering and process engineering. Each subconsultant will work directly with OK project managers and report through the project director. The subconsultants will assist the project manager with site investigations, hazard analysis and review of health and safety programs and procedures, design analysis, perform design modification and other design work including related drawings, specifications and estimates, sample gathering, testing in the field, laboratory testing, surveys, borings and monitoring.

STRUCTURE
As illustrated on the organization chart (following page), OK's team is functionally and organizationally simple. Our Project Director is the head of our team. Reporting directly to the Project Director will be each Project Manager and Project Engineers assigned to a Task Order. The level of involvement for each individual is based on the nature, size and complexity of the claim, and his/her level of experience and specific expertise relative to the task. The chart depicts a matrix organization and was developed to show our depth of resources and the structure in which we operate. A simple change order or claims task order may only require one or two individuals, but, OK's full resources are available to support this project in the event a larger staff is required.

FIGURE 10–2   Continued

129

PRECONSTRUCTION SERVICES

Labor	Hours	Rate	
Project Manager	1080	$40	$43,200
Architect	240	$35	8,400
Estimator	320	$25	8,000
General Engineer	960	$30	28,800
Structural Engineer	160	$35	5,600
Electrical Rngineer	360	$35	12,600
Mechanical Enginner	350	$35	12,600
Certified Value Specialistt	136	$40	5,400

Direct Labor Subtotal	S124,640
Overhead 1.2 x Direct Labor	149,568
Subtotal	$274,208
Direct Expenses: Per List Attached	15,000
Subtotal	S289,208
Fee 10%	28,921
Total	**$318,129**

FIGURE 10–3   Cost Proposal

The successful proposal is usually appended to the contract and becomes binding upon the proposer. The project-management risk group should review the proposal to be certain that the proposal team has not volunteered to add undue risk to the scope.

Contract Costs

Construction contracts in both public and private work are awarded on the basis of the lowest sealed bid. In selecting a project-management team, an owner can consider the professional capabilities and select on that basis, rather than on price alone. Most project-management contracts are selected on a professional-services basis. Progress invoices are typically

Tasks	PM	CVS	Arch.	Gen. Eng.	Struct. Eng.	Elec. Eng.	Mech. Eng.	Estimator
STAFF HOURS								
Project Pocedures Manual				320				
PM Oversight:								
Schematic	160							
Design Dev.	320							
Const. Documents	320							
Design Review - Schematic	40				80			
Estimate Schematic								80
Prepare for Schematic VE		16						
Schematic VE		40	40		40			40
Constructibility Review Des. Dev.	40			160				
Design Review Design Dev.	40					80	80	
Prepare for Design Dev. VE		40						
Design Dev. Estimate								160
Design Dev. VE		40	40		40	40	40	40
Draft General - Supp. Specifications				240				
On Board Review Const. Doc.	160		160			240	240	
TOTALS	**1080**	**136**	**240**	**960**	**160**	**360**	**360**	**320**

FIGURE 10–4   Staffing Plan—Preconstruction Service

issued on a monthly basis. Billing is for direct labor (as identified in the proposal staffing plan) at an hourly rate. (Figure 10–4 shows a staffing plan.) Project-management personnel are usually salaried. Although federal law requires payment on a time-and-a-half basis for all time worked over forty hours per week, management personnel are exempt from this and can be required to work overtime as part of their base salary. The usual practice, however, is to pay managers for overtime on a straight time basis rather than on a time-and-a-half basis. That is, managers are typically paid what they earn per hour for time worked beyond forty hours a week. An hourly rate is created by dividing annual salary by 2,040 hours. Payroll verification of the hourly rate is usually required by the project contract.

On the progress invoice, the sum of the direct labor is multiplied by one plus the overhead multiplier. This subtotal is multiplied by the agreed fee percentage (the agreed-to profit percent); this figure is added to the subtotal. Expenses, usually at cost (and in accordance with the proposal), are then added to complete the invoice (see Figures 10–5 and 10–6).

The professional-services contract is essentially a cost-plus contract, but in the proposal, the customer typically requires a cap figure. The progress invoices are for actual services rendered within the cost cap.

Term Contracts

The selection and negotiation process for a contract often takes six to eighteen months. To avoid this long process, many federal and state agencies award

Progress Invoice #2

October 1997

Direct Labor

Project Manager

    Oversight - 80 Staff hours @ $40   = $ 3,200

General Engineer

    Procedures Manual - 160 MH @ $30   =   <u>4,800</u>

            Total Direct Labor   **$ 8,000**

FIGURE 10–5   Progress Invoice Direct Labor Portion

term contracts, because, once in place, the process for agreeing to work on task orders under these contracts takes about a week. The term contract is a master contract because this one contract may cover several projects—as a master key opens several locks. The master contract, known more formally as indefinite quantity (fixed) term contract covers areas such as project manage-

Progress Invoice #2

October 1997

Preconstruction Phase

Direct Labor $ 8,000

Overhead 1.2 x DL   <u>9,600</u>

          Subtotal $17,600

          Fee 10%   1,760

          Expenses at Cost   <u>1,500</u>

          Total Invoice #2   **$20,860**

FIGURE 10–6   Progress Invoice

ment, construction management, value engineering (VE), and claims management. For this contract, the general type of work is described. For example, the contract may be to manage the construction of postal facilities called a General Mail Facility (GMF) for the U.S. Postal Service (USPS). When a project team is under contract, USPS assigns work orders. The following process takes about a week to accomplish:

1. USPS gives a description of the project scope such as type of GMF, budget, time of performance, and required service (e.g., construction management, project management, and inspection).
2. The company responds with proposed staffing plan (including positions, persons, and hours) and costs with rates approved in the contract.
3. USPS accepts or negotiates the level of effort.
4. The consulting company confirms the agreement.
5. USPS issues a notice to proceed (NTP).

The difference between a traditional fixed-scope contract and a master contract is that the type of service under a master contract is specified, but the scope of service is not. After the contract is in place, the agency issues scopes of work. The consulting company responds with a proposed scope in the form of a staffing plan and a time frame. The hourly rates and the overhead markup are part of the term contract.

The typical term contract is issued with a cap amount such as $500,000 or $1 million. The contract is usually for two years with annual renewal options for several years. To accommodate this, the proposer is usually allowed to escalate the salaries and hourly rates by 5 percent per year.

Direct and Indirect Labor

The term *direct labor* relates to personnel that, per contract, can be billed to the project. From a business viewpoint, being in the direct-labor group is like being on the varsity. Key members of the direct-labor group are named in the proposal.

Indirect labor, conversely, is not billable. The positions range from receptionist, mailroom clerk, and secretary, to the chief executive officer. The indirect labor are the support and management staff known as "corporate" that either provide indirect support to the project-management team, or carry on the nonproject aspects of the company business. The project team cannot control the ratio of indirect labor to direct labor. That is the responsibility of top management. In fact, the indirect labor to direct labor ratio is the principal target in corporate downsizing and reengineering. Sometimes the project-management team gets an opportunity to transfer an indirect-labor person to a direct-labor position. Carried as an ongoing policy, this can improve the bottom line. Conversely, between projects, the project-management team (even if briefly) becomes a part of the indirect labor.

Markup

In preparing the cost proposal, the direct labor is marked up or multiplied by a factor. The factor has to cover the following:

- *Indirect labor.* This is support staff and direct labor personnel not assigned to a project.
- *Corporate functions.* These are accounting, financial, human services, insurance, legal, and other functions not directly related to the project.
- *Fringe benefits.* These are vacation time (accrued as well as taken), sick time, personal business time, and retirement programs (including profit sharing and 401(k) programs). Typically, these are 30 percent to 35 percent of the direct labor cost.
- *Travel.* Unless travel is allowed as a direct expense, travel related to the project, including relocation, is part of the markup.

Field or Office Project

When the assignment dictates that the project-management team be located at the project (i.e., the field), the client typically provides direct support to the team. This support usually includes office (or trailer) space, furniture, telephone services, utilities (e.g., air conditioning, heat, water, and sewer), and basic equipment (e.g., reproduction and computers). In return, the client requires that the markup multiplier reflect the services provided. Typically, the multiplier for a field job would be 1.0 to 1.2 times direct labor.

In addition to the physical support provided, all personnel dedicated full time at the project site are considered direct labor. This includes many positions (such as receptionist, secretary, administrator, and purchasing agent) that would be indirect labor if in the home office. Not only are indirect-labor positions moved to direct labor, but these new direct-labor positions are now part of the direct labor that is marked up.

For an office job, the consulting company provides overhead such as the office space, furniture, computers, office equipment, copy machines, mailroom, and secretarial services. Because the consulting company provides more under the office job, a higher overhead must be carried. As in the field job, this overhead is typically measured as a percentage of direct labor.

Project Organization

The proposal should include an organization chart. This should be updated to reflect changes in personnel or assigned tasks. The organization chart should be posted, made available to the project team, and included in a monthly progress report to the client. A work-breakdown structure (WBS) should be developed reflecting the following:

- Cost and hours budgeted for each task or project component
- Personnel assigned
- Breakdown of each task or project component into appropriate levels of detail.

For more on work-breakdown structures, see Chapter 7.

Project teams often include subconsultants for various purposes. One purpose is to bring special skills to the team. Another is to meet disadvantaged-owned business enterprise (DBE), woman-owned business enterprise (WBE), and/or minority-owned business enterprise (MBE) goals. Under federal equal employment opportunity law, federal (and most state)-funded projects require a minimum percentage of subcontract jobs to go to firms certified as DBE, WBE, and MBE. The goals are determined by the agency sponsor. For example, the goals may be the following: DBE 15 percent and WBE 5 percent, or MBE 10 percent and WBE 3 percent.

Recordkeeping

It is not sufficient for project managers to perform their services well. They must also be able to prove that services were well-performed. There is no substitute for comprehensive written records in managing the project process.

Throughout the project, the project manager should check that all members of the project team keep accurate records of conversations, telephone calls, and events affecting project scope, services, quality, schedule, and cost. In fact, files should contain all information generated by the project team, including copies of submittals, transmittals, approvals, project memoranda, meeting minutes, notations of telephone conversations, project correspondence, review comments, and documents generated by the team. Good records are objective, clean, and complete. They should contain facts only; personal observations should not be included. This may help avoid associated liability.

Filing

Project files must provide easily retrievable information. When the project is completed, the project manager reviews the files, purging them of redundant materials and ensuring that they provide a complete record of the project. The baseline schedule should be updated and used as part of the regular (usually monthly) progress report.

Budget

The budget for the project-management team should be based on the proposed budget as adjusted in the negotiations. It should be on a task basis.

The monthly invoice, furnished by accounting, should be accompanied by a person-by-person list of hours billed. Figure 10–7 consists of the following two plots: budgeted cost on an early basis and budgeted cost on a late basis. If the cumulative cost falls within the budget, the project-management effort is proceeding within the budget.

Another approach to monitoring cost is the earned-value approach. The budgeted value for each task is monitored. Progress is measured by a value-earned curve, as well as cost. Figure 10–8 is a sample value-earned status check. At the 50 percent point in time, the amount spent is 60 percent. This suggests that the project value of the work completed is 60 percent. However, the plot of the earned value of the completed work at the 50 percent point in time is only 40 percent. This shows that the work is behind schedule and over budget by 20 percent.

Change Orders

When changes occur, they should be identified and documented. If a change is required in the project-team scope of work, a change order should be for project time as well as money. Time requests are usually accompanied by a time impact analysis based on the schedule baselines.

The contract-management team should also monitor the manner and timeliness with which the project-management team handles contractor claims for change orders. Change orders take time—and time costs the con-

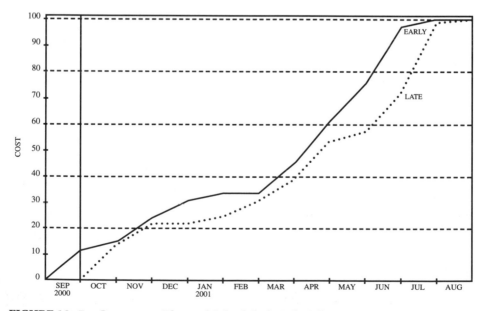

FIGURE 10–7   Current vs. Planned Scheduled - Labor Costs

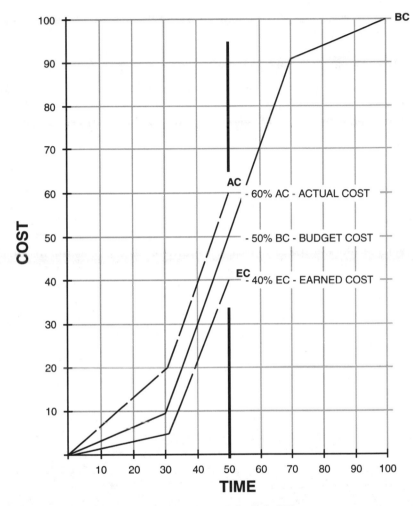

FIGURE 10–8   Value Earned at 50 percent Scheduled Time

tractor money. Job morale is definitely affected when a backlog in unprocessed change orders occurs.

Two methods are available to expedite change orders. One method is to use time and material change orders. If the project-management team and the contractor cannot agree on a fixed price for a change order, the project manager can direct the contractor to work on a time-and-material (T&M) basis. This deletes the negotiation aspect because the project is approached by doing the following:

- Labor hours by worker are listed on a daily basis.
- The base costs of labor are calculated on either a weekly or a monthly basis.
- The invoice for labor (time) is base cost plus markup for fringe benefits and workers' compensation.

- This figure is marked up as allowed by the contract for overhead and profit (usually 20 percent).
- Material is billed at cost (backed up by invoices) plus the markup allowed by the contract (usually 10 percent).

A second approach is to issue an initial unilateral change order that includes the project manager's estimate of the worth of the change. Unilateral change orders are used extensively by federal agencies. If the parties cannot agree on price, and both prefer to avoid working on a T&M basis, the project manager can issue a unilateral change order. This is issued using a project manager's cost estimate, which should be on the low side. It is understood that the contractor can continue the negotiation process and/or make a claim for cost overrun if the actual cost is higher than the estimated cost. Owners and project managers may prefer unilateral change orders because T&Ms tend to be inefficient and contractors often find that they may not cover true costs.

This keeps the contractor's cash flow moving, and makes the negotiation period less critical. It also doubles the paperwork. Why go through all this? The contractor can at least get paid in part for the change-order work.

The following case study describes a major construction-management project in which the processes described in this chapter were used to select and organize a project-management team. The project-management team carried out the three-year assignment on time and under budget.

CASE STUDY

When Southeastern Pennsylvania Transportation Authority (SEPTA) assumed operation of the former Pennsylvania and Reading rail lines in 1983, it inherited a network of bridges, track, and overhead power lines (catenary) that had already been in service for many years. Decades of deferred maintenance and virtually no dedicated capital funding had resulted in a usable but deteriorating rail system.

The commuter tunnel, completed in October 1984, connected the once-separate rail lines; it allowed all regional rail lines to access the three center-city rail stations. Several months after the tunnel's completion, an engineering inspection study indicated a need for renovation of many of the system's bridges, some of which had stood for nearly 100 years.

The four-mile stretch of track north of the new tunnel was the renovation property. The stretch consisted of track and catenary system and twenty-five rail bridges—a total of sixteen track miles—forming the main line, or throat, of the old Reading line. Six SEPTA regional rail lines fed into this central corridor.

The completed project was budgeted at about $300 million. The project, named SEPTA RailWorks, entailed major infrastructure rehabilitation of this regional rail corridor. The major components of the work included the renovation of four bridges, complete replacement of twenty-one bridges, replacement of all track, a new catenary system, and replacement of related equipment, including switches and signals. All of the bridges spanned active highway crossings in a congested urban setting.

Early in 1991, SEPTA sent letters to firms that had submitted SF 254s that demonstrated construction-management capability. The letters described the project and the availability of an RFP. About ten teams responded. A short list of five were invited to make a presentation of their proposed project team. From that short list, the O'Brien-Kreitzberg (OK) team was selected as the project team.

The contract was based on direct-labor time, plus overhead, which was calculated by multiplying 1.2 times direct labor, and a 10 percent fee on the total. SEPTA had a substantial group assigned to the field office to manage the contract. Members of this group approved the actual staffing on each task and any changes in scope. They also provided quality assurance to confirm that the construction-management team was performing according to the contract and proposal.

The OK/SEPTA team had a budget of $18 million. The team handled the base contracts and change orders. In addition, new construction scope—called supplemental changes—in the amount of $10 million, was managed by the project-management team. The team underspent the team budget by $2.5 million.

Throughout the project, the contractors were faced with a local population living in close proximity to the construction operations. Two of the bridges were actually preassembled in the yards of neighbors. The neighbors continued to use the streets in spite of the barricades and all attempts to close the streets. The entire area was laced with sanitary and storm sewers from the last century, so their existing condition was documented both before the work began and again after completion. The following list highlights facts about the project:

- Contracts: total value $140 million
- Contractors: 12 primes, 74 subs
- Start date: August 1990
- Track shutdown windows

  Phase I (April 1992–October 1992)
  Phase II (May 1993–September 1993)

- System returned to revenue service: October 1992 and September 1993
- Project closeout: December 1993
- Construction-management team (contract $15.5 million): 55 staff members

— Construction manager:	O'Brien-Kreitzberg	40 percent
— Bridges:	Michael Baker Engineers	15 percent
— Rail and power:	LS Transit Systems	15 percent
— DBEs/WBE:	Management Concepts Systems & Services; Don Todd Associates; Promatech; Vann Organization; and Mitra & Associates	30 percent

Although many different companies were represented on the construction-management team, outside allegiances were minimized. The team had its own identity in the name RailWorks, and everyone used their position title on the project rather than their home office title. Stationery, business cards, hardhats, T-shirts, and baseball caps were created for the project logo and, in general, everything feasible was done to create a sense of unity within the project team.

It was apparent from the outset that the essence of the project was the management and coordination of six prime contractors (in each phase) and their seventy-four subcontractors, combined with the sharply limited time available for the accomplishment of the work in a highly restricted and congested work area.

A project-specific procedures book was developed before the first shutdown using the OK generic procedures book as a base. In this same early time frame, a very successful partnering program was implemented. SEPTA, the construction-management team, and the initial six prime contractors were involved.

To make the transition between the completion of the general contractor's work, the corresponding start of electrical work, and the integrated system tests as seamless as possible, several mandatory milestones were included in the contract specifications. A special coordination schedule was developed by extracting relevant detailed window-schedule (the window periods during which the rail system was shut down) information from each of the contractors. This process permitted an accurate monitoring of work wherever interdependent operations by more than one contractor was unavoidable, or necessary to achieve early access.

Earned-Value System and Weekly Updates

An earned-value system was instituted based upon the detailed, resource-loaded window schedules. The windows were the times that the tracks were shut down. Within the windows, where work went on twenty-four hours a day, seven days a week, the construction project-management schedules were very detailed—they were known as Level III. Baseline target and minimum physical progress goals were established using the budgeted rate of direct labor-hours usage on the early and late schedules, respectively. Completed activities were credited with their budgeted labor hours. Credits for all completed and partially completed activities were added up on a weekly basis and compared against the baseline. Progress—baseline as well as actual—was expressed in terms of percentages to maintain a uniform yardstick throughout the project and across all contracts.

All window activities that met the criteria of physical progress were coded for cross-referencing with the project WBS, thus allowing computation of progress as a percentage of any related WBS element in a hierarchical configuration.

The construction-management team worked a weekend shift and prepared a detailed status report that evaluated progress through the close of business every Friday. This report was ready for management every Monday morning.

An OK senior principal was on-call for the project and attended thirty-three monthly progress meetings with the construction-management team and SEPTA. OK conducted an early internal audit of project procedures. Significant challenges and the greatest concerns were always twofold: (1) complete each shutdown on time and (2) restart rail lines successfully. OK considers the following results outstanding:

- All dates were met on time or early.
- The project was completed more than $20 million under budget.
- Change orders included enhancements (e.g., safe speed was increased from 40 mph to 60 mph) worth more than $10 million.
- There were no claims or lawsuits for disputed work, delays, disruptions, or disputed change orders. (Although the job was a relatively safe one, there were some workers' compensation claims and one death late in the job.)
- There was no need to apply liquidated damages (at $70,000 a day). Each summer, a window had a fixed "return to service" date. If that date was not met, each offending contractor would be assessed $70,000 a day until it was met. The first summer window was finished two days early, and the second summer window a week early.

Writing a comprehensive proposal requires the knowledge and experience to visualize how the project will progress. From this, the writer develops staffing schedules and a management plan for the project.

Developing Winning Proposals

Hans J. Thamhain

Biographical Sketch . . . **Dr. Hans J. Thamhain** is a teacher, researcher, and management practitioner in technology-based project management. Currently an Associate Professor of Management at Bentley College in Waltham, Massachusetts, near Boston, his industrial experience includes twenty years of high-technology R&D and engineering and management positions with GTE, General Electric, Westinghouse, and ITT. Dr. Thamhain has B.S.E.E., M.S.E.E., M.B.A., and Ph.D. degrees. Dr. Thamhain is well known for his research on technology-based project control and self-directed RD&E team leadership; he is a frequent speaker at major conferences, is consulted in all phases of project management, is active on the policy boards and committees of professional organizations, and has written over seventy research papers and five professional reference books in project and engineering management.

For many companies the bid proposal is a powerful competitive tool for winning new contract business. Especially for project-based firms, new contracts are the lifeblood of the organization. Among the top contenders for a new contract, the field is most often very close. Beating most of the competition is not good enough. There are no second-place winners.

The techniques for developing and winning contracts follow established bid proposal practices that are highly specialized for each market segment. They often require intense, disciplined team effort among all organizational functions, especially from operations and marketing, as well as significant customer involvement.

Many of today's managers consider proposal development both a science and an art. By understanding the process of contract acquisitions and the tools and techniques for proposal development, we can organize and manage the complexities of proposal development more effectively and predictably.

Chacteristics of Project Proposals

The following summarizes the characteristics of project proposals.

1. *Systematic effort.*   A systematic effort is usually required to develop a new project lead into an actual contract. The project acquisition effort is often highly integrated with ongoing programs and involves key personnel from both the potential customer and the performing organization.
2. *Custom design.*   Although traditional businesses provide standard products and services for a variety of applications and customers, projects are custom-designed items to fit specific requirements for a single customer community.
3. *Project life cycle.*   Project-oriented businesses have a beginning and an end and are not self-perpetuating. Business must be generated on a project-by-project basis rather than by creating demand for a standard product or service.
4. *Market phase.*   Long lead times often exist between project definition, start-up, and completion.
5. *Risks.*   Especially for technology-based projects, substantial risks are present. The contractor must not only manage and integrate the project within budget and schedule constraints, but also manage innovations, technology, and the associated risks.
6. *Technical capability to perform.*   This capability is a critical prerequisite for the successful pursuit and acquisition of a new project or program.
7. *Customer requirements.*   Projects are often unique regarding specific operational requirements. Applications in the specific customer environment must be properly understood and addressed in the bid proposal document.
8. *Follow-on potential.*   Winning one contract often provides opportunities for follow-on business such as spare parts, maintenance, training, or volume production.
9. *Complex bidding process.*   The acquisition process is often very complex and subtle, especially for larger proposal efforts. They often start a long time before the proposal writing phase.
10. *Contract negotiations.*   Although the proposal serves as a very important vehicle for narrowing the selection of potential contractors, the winning bidder is most likely selected—and its contract finalized— by negotiations. Often these negotiations involve intricate and subtle processes.

Proposal Types

Proposals are sales documents that try to persuade potential customers to buy goods or services. Although some similarities exist for selling projects and products, there is a fundamental difference. Traditional business products and services are standard and fill needs for a variety of purposes and customers. Projects, by contrast, are custom-designed items to fit specific requirements for one customer.

The majority of bid proposals prepared by companies are written documents that offer to solve a particular customer problem. They can be solicited or unsolicited. Usually, proposals are based on inquiries received from prospective clients. Most commonly these inquiries come in the form of a request for proposal (RFP). Depending on the scope and complexity of the solicitation, the RFP can range from a simple note to a highly complex document. An inquiry stipulates the conditions under which the client wishes the work to be done. The responses to these client inquiries are termed *bid proposals*. They are classified in two major categories: *qualification proposals* and *commercial bid proposals*.

THE QUALIFICATION PROPOSAL
The qualification proposal generally gives information about company organization, qualifications, working procedures, or information for a specific area of technology. Qualification proposals make no offer to perform services and make no commitments of a general or technical nature. These documents are also called *informational proposals* if the contents relate to company organization, general qualifications, and procedures. They are sometimes called *white papers, technical presentations*, or *technical volumes* if technical and economic data are provided for a specific area of technology. A special form of the qualification proposal is the *presentation*.

THE COMMERCIAL BID PROPOSAL
The commercial bid proposal offers a definite commitment by the company to provide specific work, or services, or equipment in accordance with explicit terms of compensation. A commercial bid proposal may also contain the type of information usually found in qualification proposals.

Proposal Forms

Both qualification and commercial proposals may be presented to the client in various forms under a wide variety of titles, depending on the situation, the client's requirements, and the firm's willingness to commit its resources. No sharp distinctions exist among these proposals on the basis of content. The difference is mainly in the format and extent of preparation effort. The most common forms are the *letter proposals, preliminary proposals, detailed proposals*, and *presentations*.

LETTER PROPOSALS
These are either qualification or commercial proposals. They are brief enough to be issued in letter form rather than as bound volumes.

PRELIMINARY PROPOSALS

These are either qualification or commercial proposals, usually large enough to be issued as bound volumes. They are sent to the client for the purpose of dialogue, eventually leading to a detailed proposal development, rather than for proposal evaluation.

DETAILED PROPOSALS

These are most often commercial bid proposals, which aside from the technical part, include a detailed cost and time estimate. They are the most complex and inclusive proposals. Because of the high cost of preparation and the bid commitments offered, organization and contents of these documents are defined and detailed to a much greater degree than for other kinds of proposals.

PRESENTATIONS

These are generally in the format of oral proposals. Selected personnel, specialized in certain areas, discuss their proposals verbally with client representatives. Presentation time periods may vary from an hour to an entire day. Audiovisual aids can enhance the effectiveness of these presentations.

Identifying New Business Opportunities

For many managers, bid-proposal opportunities appear unpredictable and they are in markets that are difficult to manage. Yet, in spite of the subtle nature of proposal-generated business, much can be done to drive and lead market activities consistent with a company's business objectives. For starters, effective market planning and strategizing are important. New program opportunities develop over time; for large programs, this could take as long as several years. These developments must be properly tracked and cultivated to form the basis for management actions such as bid decisions, resource commitment, technical readiness, and effective customer liaison.

The strategy of winning new business is supported by systematic, disciplined approaches, which are typically broken into six phases. These phases are often managed concurrently. They are the following:

1. Identifying new business opportunities
2. Assessing new contract opportunities
3. Planning the business acquisition
4. Developing the new contract opportunity
5. Writing a winning proposal
6. Negotiating and closing the contract

Identifying new bid opportunities is an ongoing activity that involves scanning the relevant market sector for new business. The primary responsibility for identifying new business opportunities falls on the marketing or sales department, but personnel at all levels throughout the company can help significantly in identifying new business leads. The many sources for identifying new business opportunities include customer meetings for ongoing programs, professional meetings and conventions, trade shows, trade journals, customer service, responses to advertising, and personal contacts.

For most businesses, ongoing program activities are the best sources of new opportunity leads. Not only are the lines of customer communication better than in a new market, but equally important, the image as an experienced, reliable contractor has been established. This creates a clear, competitive advantage in any further business pursuit.

In addition to sources from ongoing business activities, there are many resources available to help companies in screening the market and identifying new bid opportunities. These resources range from specialized newspapers, such as the *Commerce Business Daily*, to on-line data services and specialized consultants. Many government agencies also publish their own lists of contract opportunities together with solicitation guidelines. Major newspapers, such as *The Wall Street Journal*, are yet other important sources for new business opportunities. Table 11–1 lists some of the most popular sources of new contract opportunities for U.S. markets.

Assessing New Contract Opportunities

Pursuing new contract opportunities can be a risky business. It often requires substantial resources, yet its win probability is low. Companies with marginal success of winning new business often find themselves in the quandary of bidding on too many opportunities, without realizing the amount of resources necessary for seriously competing for any one of the contracts. As with other investments, investments in new bid opportunities must be carefully analyzed and assessed.

The objective of this analysis is to develop an *acquisition plan* and eventually a *bid decision*. Table 11–2 describes the bid decision, and Table 11–3 describes the acquisition plan. Analyzing a new opportunity and preparing the acquisition plan is usually an interactive effort. Often many meetings are needed between the customer and the performing organization before a clear picture emerges of both customer requirements and contractor's capabilities. A major benefit of such customer involvement is the potential for building confidence and credibility with the customer community. It shows that an organization understands the requirements and has the capability to fulfill them. This is an important prerequisite for eventually winning the contract.

The *assessment phase* often runs concurrently with the acquisition planning effort and leads to a preliminary bid decision. The acquisition plan, as outlined in Table 11–3, provides the basis for positioning a company favorably to win a contract. Typical development activities for positioning a company

Table 11–1. Sources of New Contract Information

Catalog of Federal Domestic Assistance, General Service Administration, Washington, DC 20402

Commerce Business Daily, U.S. Department of Commerce Office of Field Services, U.S. Government Printing Office, Washington, DC 20402

Defense Market Measurement System, Frost and Sullivan, 109 Fulton Street, New York, NY 10038

DIALOG OnDisc® The GRANTS Database®, Dialog Information Services, Inc., 3450 Hillview Avenue, Palo Alto, CA 94304

Directory of Government Production Prime Contracts, Government Data Publication, Washington, DC 20402

Directory of Research Grants, The Oryx Press, 4041 N. Central Avenue, Phoenix, AZ 85012

Federal Grants and Contracts Weekly: Project Opportunities in Research, Training and Services, Capitol Publications, 1101 King St., Alexandria, VA 22314

Federal Register, National Archives and Records Administration, Washington, DC 20400

Forms of Business Agreement, Institute of Business Planning, IPB Plaza, Englewood Cliffs, NJ 07632

Government Contractor, Federal Publications, 1120 20th Street NW, Washington, DC 20036

Government Contracts Directory, Government Data Publications, Washington, DC 20402

Government Contracts Reports, Commerce Clearance House, 4025 West Peterson Avenue, Chicago, IL 60646

National Contract Management Association, 6728 Old McLean Village Dr., McLean, VA 22101

New Business Report, Executive Communications, Inc., 919 Third Ave., New York, NY 10022

NCMA Newsletter, National Contract Management Association, 675 East Wardlow Road, Long Beach, CA 90807

United States Government Purchasing and Sales Directory, U.S. Small Business Administration, 409 3rd Street, NW, Washington, DC 20416

Internet Web Sites:

Government Contract Alerts, http://cfr.counterpoint.com/grams/taugram/out831502084.html (plus others).

Government Contract and Business Resources, www.uscontracts.com/

Government Contract Services, www.hps.com/minneapolis/gcs/

Government Contracting, www.guvcon.com/

Government Contracting Internet Resources, http://ftplaw.wuacc.edu/listproc/net-lawyers/001/msg00232.html

Government Contracts Advisor, www.counterpoint.com/taurus.html

Rock Island District, www.ncr.usace.army.mil/ncrpa/panr.html

---

favorably include significant customer contact, prior relevant experience, technical readiness to perform, and organizational readiness to perform.

SIGNIFICANT CUSTOMER CONTACT

Customer liaison is vital for learning about specific customer requirements and needs. It is necessary to define the project baseline, potential problem areas, and risks involved. Customer liaison also allows participation in cus-

Table 11–2.   The Bid Decision

Few decisions are more fundamental to new business development than the bid decision. Resources for the pursuit of new business come from operating profits. These resources are scarce and should be carefully controlled. Bid boards serve as management gates for the release and control of these resources. The bid board is an expert panel that analyzes the new business opportunity and the ongoing acquisition activities to determine the readiness of the company to mount a winning proposal effort. The bid board assesses investment versus opportunity and risk. The acquisition plan provides the major framework for the bid board's deliberations.

Major acquisitions usually require a series of bid-board sessions, sometimes starting as early as twelve to eighteen months prior to the RFP. Subsequent bid boards reaffirm the bid decision and update the acquisition plan. It is the responsibility of the proposal manager to gather and present pertinent information in a manner that provides the bid board with complete information for analysis and decision. The following checklist provides a simple tool for organizing and facilitating bid board discussions:

Checklist in Support of Bid Decision

- Does company have capabilities and resources to perform the work? . . . . FAVORABLE—UNFAVORABLE
- Can company phase in the work to meet client schedule? . . . . FAVORABLE—UNFAVORABLE
- What is company's technical position? . . . . FAVORABLE—UNFAVORABLE
- What is company's approach to project execution? . . . . FAVORABLE—UNFAVORABLE
- Is project of special importance to client? . . FAVORABLE—UNFAVORABLE
- Would doing project enhance our reputation? . . . . FAVORABLE—UNFAVORABLE
- What was our past experience and contractual relationship with client? . . . . . . FAVORABLE—UNFAVORABLE
- What is company's commercial approach and price strategy? . . . . FAVORABLE—UNFAVORABLE
- What are client's future capital expenditures? . . . . FAVORABLE—UNFAVORABLE
- Who is the competition and do they have any special advantages? . . . . FAVORABLE—UNFAVORABLE
- Does client have preferred contractor and if so, why? . . . . FAVORABLE—UNFAVORABLE
- What is the probability of project going ahead? . . . . FAVORABLE—UNFAVORABLE
- Is the project consistent with long-range business plan of the company? . . . . FAVORABLE—UNFAVORABLE
- Do we expect other bid opportunities in the next six months? One year? . . . . FAVORABLE—UNFAVORABLE
- Are there any special factors and considerations? . . . . FAVORABLE—UNFAVORABLE

Table 11–3. Characteristics and Content of Acquisition Plan

The acquisition plan is an important management tool that
provides the basis for the formal bid decision and a detailed plan for
the market development of the new business. It also provides an
assessment of the resource requirements for developing and
bidding the new business. Typically, the new business acquisition
plan should include the following elements:

- *A brief description of the new business opportunity:* A statement of the
  requirements, specifications, scope, schedule, budget, customer organization, and key decision makers.
- *An understanding of why the company should bid:* A perspective
  regarding established business plans and desirable results, such as
  profits, markets, growth, and technology.
- *Competitive assessment:* A description of each competing firm with
  regard to its past activities in the subject areas, including related experiences, current contracts, customer interfaces, specific strengths and
  weaknesses, and potential baseline approach.
- *Critical win factors:* A listing of specific factors important to winning
  the new program, including their rationales.
- *Ability to write a winning proposal:* The specifics needed to prepare a
  winning proposal, including availability of the right proposal personnel, an understanding of customer problems, a unique competitive
  advantage, a bid-cost estimate that is under customer budget, special
  arrangements such as teaming or licensing, readiness to write a proposal, and ability to bid competitively.
- *Win strategy:* A chronological listing of critical milestones guiding the
  acquisition effort from its present position to winning the new program. It should show those activities critical for positioning yourself
  uniquely in the competitive field, including timing and individual
  responsibility for each milestone.
- *Capture plan:* A detailed action plan that supports the win strategy
  and is integrated with the overall business plan. All activities should
  include timing, budgets, and responsible individuals. The capture plan
  is a working document to map out and guide the overall acquisition
  effort. It should be updated as the acquisition effort progresses.
- *Ability to perform under contract:* This is often a separate document,
  but a summary should be included in the acquisition plan stating technical requirements, key personnel, facilities, teaming and subcontracting, and program schedules.
- *Problems and risks:* A list of problems critical to the implementation of
  the capture plan such as risks related to technology, staffing, facilities,
  schedules, or procurement.
- *Resource plan:* A budget summary, including key personnel, support
  services, and other resources needed for capturing the new business.

---

tomer problem solving and building a favorable image as a competent, credi-
ble contractor. Today's complex customer organizations involve many people
in bid decision-making. Conflicting requirements and biases are realities and
must be dealt with. Multifunctional involvement at various levels of both companies is often necessary to reach all decision-making parties in the customer

community. The new business acquisition plan is a good source of information and road map for this development effort.

PRIOR RELEVANT EXPERIENCE

Nothing is more convincing to a potential customer than demonstrated prior performance in the area of the proposed program. It reduces the perceived technical risks, as well as the associated budget and schedule uncertainties. This image of an experienced contractor can be communicated in many ways: (1) field demonstration of working systems and equipment; (2) listing of previous or current customers, their equipment, and applications; (3) model demonstrations; (4) technical status presentations; (5) product promotional folders; (6) technical papers and articles; (7) trade show demonstrations and exhibits; (8) audiovisual presentation of equipment in operation; (9) simulation of the system, equipment, or services; (10) specifications, photos, or models of the proposed equipment; and (11) advertisements. Demonstrating prior experience is integrated and interactive with the customer liaison activities.

TECHNICAL READINESS TO PERFORM

Once the basic requirements and specifications of the new program are known, it is often necessary to mount a substantial technical preproposal effort to advance the baseline design to a point that permits a clear definition of the new program. These efforts may be funded by the customer or borne by the contractor. Typical efforts include (1) feasibility studies, (2) system designs, (3) simulation, (4) design and testing of certain critical elements in the new equipment or the new process, (5) prototype models, or (6) any developments necessary to bid the new job within the desired scope of technical and financial risks. Although these precontract efforts can be expensive, they are often an absolute necessity for winning new business. These early developments reduce the implementation risks to an acceptable level for both the customer and the contractor, and also might be necessary for catching up with a competitor or building credibility with the customer.

ORGANIZATIONAL READINESS TO PERFORM

Another element of credibility is the contractor's organizational readiness to perform under contract. This includes facilities, key personnel, support groups, and management structure. Credibility in this area is particularly critical in winning a large program relative to your company size. This does not require a reorganization prior to contract award, but a clearly defined organization plan, exactly detailing the procedures to be followed as soon as the contract is awarded. The following checklist defines typical organizational components that should be defined clearly and discussed with the customer prior to a major new contract: organizational structure, charter, policy-management guidelines, job description, authority and responsibility relationships, type and number of offices and laboratories, facilities listing, floor plans, staffing plan, milestone schedule, and budget for reorganization.

Writing a Winning Proposal

Bid proposals are payoff vehicles. They are among the final products of the marketing effort. Whether you are bidding on a service or hardware contract, a government or commercial program, the basic process is the same.

The proposal is one of several key marketing tools crucial for communicating the formal contract offer. The program concept and the soundness of its approach, the alternatives, the company's credibility, and so on, must be established during the face-to-face discussions with the customer, usually during preproposal efforts or contract negotiations. Yet, a superior proposal is a necessity for winning a new contract in a competitive environment. Your competition is most likely working with great intensity toward the same goal of winning this program. They, too, may have sold the customer on their approaches and capabilities. Only one company will be the winner. Therefore, writing a winning proposal is a serious business in itself. Table 11–4 shows a typical outline for a major bid proposal. It is broken into three sections: *technical, management,* and *cost.* This is a common subdivision used in formal bidding practices. The outline also shows the complexities involved in a major proposal effort.

Table 11–4. Bid Proposal Content for Major Program (Typical Bid Package Organized in Three Sections)

I Technical Section	II Management Section	III Cost Section
Executive summary	Executive summary	Executive summary
Requirements analysis	Management	Scope and cost model
Recommended solutions	commitment	Contract type
Alternate solutions	Recommended solution	Cost summary by
Scope of work	Statement of work	categories and
and limitations	Work breakdowns	workgroups
Method of approach	List of deliverables	Cost escalation
Detailed technical	Project organization	Taxes
solutions	Task responsibilities	Subcontracting
Subsystem I	Project management	Progress payments
Subsystem II	process	Options
Subsystem III	Project tracking and	Basis of cost estimate,
Prototyping	reporting	assumptions, and
Field installation	Project control	liabilities
and testing	Make-buy analysis	Overhead rates
Specifications	Subcontracting and	Support facilities
Reliability assessment	teaming	Assurances for cost
Maintenance	Quality control	effective contract
Training	Qualifications of	work
Risk analysis	personnel	Detailed cost schedules
Related experiences	Contractor qualifications	Appendix
Appendix	Appendix	Index
Index	Index	

ORGANIZING FOR GROUP WRITING

Proposal development requires hard work and long hours, often in a work environment filled with tension and constant pressure to perform. As with most projects, proposal development requires multidisciplinary efforts with an orderly and disciplined execution. Special tools are available to help particularly large programs integrate the many activities needed for developing a high-scoring quality proposal. Smaller proposals often can be managed with less formality. At a minimum, the proposal plan should include the following components:

- Proposal-team organization
- Proposal schedule
- Win strategy
- Categorical outline
- Writing assignments and page allocation
- Synopsis of approach for each topic
- RFP analysis
- Technical baseline review
- Proposal draft writing
- Development of illustration
- Reviews
- Cost estimating and pricing
- Proposal production
- Final management review

STORYBOARDING FACILITATES GROUP WRITING

Most bid proposals are group writing efforts. Organizing, coordinating, and integrating these team efforts can add significantly to the complexities and difficulties of managing proposal developments. Especially for larger efforts, storyboarding is a technique that facilitates the group writing process by breaking down its complexities and integrating the proposal work incrementally.

Storyboarding is based on the idea of splitting up the proposal writing among the various contributors and then developing the text incrementally via a series of writing, editing, and review phases, typically in the following order:

1. Categorical outline [3 percent of total proposal effort]
2. Synopsis of approach [6 percent of total proposal effort]
3. Roundtable review [4 percent of total proposal effort]
4. Topical outline [5 percent of total proposal effort]
5. Storyboard preparation [20 percent of total proposal effort]
6. Storyboard review [4 percent of total proposal effort]
7. Storyboard expansion [25 percent of total proposal effort]
8. Staff review [3 percent of total proposal effort]
9. Final proposal draft [15 percent of total proposal effort]
10. Final edit [10 percent of total proposal effort]
11. Publication and delivery [5 percent of total proposal effort]

The number and type of phases indicated in this listing, together with the relative effort, might be typical for a major bid proposal development with a 30-day response cycle. However, this listing can also serve as a guide for larger or smaller proposals. For larger efforts, more iterations are suggested among phases 5 and 10, while smaller efforts can be scaled down to eight phases, eliminating the first three steps and requiring fewer iterations. The time plan of proposal developments should be scheduled as for any other project. A bar graph schedule is usually sufficient and effective for most proposal efforts. As for any multifunctional effort, a phased approach is recommended, which can also be integrated into a *stage-gate process* for effective cross-functional integration and control. Each of the eleven phases are briefly described next.

Categorical Outline

Whether managed by storyboarding or conventional methods, the first step in the proposal process is the development of a categorical outline. This is a listing of the major topics or chapters to be covered in the proposal. The outline should also show, for each category; the responsible author, a page estimate, and references to related documents. The categorical outline can often be developed before the receipt of the RFP, and should be finalized at the time of proposal-writing kickoff. The writing kickoff occurs during this phase.

Synopsis of Approach

A synopsis of approach is developed for each proposal category by each responsible author. As an alternative, the proposal manager can complete these forms and issue them as policy papers instead of having each author develop them. This approach works especially well for proposal efforts that have a professional proposal support group that can prepare these synopses as a guideline for technical brainstorming and that can search for innovative solutions. The synopsis is a top-level outline of the approach to be articulated in each proposal category. At minimum, it should address three questions:

1. What does the customer require?
2. How are we planning to respond?
3. How is the approach unique and effective?

The typical synopsis of approach form is an 8½" × 11" sheet of paper, subdivided into five sections:

1. Proposal category and responsible writer
2. Understanding of customer requirements
3. Proposed approach and compliance
4. Soundness of approach and effectiveness
5. Risks, alternatives, and options

In preparation for the review, the completed synopsis forms and categorical outline are posted on a wall, in sequential order. This method of display facilitates effective open group review and analyses.

Roundtable Review

During this phase, all synopsis of approach forms are analyzed, critiqued, augmented, and approved by the proposal team and its manager. This is the first time that the proposed approach is displayed in a complete and continuous summary form. Besides the proposal team, key members of functional support groups, such as technical resource managers, marketing managers, contract specialists, and upper management, should participate in this review. The review typically starts four days after the proposal kickoff.

Topical Outline

Concurrent with the review and revision of the synopsis, or afterward, the categorical outline is expanded into the specific topics to be addressed in the proposal. This topical outline forms the Table of Contents for the bid proposal. Similar to the categorical outline, each topic should be defined, and a writer should be assigned to the topic. The number of pages needs to be estimated and references documented.

Storyboard Preparation

Storyboards are summary proposals. Preparation is straightforward. Typically, a one-page storyboard is prepared for each topic by the assigned writer. As shown in Figure 11–1, the storyboard represents a detailed outline of the author's approach to the writeup for that particular topic. Often the storyboard form is divided into the following three parts:

1. Topic and theme section
2. Text outline on the left side of the form
3. Summary of supporting art to be prepared on the right side of the form

The storyboard takes a first cut at the key issues of each topic. The problem statement and exit or conclusion must be written out in full, just the way they might appear in the final text. Expression of these key sentences is important; they must be relevant, responsive, and emphatic.

The storyboard composition of text and art is arranged in this format for convenience only. As shown in Figure 11–2, the text format of the proposal document can be either modular or nonmodular. For the modular concept, the storyboard format is copied directly into the proposal layout, with the text on the left, and the illustrations on the right. In nonmodular form, the art becomes an integral part of the text. The final layout should, however, be of no concern to the authors at this point in the proposal-development cycle. Storyboards are one of the most important elements in the proposal-development process. They should be typed for clarity and easy comprehension during the review sessions.

Storyboard Review

The completed storyboard forms are pasted on the walls of the review room in a logical sequence, together with the earlier displays of outlines and synopses. The set of storyboards is in essence the bid proposal. It presents the total story we want to tell to the customer.

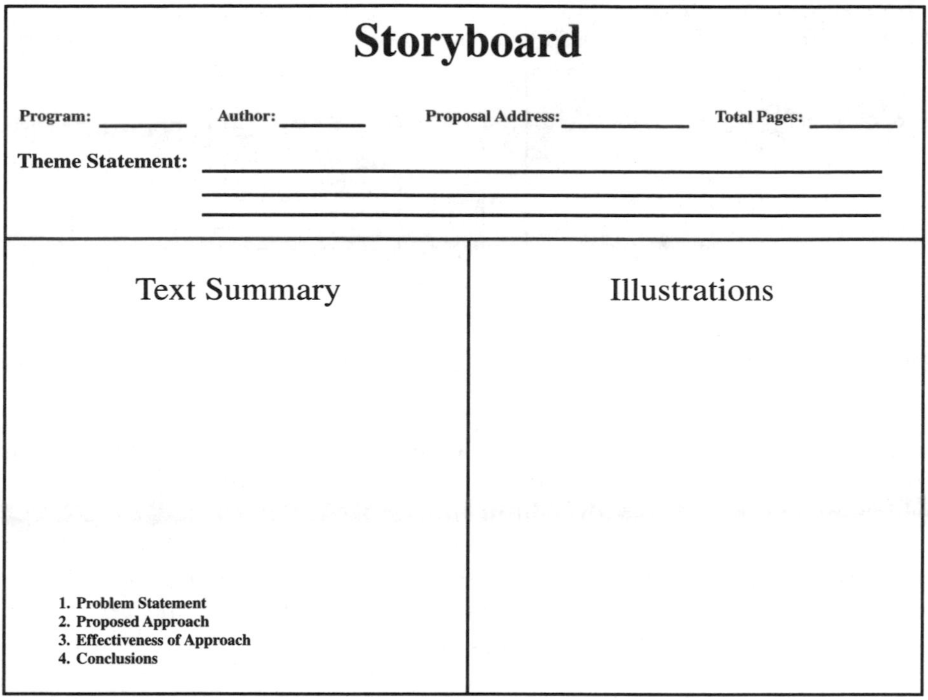

Storyboard

Program: _____   Author: _____   Proposal Address: _____   Total Pages: _____

Theme Statement: _____

_____

_____

Text Summary	Illustrations

1. Problem Statement
2. Proposed Approach
3. Effectiveness of Approach
4. Conclusions

FIGURE 11–1   Storyboard Format

Typically, storyboard reviews should start within ten working days after the proposal writing kickoff that takes place during the first phase, categorical outline. The reviews are held in the review room and are attended by the author, the proposal team, and key members of the functional organization. The storyboards are hung on the walls. The storyboard review permits a dialogue to take place between the author, the proposal team, and its management. Because participation in these reviews is critical to success, review schedules should be properly communicated via both the daily bulletin and microschedule.

The storyboard review permits the proposal team to insert, modify, or correct an approach taken by an author. The storyboard review provides the team with the single most important opportunity to change direction or change approaches in the proposal preparation. Similar to the synopsis review, storyboarding is an interactive process. During the reviews, a copy of the latest storyboard should always be on display in the control room.

Storyboard Expansion
After the storyboard review, each author prepares a storyboard expansion. Storyboard expansion is the development of each topic from the original storyboard into a narrative of approximately 500 words. As part of the storyboard expansion, all authors should finalize their art work and give it to the publications specialist for processing. This is the first draft of the final

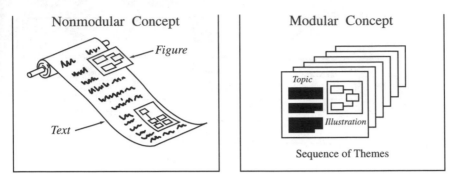

FIGURE 11–2   Nonmodular and Modular Concept of Proposal Presentation

proposal. The material is given to the technical editor who will edit the draft for clarity. Each responsible author should review and approve the final draft, which might cycle through the editing process several times.

This final text generation is the major activity in the proposal development process. All prior activities are preparatory, yet incremental to this final writing assignment. If preparations are done properly, writing the final text should be a logical and straightforward task without the hassles of conceptual clarification and worries about integration with other authors.

As a guideline, ten working days out of a proposal-development cycle of thirty working days may be a reasonable time for this final text generation. Because of its relatively long duration, it is particularly important to set up specific milestones for measuring intermediate progress. The process of final text generation should be carefully controlled. The proposal specialist, if available, will play a key role in the integration, coordination, and controlling of this final text generation and its publication. The final text should be submitted incrementally to the publication department for editing, word processing, and art work preparation.

Staff Review
The final proposal review is conducted by the proposal team, its management group, and selected functional managers. In addition, a specialty review committee may be organized to check the final draft for feasibility, rationale, and responsiveness to the RFP. Typically, this staff review is completed in less than a day. The comments are reviewed by the original authors for incorporation. The staff review can be repeated if necessary.

Final Proposal Draft
Each author finalizes his or her section of expanded storyboards, incorporating the staff review comments and recommendations.

Final Edit
After these final revisions, the entire proposal is turned over to the publication department for final editing, completion of art, and word processing. The authors should be given a last opportunity to look at the completed proposal.

Any major flaws or technical errors that may have slipped into the document are corrected at this time.

Publication and Delivery
The proposal is now ready for layout, printing, binding, and delivery to the customer.

Negotiating and Closing the Contract

Sending off the bid proposal signals the start of the postsubmission phase. Regardless of the type of customer or the formalities involved, even for an oral proposal, the procurement will go through the following principal steps:

1. Bid proposals received
2. Proposals evaluated
3. Proposal values competitively compared
4. Alternatives assessed
5. Clarifications solicited from bidders
6. Negotiations conducted
7. Contract awarded

Although bidders usually have no influence on the proposal evaluation or source-selection process, they can certainly prepare properly for the upcoming opportunities of customer inquiries and negotiations. Depending on the type of procurement, opportunities for improving the competitive position come in many forms, such as the following:

- Follow-up calls and visits
- Responses to customer requests for additional information
- Fact-finding requested by customer
- Oral presentations
- Invitations to field visits
- Samples or prototypes
- Supportive advertising
- Contact via related contract work
- Plant or office visits
- Press releases
- Negotiations

Postsubmission activities can significantly improve the bidder's competitive position. Any opportunity for customer contact should be used. Follow-up calls and visits are effective in less formal procurements, whereas fact finding and related contract work are often used by bidders in formal procurements. The proposal evaluation period is used by the customer to rank-order proposals. During this period, the bidder has the opportunity to improve his or her position in the following three principal areas: clarifying proposed program scope and content; building the image of a sound, reliable contractor; and counteracting advances made by competing bidders.

Only through active customer contact is it possible to assess realistically the competitive situation and organize for proposal-score improvement and winning negotiations.

The proposal evaluation period is highly dynamic in terms of changing scores, particularly among the top contenders. The bidder who is well organized and prepared for interacting with the customer community stands the best chance of being called first and of negotiating an equitable contract.

Recommendations to Management

Winning a bid proposal depends on more than just price, market position, or luck. Winning a piece of business depends on many factors that must be carefully developed during the preproposal period, articulated in the bid proposal, and fine-tuned during contract negotiations. Success is geared to hard work, which starts with a keen assessment of the bid opportunity and a sound bid decision.

Although a price-competitive bid can help in many situations, research shows that a low price bid is advantageous toward winning only in contracts with low complexity, low technical risk, and high competition. In most other situations, price is an important factor toward winning only within the context of many other competitive components, including compliance with customer requirements for the best-fitting solution, past experience, soundness of approach, cost credibility, delivery, and after-sale support. The better a firm understands its customer, the better it will be able to communicate the strength of its organization and the proposed contract to the customer. The following specific recommendations can help business managers responsible for winning new contracts and professionals who must support bid-proposal efforts.

- Develop a detailed business acquisition plan that includes a realistic assessment of the new opportunity and the specific milestones needed.
- Involve the right people by forming a committee of senior personnel early in the acquisition cycle.
- Maintain closeness to the customer to understand the customer requirements better and develop credibility regarding your capacity to perform.
- Select bid opportunities carefully. Submitting more proposals does nothing to improve your win ratio. It only drains your resources.
- Make bid decisions incrementally to narrow opportunities down to a short list without spending a lot of time and resources.
- Be sure you have the resources to go the full distance and develop a detailed cost estimate for the entire proposal effort. Decide what to do in case the customer extends the bid submission deadline, which will cost the bidding company more money as it refines its proposal.
- Obtain commitment from senior management. Make the necessary resources and facilities available when needed.
- Before the proposal writing starts, have a clear picture of the strengths, weaknesses, and limitations of the competing firms and of your company.

- Manage the proposal development as you would any other project.
- Enhance the effectiveness of the proposal effort with a professional proposal specialist.
- Gather marketing intelligence about competition from trade shows, bidder's briefings, customer meetings, professional conferences, competitors' literature, and special market service firms.
- Define your niche or "unfair advantage" over your competition and build your win strategy around it.
- Develop the proposal text incrementally by using the storyboard process.
- Don't allow exceptions to the customer requirements unless it is absolutely unavoidable.
- Demonstrate your ability to perform. Show past related experiences to score the strongest points. Showing that your company performed well on similar programs, that you have experienced personnel, and that you have done analytical homework on the requirements, may rate very favorably with the customer, especially when you have other advantages such as an innovative solution, or favorable timing, or competitive pricing.
- Review proposal effectiveness. As part of the incremental proposal development, assure effective reviews that check compliance with customer requirements, soundness of approach, effective communication, and proper integration of topics into one proposal.
- Use red-team reviews. Set up a special review team for must-win proposals. This review team evaluates and scores the proposal using a process similar to the process used by the customer. Deficiencies that may otherwise remain hidden can often be identified and dealt with during the proposal development. Such a review can be conducted at various stages of the proposal development. It is important to budget the time and money needed for revising the proposal after a red-team review.
- Use editorial support. Have a competent editor work side-by-side with the technical proposal writers.
- Price competitively. For most proposals, a competitively priced bid has the winning edge. Pricing should be considered at the time of the bid decision.
- Prepare for customer inquiries and negotiations immediately after proposal submission.
- Conduct postbid analysis. Review the proposal effort regardless of the final outcome. The lessons learned should be documented for the benefit of future proposal efforts.

Winning New Business

Winning new contract business is a highly competitive and resource-intensive undertaking. To be successful, it requires special management skills, tools, and techniques that range from identifying new bid opportunities to making bid decisions and developing proposals. Companies that win their share of new business usually have a well-disciplined process that is being fine-tuned and improved continuously. They also have experienced personnel who can manage the intricate process and lead a multifunctional team toward writing a unified winning proposal. Their managements target specific opportunities selectively and use good judgment in deriving bid decisions. They position their companies uniquely in the competitive field by building a quality image with the customer and they make few fundamental mistakes during the acquisition process. These are the managers who win their fair share of new contracts in today's highly competitive business environment by submitting a responsive bid proposal that is competitively priced.

BIBLIOGRAPHY

Arkebauer, James B. *The McGraw-Hill Guide to Writing a High-Impact Business Plan: A Proven Blueprint for First-Time Entrepreneurs.* New York: McGraw-Hill, 1994

Behling, John H. *Guidelines for Preparing the Research Proposal.* Lanham, MD: University Press of America, 1984

Boles, James S., Hiram C. Barksdale, and Julie T. Johnson. What national accounts decision makers would tell sales people about building relations. *Journal of Business and Industrial Markets,* Vol. 11, No. 2 (1996), pp. 6–19

Boughton, Paul D. The competitive bidding process. *Industrial Marketing Management,* Vol. 16, No. 2 (May 1987), pp. 87–94

Bowman, Joel P. and Branchaw, Bernadine P. *How to Write Proposals That Produce.* Phoenix, AZ: Oryx Press, 1992

Burns, Michael. *Proposal Writer's Guide.* New Haven, CT: D.A.T.A., 1989

Campanelli, M. Writer's block: Writing proposals can be easy. *Sales and Marketing Management,* Vol. 147, (Spring 1995), p. 114

Charland, Thomas C. *Proposal Writing and Costing Techniques Handbook.* Manassas, VA: Manage Co., 1995

Freed, Richard C. *Writing Winning Business Proposals: Your Guide to Landing the Client, Making the Sale.* New York: McGraw-Hill, 1995

Greco, Alan J. and Hogue, Jack T. Developing marketing decision support systems. *Journal of Business and Industrial Markets.* Vol. 5, No. 2 (Summer/Fall 1990), pp. 27–36

Green, R. F., Zimmerer, J. W.; Steadman, M. E., The role of buyer sophistication in competitive bidding. *Journal of Business and Industrial Marketing.* Vol. 9, No. 1 (1994), pp. 51–59

Hamper, Robert J. and Baugh, Sue L. *Handbook for Writing Proposals.* NTC Publications Group, 1995

Hartmann, How to write a proposal. *Dunn & Bradstreet Reports.* Vol. 42 (March–April 1993), p. 62

Helgeson, Donald. *Engineer's and Manager's Guide to Winning Proposals.* Norwood, MA: Artech House, 1994

Holtz, Herman and Schmidt, Terry. *The Winning Proposal . . . How To Write It.* New York: McGraw-Hill, 1981

Holtz, Herman R. *The Consultant's Guide to Proposal Writing: How to Satisfy Your Clients and Double Your Income.* New York: John Wiley & Co., Inc., 1990

Kerzner, Harold and Loring, Roy J. *Proposal Preparation and Management Handbook.* New York: Van Nostrand Reinhold, 1982

Morris, Michael and Schurink, Corine Van Erkom. Pricing behavior in industrial markets: The impact of environmental dynamics. *Journal of Business and Industrial Markets.* Vol. 8, No. 3 (1993), pp. 28–43

Newport, J. P., Jr. Billion dollar bids in sealed envelopes. *Fortune*, 42 (April, 1985)

Polley, Paulette J. and Shankin, William L. Marketing high-technology medical equipment to hospitals. *Journal of Business and Industrial Markets*. Vol 8, No. 4 (1993) pp. 32–42

Porter-Roth, Bud. *Proposal Development: A Winning Approach*. Grants Pass, OR: PSI Research, 1986

RMA Ltd. Staff. *Proposal Strategies That Work*. Dallas: Kendall-Hunt, 1993

Sant, Tom. *Persuasive Business Proposals: Writing to Win Customers, Clients & Contracts*. New York: AMACOM, 1992

Steward, Rodney D. and Steward, Ann L. *Proposal Preparation*. New York: John Wiley & Sons, Inc., 1984

Thamhain, H. J. Developing Winning Proposals. *Engineering Management Review*, Vol 7, 1989, pp. 19–33.

Thamhain, H. J. Managing Bid Proposal Developments, *In Project Management Handbook* (Cleland and King, eds.). New York: Van Nostrand Reinhold, 1988.

Wall, Richard J. and Jones, Carolyn M. Navigating the rugged terrain of government contracts. *Internal Auditor*. Vol 52, No. 2 (April 1995), pp. 32–36

Risk Management: Techniques for Managing Project Risk

John E. Martin and
Pierre-François Heaulme

Biographical Sketch . . . **John E. Martin** works for the IBM Corporation, IBM Consulting Group, Milwaukee, Wisconsin, and has been certified as a professional project manager both by IBM and the Project Management Institute. He has twenty years of field project-management experience in the information systems arena. Currently, Martin is on assignment to IBM's A. J. Watson International Education Center in Brussels, Belgium, where he is the program manager for the IBM Solution Institute's (ISI) project management curriculum. In addition, Martin is an adjunct faculty member of the Keller Graduate School of Management where he teaches courses in Keller's Masters in Project Management program.

Pierre-François Heaulme works for the IBM Corporation, IBM France. Heaulme is on assignment to the A. J. Watson International Education Center in Brussels, Belgium, where he is in charge of the IBM Solution Institute's (ISI) New Employee Training Program. Heaulme has twenty-five years of experience in information technology—including application development, project management, and education—in several countries, including the United States. He recently was the program manager for the project management curriculum at IBM's A. J. Watson International Education Center.

"It is only by risking our life from one hour to the other that we live at all."
William James (1897)

Perhaps it is this risk-taking attitude that has allowed the human species to develop quite a remarkable record of continued adaptability. We have been able to move beyond the fundamental Darwinian law where we had to "adapt to the environment" to a higher order where we have actually been able to "adapt the environment."

Corporate adaptability and survival in a free-enterprise economy depends upon the pursuit and exploitation of the right opportunities. With time becoming an increasingly delimiting factor, corporations have been forced to change their approach in exploiting these opportunities.

What this means is that enterprises must now analyze their business activities from a different perspective. For those activities that exhibit the characteristics of a project, they must employ the appropriate project-management model. But just what are the characteristics that make an activity a project? For a start, consider those characteristics listed in Exhibit 12–1.

Risk and Project Management

Depending on the context and situation, risk can have different meanings. One meaning that defines risk and the impact of a risk event for project management is "The probability that an event or events will occur that will adversely affect the attainment of one or more of the project's objectives."

This has profound implications for the project manager. Critical to the management of every project is the proper understanding and evaluation of risk, and the prescriptive action to deal with it. In other words, risk is a project factor that, like every other factor on a project, must be managed. However, risk is a particularly complex factor because it can affect one or more of the key dimensions of a project: scope, quality, schedule, and budget. If the *product* or the *process* involved in creating the product are unique, or if the *opportunity* is not actually a real one, risk can have an adverse effect.

1. Unique Product. The desired output may be impossible to achieve. For example, inventors and scientists have been intrigued with the idea of producing a perpetual-motion machine. Until someone can produce a device that will reverse certain laws of physics, this perpetual-motion product will remain undiscovered.

Exhibit 12–1. Characteristics of a Project

✔	A unique output is produced. The output may be entirely new, or a significant variant of an output produced previously.
✔	A unique process or procedure is used.
✔	The basis for initiating the activity is an opportunity that will result in some form of quantifiable benefit.
✔	One or more resources required to produce the output is limited.
✔	The task activities are performed by people.

2. *Unique Processes.*   The processes used to generate the output may not be capable of producing a sustainable output. That is, the output will fail to meet one or more of its requirements. For example, in the Middle Ages, the "science" of alchemy developed because people believed that lead could be turned into gold. Whatever the alchemists' motivations, opportunities, skills, perseverance, and justifications, their efforts never succeeded. Alchemists could produce a substance that appeared very much like gold, but it was not the real thing. Why? The processes were faulty.

3. *Opportunity.*   The opportunity may not be as real or as lucrative as originally envisioned. For example, in the 1980s, the Coca-Cola Company spent hundreds of millions of dollars to develop New Coke; a product Coca-Cola believed would allow it to replace its existing cola drink and capture new customers. New Coke was introduced with much fanfare. Unfortunately, Coke's customers were not impressed. This new cola product literally "lacked fizzle" because Coca-Cola had misread or misunderstood the market opportunity.

Elements of Risk

The previous examples of risk were purposely chosen to allow the different components of risk to be highlighted. This is important, because before you can manage a dimension of a project, you must understand how it works. There are four fundamental components of risk:

1. Risk events
2. Time
3. Probability
4. The amount at stake

RISK EVENTS

Risk events are situations that can have a negative influence on the outcome of a project. These situations can affect any of the goals of a project in the areas of scope, cost, schedule, or quality. Risk events can also arise from different sources, or categories of situations. This is important, because risk-control strategies are based upon the category, or source, of the risk event. Two categories of risk are:

- Insurable versus business. Insurable risks are risks where protection or insulation is available through insurance. The impacts of natural disasters can be minimized with insurance. Other risks such as failure to complete the project—or, as in the Coca-Cola example, improper analysis— are typically beyond the scope of insurance and are referred to as business risks.
- Endemic versus self-imposed. There are certain risks inherent with every project: risk of completing on time, completion within budget, and so on. However, it is also possible for projects to have risks that are self-imposed through decision, ignorance, or management inertia.

TIME

Time is a fundamental factor of risk. Uncertainty is associated with future events—not the present or the past. Past events may influence the occurrence of certain future events, or—as in economics—may represent leading indicators. But risk management must be careful to focus on the management of future events. Dwelling on the past is like trying to drive a car by looking in the rearview mirror. Although you must pay occasional attention to what is going on behind you, you must focus your attention on what is in front of you. You must look ahead to move ahead.

PROBABILITY

Simply stated, probability is how likely or unlikely it is that an event will occur. Mathematically, the probabilities of an event occurring can range between zero (the event will definitely not occur) and one (the event will definitely occur). The calculation of probability is fairly simple. It is the ratio of the number of chances that an event has of occurring (or not occurring), to the sum of all chances (the total of occurring plus not occurring) of that event. Exhibit 12–2 allows this definition of probabilities to be demonstrated.

Say there are a total of 36 possible combinations of numbers represented with a pair of die. These 36 numbers represent the sum of all chances. These 36 combinations will make the numbers 2 through 12. The probability of any number occurring is the number of combinations that make up that number over the sum of all chances. As shown in Exhibit 12–2, the probabilities range from zero to one:

1. There is a zero probability that a number other than 2 through 12 will occur. Zero means impossible; this cannot occur. And rightly so. A pair of standard die cannot return any number outside this range.
2. The probabilities for the numbers 2 through 12 depend upon the number of die combinations that will make that number. For example, the number 7 can occur with six different combinations of the die. So the probability of a seven is 6/36, or .167.
3. The probability is 1 that a number 2 through 12 will occur. One means absolutely certain. Again, this is fairly obvious given a pair of standard die.

As one might expect, calculating the probability of a risk event occurring on a project is never as simple as looking at a table of probabilities. In reality, projects are subjected to many risk events that need to be analyzed together as a *risk scenario*. In order to analyze these risk scenarios, one needs to understand the behavior of these risk events; i.e., are two or more risk events dependent, or are they independent? To demonstrate, we will use the die example from Exhibit 12–2.

With two rolls of a pair of die, consider the probabilities of the following scenarios: risk scenario #1: rolling a 6 *and* a 7 or risk scenario #2: rolling a 6 *or* a 7.

In the first scenario, what we are saying is that we have two rolls, or two events, but must get a 6 and a 7 with these two rolls. If a 6 shows on the first roll, a 7 must show on the second, and vice versa. The probability of this sce-

Exhibit 12–2. Probability of Combinations with a Pair of Die

Combination	Combination 1	Combination 2	Combination 3	Combination 4	Combination 5	Combination 6	Combination
Value NOT 2 thru 12							0/36 or .000
2	1 + 1						1/36 or .028
3	1 + 2	2 + 1					2/36 or .056
4	1 + 3	3 + 1	2 + 2				3/36 or .083
5	1 + 4	4 + 1	3 + 2	2 + 3			4/36 or .111
6	1 + 5	5 + 1	3 + 3	2 + 4	4 + 2		5/36 or .139
7	1 + 6	6 + 1	3 + 4	3 + 4	5 + 2	2 + 5	6/36 or .167
8	3 + 5	5 + 3	4 + 4	2 + 6	6 + 2		5/36 or .139
9	5 + 4	4 + 5	3 + 6	6 + 3			4/36 or .111
10	6 + 4	4 + 6	5 + 5				3/36 or .083
11	5 + 6	6 + 5					2/36 or .056
12	6 + 6						1/36 or .028
ANY							36/36 or 1.00

166

nario being successful (two rolls producing a 6 and a 7), is dependent upon both risk events occurring. In this case of dependent risk events, the probabilities for these events are multiplied together to determine the probability of the scenario: $.139 \times .168 = .023$.

In the second scenario, we have two rolls, or two events, to get either of two numbers: a 6 or a 7. The probability of this scenario being successful (two rolls to produce a 6 or 7) is independent of both risk events occurring. In this case of independent risk events, the probability for rolling a 6 and the probability for rolling a 7 are added together to determine the probability of the scenario: $.139 + .168 = .307$.

THE AMOUNT AT STAKE

The ultimate criteria for determining the degree and level of risk control and management is based upon what is at stake; what will be the loss to the project. Although the critical loss may not be financial, most often the loss is quantified into a financial impact. These financial amounts can then be multiplied by their respective probabilities to quantify the impact of a risk event or risk scenario, and will allow different risk scenarios to be analyzed and compared.

RISKS AND THE PROJECT LIFE CYCLE

Although probabilities and amount at stake are separate elements of risk, they have behavior dynamics that are related. Both probabilities and amount at stake vary as a project progresses in its life cycle: from concept to development; from implementation to termination. Figure 12–1 depicts the typical risk/amount-at-stake relationship over time. This relationship demonstrates three very important points about risk.

1. Risk is high in the early stages of the project. As more information becomes known about the project, and as this new information is applied in the decision process, risk decreases.
2. Amount at stake increases as resources are invested and the project opportunity begins to materialize; especially in the implementation and termination phases.
3. This behavior pattern does not imply a cause and effect relationship. This behavior does not happen automatically. It will ultimately depend upon effective risk management.

THE FOUR PHASES OF RISK MANAGEMENT

Projects are designed to pursue and exploit opportunities, which in turn bring risks. Organizations implementing projects or working in a project mode have a process to manage risks. Even if terminology is sometimes different, most organizations have a multistep process designed to address the following issues.

- Risk identification
- Risk impact analysis
- Risk planning
- Risk control

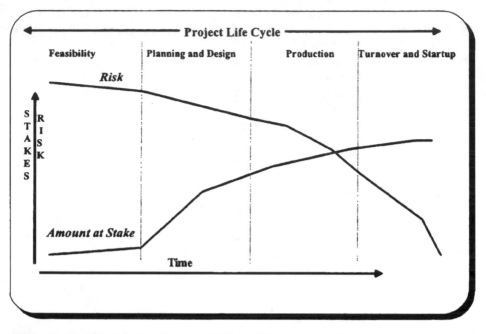

Figure 12–1   Relationship Between Risk and Amount at Stake

Risk Identification

This first step will identify the risks that could affect the project. There are several ways to do this. One way is for the project manager to conduct an individual and informal assessment when first introduced to the project. This is very much a part of human nature; analyzing facts, weighing alternatives, and, unfortunately, worrying about the unknowns. Project managers will tell you that their project is always on their minds, consciously and subconsciously.

THE INDIVIDUAL APPROACH.   Identifying risk based on your experience and skills has three advantages. It is *efficient;* no facilities or additional staff are needed. It is *expedient;* you can do it as soon as you are introduced to the project. It is *decisive;* there is no need to explain your rationale to others.

On the other hand, the individual approach has disadvantages. It is *myopic;* you see only the risks you know about or can make assumptions about. It is *biased;* you tend to minimize things you don't want to see, and amplify those items that are important to you. And last, it is *unilateral;* you do not benefit from the core knowledge of your organization, or from the experience of others.

To illustrate these advantages and disadvantages, consider the project of having a new home built for you and your family. If you have never done this before and have not had the opportunity to talk with others, your initial risk-assessment list might look like this:

- My financial plan may not be accepted by the bank.
- A job layoff may affect my ability to pay.

- The general contractor could be late in building.
- The installation of utilities may be late.
- There may be problems with the well.

This is one view of the risks. However, what about things that you may not be aware of?

- The general contractor could go out of business.
- The person who sells you the lot may not have the legal right to do so.
- The ground or underlying bedrock may not be stable.
- The state has pending plans to sell a right of way to the railroad, which will come within 100 feet of your front door.
- There has been a recent rash of burglaries in the neighborhood.
- The wetlands nearby are idyllic and attract wildlife, but perhaps they may not be the best thing for your chronic hay fever.

These additional risks did not occur to you. You only saw the risks in the area that was of interest to you: your house. This is the most common mistake: a myopic view. One of the key concepts of managing risks, as shown in Figure 12–2, is that each project can be seen from different views, or levels: There is *your project* as you see it—in our example, your house and the immediate tasks necessary to complete your house. This is usually part of a *bigger project*; for example, the twenty-house subdivision being undertaken by the developer. Then there is the *project environment*, which will affect both you and the developer.

It is very important, therefore, that when you first try to identify risks, you look at risk as three projects, and ask yourself:

- What can go wrong on my project?
- What can go wrong on the bigger project?
- What can go wrong elsewhere?

THE TEAM APPROACH. Working alone, although providing a good start, is not the recommended approach for identifying risk. You will only be able to identify those risks that are part of your experience. You need other people to provide their perspectives.

- *Your peers:* Perhaps they may have done something similar in the past.
- *Your project team specialists:* Collectively, they may have more background, may have seen more projects.
- *Your project organization:* If you work for an organization that is used to doing projects, they probably have a project-assurance organization; sometimes called quality assurance. This department is generally comprised of practitioners who have had experience with many projects. Their role is to assess what can go wrong in company projects and prescribe actions that will avoid repeating old mistakes.

With these project experts, you are in a position to conduct a risk-assessment workshop. The intent of this workshop is to tap the collective wisdom and experience of these experts. Basically, each attendee will be asked to prepare a

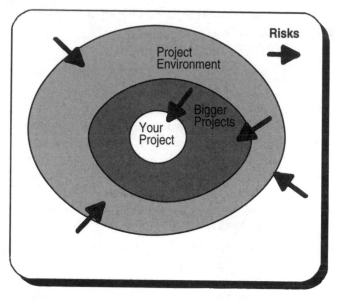

FIGURE 12–2   The Dimensions of Risk

predefined list of risks that could potentially affect his or her area of the project, and then will be asked to discuss which of these risks apply to this project.
This workshop should be conducted as a facilitated session. To be effective,
this session should use an experienced moderator to facilitate and should
select someone to take minutes.

There are seven steps to follow in conducting the risk-assessment workshop:

1. Review the ground rules for the session. In addition to covering the basic
   rules for effective meetings, make sure that everyone realizes that this is
   a brainstorming and discovery session and that certain rules apply.
2. The project needs to be explained. It might be advantageous to distribute material for review beforehand so that everyone can come to the
   session prepared.
3. Ask the attendees to record on either 3 × 5 cards or Post-It notes, the
   project risks that they foresee.
4. Group these risks into categories. To help facilitate and guide the discussion, it is best to have a preconceived list of these categories. In addition,
   as another way to make sure that all risk areas are analyzed, you might
   want to have a list of potential risk events common to projects. The risk
   events in Exhibit 12–3 are a good starter set for risk identification.
5. Review the recorded risks. Make sure that risk impacts can be related to
   the standard project elements that must be managed: scope, time, cost,
   quality, resources, communications, and procurement.
6. Rephrase, regroup, and condense the risks until there is consensus that
   the risk list is complete.

Exhibit 12–3. Risk-Event Checklist

Risk =	A. Risk Categories
✔	n. Potential Risk Events

A. Business Environment

1. Project has not been budgeted.
2. Project funds have not been allocated.
3. Project has not been justified.
4. Senior executives have not endorsed project.
5. Project is critical to the business.

B. Project Environment

1. Project objectives are not clear, or have not been identified.
2. Project scope is incomplete or is not defined in detail.
3. Scope includes performance requirements.
4. Estimates and costs have not been validated.
5. The completion criteria are not well understood.
6. Project has a fixed completion date with no contingencies.
7. There are project team health and safety issues associated with the performance of the project.

C. The Customer

1. Customer does not understand a project environment.
2. Customer does not have the ability and authority to make decisions.
3. Customer staff will not be involved in project.
4. Customer does not have prior experience with projects like this.
5. The customer is not a stakeholder in the project.

D. The End User

1. End user was not involved in generation and approval of requirements.
2. End user will not be involved in project.
3. End user does not understand the impact of changes that project will bring.
4. End user does not have prior experience with projects like this.
5. End user does not understand a project environment.
6. The end user is not a stakeholder in the project.

E. The Technical Solution

1. Solution is not known; i.e., has not been done before.
2. Development will use unproven methods, tools, or techniques.

F. Subcontractors and Other People Resources

1. Project will use subcontractors.
2. Subcontractors have a major role on the project.
3. Subcontractor is not known in the industry.
4. Subcontractor has not done projects for the company before.
5. Subcontractor is not financially stable, or financial base is unknown.

Exhibit 12–3. *(Continued)*

---

    6. Staff will not have the required skills.
    7. Staff with required skills are generally not available in the labor market.
    8. Strikes and work stoppages are a factor.

G. Quality

    1. Quality requirements have not been documented.
    2. Quality requirements are not understood.
    3. There is a not quality assurance function that will monitor project.

H. Project Management

    1. An experienced project manager has not been assigned to the project.
    2. Assigned project manager has no experience with a project of this scope.
    3. A formal project management methodology will not be used.
    4. Project management will be handled solely by the subcontractor/general contractor.

I. Contracts and Legal Issues

    1. There are warranties/guarantees associated with this project.
    2. There are performance penalties associated with this project.

J. External Factors

    1. Acts of God, forces of nature
    2. Acts of government
    3. Currency inflation
    4. Market changes
    5. Legal issues
    6. Force majeure

---

7. Once the risks have been finalized, they should be documented. At minimum, the following information will prove helpful.

- Risk identification number. This identification will prove to be quite useful later on for documenting in a formal management reporting system.
- Description of the risk. Use the risk statement from the risk checklist plus any information necessary to qualify the risk.
- Risk date. The date when the risk was first identified.
- Risk identifier. Name of the person who first identified the risk.
- Risk owner. The person or department responsible for managing the risk.
- Potential impact. A helpful approach is to give best case, worse case, and expected case. It is very important to include any assumptions that were made in determining the impact.
- Probability of the impact. Here, too, include any assumptions.

As with the individual approach, there are advantages and disadvantages to holding a risk-identification workshop. One advantage is *efficiency;* sessions can be completed in a reasonably short time frame. Another is *ownership;* there is a feeling of acomplishment and ownership by the participants.

On the other hand, one disadvantage is *reaching consensus;* depending on the mix of personalities, this may be difficult to do. A second disadvantage is *agreement;* strong influencers in the meeting may have a tendency to focus the team on their specific areas. This can result in a misguided consensus.

RISK-IMPACT ANALYSIS.   This step explores the impact risk events have on the project. Cost is the obvious impact, but this is not the only issue. For example, delivering a new product with a faulty design has the potential for immediate impacts that are not readily translatable into money, such as negative publicity, erosion of customer base, or litigation.

IMPACT OF INDIVIDUAL RISK EVENTS.   There are two ways to look at the impact of a risk event: the *qualitative approach* (yes or no; small, medium, or large; low or high; few, some, or many) or the *quantitative approach* (using money, number of customers, percentage of market share—basically anything that can be measured).

Again, you will find several models to size impacts and probabilities. To simplify, we will use a qualitative approach. Figure 12–3 is an example of a very simple 2 × 2 matrix that can be used for plotting risks.

1. *Quartile 1 (high risk, low impact):*   This could be called the craters-of-the-moon quartile. The small impact of individual risk events are not the concern here. However, the cumulative impact of many small risks can be significant.

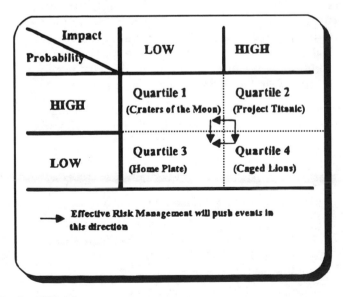

Figure 12–3   2 × 2 Matrix

2. *Quartile 2 (high risk, high impact):*   This is where the project disasters reside—the "Project Titanic" area. Individually, these events can have significant impact. Several together will destroy a project.
3. *Quartile 3 (low risk, low impact):*   This could be called the home-plate quartile. As an initial risk-management strategy, this is the area where risk management should strive to position all risks. Analysis and reality will ultimately dictate which risks can be positioned here.
4. *Quartile 4 (high impact, low probability):*   These risks are like the caged lion. There is no problem as long as the lion is under control. However, if it ever gets out of the cage, watch out! Potentially, these events can have the same impact as events in Quartile 2. There could be a project disaster lurking.

EVALUATING PROJECT RISK.   This matrix approach can also be used to evaluate the overall riskiness of a project. By numerically weighting the risks in each quartile, we can calculate an approximate risk value for the entire project. As an example, we have a project with a total of eighteen risk events that have been identified and evaluated. These have been recorded as shown in Table 12–1. By establishing weights for risks and boundaries of project-risk categories, we can gauge the overall riskiness of the project. Using this approach, this project, with an average risk value of 3.05, is in the medium category.

In practice, a 2 × 2 matrix for risk assessment is probably too simplistic. What is really needed is a scheme that allows finer gradients between the upper and lower bounds of the impact and probability axes. Of course, the more grades, the more work that needs to be done to establish the boundaries and break points. One matrix scheme that you might find effective is a 5 × 5 that has the characteristics shown in Figure 12–4. If impact quantities are known, they can be substituted for the numeric weighting scale on the impact axis. Regardless of the number of gradients, the mathematics and evaluations are the same as in the 2 × 2 matrix. The values in the cells are a suggested weighting scheme. In addition, you can overlay the matrix with the four-quartile template, as we have done in Figure 12–4 with the dotted lines.

RISK PLANNING.   At this point the risks and their probable impacts on the project have been identified. The next step is to develop a plan for managing

Table 12–1. **Project Risk**

Quartile	Weight	# Risks	Risk Value	Project Risk Category	Range of Risk Value
1	2	4	8	Low	0–1.49
2	8	3	24	Medium–Low	1.5–2.99
3	1	7	7	Medium	3.0–4.99
4	4	4	16	Medium–High	5.0–6.49
Total		18	55	High	6.5–8.0
Average			3.05		

Impact Probability	Minimal 1	Slight 2	Moderate 3	Heavy 4	Extreme 5
Highly Likely 80 - 100%	(2.0)	(3.5)	(7.0)	(8.0)	(9.0)
Likely 60 - 80%	(1.5)	(2.0)	(5.0)	(7.0)	(8.0)
Maybe, Maybe Not 40 - 60%	(1.2)	(1.8)	(4.0)	(5.0)	(7.0)
Unlikely 20 - 40%	(1.0)	(1.5)	(3.0)	(4.0)	(5.0)
Highly Unlikely 0 - 20%	(.5)	(1.0)	(1.5)	(3.0)	(4.0)

Figure 12–4   5 × 5 Matrix

these risks. Basically, all projects use the same two strategies for managing risks: decrease or eliminate the probability of the risk event occurring; and decrease or eliminate the potential impact of the risk event.

However, in order to develop effective tactics around these strategies, information is required about sources of risk and risk events.

SOURCES OF RISK.   Following is the most common scheme for categorizing sources of risk.

- *External versus internal:* Risk events can arise through circumstances or factors internal to the project, such as management (in)effectiveness or staff productivity, or from external influences such as government regulations or natural disasters.
- *Predictable versus unpredictable:* Some risk events can be predicted in terms of probability of occurrence and some even in terms of the timing of that occurrence. Other risk events cannot be predicted. Market shifts and currency changes are predictable both in timing and impact. Other events, most notably natural disasters, are unpredictable both in timing and impact.
- *Insurable versus business:* Insurable risks are risks where protection or insulation is available through insurance. Direct property damage, indirect consequential loss, legal liability, and the loss of critical personnel can be obviated with insurance. Losses due to (bad) business decisions are business risks.

- *Endemic versus self-imposed:* Endemic risks are a natural part of any project. Other risks occur as a matter of choice, ignorance, or, unfortunately, poor management or decisions.
- *Known versus unknown:* Projects, because they are unique, can spawn as yet unknown risks.

DEALING WITH RISK EVENTS.　　There are basically four tactics for dealing with risk events.

1. *Assume* the risk and its potential consequences as they currently exist. For risk events of minimum impact, this tactic is ideal. Quartile-3 risks are a candidate for risk assumption.
2. *Mitigate* the project circumstances such that either the risk probability, risk impact, or both will be reduced or eliminated completely. Changing any of the four key project dimensions (scope, budget, schedule, or quality) can accomplish this. Any predictable risk event can be managed with this tactic.
3. *Transfer* the impact through insurance, performance bonds, warranties, or subcontracting. Any insurable risk can be managed this way. Care must be taken here that the insurance does not cost more than the impact; in other words, that the cure is not worse than the disease.
4. *Establish contingency plans* and reserves to be employed in case the risk event occurs. This does not affect probability, but it does reduce the potential impact by minimizing the time required to recover from the risk event. Natural disasters and other unpredictable events, or any future unknown event can be managed with this tactic.

All the risk information is now available to develop a plan for managing risks. To demonstrate the process, assume that a risk identification and risk assessment has been performed for the project. The results are shown in Figure 12–5. However, before actually generating the plan, remember three very important rules about managing risks.

1. Risk is organic. Its probabilities and impact can change over time, at any time. Therefore, tactics for an event will potentially change over the project's life cycle.
2. More than one tactic can be employed to manage a risk. Which tactic or combination of tactics is employed is a matter of effectiveness, cost, and availability.
3. Contingency should never be a substitute for a thorough analysis of the risk.

Fundamentally, the process for developing the plan for managing risks is an analytical one; to develop the best balance between the cost of the risk, and the cost of containment. To do this, one should:

1. Review the existing risk and impact information for completeness.
2. Develop a preliminary spreadsheet that pulls the different information together. Table 12–2 is such a summary of your project.

Impact / Probability	Minimal 1	Slight 2	Moderate 3	Heavy 4	Extreme 5
Highly Likely 80 - 100%					
Likely 60 - 80%		B4		A4 C4	
Maybe, Maybe Not 40 - 60%	····C2····			···J2···	
Unlikely 20 - 40%		D6			J1
Highly Unlikely 0 - 20%					

Figure 12–5   Probability × Impact Matrix

3. Review the risk plan with the resident experts. Determine the plan's impact on the risk items. Replot the risks on a risk-impact matrix and analyze changes (Figure 12–6). Table 12-2 shows how the risk plan that we developed might change the overall risk profile of the project. Notice that for the three risks in Quartile 2 (A4, C4, J2), the tactics are very prescriptive. Quartile-2 risks are the Project Titanics and need to be dealt with aggressively. As shown in Table 12–3, our plan resulted in Quartile 2 being completely vacated, and overall project risk being reduced from medium to medium-low.

4. Continue to replan and analyze the impact until you are satisfied that the risk plan can be effective. Pay particular attention to risks in Quartile 2. These are the Project Titanics. If you can do nothing else, establish a plan that moves these risks out of that potentially fatal impact area.

5. When you are satisfied with the risk-containment actions, translate these actions into project tasks and add them to your project plan. Remember that a task must identify the following:

- *What* is to be done
- *Who* is to do it
- *How* everyone will know that the task is finished
- *How many* resources (time, etc.) are needed
- *When* this task is to be completed

Table 12–2. Risk Summary

Risk	Description/ Impact Area	Probability/ Impact	Category	Possible Tactics
A4	Senior executives have not fully endorsed project. *Scope*	Likely (60–80%) Heavy (4) Quartile 2	Internal, Business Risk	*Mitigate* Phase project to allow conceptual prototype to be developed.
B4	Estimates and costs have not been validated. *Cost*	Likely (60–80%) Slight (2) Quartile 1	Internal, Self-imposed	*Mitigate* Validate costs and estimates as part of conceptual prototype phase.
C2	Customer does not have authority to make decisions. *Communication*	Maybe, Maybe Not (50%) Minimal (1) Quartile 1,3	Internal, Endemic	*Assume* Monitor for developing problem.
C4	Customer has not had any prior experience with projects like this. *Time*	Likely (60–80%) Heavy (4) Quartile 2	Internal, Endemic	*Mitigate* Establish steering committee to help provide guidance.
D6	The end user is not a stakeholder in the project. *Quality*	Unlikely (20–40%) Slight (20–40%) Quartile 3	Internal, Self-imposed	*Assume* Monitor for developing problem.
J1	Work site is in flood plain. *Cost*	Unlikely (20–40%) Extreme (5) Quartile 4	External, Unpredictable	*Transfer* Purchase insurance against flooding and for work interruption.
J2	Pending legislation may require design changes. *Scope*	Maybe, Maybe Not (50%) Heavy (4) Quartile 2,3	External, Unpredictable	*Contingency* Establish tasks and funding for redesign

Risk Control

Risks are dynamic. Events will occur that will change risk-event probabilities, or impacts, or both. This means that there must be continuous monitoring of risks. Monitoring means paying attention to those changes that might have an effect on your risk plan. Changes include the following:

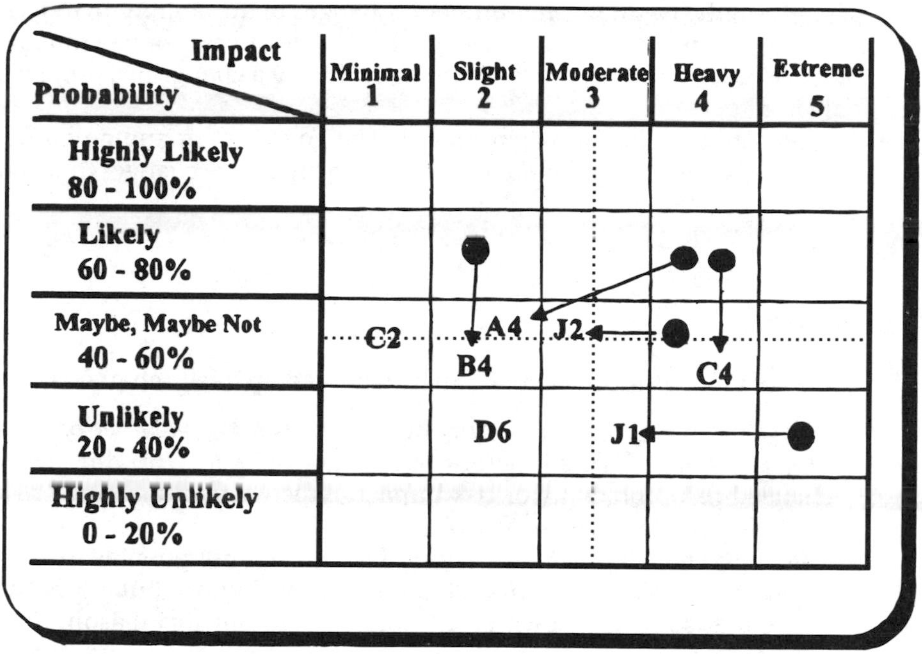

Impact / Probability	Minimal 1	Slight 2	Moderate 3	Heavy 4	Extreme 5
Highly Likely 80 - 100%					
Likely 60 - 80%		●		● ●	
Maybe, Maybe Not 40 - 60%	C2	↓A4 B4	J2	● C4	
Unlikely 20 - 40%		D6	J1		●
Highly Unlikely 0 - 20%					

Figure 12–6   Risk Impact Matrix

- Project objective changes. Changes to any of the key scope, budget, calendar, quality dimensions will introduce risks.
- Changes in the project environment. Staffing changes, project management changes, and technical changes are particularly notorious for introducing new risks, or amplifying the impact of existing risks.

Table 12–3. Risk Plan Evaluation

Risk	Initial Risk Evaluation (quartile)		Post-Plan Evaluation (quartile)		Project Risk Category	Range of Risk Value
* A4	7	(2)	1.8	(1)	Very-Low	0–.49
B4	2	(2)	1.8	(1)	Low	.5–1.49
C2	1.2	(3)	1.2	(3)	Medium-Low	1.5–3.99
* C4	7	(2)	5	(4)	Medium	4.0–5.99
D6	1.5	(3)	1.5	(3)	Medium-High	6.0–7.49
J1	3	(4)	3	(4)	High	7.5–8.49
* J2	5	(2)	4	(1)	Very High	8.5–9.0
TOTAL	28.718.3					
Project Value	28.7/7 = 4.1 = Medium		18.3/7 = 2.6 = Medium-Low			

- Changes in the business environment. Changes in the competitive environment, the introduction of new products, shifts in corporate strategy, new executive management are sure indicators of a change in a project's risk profile.
- Changes in the external environment. The government and any of its administrative or enforcement functions can introduce changes that will translate into risk events.

Conclusion

The process of managing project risk can be summed up in eleven points.

1. *Risk is really a guy named Murphy, and he is a key member of your project team.*   Risk is inherent with every project. Worrying never changed risk probability or risk impact. Effective planning and crisp execution will take care of Murphy.
2. *You don't know that what you don't know.*   It is not possible to anticipate and plan for every risk. Plan for those you know, but always be aware that some unknown event might occur. For this reason, risk-response systems must remain flexible to react to these unknown and unanticipated events.
3. *Risk is the pot that must be watched.*   Risk management is a continuous process. Formalize the implementation of this process. Risk events can occur at any time, and therefore must be managed as such.
4. *It's not "What you see is what you get," but "What you don't see will get you."*   Although the project manager has ultimate responsibility for making a risk-based decision, savvy project managers will always seek the guidance and counsel of their teams. Independent, third-party reviews can be particularly effective.
5. *You cannot manage what you cannot measure.*   The key to managing risk is understanding the impact and potential loss. Impact and loss are dimensions that must be quantified. For potential risk events where information is missing or imperfect, solid quantifiable assumptions are a reasonable substitute. Never fall into the trap of believing that simply by assigning a large contingency, you are covered.
6. *A right decision for the wrong reason can be dangerous.*   Risk-control decisions and their subsequent results should always be reviewed. This review should verify that the risk results were indeed the results of the risk-control actions and not a function of other factors, or serendipity. To depend on luck and happenstance is akin to gambling with the project's success.
7. *If you measure risk with a micrometer, don't then cut it with an ax.*   A plan's effective can only be measured by the results of carrying out that plan. Follow the plan details and don't second-guess.

8. *Risk management is an "-ify" process.*   Remember the following four steps of risk management:

- Indent-ify the risks.
- Quant-*ify* the probabilities and impacts.
- Class-*ify* the risks, then plan control tactics and establish risk-control plans around these classes of risk.
- Mod-*ify* as necessary, the risk-control plans.

9. *Risk is a predator.*   Invest early in prescriptive risk management. Risk events will consume your project if you don't.

10. *Beware of the "fool with a tool." Think!*   Although there are commercially available software tools that can help with risk assessment, ultimately the risk decision making must be a human thought process. Do not let these tools' seductive presentation convince you that they can do your thinking for you.

11. *Opportunity has an "evil twin" named Risk.*

Have I not walked under stars with an upward look
Of caution under stars that very well
Might not have missed me when they shot and fell?
It was a risk I had to take—and took.
Robert Frost (1947)

If you are ever able to glimpse the Perseid meteor showers during the month of August, you will be treated to an awesome display of nature. Is there a risk in this event? Yes, there have been documented cases of meteors striking people and buildings. But what are the real chances of that happening? Always remember that what is balancing risk is an opportunity. Therefore, risk and opportunity should always be analyzed together. However, the analysis of risk and opportunity must be real and objective. It is foolhardy both to take great risks for small gain, and to believe that great gains are not accompanied by significant risks.

BIBLIOGRAPHY

Boehm, B. W. A spiral model of software development and enhancement. *Computer,* May, 1988, pp. 61–72

Bowe, R. F. and Devaux, S. Achieving enterprise project control. *PM Network,* February, 1996, pp. 31–36

Dickson, G. *Risk Management Principles and Practice.* Course presented at The Risk Management Forum, Monte Carlo, Monaco, October, 1993

Down, A., Coleman, M., and Absolan, P. *Risk Management in Software Projects.* New York: McGraw-Hill, 1994

Harvey, J. B. *The Abilene Paradox.* New York: Lexington Books, 1988

Project Management Institute. *A Guide to the Project Management Body of Knowledge.* Upper Darby, PA: Project Management Institute, 1996

Project Management Institute. *The PMBOK Glossary.* Upper Darby, PA: Project Management Institute, 1987

Raftery, J. *Risk Analysis in Project Management.* London: Chapman & Hall, 1994

Waller, R. *Uncertainty, Analysis, Decision Support Techniques and Risk Management.* Presentation at the Project Management Institute Conference, Lake Geneva, WI, June 3, 1994

Wideman, R. M. *Project and Program Risk Management.* Upper Darby, PA: Project Management Institute, 1992

Legal Considerations for Project Managers

Randall L. Speck, ESQ

Biographical Sketch . . . **Mr. Speck** is a partner in the Washington, D.C. office of the law firm of Kaye, Scholer, Fierman, Hays & Handler, LLP. He specializes in complex litigation and arbitration involving project-related disputes. His cases have included disputes that arose from the construction of the Trans-Alaska Pipeline, the Diablo Canyon Nuclear Power Plant, the Seabrook Nuclear Power Plant, and the Bataan (Philippines) Nuclear Power Plant.

roject managers develop, execute, and complete their projects within a tangled framework of laws, regulations, and conventions.[1] To the hapless project manager, that jumble sometimes appears to be a virtually indecipherable maze that defies rational management. Acrimonious disputes—culminating in debilitating lawsuits—descend like a plague, striking down an apparently successful project in its prime. The project manager can summon his wizards (a.k.a. the dreaded lawyers) in an effort to lift this spell, but rarely does the project recover fully.

Fortunately, the adept project manager has an effective remedy. Although the specific nature of looming legal problems cannot be known at the project's inception, the project manager can rely on two facts. First, given the litigious nature of late-twentieth-century society (both in the United States and, increasingly, abroad), disputes are almost certain to arise in any significant project, and the parties will often seek vindication for perceived assaults on their rights. And second, for all its shortcomings, the legal system usually provides a reasonably predictable set of rules that can be identified and integrated into the project's structure. Like other serious risks to the project's

---

[1] Because of the variations among projects and the difference in laws from jurisdiction, this chapter provides a general overview and does not purport to provide legal advice for any specific project. For particular legal advice, a project manager should consult counsel retained for that purpose.

success (e.g., an innovative design or ambitious schedule milestones), the project manager's planning and implementation should attempt to minimize potential legal hazards.

Assessing the Legal Framework

At the inception of the project, before any substantial commitments have been made to proceed, the project manager should fully appreciate the numerous legal relationships that may require significant management attention as the project progresses.

PROJECT-SPECIFIC AGREEMENTS

A binding legal document—usually a contract—defines the terms under which one organization will make its resources available to another organization for the project. Obviously, the terms of each contract should be shaped to reflect the needs and priorities of the project. The following are typical agreements used by project managers to define project relationships.

1. Agreement with Project Owner.   The most familiar project relationship is between its owner and the contractors whom the owner engages directly to perform aspects of the work. That customary arrangement is subject to many variations, however. For example, the owner may contract with a project manager who subcontracts to others who will actually conduct the work. Alternatively, the owner may contract directly with a project-management contractor as well as with each of the other implementation contractors. Of course, each of these arrangements creates different legal obligations between the owner and contractors and among the contractors.

2. Joint Venture.   Other project-specific relationships are often equally crucial to success. For example, multiple owners frequently undertake large projects jointly. In those cases, the joint venture or partnership agreement is vital to harmonious management of the project. Without a clear understanding of each partner's role at the inception, the owners may not be able to make timely, prudent decisions in the project's best interest.

3. Finance Agreement.   If the project is financed externally, the project finance agreement is also significant. Because the financing institution risks its capital, it may insist on some control over a major project. For example, the financing institution may require compliance with certain scheduling milestones or may demand its consent to budget increases. In effect, the financing institution assumes some of the responsibilities of a partner in the venture, and the project manager must accommodate the financier's rights to monitor and to exercise limited control over the project.

4. Insurance Policies.   The project manager also minimizes the project's financial risks through insurance policies (which are also binding legal contracts) to cover potential hazards. The project manager can reduce the chances of a calamity by defining the following:

- The scope of the coverage (e.g., negligence, environmental damage, and directors' and officers' liability)
- The limits of liability (e.g., the amount of deductibles)
- The parties who are responsible for insuring against particular losses (e.g., the owner or the contractor)
- The measure of damages (e.g., lost profits as well as property loss and replacement value versus actual cash value)

5. *License for Technology.*   Some projects will require a license for the use of proprietary technology. Such a license agreement may limit the project manager's flexibility. For example, a license permitting use of a patented technique may include geographical restrictions. Thus, the project manager may be able to apply the technology to development of a project in the United States but may be precluded by the license from using the same approach in Europe.

NONCONTRACTUAL STAKEHOLDERS

Not all of the project's legal relationships are reflected in contracts or similar documents. Some of the project's stakeholders—such as governments, end users, competitors, interest groups, investors, and employees—have their own parochial objectives and demand that the project manager conform to their expectations. Although there is typically no formal contract defining their specific roles and responsibilities for the project, the following third parties may have significant, legally protected rights that the project manager must respect.

1. *Government.*   As a result of its power to regulate and to grant licenses or permits, the government plays a crucial role in the development and execution of many projects. That role may be as straightforward and predictable as the application for a city construction permit for an addition to a residence, or it may be as complex and uncertain as the process for obtaining U.S. Nuclear Regulatory Commission approval for novel modifications to a nuclear power plant. It is the project manager's task to identify the intricacies of the government requirements and to fashion the project's planning to satisfy them.

In some instances, the government's regulatory role makes it a self-proclaimed watchdog over the project manager's performance. For instance, under both state and federal law, regulated industries can only recover their "prudent" expenditures from ratepayers. (In effect, the regulators act as surrogates for competitors in a monopolistic industry.) Thus, regulatory bodies sometimes conduct extensive post-hoc critiques of projects to determine whether expenditures were prudently incurred. That evaluation is generally based on a comparison with best practices, not merely with average or minimally acceptable performance. Any project subject to such scrutiny should prepare from the earliest stages to justify every significant decision with documentation and analysis. To the extent possible, the project manager should inform government regulators of key decisions as they are made and, if possible, obtain their contemporaneous concurrence.

When there is any doubt about the interpretation of local law, the project manager, with the advice of a local lawyer, should include a provision in project contracts and other agreements specifying that those documents will be construed based on a particular state or national law whose application will produce a predictable outcome.

2. End Users.   The ultimate consumers of a project (e.g., the purchasers of a new drug who will pay indirectly for the cost of its development) have an obvious stake in a project's success, but they are typically unrepresented during its inception and implementation. Nevertheless, they may make demands that can ripen into legal disputes as the project progresses, and their impact should be evaluated during the feasibility phase of the project. For example, AIDS victims have organized, brought lawsuits, and sought legislation in an effort to speed the development of pharmacological treatments for HIV and to reduce the costs of those therapies. Pharmaceutical project managers who fail to take these pressures into account may not be able to recover all of their research costs as anticipated, possibly making product development less attractive or marketing more difficult.

3. Competitors.   Since the trust-busting era at the beginning of the twentieth century, competitors have acquired significant rights to attack what they perceive to be anticompetitive activity. For instance, a competitor may seek to enjoin a joint-venture project that it believes will violate antitrust or price-fixing statutes. The project manager may be able to take steps during the feasibility stage to foreclose a successful challenge to the venture.

Competitors may also have rights to contest the project manager's choice among bidders, especially for government projects. Government contract awards are subject to strict regulation, and any deviation from those regulations can provide fodder for a competitor's challenge. Both the project manager and prospective contractors should take great pains to comply with all bidding strictures to foreclose disputes related to contract awards.

4. Interest Groups.   A project often affects the community at large, and the project manager must account for that impact in assessing project feasibility. The legal mechanisms for an interest group to vent its displeasure over a project are legion. Examples are creative application of zoning regulations, rigorous scrutiny of environmental impacts, and proscriptions on development of the required infrastructure. It behooves the prudent project manager to anticipate areas of potential community opposition and to persuade antagonists to cooperate as much as possible by making reasonable accommodations. For example, a project manager was able to assuage community concerns about traffic congestion that threatened the viability of the project by agreeing to pay the city to install traffic signals. If such an accommodation strategy is not successful, the project manager should expect and plan for implementation delays by providing contingencies for belated approvals so that the resulting delay period can be used effectively. During the delay period, the project team may be able to advance a design or complete a necessary infrastructure.

5. Investors.   Major projects often assume such a conspicuous standing within a company that their success becomes material to the company's profitability. In those projects, the company's shareholders have a right to accurate and complete information about the project. The Securities Exchange Act of 1934, 15 U.S.C. § 78j(b), permits shareholders or the Securities and Exchange Commission to sue for damages if a company's annual reports or other public documents materially misrepresent the company's status. If a material misrepresentation about the project's progress could influence a shareholder's investment decision, it may provide grounds for litigation. The project manager should take particular pains to ensure that any public representations about the project are scrupulously correct.

6. Employees.   Employees are hardly a fungible resource that project managers can reassign or displace with impunity. Many managers, whose spouses often have equally desirable jobs, are no longer willing to relocate simply to suit a project's needs. Collective-bargaining agreements and nondiscrimination statutes may also restrict the project manager's ability to assign particular employees to the project without the risk of a lawsuit. Employees are typically well-informed about their rights and will not hesitate to assert them. The threat of a grievance or suit, therefore, is a very real limitation in making personnel assignments.

OPERATING ABROAD

The very fact of operating outside the United States carries legal implications for a wide range of project activities. For instance, personnel operating abroad will have to comply with local tax, immigration, and customs laws, but the project will usually have to make those arrangements for its employees to attract them to overseas projects. The project may also have to obtain special permits to export sensitive technology.

The economic and political uncertainties of operating in some countries extend to their legal systems as well. Emerging countries frequently have not yet developed the sophisticated legal tradition that is necessary to support large commercial projects. As a result, a project manager may not be able to rely on the consistent, fair resolution of disputes using a still embryonic legal system. Thus, it may be preferable to seek an alternative forum to the local courts. For example, contracts may specify that disputes will be resolved through mediation or arbitration under the auspices of an international body such as the International Chamber of Commerce. Contracts may also specify that disputes will be resolved by reference to a neutral law. One of the most promising recent developments is the promulgation of the 1994 UNIDROIT Principles of International Commercial Contracts. Project managers may specify this authoritative compilation of internationally accepted concepts as a mutually acceptable law for the resolution of disputes, particularly when dealing with foreign governments that are reluctant to submit their sovereignty to any other country's national law.

Because many non-U.S. projects are conducted for government entities, U.S. project managers must also be sensitive to the requirements of the Foreign Corrupt Practices Act (FCPA), 15 U.S.C. § 78dd. This statute prohibits a U.S. company from using sales representatives or other intermediaries when there is reason to believe that such agents may transfer part of their commissions to foreign government officials in exchange for favorable treatment. In some circumstances, the FCPA may also proscribe "grease" payments made to obtain a license or permit. Because the FCPA is a criminal statute, it demands very serious consideration by project managers operating abroad, and project managers should be fully cognizant of its sometimes ambiguous requirements. Because of these uniquely American restrictions, U.S. companies are sometimes at a disadvantage in bidding for government projects in countries where bribes are the norm, and that fact should be considered during the feasibility phase.

Legal Issues for Project Planning

It is a truism that the quality of a project's planning often dictates its success or failure. The project manager[2] should establish at the beginning the project participants' legally enforceable rights and obligations so that they are consistent with the parties' assigned roles and responsibilities on the project.

DEFINING RIGHTS AND OBLIGATIONS
Project managers have a variety of tools to assist them in defining and later controlling the project effort. These tools include work-breakdown structures (WBS), network schedules, linear-responsibility charts, cost estimates, technical criteria, and quality-control measures. If these tools are to be effective, however, the project manager must take steps to translate the project's objectives into the project participants' legal obligations. Both human nature and a profit-based economy ensure that the players in a project will take actions that they believe will be rewarded and will avoid actions that they expect will be penalized.

EXAMPLE.   In North Carolina, an entire project to repair a multimillion-dollar wooden blimp went up in flames in August 1995. The repair contract did not assign responsibility for a fire watch. If the contract had expressly assigned responsibility to a welding subcontractor for establishing a fire watch to prevent incipient sparks from igniting nearby flammable materials, the subcontractor would have instituted the fire watch.

---

[2] Organization may define the project manager's role broadly or narrowly. This chapter focuses on essential project-management functions, whether they are performed by the designated project manager or by other corporate managers.

By including such contract language, the project manager would have accomplished the following:

1. Identified the need for a fire watch
2. Assigned responsibility for it to the welding subcontractor
3. Communicated that assignment to the welding subcontractor in the most forceful terms available: a contract condition that specifies rewards and penalties

For the North Carolina blimp repair, however, the contract was silent about this responsibility. The welding subcontractor may have legitimately assumed (consistent with its economic interests) that a fire watch was the general contractor's assignment. Because of this ambiguity, both contractors seemed to have neglected to take this necessary fire prevention step—with the consequences that a stray spark smoldered unattended until after all the workers had left, and the project literally went up in flames.

Contracts to Fit the Plan

Formal contractual obligations are the project manager's most effective mechanisms for communicating and enforcing project responsibilities. In fact, because contractual language creates legally enforceable obligations, the parties will almost always follow the letter of the contract rather than a tacit assumption that the parties neglected to include in the written agreement. Many agreements even contain a boilerplate "integration" clause providing that the contract represents the parties' entire agreement and cannot be changed or modified except by a written document signed by both parties. Such a provision places a premium on drafting a complete, precise agreement that reflects the way the project will actually be managed and implemented. With a clearly written agreement, the parties ensure a mutual understanding of their respective duties.

During the planning phase of a project, the proficient project manager will develop a detailed definition of the project in terms of its expected scope, cost, schedule, and technical performance. As a part of that process, the project manager will also allocate responsibility among the project's participants and assign authority over aspects of the work, in accordance with the project's WBS. It may be appropriate to incorporate a linear-responsibility chart, for example, as an integral component of the formal agreement to ensure that the parties are aware of their obligations and that the assumption of those duties can be enforced.

Contracts to Ensure Project Control

Given the variations in project requirements, it is impossible to construct a contracting template that will fit every project. As a general rule, however, anything that is important to the project's success—particularly the mechanisms for exercising control—should be reflected in its legal documentation.

For example, first and foremost, the project's contracts and agreements should affirm the project manager's authority. This designation may take a variety of forms, including a provision permitting the project manager to direct a contractor's work or a joint-venture agreement designating the project manager as the owner's sole representative. There should be no ambiguity over who is in charge.

The project's legal documentation should also anticipate changes in roles and responsibilities over the course of the project. For example, during the design phase of a construction project, it is appropriate for the architect or engineer to have primary responsibility. Once the design has moved to the field, however, the construction contractor should ordinarily take the lead, and the architect/engineer should assume a more supportive role. That planned evolution of roles should be reflected in the contract so that when this change occurs, all the parties will support a smooth transition.

If intermediate schedule milestones are significant (as they usually are to maintain appropriate control), they should be explicitly included as a part of the contract. It may not be enough, however, merely to tie progress payments to successful completion of broadly defined milestones. Each triggering event should be defined precisely and objectively so that there can be no doubt whether it has been achieved. The rewards or penalties associated with the milestone should make its attainment worthwhile. If regulatory or owner approval is necessary or desirable at a particular stage in the project, the required documentation for that approval should be expressly specified in the contracts.

It is sometimes tempting at the inception of a project—when planning is not yet complete—to leave parts of the contractual relationships ambiguous, with the expectation that they can be defined more precisely as the project progresses. However, if a plan is not developed enough to define responsibilities, this may be a warning sign that it is premature to establish binding legal commitments.

EXAMPLE.   If the owner is unable to identify subsurface conditions that a contractor may encounter in building a foundation, and, therefore, the parties cannot specify the cost or schedule that will be used to control the work, it may be appropriate to postpone contracting until the owner conducts further geological studies.

RESOLVING UNCERTAINTY
Despite reasonable planning, occasionally some significant uncertainty cannot be firmed up until the project proceeds. In that case, the contract should spell out a method for resolving the uncertainty and fixing control criteria once the scope becomes clearer. In the foundation example, for instance, the parties might agree on cost and progress unit rates for various types of materials that could be encountered and on an objective test to identify the material type. Thus, the project could proceed based on an understanding about how the parties will deal with evolving conditions.

PERFORMANCE MEASURES
One of the project manager's primary tasks is to strike a balance among the project's schedule, cost, and quality goals. That objective can be promoted

during the planning phase by establishing appropriate performance measures and creating effective contractual mechanisms that will facilitate the level of monitoring and control needed on the project. The contract structure itself can either assist or frustrate the project manager in controlling the project. There are four basic types of contracts (along with many hybrid variations), each of which has implications for the project manager's ability to direct and control the work and for the parties' legal duties and liabilities.

1. Fixed-Price Contracts.   In this contract, the contractor agrees to perform a specified scope of work for a specified price within a specified schedule. The owner assumes the risk that the scope of work may change, thus requiring negotiated changes in the cost and schedule. The contractor assumes the risk that it has underestimated the cost or time required to complete the defined scope of work. This contracting form is appropriate when project planning has produced a reliable scope of work that can be accurately bid. It would be inappropriate (and much more expensive), however, if the project has not been sufficiently defined and the contractor must include a substantial contingency to cover the risk that its cost and schedule estimates might be mistaken.

In a fixed-price contract, the owner delegates the responsibility for cost and schedule control to the contractor. Thus, it would be improper under this contracting scheme—and a possible breach of the contract—for the owner's project manager to attempt to exercise day-to-day direction or cost and schedule control over the contractor's work. Of course, the owner should always retain control over the quality of the work, even under a fixed-price contract.

2. Cost-Reimbursable Contracts.   This form of contract falls at the other end of the spectrum from fixed-price contracts. Because the scope of work is not well-defined, the owner assumes all of the risk that cost and schedule will exceed estimates. The owner reimburses the contractor for all of its costs plus an allocation (often a percentage) to cover its overhead and profit. The contractor has little financial incentive to minimize costs or even to perform efficiently. However, most contractors are motivated to perform in order to protect their reputations. Even if the contract is fully reimbursable, it is sometimes possible to fix the contractor's fee, thereby providing a specific financial incentive to complete the project sooner.

In effect, the owner simply rents the contractor's resources for the project. Thus, under most cost-reimbursable contracts, the owner must assume responsibility for directing and controlling key aspects of the work and must include explicit reporting and monitoring requirements in the contract (even to the point of access to the contractor's books to confirm its underlying costs).

3. Unit-Price Contracts.   This contract type combines elements of both fixed-price and reimbursable contracts. The owner assumes all risk of changes in the amount of work to be performed, and the contractor assumes the risk that the cost of performing a unit of work (or the amount of time required to complete a unit of work) may be greater than estimated. This contract is best suited to a project in which the type of work is well-defined and can be reliably estimated (e.g., hauling a ton of concrete to a landfill), but the total quantity of the work (and thus its total cost or duration) is uncertain. This contract should provide for the owner's project manager to direct the work and to monitor and control quantities and progress rates. The contractor's project manager retains control, however, over the allocation of resources (i.e., the costs) to complete a unit of work.

4. Target-Price Contracts. Under this form of contract, the parties establish cost and schedule goals with accompanying rewards and penalties. The parties recognize that there are some uncertainties in scope, cost, and schedule, but they agree to share those risks. A target price may provide for the contractor to be reimbursed for its costs but to receive a bonus if final costs are below agreed-upon estimates. A target schedule may be structured so that when the contractor completes the work on the proposed date, it receives a specified payment, but if it finishes before or after that date, it will receive a bonus or pay a penalty, respectively.

This contract form attempts to unify the parties' incentives, but more than any other contracting relationship, it creates a virtual partnership. Because both the owner and the contractor have a common stake in the outcome, they must share direction, monitoring, and control. Without clearly defined roles and responsibilities (and usually a history of working well together), a target-price contract may spawn serious conflicts over the basic question of who is in charge.

DISPUTE RESOLUTION

Disputes are a fact of project life, but their resolution can be planned to avoid significant disruption or unsatisfactory project outcomes. A project manager may choose among four primary dispute-resolution approaches: mediation, arbitration, litigation, or a standing dispute-resolution board—each of which may be tailored to meet project needs. Regardless of the approach chosen, however, the project manager should use the planning phase to devise and agree on a particular method for resolving disputes.

Mediation

Mediation is a nonadjudicative process that requires parties to analyze their differences and, with the assistance of a neutral third party, attempt in good faith to resolve them. The parties are not bound to accept any proposed resolution, however, and mediation is the least coercive dispute-resolution mechanism. Thus, in order to succeed, mediation requires a firm commitment by both parties to the process and a skillful mediator who can guide them to a mutually acceptable solution. It is best suited to resolve disputes between project participants who have a continuing relationship (and, therefore, have incentives to work out their short-term differences to achieve long-term harmony).

Although mediation does not bind the parties to a particular outcome, it should be a mandatory step in the contractual dispute-resolution process. The following contract provision is typically used to obligate the parties to mediate their disputes:

> All disputes arising in connection with or related to this Agreement (including its formation and validity) that cannot be settled within thirty days by good-faith negotiations between the parties shall be submitted to *[a specified mediator or organization]* for nonbinding mediation.

Mediation can be structured to reach a quick end point—either satisfactory resolution or an unsettled dispute that must be resolved by another means. For example, the contract may also specify the following:

- The period within which one party must notify the other that it seeks mediation
- A representative with authority to bind the party to be made available for the mediation by each party
- A specified period within which the mediation will be completed (e.g., thirty days) unless the parties agree in writing to continue within which the mediation will be completed
- Sharing of the costs of the mediation by the parties

Arbitration

Arbitration provides for an impartial, binding adjudication of a dispute without resort to more formal court procedures. Arbitration has been touted as a faster, cheaper, simpler means of resolving disputes, but it does not always live up to that billing. In theory, arbitration should be an improvement over traditional litigation because the parties cannot compel extensive discovery of each other's documents or witnesses, and arbitration hearing procedures are generally streamlined. In practice, however, for major disputes where the stakes are high and the issues are hotly contested, arbitration can prove to be as lengthy and expensive as litigation.

Moreover, the arbitrators' decision is final for all practical purposes. Even if the arbitrators make serious factual or legal mistakes, their award will generally be affirmed without a substantive review by the courts. That means that for significant, complex disputes, one or both of the parties may prefer to have disagreements resolved by a court, where there are greater safeguards against an erroneous outcome. Because of these drawbacks, project managers should be cautious in committing to arbitrate significant disputes on major projects.

Nevertheless, some projects are particularly suited to arbitration. Arbitration is virtually the norm in international projects, for instance, because neither party is willing to submit disputes to the other's (presumptively biased) courts. Routine disputes are also prime candidates for arbitration because they can be resolved quickly, with little need for discovery or for sophisticated analysis.

A project manager can adapt arbitration to the needs of the project (e.g., by adjusting the number of arbitrators or by specifying the types of disputes that will be arbitrated). The following contract language is typically used to designate arbitration as the dispute-resolution mechanism of last resort:

> All disputes arising in connection with or related to this Agreement (including its formation and validity) shall be finally settled under the rules of the *[specified arbitration organization, e.g., the American Arbitration Association or, for international contracts, the International Chamber of Commerce]* by three arbitrators. Each party shall select one arbitrator within thirty days and the third arbitrator shall be selected jointly by the two arbitrators, or, in the event of their failure to agree within thirty days, by *[the specified arbitration organization]* in accordance with its rules. The arbitration shall take place in *[a specified city]*.

The arbitration agreement may also provide the following:

- The costs of the arbitration will be shared by the parties or borne by the losing party
- The remedies available in binding arbitration will be limited to selecting from among the parties' last-submitted positions (a format commonly known as "baseball arbitration" in which the arbitrator may only choose between the parties' final offers)
- Any demand for arbitration must be submitted within one year of such action's accrual or it will be forever barred. (In effect, this sets a statute of limitations without regard to any state or national law.)

Such a broad arbitration agreement will be binding on the parties for all of their disputes and may even continue to apply after expiration of the underlying contract. Under the Federal Arbitration Act, 9 U.S.C. § 1 *et seq.*, U.S. courts must enforce such an agreement and will not permit a party to bring suit in U.S. courts to adjudicate an arbitrable dispute. Thus, before including an arbitration clause, a project manager should be certain that arbitration is the appropriate forum for resolving the project's potential disputes.

Litigation
Litigation is much maligned as a tool for resolving project disputes, but it remains effective if used judiciously and efficiently. It should be the forum of last resort, however, after informal negotiations and mediation have failed. When at least one of the parties is unwilling to relinquish its rights to a thorough hearing, litigation may be the only available means for resolving disputes. If managed efficiently, litigation may actually be cheaper than arbitration because the parties do not pay the courts for their adjudicative services. In contrast, the parties must pay the arbitrators, and the administrative fee for arbitration is frequently significant.

Standing Dispute-Resolution Board
For large, time-sensitive projects, it is particularly important to resolve disputes as they arise and to prevent ongoing conflicts from having an impact on the work. That objective can sometimes be achieved by establishing a standing

board at the beginning of the project to evaluate and decide disputes on a real-time basis. This standing board is usually part of the contractual relationship.

The details can vary greatly, but, typically, disputes that cannot be resolved by the parties within a short time are presented to a standing board of neutral experts (e.g., engineers, accountants, lawyers) who have acquired some familiarity with the project. Using expedited procedures, the parties submit their positions, and the board issues its decision (which may be binding, as in arbitration, or merely advisory, as in mediation).

This approach permits very rapid resolution as controversies arise, before memories of the events become stale and before the parties' views become rigidly fixed. Such a board requires a substantial investment in both time and money, however, and is normally practical only on very large projects with durations measured in years.

Project Implementation

The project manager's legitimate focus during project implementation must be on completion of the project to meet cost, schedule, and quality objectives. As a result, the legal ramifications of project actions often get less attention. Nevertheless, because legal disputes can transform a successful project into a failure, the project manager should take judicious steps during the project to mitigate or avoid adverse legal consequences. In most instances, that simply means implementing reasonable project-management techniques.

COMMUNICATIONS AMONG PROJECT PARTICIPANTS

Disputes arise most often as a result of inadequate communication. For example, failure to give the construction contractor timely notice of a design change will usually disrupt and delay the work, thus precipitating a claim. If a project participant has been given the information required to manage the work effectively, however, the participant most likely will have no reason to complain. Thus, as a general proposition, the project manager should ensure that each project participant with potential legal rights (e.g., contractors, subcontractors, vendors, lenders, partners, regulators, interest groups, investors, etc.) is apprised of project developments that affect those rights.

There are several caveats to this general rule, however. First, the project manager should be cautious in communicating raw internal projections or goals that might be misunderstood or misused by outsiders. For example, to motivate managers to attain maximum performance, a project manager may set ambitious internal schedule goals that are just out of reach. If those goals are distributed to outside contractors without explanation, a contractor may alter its behavior based on that projected (but aggressive) plan. When the goal is not met, the contractor may claim that it was misled to its detriment.

Second, some information is confidential and should not be shared with outsiders. For instance, legal advice obtained from counsel is privileged and should not be divulged to others. Indeed, partial disclosure of that legal advice could result in a waiver for all communications with counsel on that same subject. Similarly, the fact that parties work together on a project (even as partners or joint venturers) does not mean that they can divulge trade secrets or other business confidences without risking a broader disclosure. Absent an agreement by the parties to maintain confidentiality or to return confidential data, whatever information is disclosed to third parties during the project—including trade secrets—may become part of the public domain after the project is completed.

Third, the project manager's most candid written communications (e.g., confidential reports to management or uncomplimentary admonitions to project staff) may become the fodder for an antagonist's litigation strategy. Although such blunt, sometimes overstated documents may be appropriate in context, they may have to be produced to an adversary in a decidedly hostile arbitration or litigation setting. Thus, project managers should avoid committing to paper comments that could later be embarrassing or troublesome to explain.

RECORD KEEPING

Because most legal questions turn on the underlying facts, it is crucial that the project manager preserve a documented history (not merely records of the final results) demonstrating the project's performance on the key parameters of schedule, cost, and quality. It is often difficult to anticipate which project decisions will later be the subject of a legal controversy. Thus, a prudent manager should compile a complete record of performance as the project develops, rather than relying on an after-the-fact reconstruction.

Some project decisions should raise red flags as the potential topic of later disputes, however, and those decisions warrant more careful documentation. Project disputes arise most frequently over the cause and effect of delays. To be able to respond to such claims, the project manager should compile a comprehensive dossier for each significant deviation from plan (e.g., a delay that affects key schedule milestones). That factual dossier should include at least the following materials:

- The root cause of the deviation
- The cost, schedule, and quality impact of the deviation on the project
- The expected costs and benefits of various recovery measures that were considered
- The justification for the recovery effort that was chosen
- The results of the recovery steps that were taken
- Identification of the project personnel who have the most first-hand knowledge about the deviation

Of course, such a rigorous analysis facilitates the project manager's response to the delay, but a thoroughly documented synopsis of the reasoning at the time will provide the most persuasive evidence if the delay precipitates a legal dispute.

ADJUSTING THE CONTRACT TO CHANGE

Change is endemic to all projects, and when conditions change unexpectedly during project implementation, the project manager should promptly adjust the legal documentation to reflect those new circumstances. In a rapidly developing project, the project manager may mistakenly assume that the parties can continue to work under a now obsolete contract and that modifications can be made after the fact to reflect the reality of the project. This is a risky approach and should be avoided, if possible.

The project manager typically tracks and controls design or criteria changes through a formal configuration-management system, and that same structure should be used to ensure that the formal contract language reflects a common understanding of the parties' evolving responsibilities. The project manager should implement mechanisms that do the following:

- Authorize changes
- Communicate changes to the appropriate parties
- Modify the applicable contract documents as necessary

Handling Potential Claims

A project's success is not assured until all potential disputes have been resolved. Too many project managers have reached the end of a project believing they had met their cost, schedule, and quality objectives, only to see those accomplishments tarnished by the protracted, expensive defense of legal claims that swallowed most of their expected gains. Conversely, project managers who fell short of their goals may be able to recoup some or all of their losses through affirmative claims if the actions of others contributed to those losses. The project manager's job is not complete until possible claims arising during the project have been resolved.

Near the end of the project, the project manager should evaluate both affirmative and defensive claims that might be brought. The usual project controls should have already identified the causes of significant deviations from plan, and those are the likely sources for claims. The next step is to prepare a thorough analysis of the claim (or defenses to the claim) accompanied by detailed documentation. This analysis should be rigorous and objective. At this stage, the project manager needs a dispassionate evaluation, not an adversarial argument.

Most disputes can and should be resolved through project closeout negotiations. If those negotiations are successful, the parties should execute formal releases to ensure that no further allegations will be raised. If productive negotiations continue but do not yield a final resolution, the parties may enter a *tolling* or *stand-still* agreement to avoid the expense and acrimony that would be generated by a suit or arbitration. A tolling agreement suspends the running of any statute of limitations and permits the parties to continue fruitful negotiations. Even if the parties had not previously contracted to resolve disputes by mediation, they may at any time agree to use a mediator in an effort to bridge the remaining differences.

If informal efforts at resolution are unsuccessful, the parties may invoke their agreed-upon dispute-resolution mechanisms. The resulting arbitration or litigation should be treated as another project and should be planned, staffed, and implemented with the same care that would be accorded to any project of similar size and complexity. As with any other project, the manager in charge of the litigation project should insist on budgets, schedules, and controls from the lawyers. Regular reassessments should identify strengths or weaknesses and dictate strategy (e.g., press ahead or attempt settlement). With application of appropriate project-management tools, litigations or arbitration can be managed successfully to achieve realistic goals.

MANAGING LEGAL COMPONENTS

A project's legal components are no different from its other aspects that must be planned, managed, and controlled. A project manager does not hesitate to apply her or his skills and relevant expertise to control risks related to technology, financing, or human resources. The same enthusiasm and expertise can manage project legal issues successfully. The skilled project manager's customary tools provide the most effective prophylactic to avoid myriad legal woes that can afflict a project.

BIBLIOGRAPHY

Corporate Counsel Section of the New York State Bar Association. Legal developments: report on cost-effective management of corporate litigation. 59 Alb. L. Rev. 263, 1995

Foreign Corrupt Practices Act of 1977, 15 U.S.C. §§ 78m, 78dd-1, 78-2, 78ff (1988) (Public Law 95-213, 91 Stat. 1494, as amended by the Omnibus Trade and Competitiveness Act of 1988, Public Law 100-418, sections 5001-5003 (H.R. 4848))

Impert, J. A program for compliance with the Foreign Corrupt Practices Act and the foreign law restrictions on use of sales agents. 24 Int'l Law 1009, 1990

Rau, A.S. and Sherman, E.F. Tradition and innovation in international arbitration procedure. 30 Tex. Int'l L. J. 89, 1995

UNIDROIT Principles of International Commercial Contracts

Project Leadership

Making Optimal Use of the Matrix Organization

Charles J. Teplitz

Biographical Sketch . . .   **Dr. Charles J. Teplitz** is the Clarence L. Steber Professor of Project Management and Director of Graduate Programs in the School of Business Administration at the University of San Diego. Since 1986, he has also headed the University's Certificate in Project Management program, which offers project-management training to practicing project managers. Dr. Teplitz is certified as a Project Management Professional (PMP) by the Project Management Institute. He has served as reviewer for PMI publications, and as President of the San Diego chapter of PMI. He also established the Training\Education SIG at PMI. Dr. Teplitz is a frequent speaker, trainer, and consultant in the United States and Europe and has published numerous articles on project management.

A love-hate relationship explains management's attitude toward the matrix organization. For over thirty years, organizations have vacillated between using the matrix structure in managing their firms and opting for the traditional functional organizational design. Although project managers have little influence over the design of the corporate organization, they do have to be able to operate optimally in a variety of situations. Project managers can use the nuances of the matrix organization to their advantage when managing projects.

What Is the Matrix Structure?

The organizational design of a matrix structure represents the hybrid of a functional organization and a pure-project organization. The functional structure is perhaps the most familiar. As seen in Figure 14–1, this hierarchical form demonstrates the type of command structure seen in a military environment, with

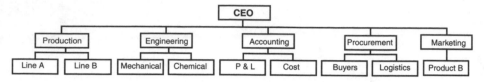

Figure 14–1   Fundamental Organization Structure

each subordinate reporting to a singular superior. Each parallel structure represents a significant function within the organization, such as marketing, accounting, production, logistics, and finance. The pure-project structure looks quite similar to the functional structure, as can be seen in Figure 14–2. The only difference is that, whereas the diagram describing the functional structure represents the entire company, the diagram describing the pure-project structure only represents those functions used by the specific large-scale project depicted. In other words, the project is shown as a miniature organization, which is that of the project. This format is used when a project is of sufficient size and duration to warrant an entire organization of its own.

The matrix organization chart appears similar to the functional chart. The difference is that there is a project manager (usually reporting to a director) whose responsibilities cut laterally across many of the functions. The result is a "matrix" of superior and subordinate relationships as shown in Figure 14–3. It is a hybrid of the functional and pure-project organization in that functional personnel report to the project manager, even though the functional personnel belong to an existing department with its own manager.

Niche Filled by the Matrix Structure

As a hybrid, the matrix structure takes advantage of the fluidity of the hierarchically aligned organization while being flexible enough to fulfill the objectives of distinctively different projects. With this form, the functional departments are maintained as repositories of specialized resources and each project is provided a manager accountable for project success who reports directly to top management. This arrangement places the project manager on the same level of hierarchy as the functional managers, providing the project manager with legitimate power in negotiating for needed resources. Thus, although project and functional components are interdependent with regard

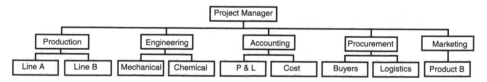

Figure 14–2   Pure-Project Organization Structure

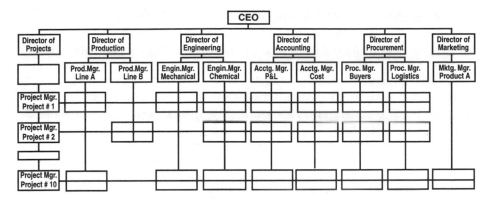

Figure 14–3   Matrix Organization Structure

to the performance of the project, they remain administratively independent. This division of responsibility can create conflict. Despite the potential problems, the matrix structure attempts to preserve the strong points of both the functional and the pure-project structures while avoiding the inconveniences of each. Organizations find that the matrix structure is the most economical for a project environment.

Economics of Organizational Design

Each organizational design option such as functional, pure-project, and matrix has its unique cost consequences. The functional structure is the most cost effective. Economies of scale are obtained within each department by staffing to efficient levels with well trained and qualified individuals. The departments can focus on training and technological improvements that will lead to enhanced departmental abilities as well as additional cost efficiencies.

Under the pure-project organization, each "mini-organization" must contain sufficient departments and personnel to fulfill the demands of the project. There are as many mini-organizations in the company as there are projects. The problem is that not all projects require an entire department or even a whole person dedicated to a particular function. This exposes the company to cost inefficiencies because of redundancies in resources. For example, one company using the pure-project structure found that one of its projects would require the services of a mechanical engineer. Under the pure-project design, they would need to establish a mechanical engineering department for this project and staff it with the appropriate number of mechanical engineers. Unfortunately, this was a small project requiring approximately three hours a day of mechanical engineering. The structure required them to hire a "whole" mechanical engineer even though the workload was only three hours per day. This example is certainly not unique to this project or this company. The possibility of such a scenario repeated many times throughout an organization leads most companies to avoid this structure. The company in this example decided to cross-train the engineer to perform other functions during the day, thus reducing its cost per hour for mechanical engineering for this project.

The matrix structure, being a hybrid, is economically somewhere between the other two designs. By maintaining departments of resources to be *shared* by all projects, resource costs are much lower than under the pure-project method of organization. It is true that under the matrix structure, departments have to contain more people than under the functional structure to ensure adequate resource availability for all projects. But the lack of efficiency is offset by the possibilities for synergy and improved methodologies within the departments. Thus, the matrix structure is often found to be the most economical for a company performing much project-oriented work.

The Matrix Continuum

Firms employ the matrix structure to varying degrees depending on the significance of work performed as projects. It would not be appropriate for a firm that only occasionally performs projects to restructure the entire organization into a matrix format. Likewise, a company obtaining most of its revenue from one major project would be well-advised to take a pure-project approach to organizing this megaproject. With project managers and functional managers having a different set of objectives, the appropriate organizational structure will depend upon the weights that top management gives to each objective. Therefore, the matrix structure employed by a firm may more closely resemble a functional structure or a pure-project structure, depending upon the company's needs.

FUNCTIONAL MATRIX
The functional matrix, also known as a weak matrix, is appropriate when overall quality or technical expertise is more important on the project than low cost or schedule maintenance. In this environment, the balance of power between the project managers and the functional managers is definitely in the functional managers' favor. That is, the functional managers have a greater degree of decision-making influence than do the project managers. Under this structure, when push comes to shove, the project managers will likely have to bow to the demands of the various functional managers with whom they are negotiating.

PROJECT MATRIX
The project matrix, also known as a strong matrix, is appropriate when project cost and schedule are more important than overall quality. Here, the project manager possesses a greater degree of decision-making influence because the project is deemed significant to the company. It is also not unusual to see project-team members removed from their functional departments and physically located together for the duration of this important project. The extreme in

relocation is referred to as "skunk works." This has been used very successfully by companies such as Apple and IBM for the development of a whole new product line. By physically moving the project-development team to a location off-site, the team bonds as a unit and is freed from the home organization's bureaucracy, policies, and procedures.

BALANCED MATRIX

The balanced matrix exhibits a balance of decision-making influence between the project manager and the functional managers. In this environment it is believed that cost, schedule, and quality are equally important. It is here that the project manager possesses the same degree of decision-making influence as do the functional managers. Because of the apparent equality of the managers, this structure results in the need for continuous negotiations and trade-offs between the managers. Such interactions often result in considerable conflict between the project managers and functional managers. This issue will be addressed in greater detail later.

Critical Look at the Matrix

As a hybrid, or more accurately, a compromise, the matrix does indeed possess some of the positive as well as the negative features of other organizational designs. Project managers trying to successfully complete projects in this environment must understand the conditions under which they are attempting to operate.

RESPONSIBILITIES OF THE PROJECT MANAGER

Project managers are responsible for planning what has to be done for the project, when it has to be done, and how much can be spent to do it. Then project managers are responsible for making sure the plan is met. Thus, the project manager is a very busy person. Most of the project manager's time will be spent developing sound relationships with the customer, functional departments, and team members, to name a few. The purpose is to ensure that what needs to be done is being done in a timely fashion and within budget.

Under the matrix structure, project managers have no direct subordinates. Project managers can only get work done through functional managers' subordinates. To do this, project managers must not only negotiate with functional managers for the use of their subordinates, but must also convince functional managers of the importance of timing the subordinate's availability properly. Depending upon the matrix structure (weak to strong), project managers may be facing quite a challenge. Project managers must negotiate with all the functional managers for all needed workers. Also, project managers are likely to require the same resources at the same time. Therefore, negotiating and communicating skills are essential for the successful completion of the project. After all, a project manager's job is to integrate and coordinate the various resources to meet the goals of the project.

RESPONSIBILITIES OF THE FUNCTIONAL MANAGER

Functional managers are responsible for determining how the tasks of the project are to be accomplished and who will accomplish them. They are the ones responsible for maintaining the high level of competence in their organizations and for ensuring that the work done on the project is of the highest quality. One reason for leaving the functional departments in place under a matrix organization is to provide an atmosphere in which professionals can enhance their skills and the knowledge base of the organization. Functional managers *own* the resources. Project managers are simply borrowing these resources.

The functional manager's priorities are to continually improve the technical competence of the department's resources, and to provide project managers with skilled staff to perform the project's scheduled work. These goals are in conflict. Goal number one is negatively affected if the subordinates are unavailable to the functional manager while assigned to a project, which is goal number two. Unfortunately, the priorities of the department manager rarely match the priorities of the projects and the project managers. Therefore, it is to the project manager's advantage to be aware of the inherent conflicts of the matrix organizational structure and to take action to mitigate these conflicts.

The greatest source of conflict between the project and the functional managers is the fact that the functional manager owns the resources whereas the project manager owns the work. Both are dependent on the other for their own survival and yet resent this dependency. It is this ego problem that must be watched. If an organization recently shifted to the matrix, the project manager will also experience the hostility of the functional manager, who believes that his or her role as a manager has been reduced by the reorganization and by the project manager.

Perhaps the most recognized drawback to the matrix structure is that personnel are expected to report to two superiors, their functional manager and the project manager to whom they have been assigned. This dual-reporting scheme goes against all management theory for successful employee relations. The project personnel are put in a bind: At any point they might be requested (required) to perform two very different tasks for their two very different superiors. Which do they obey? Unfortunately for the project manager, even in the matrix environment, the functional manager tends to possess the power over the subordinates. The worker comes from the functional manager's department and is only temporarily assigned to the project manager.

A major cause of conflict can be attributed to a lack of clearly defined roles, responsibilities, and authorities. These roles need to be defined by top management. If they are not, project managers need to persuade top management to describe, in writing, jurisdictions of the project manager and the functional manager. This documentation will reduce much jockeying for position by these two. If both parties clearly understand each other's goals, life will be a lot better for all involved. It is vital for each to understand what makes the other tick, what things are important to the other, and what things are not.

These conflicts tend to come to a head when the project manager is given a functional staff person to work on the project. Although the functional manager's first priority is the quality of work by his or her subordinates, the project schedule often takes precedence over the availability of qualified and available department personnel. Typically, the project manager demands someone *now*. So the functional manager sends over the only person available at that time. This person could be newly hired from another company, or straight out of school with no experience, or a long-time employee who is somewhat incapable, or an old-timer who hates everyone and is just waiting to retire. Any of these scenarios can leave the project manager with a major problem, especially if, as is usually the case, the project manager has no input into the worker's annual review. When top management defines the roles of the project manager and functional manager, they should also define the project manager's role in performance appraisals, merit raises, and dismissal decisions for all personnel assigned to the project. This action will greatly reduce conflicts between the project and functional manager, and it will also reduce much of the anxiety experienced by project managers on personnel issues.

Another issue is power. In the matrix, there seems to be a constant power struggle between the project manager and the functional managers. Part of this occurs when top management does not document policies for this problem area. In some cases, top management may be oblivious to the potential for conflict or may have been in such a hurry to reorganize into the matrix that they failed to consider it. Regardless of the reason, power struggles are a fact of life in the matrix organization. Project managers need to keep in mind that even when power is given, it can just as easily be taken away.

In a 1974 study of project managers' sources of power, a survey of sixty-six project personnel revealed that they believed that their project managers derived power from the formal authority given the project manager from top management.[1] Over the last twenty years, the project-management atmosphere has changed considerably. A similar study performed in 1992 reported that project personnel believed that their project manager derived power based upon the manager's technical expertise.[2] In the new study, formal authority was rated as the fourth most likely source of power behind expertise, reputation, and work challenge (the manager's ability to assign challenging assignments). Any source of power project managers can muster will be beneficial to them. Undoubtedly, project managers' professionalism, knowledge, and expertise will help provide them with greater power in managing projects.

A third issue, in addition to conflict and power, is administration. The number and cost of administrative personnel are excessive under a matrix organization compared to the traditional functional design. Because each

[1] Thamhain, H. J. and Gemmill, G. R. Influence styles of project managers: Some project performance correlates. *Academy of Management Journal* 17, no. 2, (1974):216–224

[2] Worley, C. G. and Teplitz, C. J. The use of "expert" power as an engineering influence style within successful U.S. matrix organizations. *Project Management Journal* 24, no. 1, (1993):31–35

project operates independently, there is considerable duplication of effort under the matrix. In addition, the matrix structure, by its very nature, is much more complicated to monitor and control relative to the other organizational designs. It becomes extremely important that all projects and their resource requirements be monitored by top management as a set, rather than as individual projects. This requires additional administrative staff to coordinate all the ongoing activities. It also requires that a set of universal policies and procedures be established so all projects are managed in similar fashion using similar reporting methods and using established forms and formats. Because each project has different goals, objectives, and payoffs, the strategy described can assist in establishing priorities between projects.

Benefits of the Matrix Structure

At the corporate level, it becomes obvious that the matrix structure provides maximum efficiency in the utilization of scarce resources as compared with other structures within a project environment. This shows up immediately in the corporation's bottom line. Also, from the lofty perspective of the head office, it is apparent that a properly functioning matrix facilitates more effective dissemination of information both vertically and horizontally. Such information flow reduces conflict and enhances the working relationships across functions and between managers (including project managers).

PROJECT

The true beneficiary of the matrix is the project itself. In a matrix, the project gets respect—it has an identity. Under the functional structure, with no project manager assigned, the project is tossed over the wall from one department to another, with the hope that it will miraculously be completed on time, within budget, and as designed. Unfortunately, projects can often fall through the cracks while moving from department to department in the functional structure. Functional managers may be overseeing many projects simultaneously and cannot be expected to control the progress of the projects through the organization. When this happens, projects can often lie dormant for some time because no one has been assigned responsibility for them. In the matrix, however, the project becomes highly visible and its objectives are made known to all relevant parties with responsibilities well delegated. When the project is assigned a project manager, it tends to get better support from the functional departments than it would get under the traditional structure.

Another benefit of the matrix structure is that the customer (client, project owner) receives rapid response to inquiries about project progress or modifications. Because the project has a dedicated manager, there is a contact person available to the project owner. Under the traditional structure, it would be extremely difficult for the owner to find someone to talk with who could speak knowledgeably about the status of the project or who had authority to modify the project objectives.

PROJECT MANAGER

Project managers do not exist only in matrix environments. There are project managers in organizations designed under the functional structure and certainly in organizations designed under the pure-project structure. In fact, in the latter, project managers possess the most authority, power, and control of all project managers. However, in comparing the opportunities for success for the project manager, the matrix structure certainly provides a better chance for success than does the functional design. Under the matrix, the project manager enjoys greater control over resources used on the project. The project manager is in a better position to respond to problems or changes that come along. This affords the project manager more opportunity for balancing project time, cost, and performance. That translates into more opportunity to manage the project to a successful conclusion.

FUNCTIONAL UNITS

As compared with a pure-project environment, the matrix preserves the functional units at cost-effective levels. This facilitates the development and control of high-quality craftsmanship performed by department personnel without incurring corporatewide expenses because of redundancies. It permits the continuous improvement of methods and quality of work on all projects, not just one. The strong technical base also allows for the maintenance of a powerful corporate memory. Functional personnel will be able to recall examples of prior projects that perhaps exhibited similar characteristics and problems to the current project. A problem solved once can be more easily solved the second time it is observed.

PERSONNEL

The matrix structure affects personnel in many ways. First, functional personnel stay with a project only as long as they are needed. They are not assigned for the duration of the project. This allows the worker many opportunities to experience different types of projects as well as project managers. Second, the workers are exposed to departments other than their own while working on a project. This is an excellent way for them to see what others do, and perhaps for them to move to other departments. Third, by rotating from project to project, and project manager to project manager, the functional personnel are broadening their perspectives and experiences. This training is the best means of developing future project managers. Fourth, unlike the pure-project environment, these functional personnel know they have a home when the project is terminated. They know that when they are no longer needed for this project their jobs will not be terminated and they will be able to return to their own department to await the next assignment. All of these factors lead to improved employee morale. After all, job enrichment and job enlargement are what the management experts agree provide stimulation for the employee and success for the project.

Making Use of the Matrix

There is no one right organizational structure for all companies at all times. Companies do reorganize periodically, sometimes looking for improved operations, sometimes simply looking for change. Although the matrix structure might currently work well for a company, in a few years it might not be appropriate. Therefore, if a company is not organized around the matrix structure, there may be a good reason. One should not believe that the only way the company can operate efficiently is to reorganize to the matrix. Likewise, if a company *is* a matrix organization, one should not assume it should stay in this configuration. It is important to understand the pros and cons of the different structures. Even in a functionally structured organization, It is often possible to implement certain aspects of the matrix to improve the relationships within the company and the efficiency with which projects can be managed.

Conclusion

It appears that every aspect of business is being performed under the definition of the project, including operations to mine raw materials, construction of manufacturing facilities, procurement of parts, product manufacturing distribution through marketing channels, and sales and service. As customers demand more rapid improvements in technology and quality while insisting on price cuts and shortened lead times, firms are forced away from traditional functional organizations and procedures. They are adopting project-management methods as evidenced by the exponential growth of project-management literature, books, professional societies, and certifications. This movement will result in more firms reorganizing into the matrix structure as its advantages become more evident.

BIBLIOGRAPHY

Archibald, Russell. *Managing High-Technology Programs and Projects*, Second Edition. New York: John Wiley & Sons, 1992

Badiru, Adedeji. *Project Management Tools for Engineering and Management Professionals*, Norcross, GA: Institute of Industrial Engineers, 1991

Barrie, Donald and Paulson, Boyd. *Professional Construction Management*, Third Edition. New York: McGraw-Hill, 1992

Cable, Wayne and Adams, John R. *Organizing for Project Management*. Drexel Hill, PA: PMI, 1986

Cleland, David (ed.). *Matrix Management Systems Handbook*. New York: Van Nostrand Reinhold, 1984

Cleland, David and King, William (eds.). *Project Management Handbook*, Second Edition. New York: Van Nostrand Reinhold, 1988

Cleland, David. *Project Management*, Second Edition. New York: McGraw-Hill, 1994

Davis, Stanley M. and Lawrence, Paul R. *Matrix*. Reading, MA: Addison-Wesley, 1977

Dinsmore, Paul. *Human Factors in Project Management*, revised. New York: AMACOM, 1990

Galbraith, J. *Designing Complex Organizations*. New York: Addison-Wesley, 1973

Hobbs, Brian and Menard, Pierre. Project structures and organizations. In *The AMA Handbook of Project Management*. Edited by Paul Dinsmore. New York: AMACOM, 1993, pp 81–108

Kerzner, Harold. *Project Management*, Fifth Edition. New York: Van Nostrand Reinhold, 1995

Kezsbom, Deborah, et al. *Dynamic Project Management*. New York: John Wiley & Sons, Inc., 1989

Kimmons, Robert. *Project Management Basics*. New York: Marcel Decker, 1990

Kirchof, Nicki and Adams, John R. *Conflict Management for Project Managers*. Drexel Hill, PA.: Project Management Institute, 1986

Leavitt, Jeffrey and Nunn Philip. *Total Quality Through Project Management*. New York: McGraw-Hill, 1994

Levine, Harvey. Project initiation techniques: A strategic view. In *The AMA Handbook of Project Management*. Edited by Paul Dinsmore New York: AMACOM, 1993, pp 55–70

Lewis, James. *Project Planning, Scheduling and Control*. Chicago: Probus Publishing, 1991

Lock, Dennis. *Project Management*, Fifth Edition. Hants, England: Gower, 1993

Love, Sydney. *Achieving Problem Free Project Management*. New York: John Wiley & Sons, Inc., 1989

Meredith, Jack and Mantel, Samuel Jr. *Project Management*, Third Edition. New York: John Wiley & Sons, Inc., 1995

Nichols, John. *Managing Business and Engineering Projects*. Englewood Cliffs, NJ: Prentice-Hall, 1990

Oberlender, Garold. *Project Management for Engineering and Construction*. New York: McGraw-Hill, 1993

Obradovitch, M. M. and Stephanou, S. E. *Project Management Risks and Productivity*. Bend, OR: Daniel Spencer, 1990

Porter, Lyman, et al. *Behavior in Organizations*. New York: McGraw-Hill, 1975

Stewart, Thomas A. The corporate jungle spawns a new species: Project manager. *Fortune*. July 10, 1995

Shtub, Avraham et al. *Project Management*. Englewood Cliffs, NJ: Prentice-Hall, 1994

Stuckenbruk, Linn. The matrix organization. In *The Implementation of Project Management*. Edited by Linn Stuckenbruk. Reading, MA: Addison-Wesley, 1987, pp 69–93

Thamhain, H. J. and Gemmill, G. R. Influence styles of project managers: Some project performance correlates. *Academy of Management Journal* 17:216–224, 1974

Worley, C. G. and Teplitz, C. J. The use of "expert" power as an emerging influence style within successful U.S. matrix organizations. *Project Management Journal* 24:31–35, 1993

Youker, Robert. Organizational alternatives for project management. In *A Decade of Project Management*. Edited by John Adams and Nicki Kirchof. Drexel Hill, PA: Project Management Institute, 1980

How to Motivate All Stakeholders to Work Together

R. Max Wideman

Biographical Sketch . . .   **R. Max Wideman** is a practicing project-management consultant. During his career, he has served in the capacity of executive, project director, and project manager to a range of clients responsible for a wide variety of project work. He is an internationally recognized speaker and has presented papers or seminars on a variety of project-management topics in Canada, China, Egypt, Iceland, India, Jamaica, the Philippines, Saudi Arabia, the United Kingdom, and the United States.

W hy worry about stakeholders? The objective of project management is to conduct a successful project. The problem is, the meaning of success varies. Success is a question of which project objectives are the most important, which have been met, and how well they have been met. Whether the completed project is considered successful is a subjective perception of the stakeholders. Nevertheless, anything that can be done within the scope of the project to influence stakeholders to take a positive view will help considerably in managing the project. It will also contribute to achieving the project's objectives.

Why Does Success Vary with the Type of Project?

Isn't success a question of being on time and on budget and meeting specifications? Important though these criteria are, the real measure of project success is to be found in customer satisfaction. This depends on whether the project will meet customer expectations and this in turn depends on the type of project. There are several radically different types of projects.[1] The following are some examples:

- A project that results in a tangible product and is the result of craft work, such as traditional building construction
- A project to develop a new physical artifact resulting from intensive intellectual work, such as a new invention
- A project in which the value of the product is in its intangible and intellectual property, such as the development of new software

The workforce and the recipients of these kinds of projects are very different and need different styles of management. Therefore, it is a good idea to identify the project stakeholders during early project planning and develop a list of related critical success indicators (CSIs) that reflect their reasonable expectations.

CSIs are those key indicators specific to the particular project by which the project is judged a success or failure. Project managers must identify and plan for these as part of the project planning process. One can maintain better focus on ensuring a successful project outcome if the chosen CSIs are measurable, though this is not always easy. If CSIs are measurable, project managers can make better, more well-informed decisions during the project. Typically, CSIs measure the way people think about the results of the project.

For example, a major objective on a particular public engineering project is to create local employment. However, the real value of the project is its cost-effectiveness over many years in service. For this project, the use of labor would be preferable to the use of plant, especially where the total real costs are about the same. Given the CSIs, one should be better able to observe when the success focus changes and shifts direction accordingly. For instance, market conditions or ownership may change during the project. This avoids a short-term successful project becoming a white elephant in the long term.

CSIs are not the same as critical success factors (CSFs). CSFs are those factors in the project and organizational environment that militate toward project success, whereas their absence may militate against it. They are an integral part of the project's environment and generally beyond the control of the project team. They certainly have a significant impact on the way stakeholders think. Examples are favorable labor or economic conditions. In contrast, CSIs are essentially proactive and are within the planning and control of the project team.

Who Are the Stakeholders?

Stakeholders can be many and called by different names. The following are some of those names: project owner, client, customer, or financial source; project sponsor or director; program manager, project manager, leader, or coordinator; project team, group, or workforce; the project's users; authorities having jurisdiction; professional and business groups; the public, taxpayers; the media; and special-interest groups.

Networking with these stakeholders occurs in two very different types of project environments. The first type, an internal project, is undertaken within the organization or enterprise for its own internal purposes. The second type of project, an external project, is undertaken for an outside client and is usually based on some legal agreement or contract.

INTERNAL PROJECTS

Many organizations undertake projects entirely in-house for their own benefit. Typical projects develop information systems and technology changes, organizational changes, or the addition of physical plant. Whatever the project, it is vital to ensure that the project's stakeholders are all identified and brought into the network of contacts. If the project is to be successful, these people must be fully committed and behind the project for its duration.

Obviously, the project manager is an important stakeholder. However, from the project manager's point of view, the most important stakeholders are the project's owner (the client) and the project's sponsor. Note that these two are not necessarily the same.

The project owner is the ultimate beneficiary of the fruits of the project. The project owner is the one who will pay the bill, though the money to support it may be borrowed from someone else. Therefore, the project manager must ensure that:

- Project objectives are clearly spelled out
- Project concepts are effectively developed and planned
- The project itself is efficiently executed
- The project is properly transferred back to the owner on completion

The problem with most project owners is that the ownership does not belong to one individual but to a group of people. The project owner may be an executive committee, company board, or even the company's shareholders. This does not make for the easy and rapid communication that the project manager needs to run a project efficiently. Therefore, in a well-organized project environment, there is a project sponsor, a separate individual who holds a more focused, liaison position.

If the project does not have a specific sponsor, it is a good idea for the project manager to lobby to get one immediately. This is true no matter how brief or small the project is. The project manager should ask, "Who is my direct contact person?" That person is the de facto project sponsor.

The project sponsor is the individual, usually an employee of the owner or client, who holds the authority and responsibility to act for them on the project. At first glance, it may appear that a project sponsor duplicates the efforts of the project manager. In reality, even on a small, short project, a well-briefed project sponsor can improve communication without an overlap of responsibilities. The project sponsor's job is to:

- Participate in senior management's overall project prioritization and resource allocation

- Establish the project's level of priority and maintain that level of management's interest in the project
- Alert the project manager if circumstances or the environment changes and, if necessary, arrange to either accelerate, slow down, abort, or redirect the project
- Be responsible for general overseeing of the project, its progress, control, and successful delivery
- Report progress to management

Thus, the project sponsor has a vital role to play. It is one that can greatly relieve the burden on the project manager, whose primary responsibility is to manage the work on the project.

Hidden Stakeholders
The list of the project stakeholders typically is not complete at first pass. Unsuspected stakeholders have a habit of popping out of the woodwork at inconvenient times, often with very negative attitudes because they were not recognized. A checklist of stakeholders of internal projects will typically include:

- People recruited directly to work on the project team
- People seconded to the project, full-time or intermittently, who normally work for other departments.
- Managers of those other departments who will be contributing human resources or services to the project, sometimes reluctantly at first.
- People who represent other departments because the project will affect those departments. These people may be the users or operators.
- Representatives from other remote-location divisions, subsidiary companies, or even overseas branches who will be affected by the project or required to conform to it.
- Project managers and their teams working on other projects within the organization who may be competing for the same resources.

In each case, it is the project manager's job to get these individuals enthusiastic about the project and contributing their best. It is a question of motivation. The project manager can greatly improve working relationships with these stakeholders through several personal strategies. The following are some examples:

- Invite people to join the project team, with the option of turning down the offer without fear of retribution. A person who joins the team voluntarily, as a privilege or opportunity, will do so with a positive attitude and will offer his or her best.
- Interview every team member, preferably individually, to ensure everyone's support for the project. If support is lacking, bring out and resolve obstructing issues.
- Sell managers of the functional departments, who contribute people or services to the project, on the project's importance, and relative priority within the enterprise.

- Have users form their own users' group, particularly if the users will be many and various. The group can then have a designated spokesperson formally representing them on the project team. This tactic may or may not be successful depending on the following:

  - The perception of isolation
  - The extended line of communication
  - The potential lack of discipline in conforming to the project timetable

The issue of discipline may require the intervention of the project sponsor. If other project managers are competing for the same resources, a project managers' coordinating committee should be formed. If this group is unable to agree, then call on the project sponsor to resolve the issue with senior management.

These recommendations require the project manager's personal and individual attention. It is time-consuming but well worth the effort.

Keeping Internal Stakeholders on Your Side

Having recruited members to the project team, the next step is to form a viable working group. It is a question of team building. (See Section V, "Team Management.") A few pointers are worth mentioning:

- Make sure that the project is in alignment with the enterprise's strategic plan.
- Decide on and maintain an appropriate level of stakeholder involvement, particularly on the part of those who are not a direct part of the project team.
- Start the team-building process by holding a project start-up workshop involving the principal stakeholders, or those who will be principally involved in the work. A checklist for this workshop will typically include:

  - Description of existing situation
  - Goals and objectives of the project, or problems the project is designed to solve
  - Consequent assumptions, benefits, risks, and constraints
  - Tentative overall schedule and work plan or operating mode
  - Allocation or delegation of responsibilities
  - Project communications
  - Interactive project development

- Working as a team, develop the intent of the project into a workable scope that obtains buy-in to the project's objectives.
- List the project's CSIs. Examples might include the following:

  - Reduced customer complaints as measured by the number of entries in the complaints log
  - Improved processing of accounting as measured by time to invoice
  - Improved product quality as measured by reduced mean time between failure

- Better public image as measured by increased positive publicity and reduced negative publicity
- Improved profitability as measured by reduced processing costs
- Better market penetration as measured by increased market share

- Encourage full and part-time team members to continue doing their best by maintaining a positive project culture. This requires the following:

  - Visibile, clear objectives that are well understood and worthwhile
  - Open, honest, accurate, and continuing communication
  - Evident benefits to individual team members by way of experience and enjoyable effort
  - Removal of obstacles to performance
  - Recognition and reward for excellence

EXTERNAL PROJECTS

External projects are those undertaken by the enterprise for an outside party such as a client. Alternatively, external projects are undertaken by an outside party for the enterprise. In either case, legal agreements are involved, which are said to be at arm's length. This simply means that the parties to the contract are completely independent of one another.

These parties have become stakeholders in the project. Of course, the internal project stakeholders of external projects still require considerations such as those described in the previous section. However, because of the ramifications of the legal agreements, project management's emphasis will be on the external stakeholders.

Why External Project Stakeholders Are Different

Jack Lemley, formerly chief executive of Transmanche-Link (TML), had this to say about image versus reality in managing the immense channel tunnel project:

> Today managing the public image of major civil engineering projects is at least as important as managing their physical creation. Poor public perception can damage or stop a project as surely as bad ground or shortage of labour and materials. The Channel Tunnel is a classic example: for much of its formative period it existed in an often destructive climate of adverse public opinion. Most of this was avoidable, but it resulted in the project team spending much of its time fighting a rearguard action rather than simply getting on with the job.[2]

There is a big difference in external project stakeholders. This is because all communications in an external project are subject to the terms of the legal agreements involved. Also, external projects characteristically include many public stakeholders.

It is wrong for the project manager to think that the client is the only external stakeholder to worry about. For example, on a construction project there are many stakeholders involved.[3] They may include the following:

- Prime contractor
- Subcontractors
- Competitors
- Suppliers
- Financial institutions and bonding companies
- Government agencies and commissions; judicial, legislative, and executive bodies

Of course not all these turn up on every construction project, but many of them do. Figure 15–1 shows the potential complexity of this type of project.

Just as important are the members of the public. These people can have a significant influence over the course of the project and the project-management process. They include the following:

- The local community that is affected by the project
- The general public, often represented by advocacy groups, such as consumer, environmental, social, political, and others

These people are not strictly stakeholders in the sense that they have invested the project or expect to get money from it. Still, different groups will have varying

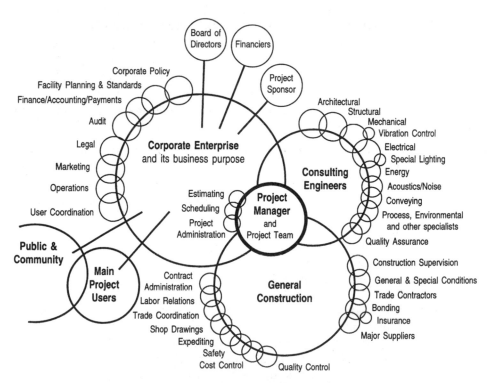

Figure 15–1   Stakeholders in a Construction Project Environment

degrees of influence over the project. Perhaps *constituents* is a better term than *stakeholders* for describing members of the public.

Through diverse legislation, members of the public may have the power to stop the project entirely if the project manager does not need their concerns and give them appropriate consideration. Therefore, even on a small external project, project managers should give some attention to the project's public.

How to Identify Public Stakeholders

The following are steps to identify public stakeholders.

1. *Examine the environment.*   The first step is to examine the public environment surrounding the project. Identify any individual or group who may be affected by the project or even have an influential opinion about it. An excellent starting point is to hold a project-team brainstorming session for this purpose. This has several benefits.

   - It enables people to contribute ideas and suggestions from their knowledge and experience of local conditions and politics.
   - It may be one of the first opportunities for members of the project team to show they can make a positive contribution.
   - The process starts the feeling of community of interest and team building for the project.
   - The process is fun and the project manager can put the results to good use.

     If the project is significant, the project manager might seek expert advice after brainstorming exercise.

2. *Determine the type of influence.*   The second step is to sort the findings into groups according to the type of influence they may have. These groups can be described as:

   - Those who come into direct contact as suppliers of inputs or consumers of outputs
   - Those who have influence over the physical, infrastructural, technological, commercial, financial, socioeconomic, or political and legal conditions
   - Those who have a hierarchical relationship to the project such as government authorities at local, regional, and national levels
   - Those individuals, groups, and associations who have vested interests that are sometimes quite unrelated to the project, yet who see the project as an opportunity to pursue their own ends

3. *Categorize the level of influence.*   The third step is to categorize the people in each group according to the level of influence they may have over the project. The following are examples:

   - Those over whom it may be possible to exercise some degree of control by way of compensation

- Those who can be influenced by some form of communication
- Those who need to be appreciated and, if necessary, planned for

4. *Gather information.*   This fourth step can be systematized. The following questions should be asked when developing stakeholder information.[4]

- What do you need to know about each stakeholder?
- Where and how can you obtain the information?
- Who will have responsibility for gathering, analyzing, and interpreting the information?
- How and to whom will you distribute the information?
- Who will use the information to make decisions?
- How can you protect the information from misuse?

It is quite possible that some information collected will be sensitive material. One cannot conclude that all stakeholders and constituents operate ethically. Consequently, treat all information as if it were sensitive. This poses a problem for some government operations, which may be subject to requirements of the Freedom of Information Act (FOIA). Whatever the circumstances, project managers should observe strict security.

The following are typical sources of stakeholder information:

- Project team members
- Key managers
- Business periodicals such as *The Wall Street Journal, Business Week,* and *Forbes*
- Business reference services such as *Moody's Industrial Manual* and *Value Line Investment Survey*
- Professional associations
- Customers and users
- Suppliers
- Trade associations
- Local press
- Trade press
- Annual corporate reports
- Articles and papers presented at professional meetings
- Public meetings
- Government sources

The next step after gathering information is to do something with it.

How to Deal With Public Stakeholders

If the project is small, project managers can share the communication workload among members of the project team. Each team member can assume responsibility for specific areas and groups. By maintaining stakeholder and constituent linkages in this way, the project has the best chance for ultimate success. Project managers should document communication responsibilites in a project-communication plan.

Mounting a Project Public Relations Program

If the project is large, significant, or critical, it may be advisable to mount a more formal program to establish and maintain stakeholder and constituent linkages. Such a program is often called a project public-relations program (PPRP) and is designed to deal with the public and the media. Expert staff should undertake this work.

Public relations may be defined as a set of activities calculated to improve the environment in which the enterprise operates, which in turn improves the performance of the enterprise. In the following text, the term *stakeholder* is used to refer to stakeholders and constituents collectively.

Dynamic managers recognize that opening communications in both directions—for top management and for employees—is a powerful motivator. Providing that information of high quality is exchanged—whether verbal or written, or better still, in graphical form—project managers should expect a remarkable improvement in team performance and in the progress of the project.

To a surprising extent, the project team's ability to exercise positive communications can have a significantly favorable impact on the team's ability to control the project's schedule and cost. If the project is a major one, especially if it is publicly funded, establishing such a program is essential.

On some sensitive projects, the term *project public relations* may be viewed as vague and self-serving. The image of a smooth, fast-talking individual replete with well-worn clichés is not a desirable one. The term may therefore be unacceptable; a possible alternative is *public participation*.

Unfortunately, this, too, has negative connotations. For many, it may conjure up the perception of interference with project objectives, escalating costs, and schedule delays. Nevertheless, whatever the activity may be called, the purpose is the same: to obtain people's understanding and positive, active support.

Every project team should bear in mind that projects have a habit of becoming the target of negative information. The negative information may be circulated by those with conflicting interests. Special-interest groups may seek to have the project delayed or canceled to preserve the status quo, or otherwise "held to ransom" to serve their own ends. Like bees to the honey pot, the news media is much more attracted to controversy, which they find more newsworthy than any official project press releases.

The cry of the critics will likely include the following:

- The technology is untried.
- Safety is at stake.
- The environment will be destroyed.
- Additional indirect costs will be incurred by the community.
- Taxes will increase.

There may well be some individual hardship cases that will attract political and media attention, especially if property has to be acquired. Some people's homes, businesses, or lifestyles may be affected. Construction projects, for example, may cause noise, dirt, trucking, road restrictions, and congestion.

All these require immediate and effective responses. The project manager needs to foresee these issues, recognize them as part of the project responsibility, and deal with them honestly and fairly. It is important to understand that everyone who works on the project contributes to its image, and all contributions should be positive.

An effective PPRP requires a strong identity within the project setup, concrete goals, and a well-planned strategy to achieve the setup and goals.

A PPRP must also recognize, reinforce, and actively promote the objectives of the project. The PPRP must be evident at all levels of the project organization and should aim at improving the credibility of the project team and therefore the team's ability to perform. Whether the project is publicly or privately funded, the primary benefits will undoubtedly go to the project's owners. Nevertheless, there will be secondary benefits for the public, so the PPRP should be designed to promote them. Such benefits may be:

- Increased employment
- Improved services
- Increased demand for local goods and services
- A trickle-down effect of related commercial activities
- Increased primary and secondary contributions to taxes

A PPRP has all the characteristics of a project in its own right, but it is conducted within the main project. It requires a leader who is outgoing and positive about the project, yet able and willing to listen. Such a leader must be capable of preparing carefully constructed text and presentations; of responding to media questions rapidly and honestly; and of working through a PPRP steadily and systematically.

There are eight steps in developing a PPRP plan.[5]

1. Know the enterprise and its objective thoroughly.
2. Identify the interested public stakeholders, and the characteristics of each.
3. Establish stakeholders' relative importance to the project. In particular, determine the high-risk areas.
4. Assess the current reputation of the sponsoring organization as it is perceived by each of the public stakeholders.
5. Decide appropriate action in each case.
6. Develop an integrated strategy that includes resource requirements, priorities, and a schedule consistent with the project for which the PPRP is being developed.
7. Carry out the plan.
8. Continuously monitor the effectiveness of the program during its application and adjust as necessary for optimum results.

It should be kept in mind that the public that stands to gain from a public project is not necessarily the public that is most affected by the project. Vocal minorities may create difficulties while the silent majority sit on the sidelines, leaving others to resolve the issues.

A typical philosophy behind a PPRP would include the following goals:

- To maintain internal project communications that promote a good understanding of the project by the workforce and members of the project team
- To keep the public up-to-date on the progress and performance of the project
- To be open with public information
- To promote and effectively respond to any misleading information that may be circulating about the project or its people
- To develop audio and visual aids and information sources that give substance to the above

Project managers need to design visual presentations to create confidence, trust, and pride in the project. Presentations should not be more than four to six minutes. If there is a technical story to tell, it should be told in terms that a third-grade student can understand. The technical story should be in keeping with the short TV commercials to which we have become so accustomed. Too much detail must be avoided, but the presenter should be ready with such details for the time when an expert comes along to question the project. A scale model, whether of the physical entity or of the underlying concept, is an excellent demonstration tool and well worth considering.

The primary target audiences for a PPRP on most major projects will likely include:[6]

- The project workforce
- The eventual users
- The local community
- The community at large
- Special-interest groups
- Elected representatives and government administrators
- The news media

Secondary target audiences may include:

- Business and professional groups
- Business media
- Labor groups
- Educators and school groups
- Taxpayers
- The industrial sector of the project

Those responsible for the PPRP on a high-profile project must be prepared for some typical issues and concerns that will inevitably be raised by the various target groups. These will depend on a variety of factors:

- The critical project assumptions
- Real and imagined situations
- Trends based on various public indicators

- Experience with similar projects
- The latest fashionable issues currently being pursued by the media
- Irresponsible news reports
- Fallout from any disputes or litigation on the project

Project managers should develop responses that are in tune with the current political climate. A sampling of typical questions encountered in the past includes:[7]

- Will the project cause safety risks?
- What happens in an emergency?
- How many jobs will be lost through automation?
- How reliable is this latest technology?
- Will there be dislocation because of land expropriated for the project?
- How much congestion and noise will there be in local neighborhoods during construction?
- What is the real cost to the taxpayer, including subsidies and the costs of budget and schedule overruns?
- Will the project become an issue in an election campaign and, if so, will the winning party terminate it?

Careful and constructive attention to these kinds of details are of enormous value in enabling the project to proceed in a smooth and orderly way. However, the PPRP should not become an end in itself, and therefore a target for public outcry.

With a PPRP plan prepared in outline, the team member responsible for the PPRP should obtain approval from the project's management. The PPRP should be part of the project's work-breakdown structure (WBS) with its own line item in the project budget. (See Figure 15–2.) If the project is very important, the PPRP should not be left to an existing department as an added workload, lest it gets overlooked or becomes secondary in importance.

The PPRP must be complete with detailed objectives, target dates to match the progress of the project, the resources required, detailed costing, and identification of performance measures. For example, a detailed set of PPRP objectives[8] might look like the following:

1. Develop and maintain a PPRP that ensures that timely, accurate, consistent, and relevant information is presented to the project's primary audiences.
2. Develop internal project procedures that ensure the availability of accurate and consistent information that emphasizes the team approach.
3. Establish a resource facility that monitors, researches, collects, and collates information as it relates to the project.
4. Develop material that clearly explains the economic benefits of the project to business, labor, and others.
5. Develop and maintain information packages, presentations, and events that show pertinent information, including safety on the project, to community groups, educators, professionals, school groups, and others.
6. Identify and monitor milestones during the project and their impact on, or opportunities for, the PPRP.

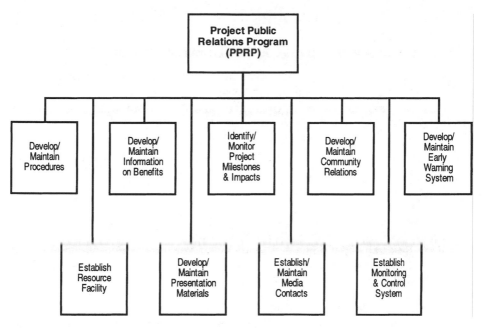

Figure 15–2   Project Public Relations Program Work-Breakdown
Structure

7. Establish news media contacts that keep key writers and editors fully informed, especially those who appear sympathetic toward the project.
8. Develop a community-relations program that responds to public issues and concerns relating to the project.
9. Monitor and control the PPRP to ensure optimum benefit to the project.
10. Develop a system of review and contacts that can provide an early warning about activities by outsiders that may adversely affect the project.

Each of these objectives are elaborated into a detailed task list. For example, item 7, which suggests establishing and maintaining media contacts, may require completion of the following tasks:[9]

- Develop a telephone listing of local television stations, radio stations, news wire services, newspapers, local politicians, and other frequently called numbers.
- Develop and maintain news media mailing lists suitable for the circulation of project news releases, articles, or features intended for the audiences in the primary and secondary target areas.
- List names and addresses of elected representatives, administrators, and others who will receive project news releases.
- Schedule a series of contact meetings with key media representatives who have appropriate spheres of influence.
- Notify key project personnel who will attend such meetings.
- Hold a seminar to discuss the advantages of the latest technology incorporated into the project.

- Arrange to hold an open house when work on the project is sufficiently well advanced.
- See that notices go out in good time for maximum impact.

A PPRP effort is significant, especially a large project with public involvement and sensitive issues. At critical times, or at specific locations, a weekly newsletter can be very helpful to inform local people of unavoidable temporary disruption. People are willing to put up with a lot more, if they know what is going on and that it is only for a limited period. The key to the success of a PPRP is the constant garnering of opinion and adjustment of the program details accordingly.

ENDNOTES

1 From *Civil Engineer International*, April 1996, p 34
2 Shenhar, A. J. and Wideman, R. M. *Towards a Fundamental Differentiation Between Projects*, Research paper under development, University of Minnesota, 1996
3 Cleland, D. I. *Project Management: Strategic Design and Implementation*. Blue Ridge Summit, PA: TAB Professional and Reference Books, 1990, p 105
4 Ibid., p 107
5 Wideman, R.M. Managing the project environment, in *Dimensions of Project Management,* Edited by H. Reschke & H. Schelle, Berlin: Springer-Verlag, 1990, p 64
6 Cleland, D. I. *Project Management: Strategic Design and Implementation*. Blue Ridge Summit, PA: TAB Professional and Reference Books, 1990, p 98
7 Wideman, R. M. Good public relations: An essential part of successful project management. *Proceedings of the Project Management Institute*, Vol 1, Track 1/11, 1985, p 8
8 Ibid., p 10–11
9 Ibid., p 14

BIBLIOGRAPHY

Cleland, D. I. *Project Management: Strategic Design and Implementation*, Blue Ridge Summit, PA: TAB Professional and Reference Books, 1990

Cleland, D. I. project stakeholder management. *Project Management Journal*, Sept. 1986, pp 36–43

Padgham, H. F. The Milwaukee water pollution abatement program: Its stakeholder management. *PM Network*, April 1991, pp 6–18

Tuman, J. Jr. Models for achieving project success through team building and stakeholder management. In *The AMA Handbook of Project Management*. Edited by Paul Dinsmore. New York: AMACOM, 1993, 207–223

Verma, V. K. *Organizing Projects for Success*. Upper Darby, PA: Poject Management Institute, 1995

Wideman, R. M. *Cost Control of Capital Projects. Richmond, BC*, Canada BiTech Publishers Ltd., 1995

Wideman, R. M. *Managing the Project Environment: Dimensions of Project Management*, Edited by H. Reschke & H. Schelle, Berlin: Springer-Verlag, 1990, pp 51–69

Wideman, R. M. Good public relations: An essential part of successful project management. Proceedings of the Project Management Institute, Vol 1, Track 1/11, 1985 pp 1–16

Political Strategies
for Project Managers

Bud Baker

Biographical Sketch . . . | **Dr. Bud Baker** is Associate Professor of Management at Wright State University, where he also directs the graduate program in project management. Prior to arriving at Wright State, Dr. Baker served as a program manager for a major Air Force acquisition effort. He writes frequently for such publications as *The Project Management Journal* and *PMNetwork.*

T he planning phase for a project is where basic, fundamental political strategies must be set. These will carry over, in large measure, to the execution phase of the project.

There are at least six aspects of politics to be considered when planning a project. These apply to all projects, not just those that are large or publicly visible. However, each of these takes on particular meaning based on the individual project at hand.

1. Listening actively. Project managers must do a lot of listening to determine the answers to these questions: What do stakeholders really want? What needs must the project address? Are those needs real? Where do stakeholders' needs coincide, and where do they conflict?

2. Structuring the project. Only after thoroughly understanding the needs of stakeholders can the project be successfully structured. Subcontracting, for example, may need to be spread out geographically to ensure broad legislative support. If risk is believed to be unacceptable, then risk reduction can be pursued through strategies such as joint ventures, partnerships, and teaming arrangements. An uncertain funding future may cause a long-term project to be planned in discrete chunks so that inevitable changes of business or government leadership are more likely to mean project slowdown, and less likely to mean project termination.

3. *Building coalitions.* Where stakeholder interests converge, joint action is possible. We live in a world where such long-time antagonists as General Motors and the United Auto Workers can join forces to make possible a project like the Saturn. If that coalition can work successfully, it certainly supports the idea that other diverse project stakeholders can find enough agreement to join forces in a common cause.

4. *Dealing with government.* This goes beyond widely practiced activities such as lobbying and targeted campaign contributions. Such issues as zoning, environmental restrictions, and regulatory limits all have the potential to stop a project in its tracks. Ideally, such constraints can be shaped by a proactive effort. But before that can even be a possibility, the government environment must be thoroughly understood.

5. *Setting expectations.* Clement Studebaker, the American automaker, lived by the motto, "Always underpromise and overdeliver." We tend to forget that sometimes. In the zeal that so often characterizes the start of a project, when all things are possible and the laws of physics and economics are but distant clouds on the horizon, we tend toward overoptimism. Sometimes our optimism is calculated to gain support. If all the project's potential catastrophes were known up front, we might be unable to get the political support necessary to begin. Further, if we don't believe in our own project, who will? But whatever the cause, overly rosy expectations will come back to haunt the project later when—to twist Mr. Studebaker's words around—the project is seen to have overpromised and underdelivered.

6. *Communicating with all stakeholders.* This can take the form of town meetings, media appearances, press releases, and advertising. Many projects fail because project leaders, especially in contentious situations, forget that the opponents of a project are at least as important as its proponents. It's human nature to want to maximize time with our friends and minimize it with our foes. The tendency may be understandable, but that doesn't make it correct.

Politics is synonymous with effective stakeholder management, and stakeholders create the environment in which a project must develop. The following case studies explore the political environment of project management.

CASE STUDY
THE SUPERCONDUCTING SUPERCOLLIDER

The Superconducting Supercollider (SSC), located near Dallas, Texas, was designed to conduct experiments within a 54-mile underground circular chamber, accelerating subatomic particles to 99.9999 percent the speed of light and smashing them together at combined energies of forty trillion electron volts. The thought was that this would provide answers to fundamental questions about the formation of the universe. Many believed that the benefits of such research could be enormous. In their view, such pure science research was comparable to the first atom splitting, which led to the discovery of nuclear energy, quantum theory, and most of the electrical and computer technology we take for granted today.

But all that will remain mere speculation. After spending more than $2 billion on the SSC project, Congress unceremoniously pulled the plug in 1993. This ended eleven years of effort and put two thousand people out of work. Certainly there were problems with the SSC. Cost had ballooned, largely because of increasing technical requirements, and the schedule was slipping correspondingly. But the real problem facing SSC management was not technical, budgetary, or schedule-related. The real problem was politics.

One political problem facing the SSC was the lack of support from the Clinton administration. The SSC was begun under a Republican administration. There was never more than a lukewarm acceptance of the SSC from the Clinton White House, and when the going got tough there was only concern for the budget deficit.

The SSC became, in fact, a symbol of fiscal irresponsibility. For all the billions spent, the truth was that the SSC produced very few jobs, at very high cost, in a limited geographical area. With limited economic importance beyond Texas, the SSC had few backers in Congress. And when the respected Texas Senator Lloyd Bentsen left the Senate for President Clinton's cabinet, the SSC became a prime target of Congressional budget cutters concerned with a $4 trillion deficit and unmoved by the SSC's limited appeal as a Texas project.

The project's negative press wasn't helped by news of millions of taxpayer dollars spent on ritzy hotels, liquor, decorative plants, and art work. The widespread dislike of the senior SSC officials in the Clinton administration didn't help either. Top SSC officials were perceived as self-important and arrogant. And they denied access to confidential information requested by auditors from federal agencies. Other scientists—perhaps jealous of the SSC budget—claimed that the SSC was undermining the credibility of all science. Worse still, the SSC's wastefulness was singled out from a list of hundreds of government projects.

One last difficulty probably sealed the SSC's fate. As opposition to the project grew, leaders of the effort persisted in their tendency to speak primarily to pro-science groups at universities around the country. At the same time, they avoided hotbeds of opposition, including Capitol Hill. In fact, project leaders had so little regard for Congress that after legislators finally killed the project, one senior project leader reportedly referred to the cancelation as "the revenge of the 'C' students."

CASE STUDY
THE DEATH OF THE TIGERSHARK

Long a power in the business of selling fighter aircraft to foreign governments, Northrop had sold thousands of its F-5 Freedom Fighters to countries around the world. By the mid-1970s, they had developed the newest version, the F-5G Tigershark.

At the same time, the Carter Administration was expressing concern about selling more advanced U.S. fighter aircraft to foreign governments. There were at least two reasons for the concern. First, such weaponry had a way of later being used against U.S. interests. This was a potential risk with Ayatollah Khomeini's Iran. Second, there was genuine concern about fueling arms races between unstable third-world governments.

So the stage seemed set. Northrop had a good, affordable design, arguably less capable and thus less threatening than other, more sophisticated fighters. Further, the Tigershark meshed with the political desires of the Carter Administration. At this point, Northrop began to pour its own money into the Tigershark's development.

It didn't take long for trouble to develop. President Carter—the very man who had encouraged the plane's development—vetoed a proposed sale to Taiwan for fear of offending the People's Republic of China.

The election of Ronald Reagan in 1980 marked the beginning of the end for the Tigershark. The Tigershark was seen as a "Carter airplane," and Reagan seemed happy to sell the top-of-the-line fighters to pretty much anyone who could pay the bills, including South Korea, Pakistan, and a host of other less stable nations. Added to the fact that the U.S. Air Force had never ordered any Tigersharks, the overall image of the Northrop fighter began to decline.

The crashes of two of the three prototypes—neither attributable to aircraft failure—merely provided the coup de grace to an already staggering program. Northrop threw in the towel in 1986, after investing $1.2 billion. A project with impressive technical qualities, one that hadn't cost the taxpayers a cent, became one of the great product failures in history, largely because of political considerations. The Tigershark was dead.

Where had it all gone wrong? If Northrop, a politically astute firm in many ways, had listened adequately at the beginning, could the Tigershark debacle have been prevented? Certainly Northrop would have realized that the genesis of the project was not a real military need, but rather an artificial political one. And those sorts of needs can, and do, change rapidly. Certainly the military stakeholders, both within the United States and outside, had no desire for the Tigershark. Hindsight is always 20-20, of course, but it's clear that an unsound political strategy was at the core of the Tigershark's failure.

Managing Politics in the Project Execution Phase

As a project moves from planning to execution, most of the same elements that were previously important remain, but the approach changes in subtle ways. Listening to stakeholders remains important, but not for the purpose of planning and structuring the project. It's too late for that at the execution stage. Rather, listening forms the basis for midcourse corrections in the project, so that the unknowns from the planning phase can be addressed as they arise. Coalitions built earlier need to be maintained and even repaired, as the pressure of the project causes fissures to develop among coalition members.

Government liaison must be maintained. As seen in the Tigershark case, changing administrations—whether in Washington D.C. or in a local village council—can cause paradigm shifts that can undermine all the project manager's previous efforts.

Expectations set in the planning phase need to be managed carefully, so that surprises are kept to a minimum. Few factors corrode working relationships in a project as badly as the unexpected bombshell, when one project constituent is perceived as springing a surprise on the others.

Communications channels built in the planning phase need to be fertilized and even expanded during project execution. This is extraordinarily difficult, for many reasons. One reason is that the pace of the project typically picks up, and firefighting efforts tend to take precedence over longer-term issues.

Further, the interests of stakeholders can diverge in this phase. The project team wants to tell its *good* news to the world, using press releases and other tools. The world, on the other hand, finds such good-news stories uninteresting at best, self-serving at worst. But when *bad* news is involved, positions reverse: Media and other outside stakeholders are passionately interested, whereas the project team circles the wagons, just as the Superconducting SuperCollider team did when under attack.

Another political strategy rises in importance during the execution phase. It can take many forms—litigation, stonewalling, outright noncompliance are examples—but we can call this strategy "resistance." Consider a hypothetical power plant project, for example. Six years into the project, a new interest group emerges that is passionately opposed to any form of power generation, nuclear or otherwise. Most of the strategies cited earlier such as listening and building coalitions are useless in a case like this.

Rather than accommodation and appeasement, a more appropriate strategy is resistance. Defensive legal postures, offensive litigation, counterattack, and delaying tactics are all more feasible when the project is well underway, or when dealing with constituencies who are unalterably opposed to the project.

The following case study about the American interstate highway system demonstrates some of these ideas. Poor planning got it off to a shaky start, but well-conceived political strategies allowed it to recover.

CASE STUDY
THE INTERSTATE HIGHWAY SYSTEM

In the 1950s, President Eisenhower proposed a massive road-building plan, one that would bring a host of benefits to the American public. Among these benefits, Eisenhower mentioned increased productivity, enhanced highway safety, and a strengthened national defense. In addition, Eisenhower believed that the thousands of jobs created would help lift the United States out of the post-Korean War doldrums. He estimated the cost of the highway system at $50 billion.

Despite Eisenhower's personal support, the project was quickly swamped with political problems, largely related to finances. Within just four months, the cost estimates had grown to $76 billion, and they further ballooned to over $100 billion just two months after that.

But it wasn't the projected cost overrun that sidelined Eisenhower's first plan—it was politics. Truckers objected to increased taxes on tires and fuel. Western states, faced with vast expanses of highways but few drivers, objected to tolls as a financing source. Eisenhower's Democratic opponents objected to the proposed financing methods as well. In the summer of 1955, Congress killed Eisenhower's plan and adjourned.

The setback was only temporary. Early in 1956, Eisenhower adopted a more politically astute approach. He identified the key stakeholders and their demands. The result was the Interstate Highway Act of 1956. The key principles behind the Act were these:

- Tax increases on the trucking industry would be limited.
- In return for federal design control, 90 percent of the cost would be borne by the federal government
- Urban areas—where the votes were—would receive most of the construction dollars.
- Contentious issues, such as the use of tolls as a financing tool, were intentionally avoided. Both sides agreed to postpone any decisions until the project was underway. Although this is not a sound concept for most projects, it was necessary here.

In sum, the Act offered something to everyone and aroused the ire of almost no one. And therein lies one secret of political success. Certainly some tactics, such as the intentional postponement of critical decisions, aren't applicable to every project. But politics is, as they say, "the art of the possible," and the rules are, of necessity, different.

Politics matters. And effective project leaders know that politics—the effective management of project stakeholders—can spell the difference between ultimate success or failure. Early attention to stakeholder issues during the project-planning phase is a start, but it is not enough. The plans laid out and the channels opened at that time need to be maintained and enhanced throughout the life of the project. Only by those actions can project managers put politics to work for them, rather than against them.

The Role of Senior Management

Kenneth O. Hartley

Biographical Sketch . . . Kenneth O. Hartley has spent over thirty-two years in the project management field. He is currently serving in the Business Management unit of Bechtel Telecommunications. Mr. Kenneth O. Hartley holds a B.S. and an M.S. in civil engineering from the University of Missouri. He is a Fellow of the Project Management Institute, having served as its international President and Chairperson. He was recognized for Distinguished Contribution to Engineering by the University of Missouri in 1988.

Specific senior-management involvement with projects may vary among organizations. Management's involvement depends to some degree on whether the project is for internal users or external clients. However, whether the organization's core business has only an occasional project, or whether the organization is essentially project-driven, the need for top-management involvement still exists.

Although a seasoned project manager may indicate that senior management's role is to let the project manager manage the work and stay away from the project, there are several critical functions that senior management must perform in the project-management process. These begin in the preproject-management phase, continue during its execution, and conclude with the postproject phase. The following describes senior-management activities required during each of these project phases.

Preproject Phase

The stage for successful project execution is set by senior management before the project gets fully underway. This is a crucial and active period for senior management. Planning done and decisions made during this phase are fundamental to the ultimate success of the project. During this phase the critical senior-management activities include the following:

1. Select the right project.   This step must be done whether the proposed corporate project is conducted for internal purposes (e.g., installing new computer systems, changing procedures, or modifying a production facility) or whether the corporation is proposing to execute a project for another firm. It is imperative that senior management evaluate each prospective project to ensure that it fits within the overall corporate strategy and that the successful execution of the project will contribute to the short-term and long-term corporate objectives. (See Chapters 1 and 4.)

2. Commit the corporation.   It must be clear to all parties that each project has a corporate champion, typically called the corporate sponsor. This is someone who believes in the project and is committed to its success. The corporate sponsor is ultimately responsible to the other members of the senior-management team for the success or failure of the project throughout all of its phases. It is the responsibility of this individual to clearly convey the corporate commitment to the success of the project—not only to the other senior managers and shareholders, but also to the project team, client, outside agencies, and the general public as well.

3. Obtain needed technical and management skills.   Here, senior management must evaluate its own corporate resources to determine if they are sufficient to perform the project. If resources are lacking, the corporation must arrange for the appropriate teaming with another firm or specialists to supplement the existing corporate resources. It may be necessary to establish contractual arrangements in a joint venture, partnering, or contractor mode so that these resources are available as they are needed.

4. Select the right project manager.   Senior management must carefully examine its candidates for the project-manager position before selecting the individual to fill this important role. The right candidate must possess a combination of technical expertise, management experience, and personnel skills to be able to manage the specific project type and size. This is the individual the corporation will hold accountable for directing the project's day-to-day activities as well as communicating daily with the client and others involved in the project. Therefore, the importance of selecting the right person for the right job cannot be overemphasized.

5. Provide sufficient support systems.   Senior management should ensure that the functional support systems are in place for access by the project team as needed during performance of the work. These support systems include policies, procedures, and standards. Although it is recognized that unique project requirements will likely demand that adjustments be made to these corporate systems in order for them to be thoroughly applicable to the specific project, the structure must be in place at the beginning of the project. Equally important is the need to have support staff in place who are experienced in using these systems so that assistance can be made available to the project as required.

6. Establish effective incentives. Projects are often disruptive to corporate operations, functional activities, employee relations, and personal lives. Prior to the commencement of each project, potential incentive systems should be examined in the context of the particular project to determine their applicability to the work and to create the appropriate reward structure for successful project completion. The project-incentive program may be established either for key personnel only or for the entire project team. However, the parameters should be clearly established at the outset.

Project Execution Phase

The project-execution phase is the phase in which most practitioners see senior management as having an enabling relationship to the project team. That is, the corporate sponsor enables the project manager to focus attention on the specifics of the project. The project manager and team are now in place with full responsibility for day-to-day execution of work. Therefore, the corporate sponsor's role in this phase is to support the project manager by fulfilling several essential responsibilities, including the following:

1. Let the project manager manage the project. It is important that the corporate sponsor and the project manager jointly establish their specific roles and responsibilities at the start of the project. It should be clearly understood that the project manager is indeed responsible for the hands-on management of the work by directing the day-to-day efforts of the project team and ensuring that the project objectives defined in the project mission statement are met. On the other hand, the corporate sponsor is responsible for providing support to the project manager to accomplish the work. It is also important that the corporate sponsor refrain from becoming so involved in the project details that the project manager's responsibility for project execution is diluted.

2. Provide the project oversight and feedback. Even though the project manager has been assigned responsibility for performing the work, regular management reporting is required to provide the corporate organization with sufficient information to demonstrate that the project objectives are being met. These objectives may include those related to cost, schedule, quality, safety, affirmative action, Disadvantaged Business Enterprise (DBE) participation, environmental concerns, and productivity. The corporate sponsor represents the corporate interests in analyzing this management information, evaluating corrective actions taken by the project team, and suggesting alternative courses of action, as applicable. Providing senior-management feedback to the project team is essential, because typically the corporate sponsor has had previous experience in managing similar projects.

Furthermore, the corporate sponsor may offer a broader perspective to implications of the actions.

3. *Provide senior-management-level client contact.* The corporate sponsor provides an appropriate executive-level contact with the client's executive staff. This relationship serves as a conduit for ensuring a high level of client satisfaction, addressing concerns about the project operations, and obtaining client reactions to the performance of the project team. It is important that this critical communications link be established early in the project and continue throughout its duration. This will reinforce the stated corporate commitment to the project. Although this contact is critical, care must be taken that it does not usurp the project manager's ability to work an issues with the client's organization and that the client does not use this conduit to circumvent the project manager's role.

4. *Ensure technical and management support availability.* The corporate sponsor should ensure not only that the corporate functional organizations are available to assist the project team on an as requested basis by providing needed tools and resources to the project, but also that these units actively encourage contact with the project team. The corporate sponsor must facilitate this process, especially when corporate resources are at a premium, time constraints are critical, and near-term results are required.

5. *Promote innovative solutions.* During the course of the project, the project team will undoubtedly encounter situations identical, or at least similar, to those encountered on other projects. These projects may be the corporation's own endeavors or they may be ones highlighted in technical publications as having developed unique and innovative approaches to solve project problems. The corporate sponsor should serve as the conduit to the project for transfering innovative or unique solutions to problem areas. The corporate sponsor should encourage the exchange of lessons learned among project managers and their project teams on a continual basis while projects are ongoing.

6. *Keep the project shielded from corporate politics.* The corporate sponsor must ensure that the project team is protected from ongoing corporate politics and competing corporate organizations to minimize disruptions and ensure that the focus is on the project goals. It is recognized that there will undoubtedly be situations in which various members of senior management will have differing objectives and approaches. These should not be allowed to affect accomplishments of the project's stated and agreed-upon objectives. However, the corporate sponsor should ensure that the project team is made aware of organizational changes and events that may have an impact on the staff. Having the corporate sponsor address a project-team meeting on a planned project visit facilitates this communication.

7. *Provide staff-growth opportunities.* Although it may be expected that assigned project-team members will remain on the project throughout its duration, this is not always the case. The corporate sponsor must be cognizant of the needs and desires of the project-team members concerning career objectives, personal growth, and project burnout. The corporate sponsor must also be aware of staffing needs on other projects and the opportunities for placement or exchange of personnel between projects. Whenever possible, these personnel changes should be encouraged to develop corporate resources and enhance the ability of the corporation to execute additional projects and perform more complex ones. The corporate sponsor should also be available to meet one-on-one with project-team members to discuss career objectives and life-after-the-project opportunities.

8. Enhance staff morale.   The corporate sponsor should assist the project manager by supplying corporate funds to the project team to provide training and career-development opportunities, support morale-building efforts, recognize individual staff contributions, celebrate project accomplishments, and commemorate milestone achievements. The provision of corporate funds to the project for use by the project manager to enhance employee morale pays large dividends in personnel productivity and promotes focus on project objectives.

Postproject Phase

The role of senior management continues after conclusion of the project-execution phase when the physical aspects are complete and the project is operational. The corporate sponsor must, at a minimum, ensure that the following activities are performed:

1. Document the project.   An essential management tool that is sometimes overlooked in the rush to get a project completed is the need to compile a project history. This includes an analysis of the project successes and opportunities for improvement. Although this document needs to be started early in the project, it often languishes near the end. This typically results in the need for an expenditure of corporate resources to complete the documentation after project turnover. Of significant importance in the document is the inclusion of lessons learned, as well as cost and schedule information for future projects. Because the project team will be dispersed and the project manager, who is responsible for providing the document, will likely be reassigned immediately, this document may become the only easily accessible record of the project for future reference. Therefore, it is important that the corporate sponsor ensure that the document is completed in a timely manner and in a format that is usable by other project managers.

2. Recognize the project team.   It is very important that senior management properly recognize and reward the project team for successful completion of the project objectives. This recognition may take several forms, including publicizing the project success in corporate and public literature, relocating project personnel to other projects, promoting personnel who contributed significantly to the successful effort, reassigning personnel to functional organizational units, following through on the incentives established at the beginning of the project, and providing actual rewards, either monetary or commemorative, to celebrate the satisfactory conclusion of the work.

3. Build on the successful project.   Some of the primary purposes for undertaking any project are the long-term benefits that will accrue to the corporation in the form of enhanced professional recognition of management and technical competence in the industry, a broader satisfied client base, and development of staff skill levels. With the project objectives having been met, senior management has the opportunity to maximize these benefits to the corporation by using these seasoned project-management personnel on other projects and making them available to all senior corporate managers who have requirements for similar expertise on their projects.

Conclusion

It is clearly unsatisfactory for senior management to select a project manager, assign staff to a project, and then take a passive approach to the project. The preproject steps must be taken to increase the probability of project success well before the project begins. Provision of technical and management support, as well as close attention to overall project results compared with project goals during the project, are required to achieve the project objectives. Postproject activities are needed to maximize the benefits available to the corporation following completion of a successful project.

Building a High-Performing Project Team

Jimmie L. West

Biographical Sketch . . . **Jimmie L. West, Ph.D., PMP** is currently Director of IBM programs for Educational Services Institute. His experience includes ten years of project-management experience in the fields of telecommunications and office automation. He has been an adjunct professor of management sciences for National Louis University, Washington D.C. campus, and an Associate Professor of Management for the University of Maryland University College.

For decades, project managers have been trained extensively in the technical, tactical, and strategic components of managing projects. The skills to support these components include work identification, schedule management, resource management, risk management, and change management.

Little attention has been given to the area of human-resource management outside the parameter of using organizational resource-responsibility matrixes for assignments and scheduling people to do the work of the project. Recently, more attention has been given to the more nontechnical aspects of project management, such as leadership. This attention is important in light of the recent trend in many organizations to "right size" without experiencing a reduction of production. The trend to achieve efficiencies with fewer resources has increased the necessity for organizations to use cross-functional, multidisciplinary teams with a project manager directing their efforts. As a result, project managers have had to acquire a set of softer skills needed to lead a group of diverse individuals toward a common goal. Specifically, these skills involve coordination, delegation, collaboration, empowerment, team building, and conflict management. The purpose of this chapter is to provide active project managers with some approaches to leading project teams that go beyond the traditional management functions of planning, organizing, implementing, controlling, and reviewing. It is not intended to be a remedy for all the issues related to leadership. Rather, it is intended to help solve the variety of leadership challenges facing project managers every day.

Defining and Diagnosing Teams

Projects are essentially composed of teams. The teams are composed of individuals. Therefore, project managers must know how to deal with people as part of a team and as individuals. To get people to buy in to being team members requires understanding the elements of a team.[1] The elements include the following:

- A small number
- Complementary skills
- Commitment to a common purpose
- Common performance goal
- Commitment to a common approach
- Mutual accountability

When examining a team, project managers can use these elements in the form of questions to get a picture of the strength of the team:

- Are we small enough in number?

  - Can we convene easily and regularly?
  - Can we communicate with all members?

- Can we encourage open, honest, timely communication among members?
- Are the right skills present on the team?

  - Are the technical, problem-solving, decision-making, interpersonal skills present to achieve success?
  - Do team members have capability in one or more of these areas?
  - Which skills are critical to the success of the team?
  - Are team members willing to acquire the necessary skills to help the team?

- Do we have a common purpose?

  - Is it broader and deeper than a short-term objective?
  - Is it a team purpose?
  - Are the members passionate about it?
  - Is it inspiring and visionary?
  - Is it important?

- Do we have a specific performance goal?

  - Is our goal a team performance goal or an organizational performance goal?
  - Are the goals clear, measurable, and achievable?

- Are the goals important to all team members?
- Do members describe them in the same way?

- Do we have an agreed-upon working approach?

  - Is it clear to all members?
  - Does it maximize the skills of all members?
  - Does it provide for objective, result-based evaluation?
  - Is it subject to improvements and modifications?

- Do we have mutual accountability?

  - Is there a sense of "me" versus "we" mentality?
  - How do we measure progress as a team?
  - Does everyone feel ownership of the products of the project?
  - Is there clarification between individual responsibility and team accountability?

The answer to these questions will help project managers begin to determine the psychological climate of your team.

Stages of Team Development

The Tuckman Model for the stages of group development has been used effectively to describe the growth of a group (see Table 18–1). In that context, it lends itself quite easily to being a diagnostic tool for analyzing where a team is in terms of its maturity. The maturity scale can be logically drawn with Forming at one end of the scale representing immaturity, and Performing at the other end of the scale representing maturity. All teams typically go through these stages and it is important to recognize that dysfunctional teams will linger at the immature end of the scale and healthy, functional teams will move quickly to the mature end of the scale.

Table 18–1 presents enhancements to the model to include interpersonal and leadership issues. This table is a summary of how to diagnose and move a team to maturity. It can be used to quickly identify where a team is by examining the behavioral patterns for each stage. Corrective actions are listed in the group task issues for each stage.

The interpersonal issue of inclusion deals primarily with membership on a team. This means that the team members have to answer the personal question "Do I want to belong to this team?" To get a "yes" from the team member, it is essential to provide the environment that will solicit that response. As project manager you can do the following:

- Define the goals and objectives by using team input.
- Clearly define the organizational structure for the project.
- Identify the responsibilities of the various groups.
- Provide opportunities for recognition for team members.
- Organize social get-togethers to encourage team identity.

Table 18–1. Stages of Group Development

Group Stages	Interpersonal Issues	Group Behavioral Patterns	Group Tasks Issues	Leadership Issues
Forming	Inclusion	Hesitant climate, testing boundaries, superficial, polite ambiguity, confusion	Clear lines of membership; focus on commonalities, orientation, and introductions	Dependence on others to assume leadership role
Storming	Control	Establish operating rules; attempts to create order; emergence of conflict; seeking for status, prestige, power	Decision-making process clarified, power and influence issues emerge	Counterdependence, alliances, subgroup formation
Norming	Affection	Cohesion; negotiation; hostility reduction; open communication; increased harmony regarding attitudes, values, and expectations	Development of functional working relationships	Interdependence between team members
Performing	Affection	Growth, insight, collaboration, freedom of communication, shared responsibility, personal accountability, more informality	Production, creativity, shared ownership	Interpendence between team members
Reforming	Inclusion, control, and affection	Hesitant climate, polite ambiguity, confusion, emergence of conflict, growth, insight	Orientation and introductions, development of functional working relationships	Alliances, subgroup formation, interdependence between team members

The interpersonal issue of control has to do with the degree of control team members need to satisfy their search for order or the amount of control the team members want to exert on the project team. Some project members need a clear structure in which to function, whereas others want to assume leadership roles by assuming decision-making authority. For those members who require structure, project managers can do the following:

- Provide a clear organizational chart with lines of authority outlined.
- Provide a team operating manual with procedures for ordering, purchasing, time-sheet preparation, and status reporting.
- Provide job descriptions detailing what team members are to do, who they are to report to, and what the deliverable will look like.
- Provide work-package descriptions that identify what will be done, who will give inputs, who receives the output, and how long they have to produce the deliverable.

If team members look for and respond well to control, a project manager can do the following:

- Describe what is required, not how it should be done.
- Give team members responsibility for supervising the completion of several work packages.
- Have team members report the progress of their work packages in team meetings.
- Provide team members with more support, and allow them to make decisions for their areas.

The interpersonal issue of affection deals with the need to be accepted by the group and included as a valued member. This feeling can be achieved primarily through both the social and office environment. Socially, project managers can encourage the feeling of affection by doing the following:

- Arrange for social gatherings during lunch, after work, or at company functions.
- Organize teams, which can be co-ed, and encourage participation.
- Recognize significant events such as birthdays, anniversaries, and births.
- Encourage group togetherness in the office by trying the following:

  - Create a "war room" where members can gather for project functions.
  - Position the team so they can have daily interaction with other team members.
  - Schedule team meetings to get maximum attendance.
  - Communicate using a team newsletter or electronic bulletin board.
  - Create a home page on the World Wide Web.

As a group goes through the stages of development, it is the project manager's role to facilitate movement to performance. Using the Tuckman model as a benchmark, project managers can easily determine where their teams are functioning. Once that is determined, the project manager can decide to nurture the group to maintain that level or encourage the group to move to the next phase. Simply put, if the team is stuck in forming or storming, the project manager needs to assist the group by being more directive. When the group is in the norming or performing stage, the group needs less direction and more support in terms of encouragement and recognition. The last two phases require the project manager to abandon micromanagement attitudes and adopt macromanagement attitudes.

FORMING STAGE

To determine where the group is functioning, project managers should examine the types of behaviors that are being displayed. A group in the forming stage will exhibit the following behaviors:

- Hesitancy on the part of team members to interact with each other
- Uncertainty about boundaries in terms of behaviors, and commonalities
- Questions by members to determine possible alliances
- Superficial conversation and hesitancy to come forth with information or revealing insights
- Confusion about the reason for being together and the direction of the project.

To overcome some of the initial fears and questions of a group in the forming stage, the project manager must step up and provide boundaries, direction, purpose, and objectives. A project manager can accomplish this using a variety of approaches. One approach is to document everything about the project and publish a project handbook. Another is to have the project team deal with some of the issues of membership. Specifically, the project manager can have the team develop the following:

- A team name to create a sense of uniqueness

- A set of project ground rules that outline the expected behaviors, such as
  - having respect for each other
  - being on time
  - keeping communication open

- A project binder that contains the group charters, ground rules, decisions made, and escalation procedures

The forming stage is critical to get a project team moving toward achieving its goals and objectives. The primary issue for group members is inclusion. Project managers need to provide them with opportunities to wholeheartedly join the team. Additional ways of accomplishing this are the following:

- Kick-off meetings to disseminate information about the project
- Small-group exercises that allow team members to interact with each other less formally
- Team members pairing up and interviewing each other, then introducing their partner to the larger group using information gathered from the interview

- Small groups to clarify the project objectives for individuals
- An organizational breakdown structure with team members' names in the appropriate areas.

STORMING STAGE

As the group progresses to the storming stage, project managers can view it as the natural progression of a high-performing group. Remember that the issue of inclusion is settled by now and the issue of control begins to emerge in the group. The issue of control centers on both structure and authority/responsibility. The signs that a group is entering the storming stage are:

- Rules begin to emerge by default or by practice.
- More assertive people begin attempts at creating order.
- Conflicts emerge, some centering on personalities, most on process and position.
- Individuals begin to search for power, status, or prestige.

To deal with the issues in this stage, project managers must accept the fact that conflict is inevitable and can be managed. Essentially, the project manager must be able to use conflict-management techniques effectively to overcome the tendency for teams to use conflict as a roadblock to progress. Some useful conflict-management approaches are:

1. *Avoidance.*   Use the avoidance approach when the conflict is meaningless, not critical to the project's activities, or when the conflict is focused on unrealistic outcomes and involves a procedure that is documented.
2. *Accommodation.*   Use this approach when the issue involves mutual gain, when the issue focuses on minimal differences in approaches, methodologies, or precedence, and when the only resolution presents an interim solution.
3. *Compromise.*   Use compromise when it represents the best outcome for both parties at that time, when further pursuit of a resolution would impede progress of the project or damage the relationship of the parties involved.
4. *Force.*   Use this approach when there is not enough time to involve others in resolution of the conflict, when there is a predetermined solution to the conflict, and when neither of the parties can come to an agreement. (When using this method, it is always prudent to follow up with the parties involved to explain one's actions.)
5. *Collaboration.*   Use this technique whenever there is enough time to involve team members, when seeking the best long-term solution, when the impact on the team may be significant, and when there is a need to boost team morale and commitment.

This phase is the ideal time to use delegation to move decision making to more appropriate levels. This will encourage team participation and ownership of members.

NORMING STAGE

During the norming stage, the interpersonal issue is affection. Both inclusion and control issues have largely been resolved, and the group starts to focus on satisfying its social needs of being accepted and valued. This is the stage where the first signs of productive work begin to emerge. The real purpose of the project manager during this stage is to maintain the momentum of the group by encouraging further growth. The signs of a group in the norming stage are the following:

- More cohesiveness among team members
- More open communication so that people are willing to voice differences, suggest alternatives, and offer critical reviews
- Reduced hostility so that conflicts are more focused on issues and less on individuals
- A visible emergence of common attitudes, values, and expectations

Again, the job of the project manager is to sustain this atmosphere of collegiality. A project manager can accomplish this by doing the following:

- Supporting the group process by acting as its champion to people outside the project team, such as those in upper management, functional management, and supporting functions.
- Creating small work groups to tackle difficult problems and making these teams cross-functional. (The characteristics of teams described earlier can be used as guidelines for forming these teams.)
- Focusing the group's energy on achieving the performance objective established by the team.
- Creating opportunities for teams and team members to be recognized for their contributions. These opportunities may include having them make presentations to the customer, to upper management, and to other team members; and allowing them to conduct product demonstrations or attend conferences to make presentations.

PERFORMING STAGE

The most productive stage for a team is the performing stage. To get to this point, all groups have spent some time in each of the other phases. The time spent in each phase will vary, and the project manager can support the development of the group by observing and intervening when necessary. This last stage represents the atmosphere of high-performing teams. Again, the primary role of the project manager is to sustain this level by actively supporting the group. A group in this stage does not normally require direction; rather, it requires support. A project manager can determine when a team is in this stage when the following behaviors are observed:

- There is more collaboration between and among team members.
- There is more freedom of communication so that there is less of a need to seek approval of letters and memos from the project manager.
- There is a "we" mentality, rather than a "me" mentality.

- More statements are made about team performance and accountability and less statements are made about individual performance requirements.
- There is a mutual accountability mentality concerning whether the team succeeds or fails.
- Job titles become transparent and lines of authority are delegated to the appropriate level.

The job of the project manager now is to sustain this atmosphere. The project manager can do this with the following approaches:

- Maintaining group morale through the use of team bonuses and letters of recognition to reward performance
- Allowing teams to generate solutions to problems
- Providing more opportunities to share in decision making
- Developing and using more self-directed teams
- Providing more challenging performance objectives
- Using collaboration to solve complex problems

GROUP BEHAVIORS

In addition to observing stage-related behaviors, project managers should watch for two other specific behaviors that indicate the health of the group: maintenance behaviors and task behaviors. Teams that have matured to the performing stage have a balance between the maintenance and task behaviors. The role of the project manager is to facilitate that balance in the team.

Maintenance Behaviors

Maintenance behaviors are directly aimed at maintaining the health of the group in terms of processes, interactions, decision making, conflict resolution, and creativity. These behaviors directly contribute to creating a good work environment and establishing relationships that encourage the maximum use of the individual members' skills and abilities. When observing a team, project managers should look for these types of behaviors:

- *Encouraging or praising:* Expressing support or warmth, and recognizing the value of group members' ideas or suggestions
- *Harmonizing:* Mediating differences between members and helping to relieve tensions
- *Encouraging inclusion:* Helping quiet team members voice their opinions and keeping the communication channels open
- *Gate-keeping:* Keeping the group on task, maintaining schedules, and providing feedback on the group's processes in terms of effectiveness
- *Standard-setting and testing:* Pointing out explicit or implicit norms that have been set, suggesting improvements, and introducing new norms

Task Behaviors

Task behaviors focus on the accomplishment of the group's task or output. These types of behaviors are directed at getting started, exploring issues, making decisions, and resolving conflicts. When observing a group, project managers can look for these behaviors:

- *Initiating:* Proposing tasks or goals, defining a group problem, and suggesting procedures
- *Seeking information or opinions:* Requesting facts, asking for relevant information, soliciting expressions of value, and seeking suggestions and ideas
- *Giving information or opinions:* Offering facts, providing relevant information, and giving unsolicited suggestions and ideas
- *Clarifying and elaborating:* Interpreting ideas, clearing up confusion, and developing alternatives
- *Summarizing:* Pulling together related ideas, restating suggestions, and offering decisions or conclusions
- *Consensus-testing:* Testing the group for agreement

Project managers must recognize that not all behaviors will be displayed by all members and not all behaviors will appear in the group. It is equally important to recognize that these behaviors can be displayed by more than one person. The giving of an opinion may also be an attempt to test the waters for consensus. When project managers see the absence of a particular behavior, they can encourage use of that behavior to further the progress of the group when appropriate.

Identifying Individual Contributions

Project managers need to have both the macro and micro view when examining their project teams. The previous discussion has dealt with the macro view, pointing out how to look at the stage of the group, and the behaviors and characteristics of the team. The micro view focuses on identifying the individual capabilities and contributions of team members. Just as group and task behaviors require balance, so do the group and individual behaviors. The context for discussing the individual contributions will be the Myers-Briggs Type Inventory (MBTI). This powerful tool can provide multiple insights on communication preferences, leadership preferences, function preferences, and team dynamics.

The MBTI is an assessment instrument that measures the strengths of each person's preference on the following four scales: Extrovert–Introvert (E–I), Sensing–Intuition (S–N), Thinking–Feeling (T–F), and Judging–Perceiving (J–P). Each person displays a single preference on each scale, which results in 16 types of combinations (see Table 18–2).

The MBTI is not an attempt to place people in confining little boxes. An ENFP is not like every other ENFP. A person's type only reflects which preferences that person chooses to use, not that they cannot use the other preference. Indeed, every person can and does use each of the letters of the scales; they just prefer to use a particular one on each scale. Each type brings

Table 18–2. MBTI Type Table

ISTJ	ISFJ	INFJ	INTJ
ISTP	ISFP	INFP	INTP
ESTP	ESFP	ENFP	ENTP
ESTJ	ESFJ	ENFJ	ENTJ

strengths to the group, and inclusion in the group should not be based on having the "correct type."

How can a project manager use the MBTI without giving each member a test? There are a few ways that will provide project managers with some insight into a person's type without using a testing instrument. Primarily, the project manager needs only to observe behaviors and listen to the language of the team member to get a good picture of the person's preference. Tables 18–3 through 18–6 provide some characteristics of each of the preferences. Project managers can review the preference characteristics for each scale and check the ones that appear to match the behavior and language of the individual. The preference on each scale with the most characteristics are combined in the individual's type. The best way to verify those preferences is to have the individual take and score the MBTI themselves. Most HR organizations have access to people who can further assist teams with administering the MBTI.

THE FOUR MBTI SCALES

The MBTI is based on the psychological theory that everyone has a natural preference for one of the two opposites on each of the scales. People use both preferences but at different times and with different levels of confidence. When people use their preferred types, they are typically at their best and feel most competent and energetic.

The four scales each measure different aspects of interaction. The E–I scale determines where people prefer to focus their attention, or how people energize. Extroverts energize by being with people, in the external world. Introverts energize by being alone or with a few select people, in the internal world. The S–N scale determines the way people prefer to collect data. Sensing people prefer to use their five senses (seeing, hearing, touching, tasting, and smelling). Intuitive (N) people use their senses also, but prefer to develop meaning from the data. The T–F scale determines the way people prefer to make decisions once they have the information. Thinkers prefer to be objective, logical, and firm-minded. Feelers prefer to be subjective, concerned with people, and warm-hearted. The J–P scale determines the preference for orienting to the outer world. People with a judging preference are more structured, organized, and planned. People with a perceiving preference are more spontaneous, flexible, and impulsive.[2]

SHORT CUTS FOR USING THE MBTI

There are two areas where using only combinations of the person's type can be useful. These areas involve the *function lens* and the *temperament lens*.

Table 18–3. Characteristics of Preferences

Extraversion–Introversion Scale (E–I Scale)

Extraverts (E) (75%)	Introverts (I) (25%)
Gregarious	Reserved
Talkative	Quiet
Public	Private
Boundless	Territorial
Speak-to-think	Think-to-speak
Expend energy	Conserve energy
Interaction	Reflection
Breadth	Depth
External	Internal
Multiple relationships	Few relationships

Sensing-Intuition Scale (S–N scale)

Sensing (S) (75%)	Intuition (N) (25%)
5-Senses	Possibilities
Facts	Meanings/Ideas
Present moment	Future-oriented
Specific	General
Concrete	Abstract
Practical	Theoretical
Literal	Figurative
Realistic	Imaginative

Thinking–Feeling Scale (T–F scale)

Thinking (T) (50%)	Feeling (F) (50%)
Objective	Subjective
Detached	Involved
Principle	Values
Critical	Impact on people
Logical	Circumstances
Analytical	Relationships with people
Firm-minded	Warm-hearted
Problem first	People first

Judging–Perceiving Scale (J–P scale)

Judging (J) (55%)	Perceiving (P) (45%)
Files	Piles
List for action	List for possibilities
Structured	Spontaneous
Control	Loose
Decided	Deciding
Organized	Process
Opinion	Options
Fixed	Flexible
Planned	Impulsive

Function Lens

The function lens is comprised of the two middle letters in an individual's type. An ENFP has the function preference of NF. The function lens is insightful because it helps determine an individual's communication style and preference for the kinds of tasks a person seeks to do and to avoid.[3]

The four functions are noted as ST, SF, NF, and NT. STs focus on details and the logical implications of those details. STs seek the team tasks such as the following:

- Monitoring progress with statistics, graphs, and charts
- Managing costs and schedules
- Showing measurable results
- Using proven methods to increase productivity
- Solving problems immediately

SFs are also concerned with details, but their focus is the impact of those details on people. They are most comfortable executing team tasks, such as the following:

- Using tried-and-true methods
- Applying experience to practical jobs
- Sharing work equitably
- Developing charts that document each person's skills or needs
- Reviewing plans and material others have formulated

NFs have a big-picture approach and typically want to make an impact on people's lives. They seek the following:

- Having fun, instilling harmony, and being innovative
- Doing work that allows for awareness and growth
- Communicating in creative ways
- Trying exercises that provide insight into things that matter to people
- Working with diversity to improve output

NTs also see the big picture but are more concerned with the logical implications presented by that big picture. NTs seek the following:

- Positioning the team for the future
- Linking systems, strategies, and models
- Finding opportunities for growth
- Conducting long-term impact studies of complex problems
- Debating challenging questions

What does all of this mean for a project manager with a large team? Essentially, project managers need to focus on their direct reports—people they have direct control over. They can use the tables to determine roughly what the preferences of their direct reports might be in light of their observable behavior. Then they can determine the function type (ST, SF, NF, NT). Once that is accomplished, project managers can start to maximize team members' contributions by matching their choices of team tasks with the requirements of the project.

Temperament Lens

Another useful combination of letters reflects the temperament of individuals. Temperament is defined simply as observable behaviors and core values that are displayed in the outside world.[4] Temperament has a significant role in determining leadership style and expectations. For that reason, when project managers can determine a person's temperament, they can determine what they expect from team members.

There are four temperaments (SJ, SP, NF, and NT). The combination of these letters allows project managers to match their leadership style with the expectations of their followers. When project managers are trying to determine how to lead a particular group or motivate an individual, understanding one's own temperament is an excellent tool to determine what behavior to use.

When a group or an individual has an SJ temperament, project managers can create an environment that has:

- Precise expectations and procedures
- Definite lines of authority
- Firm deadlines
- Clear communication channels

The project manager's behavior and approach should be:

- Decisive
- Well organized
- Hard working
- Direct and fair

And management style should include:

- Encouragement when needed
- Humor where appropriate
- Appreciation when deserved

When a group or an individual has an SP temperament, project managers can create an environment that has:

- Risk-rewarding objectives
- A variety of tasks and responsibilities
- Freedom and independence
- A flexible, self-paced, fun atmosphere
- Face-to-face dialogue

A project manager's behavior and approach should be:

- Responsive
- Open-ended and flexible
- Stimulating
- Direct and honest

And management style should include:

- Infrequent meetings and memos
- On-the-spot decision-making and risk-taking
- Rewards for initiative and risk-taking
- Action that is cleverly timed

When a group or an individual has an NF temperament, project managers can create an environment that has:

- A trusting, friendly, harmonious atmosphere
- Opportunities for personal growth
- A vision that team members can believe in
- Creative freedom
- Rapport

The project manager's behavior and approach should be:

- Inclusive
- Inspiring and positive
- Open to input
- People-centered

And management style should include:

- Acknowledgment of the team member's uniqueness
- A personal approach
- Praise and encouragement for positive efforts
- Care with human interactions

When a group or an individual has an NT temperament, project managers can create an environment that has:

- Global outcomes
- Challenging, stretching goals that are difficult to meet
- Autonomy
- Evaluation criteria that are task-based and personal
- Models and systems

A project manager's behavior and approach should be:

- Competent
- Challenging and strategic
- Convincing
- Open to change

And management style should include:

- Minimal guidelines
- Use of team members as leaders
- Use of team members' analytical skills
- Ingenuity and logic

No team is composed entirely of one type, a single function, or a single temperament. Using the MBTI helps project managers focus more effectively on ways to capitalize on the strengths of individuals and turn those strengths into team strengths. Because there are always multiple types on a team, project managers must be flexible and adaptable to get the most out of their teams. Understanding type has been one of the most effective methods in achieving that goal. Only with practice will project managers become comfortable using this approach.

ENDNOTES

1 Katzenbach, J. R., Smith, D. K. *The Wisdom of Teams.* New York: HarperCollins Publishers, 1994
2 Kroeger O., Thuesen, J. M. *Type Talk at Work.* New York: Dell Publishing, 1992
3 Hirsh, S. K. MBTI *Team Building Guide: Leaders Resource Guide.* Palo Alto: Consulting Psychological Press, 1992; Keirsey, D. and Bates, M. *Please Understand Me: Character and Temperament Types*, Fifth Edition. Del Mar, CA: Prometheus Nemesis Book Company, 1984; Myers, I. B. *Introduction to Type.* Palo Alto: Consulting Psychological Press, 1993
4 Hirsh, op. cit.

Bibliography

LEADERSHIP

Bennis, W. *On Becoming a Leader.* Reading, MA: Addison-Wesley Publishing Company, 1994
Bennis, W. and Goldsmith, J. *Learning to Lead: A Workbook on Becoming a Leader.* Reading, MA: Addison-Wesley Publishing Company, 1994
Kouzes, J. M. and Posner, B. L. *The Leadership Challenge.* San Francisco: Jossey-Bass Publishers, 1994
Myers, I. B. and Myers, P. B. *Gifts Differing: Understanding Personality Type.* Palo Alto: Davie-Black Publishing, 1980

TEAM BUILDING

Kayser, T. *Building Team Power: How to Unleash the Collaborative Genius of Work Teams.* Burr Ridge, IL: Irwin Professional Publishing, 1994
Parker, G. M. *Cross Functional Teams: Working with Allies, Enemies and Other Strangers.* San Francisco: Jossey-Bass Publishers, 1994

Motivation in the Project Environment

Robert J. Yourzak

Biographical Sketch . . .   Robert J. Yourzak, P.E., is President of Robert Yourzak
& Associates, Inc., a Minneapolis management and
engineering consulting company founded in 1982.
The company's thirty professionals serve clients in
program, project, construction, and operations management, and planning for facilities, products, and
training. Mr. Yourzak has over twenty-five years of
experience, and is a Certified Management Consultant
and Project Management Professional. He has a
Master's Degree in business administration and in
engineering. Mr. Yourzak has taught project management for over ten years at the University of Minnesota,
and is a worldwide speaker and author. He is a Fellow
and Past Chairman and President of the Project
Management Institute (PMI). He also served as
Minnesota Chapter President for PMI, American
Society of Civil Engineers, and Institute of Industrial
Engineers. He is honored with current listings in *Who's
Who in the World*, *Who's Who in America*, and *Who's
Who in Engineering*.

Often the difference between a good and an excellent project is the ability of the project manager to develop a motivated team. The challenge
for project managers is to motivate multidisciplinary individuals to
effectively work together toward a common goal as a team. The interpersonal
style of the project manager can have an impact on the project throughout its
life cycle.[1] The following are the classic leadership behavioral profile patterns:

1. *Analytical.* Project managers with this behavioral style depend on
   their own technical knowledge and ability, and often make the technical decisions for the project, which they communicate to their teams.
   One-way communication may result. Project managers will often ask
   questions to get the facts.

2. *Driver.*　Project managers having a dominant driver style are extremely self-motivated and control their teams by constantly giving directions. Their competitive attitudes drive the teams to win.

3. *Supportive.*　Project managers with this behavioral style establish formal project-reporting channels linked to their organizations' structure. These project managers understand the broad company perspective. When unsure of an issue requiring subjective judgment, they ask questions to find answers before making decisions.

4. *Influencing.*　Project managers using the influencing style emphasize teamwork, team building, and team decision making. They work with their teams to influence project implementation.

Each project manager has a mix of these styles. The mix can vary depending on experience level and the project environment. The most important skill is knowing when to apply one style (or a mix of styles) to handle a specific situation.

Research Studies

The following three research studies were led by the author.

1. In 1985, students interviewed 128 executives and 59 employees near the University of Minnesota's Institute of Technology.

2. In 1996, the same 1985 questionnaire was sent to 400 midwestern executives in manufacturing, utilities, government, consulting, and construction. However, only 36, or 9 percent, of the executives sent back the questionnaire.

3. The author conducted a study on behavioral styles by summarizing profile-instrument results from participants in company training programs since 1982.

Executives in the 1985 and 1996 survey questionnaires were asked to rank the project manager's behavioral style that would best service their organizations. Table 19–1 shows that in 1985 executives ranked influencing style as the most desired, followed by supportive, analytical, and driver. In 1996, executives ranked influencing style as the most desired followed by analytical, driver, and supportive. After a decade of desiring their project managers to develop a greater influencing style, the 1996 executives surveyed reported a 3 percent drop overall in project managers having an existing influencing behavioral style (see Table 19–2).

Results from the study on participants in the author's company-training programs since 1982 differ from the other studies. The dominant behavioral styles of existing or aspiring project managers taking the training programs are the following: supportive style (29%), analytical style (28%), driver style (25%), and influencing style (18%).

Table 19–1. Project Managers' Desired Behavioral Style

Project Managers' Desired Behavioral Style	1985 Executive (128)	1996 Executive (36)
Analytical	3 23.7%	2 24.2%
Driver	4 21.6%	3 21.7%
Supportive	2 25.0%	4 19.2%
Influencing	1 29.7%	1 34.9%

()Denotes Sample Size

Developing Leadership Skills

Project managers will change the balance of the four behavioral styles as they get more experience and as the project environment changes. In 1996, the functional organization was the most common structure, with 69 percent of organizations using this structure. (See Chapter 14 for more on organizational structures.) The matrix organization was the next most popular, with 17 percent using this structure. Project and one-owner organizations each had 7 percent. Projects had an average of eleven team members and a duration of thirteen months. Many of these organizational factors will have an influence on how project managers lead their teams and interact with other stakeholders.

A project manager working on a technical project may start with a dominant analytical style. At this stage, the project manager may have a small, single-discipline project where he or she also does the technical aspects.

As the project manager gets more assistance and directs project teams for small- and medium-sized projects, he or she may develop a dominant driver style. As the project manager gets medium- and large-sized, multidisciplinary

Table 19–2. Project Managers' Existing Behavioral Style

Project Managers' Existing Behavioral Style	1985 Executive (128)	1996 Executive (36)
Analytical	2 26.6%	1 31.6%
Driver	4 20.7%	2 27.4%
Supportive	3 25.3%	4 16.9%
Influencing	1 27.4%	3 24.1%

()Denotes Sample Size

projects, she or he may develop a dominant supportive style. This stage often includes repeat, noncontroversial projects.

As more new, controversial, difficult, large, and multidisciplinary projects are successfully completed, the project manager may develop a dominant influencing style. At this stage, the project manager especially recognizes the need to motivate and lead the team.

Project managers who desire to strengthen their influencing style to achieve greater balance among the four behavioral styles should do the following:

- Observe and understand effective influencing leaders in their organization, professional society, or civic organization. In particular, observe decision-making, controlling, motivation, communication, and planning styles.
- Gain influencing experience as a committee chair or officer in professional societies or civic organizations.
- Take courses in organization and management, human relations in organizations, psychology in management, fundamentals in management, team building, and leadership.

Motivation Factors

An improper behavioral style can lessen the impact of effective motivators. According to the survey, some motivational factors have not changed much over the last decade. Table 19–3 shows that executives and employees ranked recognition, achievement, and responsibility as the top motivators in this decade and the last. The four most demotivating factors are inadequate project-management leadership, inadequate team–peer relations, inadequate relations with the project manager, and inadequate salary (see Table 19–4). When asked to separately rank the six intrinsic motivators, as shown in Table 19–5, the 1985 executives and employees had identical rankings. The 1996 executives had the same rankings except they reversed the last two factors. The top three motivators again are recognition, achievement, and responsibility. Dr. Frederick Herzberg's two-factor theory was used as the basis for the motivator and demotivator factors listed. (Please refer to his work cited in the bibliography.)

The following lists include a host of practical motivating tips for everyday project-team use. It is recommended that organizations first place their effort in fixing the problems causing their most demotivating factors. Then, and only then, they should work on improving the motivating factors for project-team members. Some of the practical motivators listed in this chapter should be implemented as they best fit the specific situation.

RECOGNITION MOTIVATORS
- Recognize team as the key component of the organization in the company newsletter or on the bulletin board.

Table 19–3. Most Effective Motivators

Motivator	1985 Executive (128)	1985 Employee (59)	1996 Executive (36)
Recognition*	1	1	2
Responsibility*	2	3	3
Achievement*	3	2	1
Advancement*	4	9	5
Growth*	5	10	8
Salary	6	5	10
Project manager's leadership	7	7	7
Work itself*	8	8	6
Relation with project manager	9	6	9
Team peer relations	10	4	4
Work conditions	11	11	13
Team subordinate relations	12	12	12
Organization's policy	13	15	14
Title/status	14	14	15
Security	15	13	11
Personal time	16	16	16

*6 intrinsic factors (other 10 are extrinsic factors)

- Write an article or articles on the project in external publications and include team-member names.
- Send the team to seminars and conferences, especially to present successful project-team results.
- Give team awards, performance certificates, plaques, or gifts, "project of the month," "team of the month," annual awards day, traveling team trophy, 5-10-15-etc.-year service pins, watches, clocks, or pens.
- Give special parking spaces next to the building for the month; or use of the company resort condominium.
- Create a "company wall of project teams."
- Identify and associate the team with successful results; provide positive reinforcement by management, peers, and customers for being under budget and ahead of schedule with high project quality.
- Hold team dinners or lunches, picnics, social or sporting events, fishing or hunting trips; invite customers and top management.
- Give extra time off at project completion as a reward for a job well done.
- Participate in major decisions on project.
- Give additional responsibility or special assignments.
- Include in key project teams working on important issues.
- Sign reports or drawings.
- Make client or top management presentations.

Table 19-4. Rank of Extrinsic Demotivating Factors

Demotivator	1985 Executive (128)	1985 Employee (59)	1996 Executive (36)
Project manager's leadership	1	4	1
Team peer relations	2	2	6
Relation with project manager	3	1	2
Salary	4	3	3
Organization's policy	5	7	7
Team subordinate relations	6	8	8
Work conditions	7	6	5
Security	8	5	4
Title/status	9	10	10
Personal time	10	9	9

- Receive praise or feedback from management for a job well done; get an in-person "thank you" from the boss and/or the president.
- Obtain customer or client thank-you letter to the team.
- Provide profit-sharing, stock purchase, bonus, merit, or benefit increases—tangible proof of the value of the team accomplishment.

ACHIEVEMENT MOTIVATORS
- Meet or beat project schedule, budget, technical requirement, quality, or goals while working together as a team.
- Obtain satisfied customer.
- Receive sense of accomplishment seeing your project completed and working as planned.
- Solve difficult problem, find innovative process, or get new patent.
- Market project to potential customer and win, beat out competitors for a new business account.

Table 19–5. Rank of Intrinsic Motivating Factors

Motivator	1985 Executive (128)	1985 Employee (59)	1996 Executive (36)
Recognition	1	1	1
Achievement	2	2	2
Responsibility	3	3	3
Work itself	4	4	4
Advancement	5	5	6
Growth	6	6	5

- Become an industry leader.
- Develop leading-edge product that works, which customers need or want, and with a good financial return.
- Create publicly needed structures or services.
- Complete a new and difficult project.
- Complete additional education or degree.
- Feel a sense of being important or belonging to the team and organization.
- Get payoff for entrepreneurship.
- Reach or exceed team goals that are greater than the goals of individuals working alone.

RESPONSIBILITY MOTIVATORS
- Be accountable for project schedule, budget, technical work, or quality.
- Plan scheduling, budgeting, and staffing on your project.
- Set one's own work goals and be accountable for achieving them.
- Take control of team direction and project approach.
- Select one's own work method.
- Receive commensurate authority to act, along with responsibility for the project.
- Provide customer needs or wants.
- Develop a good working relationship with the customer.
- Participate in decisions affecting your project.
- Keep informed on issues affecting the project.
- Take new risks.
- Get larger and more complex projects or project-team role.
- Be trusted to perform responsibilities and achieve desired results.

WORK ITSELF MOTIVATORS
- Have interesting, varied, challenging, and important projects and work.
- Know one's work is needed and helps society; see physical results of meaningful contributions.
- Create an innovative, worthwhile, necessary, and/or tangible product with high quality for satisfied customers.
- Develop good team spirit and peer relationships, and work with knowledgeable professionals.
- Have a choice of projects.
- Make one's own decisions and have greater team and individual independence.
- Be allowed to take a risk.
- Work for one's own customers and obtain new customers.
- Have meaningful impact and ownership of work.
- Feel competent, so that one is not underemployed or pigeonholed.
- Handle job-related problems that customers care about.
- Receive clear direction and leadership.
- Have realistic goals and objectives.

- Work in a proper, positive company work environment.
- Be satisfied with the accomplishments that can be achieved in a 40-hour work week.
- Like the job and go to work with a smile.
- Adjust hours to meet personal and business demands.
- Convince customers to be environmentally supportive.
- Have work specialty(ies).
- Contribute to financial business goals.

ADVANCEMENT MOTIVATORS

- Receive job promotions for new and broader opportunities.
- Obtain more responsibility, authority, and accountability.
- Get new, more complex tasks and larger projects.
- Recommend team members on the project for promotion, and share in their satisfaction when they earn it.
- Obtain opportunities to advance by receiving reimbursement for seminars, workshops, classes, or conventions.
- Certify and approve projects.
- Get an increase in salary, obtain a bonus, a larger office, a company car, or other added benefits.
- Meet with clients or top management on the project.
- Participate in job rotational development; obtain varied experience to become well-rounded.
- Have a dual-ladder system; promote both on the managerial and on the technical sides.
- Receive one's first project to manage.
- Earn professional registration or specialty certification.
- Have a company policy of advancing from within.
- Relocate to more a desired company location.
- Be named to a corporate committee.

GROWTH MOTIVATORS

- Increase or develop new technical, multidisciplinary, or managerial skills.
- Become more competent on the job through on-the-job-learning and from projects that develop the individual.
- Attend company-paid seminars, courses, trade shows, conventions, or professional-society programs to help prepare for future changes.
- Promote life-long learning in a comprehensive career-development program.
- Diversify one's knowledge base; learn other skills in nontechnical areas and a wide variety of work tasks.
- Increase interpersonal skills.
- Contribute to one's professional society, including service as an officer and committee chair.
- Research a new area for publication on company-paid time.

- Interact with other industry professionals.
- Read or use up-to-date industry publications or books.
- Participate in a rotational development program (broadening assignments).
- Obtain more challenging and varied work assignments.
- Develop a respected reputation.
- Use new, company-paid equipment.
- Meet more people, both inside and outside the company.
- Become more marketable for other tasks, positions, and new challenges.
- Earn an opportunity to teach, and become a leader and mentor within the company.
- Be part of a growing organization that is expanding in new areas, adding new staff, and having efficiency gains and office improvements.

ENDNOTE

1 Geier, John and O'Connor, Michael. *Personal Profile System.* Minneapolis, MN: Performax Systems International, Inc., 1986.

BIBLIOGRAPHY*

Dinsmore, Paul C. Human behavior as seen by the experts. In *Human Factors in Project Management.* New York: AMACOM, 1990, pp. 31–46

Dowling, William. Conversation with Frederick Herzberg. In *Effective Management and the Behavioral Sciences.* New York: AMACOM, 1978, pp. 36–51

Geier, John and O'Connor, Michael. *Personal Profile System.* Minneapolis, MN: Performax Systems International, Inc., 1986

Herzberg, Frederick. One more time: How do you motivate employees? *Harvard Business Review* January-February 1968, pp. 53–62

Herzberg, Frederick. *Work and The Nature of Man.* Cleveland: World Publishing Company, 1966

House, Ruth Sizemore. *The Human Side of Project Management.* Reading, MA: Addison-Wesley, 1988

Lee, David R., Bohlen, George A., and Sweeney, Patrick J. Project manager influence activities: The reasons and strategies. In *1995 Proceedings of the Project Management Institute.* Upper Darby, PA: Project Management Institute, 1995, pp. 490–499

Losoncy, Lewis E. *The Motivating Leader.* DelRay Beach, FL: St. Lucie Press, 1995

Martin, M. Dean and Wysocki, Jay. Selecting a leadership style for project team success. In *1990 Proceedings of the Project Management Institute.* Upper Darby, PA: Project Management Institute, 1990, pp. 748–752

Mausner, Bernard, Herzberg, Frederick, and Snyderman, Barbara. *The Motivation to Work.* New Brunswick, NJ: Transaction Publishers, 1993

Owens, Stephen D. and Martin, M. Dean. Project team connections between job satisfaction and productivity. In *1990 Proceedings of the Project Management Institute.* Upper Darby, PA: Project Management Institute, 1990, pp. 238–243

*Portions of the author's previously cited articles are reprinted from the Project Management Institute's 1986 and 1987 *Proceedings* respectively, with permission of the Project Management Institute, 130 South State Road, Upper Darby, PA 19082, "a worldwide organization advancing the state-of-the-art in project management."

Robinson, Daniel G. Motivation. In *1992 Proceedings of the Project Management Institute.* Upper Darby, PA: Project Management Institute, 1992, pp. 522–526

Rosen, Ned A. *Teamwork and the Bottom Line: Groups Make a Difference.* Hillsdale, NJ: Lawrence Erlbaum Associates, 1989

Thamhain, Hans J. Building high performance engineering project teams. *IEEE Transactions on Engineering Management* August 1987, pp. 130–137

Thamhain, Hans J. Managing technologically innovative team efforts toward new product success. *Journal of Product Innovation Management* March 1990, pp. 5–18

Tippet, Donald D. and Peters, James F. Team building and project management: How are we doing? *Project Management Journal* December 1995, p. 29–37

Yourzak, Robert J. Leading people to project goals. In *1987 Proceedings of the Project Management Institute.* Upper Darby, PA: Project Management Institute, 1987, pp. 272–283

Yourzak, Robert J. Measuring successful motivators. In *1986 Proceedings of the Project Management Institute.* Upper Darby, PA: Project Management Institute, 1986, pp. 412–418

Chapter

20

How to Get the Right Message Across

Francis M. Webster, Jr. and
Stephen D. Owens

Biographical Sketch . . .

Francis M. Webster, Jr., is retired after eight years as editors-in-chief of the Project Management Institute (PMI), twenty-one years of teaching at the university level, and fourteen years of industrial experience. He joined PMI in 1978 and has received all three of PMI's highest individual awards. He has authored a number of articles and papers and conducted several workshops on project management. He was responsible for the PMI Software Survey for eight years and for creating *PMNETwork*. He earned a B.S. in chemical engineering from the University of Missouri, an M.S. degree from Carnegie-Mellon University, and a Ph.D. from Michigan State University. He has had work experience with Phillips Petroleum Company, Chrysler Corporation, and H. B. Maynard and Company.

Stephen D. Owens is an Associate Professor of Management at Western Carolina University (WCU). He holds a Ph.D. in management, with a concentration in the fields of industrial relations and human-resource management. He teaches in the Master of Project Management Program at WCU. His research interests are in the areas of human-resource management in projects, labor relations, and dispute resolution.

E ven the most experienced project manager is probably not competent over the entire range of variables involved in communicating. For example, most of us are only slightly conscious of the extent to which we communicate through body language. Often spoken language and body language are in conflict; for example, when a person says, "I am listening to you," but is looking around the room or out the window.

Spoken language and written communication are the most obvious ways to get a message across. How those messages are delivered are important for the effective project manager. For instance, some voices are in ranges with a timbre that is pleasing to hear. Varying the tone of voice and speed of speaking adds interest to the spoken words. Combining these with clear, crisp diction conveys the image of an educated and often sophisticated person. Adapting such characteristics to the situation can help bridge the gap between the speaker and the listener. Aspiring project managers should not hesitate to seek counsel on their voice and, if appropriate, get training.

Another important communication element is the use of plain language that everyone can understand. Typically, a project team develops its own specialized language. This may be a coded matrix that identifies locations in physical space or words that describe unique business processes. This specialized language increases the efficiency and accuracy of communicating within the team but may create significant problems in communicating with peripheral project participants or outside stakeholders. Sometimes project participants may use unfamiliar words to impress or obfuscate. Repeated insistence on speaking or writing in plain language will probably resolve the problem.

Putting It in Writing

The formal written document is a must in any organization to convey instructions, restate understandings, convey a sense of importance of the message, or cover your tracks. The competent project manager ensures that all decisions and actions are properly documented so there is a complete audit trail. Too often legal action requires proof that the project manager behaved in a prudent and rational manner.

Although e-mail is a fast method of written communication, it has its disadvantages. E-mail can get you in trouble faster and with more people. E-mail can invite you to express feelings at the wrong time or send would otherwise be considered a draft to people who matter. The probability that you will say the wrong thing or the right thing the wrong way is greater. Always assume there is an electronic copy of a message recorded somewhere in the system that can haunt you. You cannot deny having said it. On the other hand, when using a formal written letter or memo, it is relatively easy to carry it around it one's briefcase for a day or two and then revise it.

Show and Tell

"A picture is worth a thousand words" is still a relevant admonition. Data portrayed in graphic form, and the message conveyed by that data, is far more likely to be understood. However, failure to portray the data properly is more likely to lead to confusion and frustration. Probably the greatest error is trying to cram too much into the graphic. Even if the graphic must be replicated several times, it is wise to make one key point per graphic.

Communicating Well Means Career Advancement

Regardless of the communication form, good communications skills go hand-in-hand with a project manager's ability to effectively handle more complex projects. It has been posited that project managers are developed "one zero at a time." A person's first experience upon joining an organization is likely to be an assignment as a contributor on a project. That assignment may be valued at $1,000. If that person handles the job well, the next assignment may have a value of $10,000, and suddenly you are a project manager. And so it goes. If a person flubs an assignment, that person may go back down a notch or two. If a person truly shows promise, that person may skip a few steps.

The Neophyte Project Manager

An aspiring project manager has some important lessons to learn about communicating. To attract management's attention as a potential project manager, you need to demonstrate that you will be a good ambassador for the organization. The following suggestions should help the zeroes grow for your assignments. What you communicate to others and what others communicate to you, the potential project manager, are important. How you behave as a manager and how you provide visibility for what you are doing are also important.

DRESS FOR THE DESIRED ROLE

If you are to represent your organization, either internally or externally, you must present an image that is consistent with the organization's image. If you are playing in Boston, you need to be very proper. If you are in Tombstone, Arizona, you need to look like one of the outstanding leaders there. IBM once had a very rigorous dress code because it sold to executives. All who represented IBM looked like executives. Is this communicating? Most assuredly. The first impression people have is that of your appearance. If clothes are garish or unkempt, they communicate an impression of someone with poor judgment or lacking in personal pride. The message is that those characteristics will dominate in your work.

DEVELOP A POSITIVE ATTITUDE

Typically, the second impression that people get is attitude. In part that is communicated by posture, both standing and sitting. A slouchy posture says you are already defeated, so you are not likely to put forth an outstanding work effort. Standing erect, no matter what your height, gets attention. Sitting erect says you are interested in what is being said. Follow posture with a "can do, will do" attitude and you will be given the opportunity to prove yourself. To these, add high self-expectations and high work standards, and you will be saying "I'm ready, boss."

The message goes further because high expectations will be communicated to peers and the best of those will be pleased to be on your team. It will be a strong message to all on the team that great things are expected from them. It will also communicate to management that if they give you, an aspiring project manager, an important assignment, you will ensure that excellent results are delivered in a timely manner.

AVOID FOOT-IN-MOUTH DISEASE

A major trap into which many young people fall is saying the wrong things or even saying the right things at the wrong time. This can brand a person as a loose cannon. If management cannot rely on you to be discreet in choice of words and issues, management will not put you into a position of representing them either internally or externally. Does this mean being super cautious to the point of silence? Certainly not. But it does suggest that you should think carefully before speaking and especially writing.

The first opportunity to be heard will be in one-on-one discussions. After that, most likely the first chances to be heard by a variety of people will be in a meeting. Do not express an opinion on something about which you have little understanding. This point will be made abundantly clear when your boss says, "You haven't been around long enough to have an opinion on that!" If you have the basis for speaking up, you should organize thoughts well. This means jotting down key words of the points to make. These may be in the form of notations in the margin of your notes on the meeting discussion. Those notes should be prioritized so the comments sound well thought out.

LEARN TO LISTEN

Communications is a two-sided coin. One side is transmitting a message. The other side is hearing a message. Listening is an active verb, but it seems to be practiced passively by most people. Too often project assignments are misunderstood because of a lack of listening. If aspiring project managers want others to listen to them when they are project managers, they must learn to listen to the current project managers. Listening to other's ideas and suggestions, whether or not the suggestions are used, will earn you a reputation for at least considering other people's ideas.

LEARN TO OBSERVE

Communications need not be verbal or intentional. We all learn much from what we observe. Observe the techniques that more senior people use to get the job done, to manage meetings, or to convey their attitudes and expectations. Take notes on these and on how you can adapt and adopt the best practices. Learn to observe what needs to be done, where to appropriately anticipate that your services will be needed, and either do them or prepare to do them. This will communicate to management that you have the capability and the initiative to handle such responsibilities on your own projects.

The Novice Project Manager

This phase of career development may come sooner than expected. You will actually be managing your first project. The project value will be in the range of four to five zeros. Skills to develop during this phase include meeting management, controlling requirements and specifications, document control, achieving visibility, obtaining commitment, showing an effective leadership style, resolving conflicts, and communicating with stakeholders.

MEETING MANAGEMENT

At this level you will have a project team, although members probably will not report directly to you administratively. You will have to preside at project meetings, making them productive and worth attending. You should assume the others in attendance are at least as busy as yourself and could do very well without having to attend another meeting. Thus, it is essential that an agenda be distributed sufficiently before the meeting to allow everyone to be prepared to participate. It will also serve as a reminder of the meeting.

Do not just list the subjects to be discussed but identify the decisions to be made. One residential subdivision meeting drew record attendance when the agenda included a decision item for banning snowmobiles on the lake in winter.

The team may want to participate in designing the meetings. For example, members may wish to meet for one hour, whether all items have been completed or not. If this approach is taken, care should be taken to keep the agenda focused tightly, well prioritized, and on track. Another group may opt for longer and fewer meetings. If the first option is chosen, it is desirable to separate schedule and performance discussions from specific problem-solving meetings. If the second option is chosen, these subjects may be combined.

You can be relaxed or hard-nosed in running the meeting. At the extreme, for example, the relaxed approach may result in starting the meeting sometime after the appointed hour and summarizing what has been accomplished as each additional person enters. This will surely invite late arrivals and probably absences from the meeting. On the other hand, the hard-nosed approach might mean starting the meetings exactly at the appointed hour, not summarizing until the end of the meeting, and not allowing someone who enters late to repeat something that has already been discussed. Somewhere in between, though probably closer to the hard-nosed approach, may be most effective. Also, steps should be taken to ensure that each person is prepared for the meeting. That is, each person should have read the distributed materials or obtained the required information beforehand.

Care should be taken to ensure that everyone present has the opportunity to speak on each issue. Indeed, the project manager should ask specific questions of those individuals who are reluctant to speak. This encourages them to become involved in the meeting. It also serves a good purpose by letting all participants know that they, too, may be called upon, so they better be listening carefully.

The meeting should be wrapped up with a summary of what was accomplished and what was agreed upon. As soon as the meeting is over, the project manager should prepare the minutes or a memo restating the accomplishments, agreements, action required by whom and by when, and the date and time of the next meeting.

CONTROLLING REQUIREMENTS AND SPECIFICATIONS

This may be one of the most important tasks for a project manager. First, it is the basis for confirming with the customer or sponsor exactly what the team has committed to deliver. The work-breakdown structure (WBS), accompanied by appropriate text to more clearly define and limit each item, is the best way of communicating these commitments. (See Chapter 7 for more on the work-breakdown structure.) The text should start to define the criteria for accepting each deliverable. These criteria should be amplified early in the project.

Second, the WBS is the best friend of the project manager in protecting against "scope creep": the gradual expansion of the work content. This can be driven by either the customer asking for a little bit more here and a little bit more there or by participants in the project getting intrigued by esoterics or other motivations and actually performing work that is not necessary.

It is also important to verify the budget and other resources to be provided. Consider the consequences to your career of committing to upper management to achieve certain objectives only to discover that management decided to provide half the resources one expected. If this should occur, you may wish to quickly revise, or renege on, the commitments. Avoid the "superman" complex. You may not be able to do the impossible, let alone the improbable.

DOCUMENT CONTROL

As the product of the project is progressively elaborated, work-to-date is communicated to others who are dependent on it to proceed. It sometimes becomes necessary to revise certain decisions or drawings that have been distributed to other project participants. This can lead to interesting consequences.

EXAMPLE.   In building a house, it was necessary to provide the plumber with drawings to plan and estimate the work. Later, as the concrete was being poured in the garage floor of the house, a question was raised about the precise location of a sewer riser. The explanation was that it was to provide drainage for the sinks on the floor above and it was to go up inside the utility-room wall. The problem was that on a subsequent drawing, the utility-room wall had been moved out about eight inches. Realizing that it was too late to move the riser, the owner issued an "expletive" and work proceeded. Later, after the utility-room wall was roughed in, the plumber returned and installed a urinal and the "expletive" was in fact realized. Had adequate document control been in place, this error would not have occurred.

ACHIEVING VISIBILITY

One of the communication responsibilities of the project manager is to maintain support for the project. This includes support as the part of upper management to ensure that adequate resources are provided and on the part of functional managers, who control when specific resources are available.

Visibility can be achieved by displaying large-scale versions of project documents. Pictures and other messages convey the importance of the project to the organization. These are sometimes displayed in a war room but can be on the wall in a convenient hallway. By posting progress against plan on these documents, every participant on the project is aware that the world will know if they fail to perform according to the plan. The display also encourages members of upper management who happen to pass the display to ask questions about the status of the project. Thus, the project is on the minds of all these stakeholders.

One document to display is the time-scaled project network diagram. It clearly shows which activities are on, as well as behind, schedule. Another convenient tool is the WBS, with each item colored in to show planned and actual progress and planned and actual costs. These can be plotted in translucent colors on percentage scales. While the schedule information is shown on the time-scaled network diagram, the same information summarized by the WBS element communicates clearly what the impact of schedule slippages may be.

OBTAINING COMMITMENT

Novice project managers should avoid getting out on a limb. You need commitments from functional managers to provide certain resources. You also need commitments from those people that they will perform certain tasks according to time and cost constraints.

Obtaining an individual's commitment to a project can only be conducted by relating project objectives to needs, plans, and objectives of that individual. This can challenge your best skills in communicating, and it often takes considerable time. But it is worth it because the individual who is committed will need much less supervision and direction later. The following are two important ways to verify commitments: public declaration and written confirmation. The former is the strongest because when a person states before others—be they peers, superiors, or subordinates—that they will perform a specific task, the person will work very hard to accomplish that task. Such oral commitments should always be confirmed in writing, and, if feasible, distributed to relevant superiors.

SHARING AN EFFECTIVE LEADERSHIP STYLE

There are many leadership styles, such as laissez faire, participative, authoritarian, autocratic, and situational. Pure laissez faire is hardly consistent with the requirements for managing a project. Pure participative is inconsistent with timely completion of a project. The authoritarian will likely alienate the project team. The autocrat will bog the team down as members wait for decisions. The last style, situational, which is really using the other styles at appropriate times, is probably the best style for a project manager. It should be apparent that each pure style implies a different way of communicating. Some of these have unintended and unfortunate consequences.

EXAMPLE.   The owner of a construction company was concerned that his employees would never tell him about a problem until it was too late for him to do anything about it. It was suggested to him that his favorite response to bad news was, "Where is the SOB? I'll give him a new [a part of the anatomy]!" He turned away and thought for nearly a minute. Then he turned back and admitted that this suggestion was probably correct. "But I don't know if I know how to manage any other way," he said. The owner had failed to develop a broad repertoire of behaviors that he could employ as the situation really warranted.

How we communicate with people often determines what they tell us. If a project manager makes people uncomfortable when they deliver bad news, that manager can expect to get bad news only when it's too late. If a project manager reacts negatively toward anyone who suggests something other than what the project manager thought of, those manager will get a team of sycophants.

EXAMPLE.   A new manager of a refinery examined the 24-hour control charts looking for aberrations. The aberrations began to disappear. Then the process engineers began having trouble getting a material balance for the refinery. It seems the pump-house operator got tired of explaining aberrations and saw to it that he did not produce anything but perfect circular charts. The moral the story? Tell me what you want to hear, either explicitly or implicitly, and I'll see that you hear it, whether it is true or not.

It is very important that project managers develop a management style and a communication style that elicits the desired behavior. If project managers want to hear the bad news when there is still time to do something about it, they can't shoot the messenger. In fact, the most severe reprimand should be for the person who hides the bad news until it is too late. This is just one example of how important an appropriate leadership style is to the modern project manager.

RESOLVING CONFLICTS
Conflict is inherent in project. Resolving conflict is therefore an essential skill of a project manager. The best solution to a conflict is one that is arrived at by mutual agreement of the concerned parties through discussion of the issues. (See Chapter 21 for more on negotiating skills.)

COMMUNICATING WITH STAKEHOLDERS
The typical project has several stakeholders. They will require project information of various types at different intervals. Learning to understand their needs, anticipate their questions, and provide the appropriate information in a timely manner is an interesting experience for the novice project manager. A

careful analysis of the stakeholders' needs and desires plus the availability of versatile computer capabilities will go a long way toward achieving this.

The Developing Project Manager

Success on previous projects will lead to more zeros so that the project's value is probably in the range of six to seven zeros. A developing project manager will have a larger project team, more stakeholders, and likely some level of public interest in the project. In addition to the skills honed on prior projects, it will become important to develop the vision, maintain commitment, create a sense of urgency, report accurately manage conflicts, manage stakeholders, communicate with the public, and learn to listen.

DEVELOPING THE VISION
On previous projects, the vision of the product of the project and the project itself will likely have been given to the novice project manager. As the project size increases, the ambiguity of the requirements will probably increase. Part a developing project manager's job will be to work from the broadly stated requirements and define the project in more detail. It will require that the project manager develop a large part of the vision. This will probably be done with the help of the key members of the project team. The process will result in a common vision on the part of those involved, and they are likely the ones for which the vision is most relevant. Thus, the communications task is minimized in the beginning. However, the project manager must maintain a sharp and constant focus on that vision and draw others back to it as the project progresses. The price for failing to do so is the inevitable "scope creep" and deterioration of project performance.

MAINTAINING COMMITMENT
Larger projects require longer durations. As time passes, memories fade and commitments get lost. The effective project manager must continually reinforce the commitments made for and to the project. This means communicating the importance of the project to the capabilities and reputation of the organization as well as to the careers of the team members. Even the project sponsor must have the fire rekindled sometimes to ensure that resources are not drawn away to more recent crises.

CREATING A SENSE OF URGENCY
As the duration of the project increases, participants tend to see the target as being well into the future and lose the sense of urgency that often pervades the shorter project. Soon precious slack is being used up and, if not dealt with early enough, the result will be slipped activity completion dates and increasing overtime. Budgets may be overspent in expediting work that could have proceeded in an orderly manner.

There are a lot of ways to create a sense of urgency, ranging from cajoling to being a hard-nosed autocrat. Clearly, the approach selected will depend on the extent to which the problem has gotten out of hand. One good approach is to ensure accuracy and honesty in reporting.

REPORTING ACCURATELY

Few project managers would argue that percentage complete is an accurate measure of progress. All are familiar with the adage that "It takes 90 percent of the estimated duration to do the first 90 percent of the work and 90 percent of the estimated duration to finish the last 10 percent of the work." Yet percentage completion still seems to be the preferred measure for communicating progress. Some people argue that no progress should be shown for activities that are not 100 percent complete. Perhaps an intermediate position is more appropriate. This approach was used very successfully on the following example of a half-billion-dollar project.

EXAMPLE.   For each reporting cycle, the person responsible for an activity had to select one of two answers, yes or no. If the activity was due to start, the question was, "Will this activity be started on time?" If the activity was started, then the question was, "Will the activity be completed on time?" It was clear that no one would be chastised for answering "no" prior to the date the action was scheduled to be taken. It was be made even more clear that a series of "yeses" and then all of a sudden a "no" just as the activity was due to finish had to be accompanied by a very good excuse. So long as the activity was on schedule, the only answer required was "yes". If a "no" was reported, a simple explanation had to provided, along with an indication of what help was required.

To improve on meeting management, activities were coded with numbers to indicate the following:

1. This should have been completed in the prior report period.
2. This was due to be completed in this report period.
3. This should have been started in the prior report period.
4. This was due to start in the current report period.

The name of the responsible person was at the top of the report. Participants on this project practically turned handsprings to avoid having a "1" on their report. Because the reports were sorted by these codes, schedule meetings focused on the "1s," then on the "2s" for which the answer was "no", then on the "3s," and then on the "4s" for which the answer was "no". Activities in process with a "no" were discussed as time permitted. After implementing this approach, the project-team meetings went from about five hours every Thursday to about two hours every other Thursday. There were some fifteen people involved in these meetings, so the savings were substantial, both in direct costs of the meeting and in the indirect costs of the productivity of those subordinates attending the meetings.

To further increase the effectiveness of this approach, consider providing an advanced activity forecast showing the activities for which each person is responsible along with the status of all activities that are immediate predecessors of the activity. Along with predecessor activities, show the names and phone numbers of those responsible for the predecessors activities. This way, there is no excuse for lack of communication between responsible parties.

Since report formats are not included in most project-management software packages, you will have to create the report formats for your projects. The honesty and accuracy engendered in the reports will make their creation well worthwhile. One problem in using this approach is that it can create an atmosphere in which people become overzealous about starting and completing activities per schedule to the point of burn-out and possibly physical problems.

CONFLICT MANAGEMENT
Novice project managers learn how to resolve conflicts. The more adroit project managers learn how to anticipate conflict and manage problems before they become potential delaying factors for the project. One approach to this is to "manage by walking around." Learning early of a potential conflict provides time to analyze the issues, talk one-on-one to the key parties, and often achieve agreement on a solution before the "concrete begins to set." Often the seasoned project manager can anticipate the issues based on prior experience. By building up a credit balance of "wooden nickels" (i.e., favors) beforehand, many conflicts can be resolved by horse trading early on.

STAKEHOLDER MANAGEMENT
In a similar manner, the astute project manager analyzes the needs and desires of stakeholders early on and anticipates the issues. The evidence indicates that this was done very successfully on a recent rapid-transit project. Issues and constraints were made public early in the project, thus creating an environment in which all parties to conflict resolution knew they had to come to an agreement or the public would become very difficult to deal with. As a result, negotiations with several government bodies proceeded to very acceptable solutions in time to avoid delaying the project. The last issue was signed off on just hours before the first train was to run.

COMMUNICATING WITH THE PUBLIC
Key to the successful stakeholder management in the rapid-transit project was a very aggressive and carefully considered public-relations program. Representatives of the rapid-transit project attended public meetings and made themselves available to the public. They released regular announcements to the media, established local information offices, and had a booth at every possible fair, exposition, or other event where they could communicate with people. The project became a source of pride to members of the communities involved, to the point that "the project could not fail." This was combined with excellent execution of the project so that the product that was delivered fulfilled that sense of pride. There are many examples of both failure and success of this aspect of project management.

LEARN TO LISTEN, AGAIN

Project managers in the developing stage may have gained the impression that now it is time for others to listen to them. That is true, but it in no way implies that the project manager is relieved of responsibility for listening. Indeed, that responsibility has become even more important.

Project managers are the ones who must listen to clients to sense any dissatisfaction with the project or any changed or new expectations. Project managers must listen to management to sense any concerns with or slackening of support for the project. Project managers must listen to those whom they may consider to be peripheral stakeholders to the project to identify their concerns and resolve those concerns before they delay the project. Project managers must listen to potential vendors very carefully, because they will attempt to sell project managers the latest innovations with seemingly little concern for the successful completion of the project. In fact, vendors are often far more concerned about getting someone to adopt their technology to help them pay for further development and aid them in selling to other potential clients. This has been a major cause for difficulties in the implementation of management information system (MIS) projects.

Above all, project managers must listen to their teams. They must listen to those concerned with the technology of the project to ensure that planned approaches are feasible and that all risks are identified. Project managers must be the leaders of value engineering by listening for ideas on how the project can be done better, more economically, or more quickly. To maintain peak morale of team members, project managers must listen to all team members. They may not adopt every suggestion, but failure to listen will dry up the source of ideas.

In at least one organization, it is common for an ombudsman to be a part of the project team as advisor to the project manager with regard to listening as well as other behaviors.

Listening is a vital skill of the professional project manager. You can only manage those things of which one is aware.

An Experienced Project Manager

Clearly, only experienced project managers are going to be assigned the very large projects. These have very large project teams, many stakeholders, and considerable public involvement. Experienced project managers need to have strong skills in the areas of identifying conflict, selling the vision, and managing public interests.

IDENTIFYING CONFLICT

In large projects, opportunities abound for conflict to exist out of the project manager's sight. Again, managing by walking around is helpful, but using communication skills is more demanding. The project manager must understand the decisions that have to be made at various levels in the organization and recognize the potential for conflict when greater numbers of people, organizations, and issues are involved. One manager did this very effectively by arriving at the site at 7:30 AM and visiting a different area each day. He seldom arrived at his office until 8:30 or 9:00 AM, but what he learned by walking around was more important than the extra hour in the office.

SELLING THE VISION

The large number of stakeholders increases the task of creating a vision that can be sold to all the parties. As this vision takes shape, it is often the task of the project manager to be the primary articulator of that vision. Often there will be multiple sponsors for such a project, all of whom will try to "help." If their perceptions of the vision stray, or if they have not accepted some aspect of the vision, they can actually harm to the project.

In developing the vision, it may be useful to use market research tools such as surveys and focus groups. Having the results of these may be helpful in developing the vision, but the results must be shared if the vision is to be accepted by the stakeholders. The results must also be provided to the key stakeholders and sponsors in such a way as to be an authoritative source to which they refer when answering questions. The vision must be continually reinforced to ensure a constant and consistent portrayal. A briefing book is a useful way to accomplish this. It should contain, in easy-to-use format, the project charter, vision, issues and answers, progress and status information, discussion of benefits to the stakeholders, and any relevant caveats.

MANAGING PUBLIC INTERESTS

The first step in managing public interests may well be to agree to and proclaim a customer-service charter that states concisely the attitudes that are to prevail on the project concerning the customer. No matter how considerate the participants in a project, one surly individual can create a negative image of the project. There can be no misunderstanding of the project team's attitude toward the customer.

EXAMPLE.   On a recent project several communities were involved, and there was no time in the schedule for disruption by court delays. The team established and advertised a complaint system to aid in identifying individuals with complaints as well as identifying issues of concern to the public. Community information bulletins dealing forthrightly with various issues reduced misunderstandings that could have arisen if the grapevine had been the primary source of information. Community information offices can provide face-to-face opportunities to answer questions and correct misunderstandings. This project's team members participated in public events and forums such as meetings and spoke at civic organizations and other clubs. Team members had booths at fairs and expositions to take the message to where the people were. The project team offered community education, outreach programs, and safety seminars. These seminars and programs were held at public schools, community colleges, senior-citizen centers, and other forums for opinion leaders. Radio talk shows and television interviews made the information available to mass audiences. All of these are ways to increase the public's understanding of the project and its product, reduce misunderstandings, and diffuse special-interest groups who could cause substantial delays in the project.

The Art of Communicating

There is much more that could be said about communicating in projects, such as maintaining honesty and integrity and developing trust. These are major underpinnings of successful communications. Perhaps it is fair to compare the communication competencies of a project manager with those of an artist. The neophyte artist may create a crude still-life painting. The novice artist may create something that is a pleasure to perceive. The developing artist may create a more complex painting. Eventually the artist's skills develop to the point of creating a large canvas conveying complex messages on a variety of subjects.

The project manager must develop communication skills in a similar manner. Those who learn to excel in communicating in a project environment will truly be rewarded.

BIBLIOGRAPHY

Baker, Bud. The project manager and the media: Some lessons from the stealth bomber. *Project Management Journal* 24:11–14, 1993

Baker, Bud and Menon, Raj. Politics and project performance: The fourth dimension of project management. *PMNETwork* 9:16–21, 1995

Bringelson, Liwana S. and Rad, Pariz F. Electronic project group meetings: Taking advantage of technology. *PMNETwork* 9:26–28, 1995

Dinsmore, Paul G. The chicken and the egg of organization design: Information flow versus relationships. *PMNETwork* 7:37–38, 1993

Durrenburger, Mark, Nelson, Beebe, and Spring, Steve. Managing the external forces in new product development. *PMNETwork* 10:44–47, 1996

Harrell, Clayton W. Breaking the communication barrier with a WBS. *PMNETwork* 8:6–8, 1994

Huyler, George and Crosby, Kevin. The best investment a project manager can make . . . improve meetings. *PMNETwork* 7:33–35, 1993

Juliano, William J. External communications as an integral part of project management. *PMNETwork* 9:18–21, 1995

Kostner, Jaclyn and Strbiak, Christy. 3-D leadership: The key to inspired performance. *PMNETwork* 7:50–52, 1993

Kostner, Jaclyn and Strbiak, Christy. Openness: The gateway to top performance. *PMNETwork* 7:25–29, 1993

Knutson, Joan. How to manage a project launch meeting. *PMNETwork* 9:27–30, 1995

Maes, Jeanne D. and Mosley, Donald C. Public relations: Another advantage of partnering. *PMNETwork* 8:30–34, 1994

McMichael, John R. Boeing spares distribution center: A world-class facility achieved through partnering. *PMNETwork* 8:9–19, 1994

Melanson, Carolyn. The human side of project management. *PMNETwork* 7:27–33, 1993

Miller, Mark A. The great communicator. *PMNETwork* 9:45–46, 1995

Pinto, Jeffrey K. and Kharbanda, Om P. Project management and conflict resolution. *Project Management Journal* 26:45–53, 1995

Pomponio, P. A. Visual solutions for project success in the 21st century. *PMNETwork* 9:19–20, 1995

Reith, William Douglas. Communicating with a manufacturing plant. *PMNETwork* 9:21–25, 1995

Negotiating Skills for Project Managers

Stephen D. Owens and
Francis M. Webster, Jr.

Biographical Sketch . . . **Stephen D. Owens** is an Associate Professor of Management at Western Carolina University (WCU). He holds a Ph.D. in management, with a concentration in the fields of industrial relations and human-resource management. He teaches in the Master of Project Management Program at WCU. His research interests are in the areas of human-resource management in projects, labor relations, and dispute resolution.

Francis M. Webster, Jr., is retired after eight years as editors-in-chief of the Project Management Institute (PMI), twenty-one years of teaching at the university level, and fourteen years of industrial experience. He joined PMI in 1978 and has received all three of PMI's highest individual awards. He has authored a number of articles and papers and conducted several workshops on project management. He was responsible for the PMI Software Survey for eight years and for creating *PMNETwork*. He earned a B.S. in chemical engineering from the University of Missouri, an M.S. degree from Carnegie-Mellon University, and a Ph.D. from Michigan State University. He has had work experience with Phillips Petroleum Company, Chrysler Corporation, and H. B. Maynard and Company.

Rarely are project managers allocated all the resources needed. Thus, there is conflict on what and how many resources are going to be available to the project and on which aspects of the project they will be used. Negotiating is one of the fundamental methods to resolve conflict. The dominant mode for negotiating has often resulted in a win-lose situation or outcome. This mode has often led to disputes. Negotiating within a win-lose framework often results in costly and protracted legal proceedings, the creation of ill will, increased financial costs, and even the demise of successful witnesses. Because conflict in projects is likely to occur, perhaps it would be better to have a means to resolve conflict that can lead to win-win solutions. Improved negotiation skills can make this possible.

Negotiations in Projects

Typically the negotiation skills needed in projects are applicable in two broad domains: interpersonal negotiations and contract negotiations.

INTERPERSONAL NEGOTIATIONS

Interpersonal relationships with various project stakeholders will influence negotiations. For example, it is common for project managers to attend innumerable meetings, direct and motivate project members, obtain information, delegate, resolve conflicts, acquire resources, and set goals. All these activities involve interpersonal contacts with the following stakeholders: other project managers, customers, team members, peers, superiors, functional managers, and representatives of government and regulatory agencies. For activities characterized by interpersonal relationships, the project manager must use a variety of negotiation skills. Because project managers often have more responsibility than authority, such skills are vital for successful project completion.

Interpersonal negotiations require a skill called partnering, which is typically used in *external projects*. Essentially, a partnering mind-set can replace the adversarial relationship that often exists between the project organization and subcontractors. The former wants the deliverable at the least cost, whereas the latter tries to create a profitable outcome. The suspicions and antagonisms in this relationship lead to conflict. Partnering, however, can replace that counterproductive atmosphere with one of cooperation or accommodation. How does a project manager obtain this mind-set of partnering? All the parties in the project—the client firm and selected subcontractors—must commit to the partnering relationship. Also, they must all participate in workshops (sometimes called alignment meetings) where they will accomplish the following:

- Learn general principles of partnering
- Assess behavioral styles and personalities
- Examine communications principles and conflict resolution
- Discuss mutual interests, positions, and project needs
- Determine the participants' expectations and needs
- Jointly develop a mission statement and project charter
- Agree on the indicators for continuous quality on the project
- Develop a responsibility matrix for partnering actions
- Develop a partnering agreement to formalize the relationship

In developing the partnering agreement itself, the parties must engage in negotiation. However, because partnering is founded on mutual trust and openness, the negotiations must be nonadversarial.[1] Once the partnering agreement is negotiated, subsequent negotiations take on a different perspective, because the parties have placed all their cards face up on the table. Thus, a working relationship develops in which conflict is resolved through win–win negotiation techniques.

CONTRACT NEGOTIATIONS

Contract negotiations are generally more formal than interpersonal negotiations. They occur between a buyer who has a specific need and a seller who agrees to meet that need. Given the more formal atmosphere, the parties will exhibit different behaviors than would be apparent in the context of interpersonal negotiations.

Contract negotiations require the ability to develop a project charter. *Chartering* is the process that creates the project charter or mission statement. It is simply a written agreement between the project manager, senior management, and the functional managers who are committing resources and people to the project.[2]

Chartering is applicable to the *internal project* and includes statements about issues such as resources to be provided and reporting relationships. Negotiation occurs when developing the charter because the parties hammer out what is to be done, how it is to be done, what resources are to be used, and when resources are to be available.

The completed charter sets forth the expected project's deliverables, often including the project's schedule and budget.[3] The charter connotes that the parties have agreed upon what is expected of the various participants in the project. It also places obligations upon the parties not to make unilateral changes to the terms of the charter.

Conflict in Negotiations

Negotiations can permeate a project. The Project Management Institute's Project Management Body of Knowledge (PMBOK) outlines eight project-management functions, each of which can be sources of conflict.[4]

1. Scope: negotiations over what is to be accomplished
2. Quality: negotiations over the specific measures to be taken to ensure quality
3. Cost: negotiations over the parties' financial outcomes
4. Time: negotiations over deadlines and resources
5. Risk: negotiations over who assumes what risks
6. Human resources: negotiations over staffing
7. Contract/procurement: negotiations over cost, delivery, and specifications
8. Communications: negotiations are affected by appropriate communications of project status

Negotiation skills are needed to resolve conflicts in these areas, which can arise throughout the project's life cycle. (See Chapters 5 and 6 for discussions of life cycles.)

RESPONSES TO CONFLICT

How can a project team member respond to conflict? Responses can be placed on two dimensions: assertiveness and cooperativeness. There can be five approaches to conflict, each of which reflect different degrees of assertiveness and cooperativeness.[5] The five responses are the following:

1. *Forcing response.* Here the negotiator attempts to get all he can at the other's expense. Legitimate or coercive power may be used and negotiators try to manipulate the process to only their advantage. Overuse of this response will likely breed hostility and resentment in others.
2. *Accommodating response.* This results in others getting most, if not all, of their desired results. Negotiators who favor a friendly relationship over a tougher or more critical approach will not serve their constituencies very well over the course of negotiations.
3. *Avoiding response.* One's interests are subordinated or neglected outright to avoid conflict. Unresolved issues lead to frustration and a sense of powerlessness, and other project team members will likely seek to change the situation.
4. *Compromising response.* This represents a middle-of-the-road strategy for dealing with conflict. Resolving disputes is accomplished by reliance on "splitting the difference" between two positions; more concern is placed on expediency than on trying to seek out the best outcome.
5. *Collaborating response.* This is both cooperative and assertive and illustrates the parties' attempt to solve a problem for their mutual benefit. The focus is on the problem, not the personalities involved in the negotiations.

Which of the approaches a project manager uses will depend to a large extent on how the following questions are answered.

1. How important is the outcome to be gained?
2. How important is the past, present, and future relationship with the other party in the negotiation?[6]

Power in Negotiations

Power can give the project manager leverage over both the desired outcome and the ongoing relationship of the parties. Because the outcome of negotiations rests largely on the ability to influence another, and the ability to influence is a function of power, it is important to take a closer look at power.

SOURCES OF POWER

Power is described as the "ability to get another party to do something they ordinarily would not do by controlling the options they perceive open to them."[7] During negotiations it is important to consider how power can affect the other party, especially concerning the perception of options available to the participants. For example, an energetic and productive worker, once known as a slacker, was asked by an interviewer: "How long have you been working here?" His answer was, "Since the day they threatened to fire me." The employee's turnaround in work performance demonstrates how the use of power can influence behavior.[8] This example illustrates the use of coercive power. Six major sources of power are the following:

   1. Reward power.   This refers to the ability or attempt to use rewards to gain compliance. To obtain the desired compliance, one must be perceived to hold rewards that are desirable to the other party and that can be administered to obtain the compliance. Such rewards don't have to be tangible. For example, intrinsic rewards such as praise, recognition, and encouragement can be used to change behavior. Also, rewarding team members with desired work assignments that have visibility can be used. Reward power can be useful in negotiations to influence behavior through positive incentives.

   2. Coercive power.   This is the reverse of reward power in that one can influence the other by using punishment or taking something away. For example, construction superintendents have been known to forget to turn in a request for payment for a subcontractor who has been less than cooperative. Using coercive power is probably not as likely to produce the desired results in project negotiations. Under such circumstances, an unfavorable climate for future negotiations will likely be created. Although the use of coercive power is often counterproductive, it does occur in negotiations when tempers take over and efforts at persuasion fail.

   3. Legitimate power.   This occurs when a group organizes itself into a social system and someone is elected, born, or appointed to a position of authority in that system.[9] Engineers have power in the functional area of operations, whereas accountants have legitimacy in financial matters. Moreover, individuals can dispense rewards and punishments to solidify their position. In negotiations, the project manager must establish legitimate authority to be recognized by others in that social context.

   4. Informational power.   This refers to the ability to obtain and present relevant information that will change another's position or point of view. The project manager is privy to a large amount of information that can be used advantageously. For example, certain test results can be withheld until the appropriate time. Thus, the amount of information, where it originates, and its persuasiveness are all factors affecting the perceived power of the information. Moreover, the entire process of information exchange serves to define the context of negotiations for the parties. Essentially, information exchange serves as the primary medium for justifying one's own and the other's position, and eventually the information exchange leads to making concessions.[10]

5. Expert power. This stems from mastery of a large amount of information; it is the power of knowledge. It comes when the project manager has demonstrated competence in prior assignments or can do something better than others. For example, the project manager who can find the bug that has eluded the systems people has bargaining power. When someone has knowledge others don't have or has control of needed information, that person is accorded deference and power. The project manager who has access to information or possession of knowledge can manipulate options and exert greater control in the negotiations process.

6. Referent power. This accrues to the project manager who has personal qualities that others admire or want to emulate. Such power can also spring from building long-term relationships with others who develop trust and share common interests with one another. A project manager who possesses referent power should take precautions not to abuse it in negotiations because such power is only obtained after a long period of relationship-building founded on trust and honesty.

The review of the six sources of power should help project managers understand how power can be acquired. However, project managers must use care in exerting power. Project managers may achieve short-term goals if power is misused, but long-term relationships may be jeopardized or ruined. With this caveat in mind, the following list sets forth some guidelines for the prudent use of power.[11]

- The illusion of power can be as effective as real power in negotiations.
- It is easy to overestimate the power of the other negotiator.
- Using power exposes one to risks and costs.
- Power is affected by time constraints.
- Decisive and assertive action can create power.
- Creation of options and alternatives enhances power.
- Negotiators should not lose sight of their objectives.
- Negotiators should discover the needs and wants of the other person.

The subject of power is an extremely complicated one. One must not only be aware of its sources, but also be prudent in its application. In the context of project negotiations, the use of power can affect a project's success and a project manager's personal relationships with the team and with others involved in the project. Research has shown that effective project managers use their personal sources of power more often than do less effective ones.[12]

More Key Factors in Negotiations

Although power and its prudent application is a critical element in negotiations, other important variables must also be examined. Awareness of all the factors in negotiations lead to a better perspective on the process.

SUPPORT OF OTHERS IN PROJECT ORGANIZATION
The project manager (negotiator) is not without support from various con-stituencies. These supporters will encourage and assist in the negotiations by providing resources and reinforcing the objectives to be gained. However, where constituencies are not close to the action, they may have unrealistic expectations that could cause problems. Project managers who come to the table with the support of a savvy constituency have a distinct advantage.

TIME PRESSURES AND DEADLINES
In labor-management negotiations it is quite common for the parties to reach an accord at 11:59 on the night the labor agreement is to expire. Parkinson's Law often applies to project negotiations: They will usually take as long as the time limits given.

There are advantages to self-imposed time limits. For example, deadlines can serve to energize the parties as they approach the time limit. Deadlines can also make the granting of concessions more palatable because they were made to beat the time limits.

INTERDEPENDENCE
It is extremely important in project negotiations that the parties not forget they need each other to reach agreement. Conflict over differing needs can cloud the need to work together. What is essential to keep in mind is that the project manager must work with and through others to succeed in negotiations.

PERSONAL ATTRIBUTES
Not only is it important for a project manager to have cultivated a high degree of self-awareness, but it is also essential that she or he be able to "read" the other party. That is, knowing the personality traits and negotiating style of another can affect the manager's behavior in negotiations. Three personal qualities—persuasiveness, persistence, and integrity—are especially potent attributes that can positively affect outcomes in negotiations.[13]

ENVIRONMENTAL FACTORS
These factors include the location of the negotiations, the type of problems facing the parties (i.e., a simple, single issue vs. complex multiple issues), the parties' past relationship and negotiating record, the rules related to the agenda, and the negotiators' different approaches to negotiations.[14]

The Negotiating Process

To achieve success in negotiations, the project manager must be aware of the fundamental characteristics underpinning the process. Whether the negotia-tions involve informal circumstances or more formalized contractual exchanges, these characteristics are present. Essentially, the parties must not forget that one party cannot achieve their objectives without considering the needs of the other party.

Planning for negotiations can be divided into the following three types:

1. *Strategic planning.*   This involves defining long-range goals in negotiations and taking a position that will lead to the goals.
2. *Tactical planning.*   This is the use of steps in the short run to attain strategic goals.
3. *Administrative planning.*   This is the actual administration of negotiations, which requires forming teams, designating resource persons, preparing for caucuses, and getting information germane to the negotiations.

All three types of planning are important, and all tend to overlap during the process.

TWO KEY NEGOTIATION STRATEGIES

Two key negotiating strategies are *distributive bargaining* and *integrative bargaining*. Distributive bargaining can be described as win-lose bargaining, whereas integrative bargaining is more a mutual problem-solving solution or a win-win approach. In both, the premise is that the parties' behavior in negotiations is predicated upon how they perceive the issue(s) to be negotiated.[15]

Distributive Bargaining

The basic condition for distributive bargaining is that the issues involve goals that are in conflict. That is, resources are limited, and each side wants to gain as much of the "fixed pie" as possible and leave a smaller amount for the other. In projects where managers are vying for staff whose special expertise is also needed by others, a distributive situation occurs. Because the pie is fixed, the bargainers are likely to become more adversarial. As a result, the parties are going to hold their cards close to their chests and are likely to engage in bluffing and padding their list of demands. The parties seek to camouflage their positions and deliberately misrepresent their position. It is easy to see how conflict can be exacerbated in projects when the parties engage in distributive bargaining.

Integrative Bargaining

Also known as *problem-solving bargaining*, the integrative approach is a much more preferable negotiation strategy for bargaining in projects. It has been defined as a set of activities that help attain objectives that are not in conflict with the other party, and, therefore, can be integrated to some degree.[16] If both parties can agree that they share a common problem calling for a negotiated solution that will result in mutual benefit, then different bargaining behaviors will be needed. When project managers are involved in integrative bargaining, the resolution of the problem requires the parties to be open, honest, and willing to share information about their preferences for solutions. How does a project manager recognize whether integrative bargaining behaviors are appropriate to solve project problems? The following preconditions are important.[17]

- Common goals that are shared jointly so all will benefit
- Use of problem-solving ability
- Commitment to work with the other party
- Trust, which enables one to break down defensiveness
- Clear communication of needs
- Acceptance of others' positions as accurate and valid

It is quite important that these six preconditions exist in the project environment so that integrative bargaining can occur. When the negotiating parties perceive that problems can be solved for mutual benefit, both parties will be much more likely to adopt collaborative and cooperative behaviors. These approaches are much more likely to lead to win-win outcomes.

HOW TO OVERCOME NEGOTIATION PITFALLS

In *positional negotiations*, the parties tend to do the following:

- Become wedded to inflexible positions
- Take an inordinate amount of time to agree because initial positions are extreme
- Perceive the process as a contest of wills
- Have to deal with numerous constituencies
- Choose between hard or soft styles, both of which can be counterproductive

The following *principled negotiation* strategies can be used to overcome the deficiencies found in positional negotiations:

- Separate the people from the problem.
- Focus on interests, not positions.
- Invent options for mutual gain—or find a way to divide a pie so that each side gets the biggest half.
- Insist on using objective criteria to overcome the harsh reality of conflicting interests.

It is hoped that by using the methods of principled negotiation, project managers will fashion a worthwhile, acceptable, and wise agreement. It is especially important to separate the other party from the problem to be solved through negotiation. This will allow project managers to deal directly and empathetically with the other negotiator as a human being, thus making possible an amicable settlement.

ENDNOTES

1 Meredith, J. and Mantel. *Project Management: A Managerial Approach*, Third Edition. New York: John Wiley & Sons, Inc., 1995, pp. 254–255
2 Ibid., p. 255
3 Ibid.

4 Project Management Institute. *Guide to the Project Management Body of Knowledge.* Upper Darby, PA: Project Management Institute, 1996

5 Whetten, D. S. and Cameron, Kim. *Developing Management Skills*, Third Edition, New York: HarperCollins, 1995, p. 423

6 Lewicki, R. and Litterer, J. *Negotiation.* Homewood, IL: Irwin, Inc., 1985, p. 69

7 Ibid., p. 251

8 Brooks, E. and Odiorne, G. *Managing by Negotiations.* New York: Van Nostrand Reinhold Co., 1984, p. 62

9 Lewicki & Litterer, p. 248

10 Ibid., p. 251

11 Brooks & Odiorne, pp. 65–75

12 Youker, B. Sources of power and Influence, in *The AMA Handbook of Project Management.* Edited by Paul Dinsmore. New York: AMACOM, 1993, p. 245

13 Lewicki, R., Hiam, A., and Olander, K. Wise. *Think Before You Speak: A Complete Guide to Strategic Negotiation.* New York: John Wiley & Co., Inc., 1996, p. 43

14 Ibid., p. 47

15 Walton, R. and McKensie, R. *A Behavioral Theory of Labor Negotiations.* New York: McGraw-Hill Co., 1965

16 Ibid., p. 35

17 Lewicki and Litterer, pp. 109–114

Developing Project-Management Skills for the Future

Elvin Isgrig

Biographical Sketch . . .   **Elvin Isgrig** teaches project management at North Dakota State University (NDSU) in Fargo, North Dakota. He is also PMI's Director of Educational Services. He holds degrees in industrial engineering and management and in aeronautical and mechanical engineering. He studied for an academic year with the Boeing Company in an education-with-industry program. He concluded a 27-year career in the U.S. Air Force as Dean of the Defense Systems' Management College, after spending over two decades in the practice of project management and systems engineering. He has been teaching those topics for eighteen years.

Almost everyone works on projects in their personal or professional lives, but preparation for managing such efforts ranges from none for most, to haphazard for many, and formal for a relative few.

In the future, project-management professionals will need a broad base of forward-looking, highly responsible stewards. But project management is not yet included broadly in general education. A number of difficulties seem to exist. For example, educators and corporate managers don't understand each others' languages, according to a survey conducted by the University of Pennsylvania in 1994.[1] Employers have given up on schools, and by giving up, they've lost their ability to influence them.

In spite of the roadblocks, however, some efforts in formal training for project management have gotten underway. In 1971, David S. Packard, former Deputy Secretary of Defense and former CEO of Hewlett Packard, helped found the Defense System's Management College in Ft. Belvoir, Virginia. He persuaded Congress to establish this academy of management where the best of modern management practices are taught. That institution has been a dynamic contributor to the evolution, revolution, and export of project solutions for the needs of the age. It has graduated thousands. But the traditional academic community has been slow to emulate its lead. There are six academic project-management degree-granting programs available in the United States today. The University of Calgary has master's and doctorate programs that are not accredited.

Professional Organizations

Professional associations such as the Project Management Institute (PMI), the American Management Association (AMA), and thousands of consultants supplement the traditional academic world's lag in satisfying project management and training needs.

The PMI certification program is growing each year to the point that it is now processing thousands of applications for certification. Nearly 5,000 individuals are currently certified by PMI worldwide. The program is recognized internationally by all other leading project-management professional organizations.

PMI has over 25,000 members and its membership has been increasing by 40 percent every year. It has cooperative agreements with several specialty associations and has chapters and interest groups around the world. PMI's international conferences draw 1,500 registrants, and the conferences are growing in popularity. The association services almost that many in educational short courses at those conferences.

PMI's *Guide to the Project Management Body of Knowledge* (PMBOK) resulted from a highly collaborative Standards Committee effort that brought together the wisdom of practice from virtually every industry that has begun using project management.[2] Many who are close to the profession believe the PMBOK will become the foundation for an international standard. They also expect the development of more detailed standards for specialty industries and businesses.

Project management is gaining recognition from such organizations as Andersen Consulting Company, AT&T, Digital Equipment Corporation (DEC), IBM, Boeing, and US West Communications as they support PMI activities and encourage their employees to become involved in the organization and its certification program.

The International Project Management Association (IPMA) in Europe, the Association of Project Managers (APM) in England, and the Australian Institute of Project Management (AIPM) are the three largest and most influential organizations other than PMI.

Although project management is studied at the academic and professional levels, knowledge about the general discipline and the profession is beginning to be taught in secondary and vocational schools. PMI is focusing its efforts on establishing more collaborative partnerships with academia at all levels, including elementary and middle schools (K–8), high schools, undergraduate schools, and graduate schools.

Many PMI members are consultants and teachers. PMI has chartered an education committee, an educational specific-interest group, and an education foundation. One purpose is to reach and recruit people from academia such as presidents, vice presidents of academic affairs, deans and curriculum developers, and faculty to form partnerships for the adoption of project-management methods on their campuses and to join in the development and teaching of the discipline.

Elementary Schools

Children have a natural talent for recognizing and managing projects, according to an article in the June 1996 issue of *PM Network Magazine*.[3] The authors find that children have vivid expectations and manage the environment and resources available to win the game, conduct the party, and build the club house. They negotiate for "win-win" and show the ability to adjust constantly.

Kindergartners exhibit the skills necessary to be successful project managers. Robert Fulgham points out the necessary attributes in his book, *Uh, Oh*.[4] In a kindergarten classroom and on university campuses, the same opportunities and facilities exist, says Fulgham. Tools for reading, writing, and exploring are available in both classrooms. Students can use words, numbers, and areas devoted to scientific experimentation. The most apparent difference between the kindergartners and the college students is in the self-image of the students. Ask a kindergarten class, "How many of you can draw or sing?" and all hands go up. The children are confident in spirit, infinite in resources, and eager to learn. Everything is possible. Try those same questions on a college audience and only a small percentage will raise their hands. Those who do will want to qualify their response with limitations. What went wrong between kindergarten and college? The future of the disciplines, professions, society, and civilization may weigh upon the answers we accept. Those who hesitate to step forward haven't learned to accomplish tasks with confidence.

The college graduate represents the accumulation of the knowledge, skills, and maturity that society has agreed should be required for entry-level professional positions on career tracks. However, somewhere between kindergarten and college, attitudes tend to change from enabling optimism to crippling pessimism. Project managers who succeed exemplify Fulgam's kindergartner.

High Schools

High schools are rich with opportunities for projects that are both assigned and spontaneous. Recognition that projects are the way to develop knowledge and skills is coming ever so slowly. Eliot Wigginton in *Sometimes a Shining Moment* shares the following thoughts:

I believe there are many students capable of doing far more than they're doing. They must have the opportunity and stimulus to do so, if they are to get all from school they should. . . . They should learn responsibility. . . . The factual materials students carry away is negligible. Discipline, budgeting of time, enthusiasm, appreciation . . . are traits that they will carry with them into all they do, and assure them success both in studies and their chosen fields. Students should be given a multitude of opportunities to express themselves . . . to find their talents, and to be recognized, praised, and encouraged. There are numerous approaches to this, and there is no one right answer.[5]

Example of an Undergraduate Program

At North Dakota State University, a course called Integrated Capstone is required for a Bachelor of Science degree in industrial engineering and management. When the course was first offered, only seniors and graduate students were eligible to register. The concept of integration, like teamwork, is difficult to infuse in the last semester of the senior year. Pass-and-forget attitudes from the earlier years had to be addressed squarely. Now freshmen, sophomores, and juniors are included in a vertical sort of integration. The earlier-level students serve in subcontracting roles for seniors and graduate students. Over seven hundred students have taken those courses since 1981, and much good feedback has been received. Some companies, such as Andersen Consulting and Intel, recruit graduates because this preparation differentiates those candidates in positive ways from graduates of other institutions.

Under the program, students become part of a matrix organization and assume roles such as a member of an engineering functional-specialty department, a member of a functional-management department, or a member of an interdisciplinary project team. By working together in those positions, students learn how to carry out critical success factors such as the following:

- Performing a series of joblike activities within the typical stages of the life cycle of a project. These include analyzing market needs; making inputs to requirements and specifications for conceptual and preliminary designs; and planning for construction, installation, check out, and initiation of operations.
- Designing products and processes; selecting and laying out equipment in ways that simplify work; minimizing material handling; and protecting people, property, and the natural environment.
- Conceiving an employee acquisition, orientation, and training program in concert with the philosophy of total quality management.
- Preparing implementation plans for a manufacturing or service facility that optimizes quality, cost effectiveness, and market competitiveness. A family of processes and layouts are created, and resources are estimated that encompass a budget, schedule, and use of people.

- Communicating with departmental and project-team members, client representatives, and people with needed sources of information.
- Entering data and information and contributing to master files of sources concerning, among others, people, material, machines, and information. Descriptive information, cost estimates, and information on availability are obtained through personal research on marketing, product, and process development.
- Contributing narrative and quantitative inputs to draft and final reports for recommended approaches, resources, and courses of action.
- Making formal oral presentations of departmental and project reports to executives in their office setting. Those presentations are made using computer-generated visual aids. Students describe their class jobs, their departmental and project mission, and the results they achieve, such as designs, plans, schedules, resources, and budgets. A few members of the class are selected to make the final presentations to the executive council at an off-site conference location.

A team from the Accrediting Board for Engineering and Technology (ABET) reviewed the course in much detail. The team approved the curriculum and held seminars around the country on the design of Capstone courses. Papers on this topic have been given at conferences sponsored by PMI, Institute of Industrial Engineers (IIE), and American Society of Engineering Educators (ASEE).

Continuing Education

Continuing education forms a bridge between practice and academic degree programs. Concentrated opportunities for learning and sharing through conferences, seminars, symposiums, paper sessions, articles, publications, and exhibits are increasing. PMI offers the opportunity to register for a series of one- and two-day courses that could add up to ten continuous days of professional development.

An expanding stream and variety of continuing-education courses in project management and its subdisciplines (scope, time, cost, quality, procurement, risk, human resources, communications, and integration) are offered by vendors all over the world. According to PMI and the American Management Association, the most popular courses are those that introduce the student to the basic and integrative concepts of project management. More advanced courses offer to prepare students for the project-management professional certification examination that PMI offers.

Developing the Skills

Project management can be taught in every grade and every subject. Our educational system needs to develop leadership skills in tune with conflicting needs of project management. In *Liberation Management*, Tom Peters highlights the paradoxes of project management.[6]

- *Total ego versus no ego.* On the one hand, project managers must be consumed by the project before them. On the other hand, they must have almost no ego. They deal with many outsiders and insiders whom they can hardly command. This means the project manager must take a smaller share of the credit for accomplishments and give a larger share of the credit to other participants.
- *Autocrat versus delegator.* When the chips are down, the project manager must issue orders fast. At the same time, the project manager must turn ownership over to the contributors.
- *Leader versus manager.* Effective project managers must match their passion for inspiring others with a passion for grubby nuts and bolts of doing the job.
- *Oral versus written communication.* Communicating orally and on the run comes easily to effective project managers. But they must also be masters of the detailed plan and the daily checklist.
- *Complexity versus simplicity.* Nothing is more complex than dealing with a sophisticated, multiorganization project. The effective project manager must juggle, sometimes for years, hundreds of balls of differing and ever-changing shapes, sizes, and colors. On the other hand, the project manager must be adept at keeping it simple.
- *Big versus small.* Project managers must appreciate forests and trees equally. They must be able to see the relationship of the small to the big and the big to the small, and do so at every moment simultaneously.
- *Patience versus impatience.* Smart, independent leaders spend lots of time on relationship building and networking. This is as important as pushing project participants for action.

Outlook

Fortune Magazine declared project management a rapidly growing discipline.[7] Custom training and continuing education are moving into the voids left by academia. Meanwhile, project management is being added to academic majors; and in a relatively short time, project management will be added to the general-education curricula at every level of education. Those who have completed their formal academic education are improving professional skills with more training in this area. For example, people with specialties in fields where there is significant unemployment, such as architects in the United Kingdom, openly seek project-management training to enable them to reenter the job market.

ENDNOTES
1 National Center on the Education Quality of the Work Force, University of Pennsylvania. First National Survey of Hiring, Training and Management Practices in America. Aug./Sept. 1994
2 Duncan, William, ed. *Guide to Project Management Body of Knowledge.* Upper Darby, PA: Project Management Institute, 1996

3 Mars, Lavy and Ross, Joseph D. Child-like lessons for the adult-like project manager: Why my eight-year-old is a better project manager than I. *PMNetwork Magazine*, June 1996

4 Fulgham, Robert. *Uh, Oh*. New York: Villard Books, 1991

5 Wigginton, Eliot. *Sometimes a Shining Moment*. New Providence, NJ: Reed Elsevier, 1993

6 Peters, Tom. *Liberation Management*. New York: Alfred Knopf, 1992

7 Stewart, Thomas W. The corporate jungle spawns a new species: The project manager. *Fortune Magazine* Vol 132 No. 179, 1995

Project Oversight

How to Monitor and Evaluate Projects

James R. Snyder

Biographical Sketch . . .

James R. Snyder is Associate Director of Planning & Business Management, Strategic Product Development, at SmithKline Beecham Pharmaceuticals. He has thirty-seven years of experience in computer sciences, operations research, international marketing, marketing administration, and finance, within the pharmaceutical industry. He is a project-management practitioner who has been involved in developing and implementing systems as well as using project-management skills in a wide variety of projects since 1969. He is a Founder of the Project Management Institute; a Fellow of the Institute; a past Executive Director, President, and Chairman of the Board; and an active participant in the activities of the Institute. Mr. Snyder is a member of the Delaware Valley Chapter of PMI and the Pharmaceuticals Special Interest Group. He is also a member of the Publications Board of the Institute.

In the life of every project there is a point where the project has been defined, the life cycle planned, the work-breakdown structures (WBS) prepared, the activities scheduled, the costs estimated, and the team motivated. Like it or not, the project manager is faced with the real world and must now take some action to monitor project activity and evaluate the impact of both project activity and the project environment on project objectives.

There remains at least one significant issue to be resolved by project managers. The issue is whether to be concerned with monitoring and evaluating project progress. Some projects might not require monitoring processes and others will demand state-of-the-art computer systems to track their complex activities. Where monitoring is required, it is only to identify change and appropriate reactions. Monitoring, evaluating, and reacting to the real world is a project in itself. One must consider objectives and plan how to meet them as one would for any other project. This plan becomes the project control plan.

This chapter deals with the *monitoring* and *control* parts of the loop shown in Figure 23–1. At this point in the project, emphasis becomes much more important than process. All projects will be managed; it is the amount of emphasis on the control part of a project that clearly distinguishes it from other projects. Here we will look at the emphasis on control and see how it affects management of the project.

EXAMPLE.   A computer-systems project involving the implementation of a new version of a piece of software was recently undertaken by an administrative group. Although it had some knowledge of major networked software systems, the group really did not have vast systems-implementation experience. It did have good project-management skills in the team and set about using those skills to deal with the unknown. The team devoted lots of time and analytical ability defining what had to be done, how it would be done, and who would do it. At the end of the exercise, the team had a plan that was reviewed by knowledgeable systems analysts, and their comments and suggestions were incorporated in the plan.

The result was a very simple-minded plan, both to the team and to the analyst who had critiqued it. The plan was so simple and straightforward that

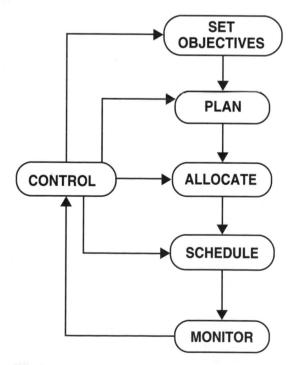

FIGURE 23–1   Project Process Flow

it was not referred to again throughout the very successful implementation of the project. Here the emphasis was on the planning aspects of the project, not on the monitoring and control processes.

In another part of the same implementation project, the team was faced with the shutdown of one facility, the movement of equipment to a new location, and start-up at the new location. The process was not complex, the activities were well-defined, and the timing was based on lots of experience. Here again, emphasis played a major role in the way the project was managed. The planning process, or how to do the job, was not as important as the control and monitoring process. If each part of the project did not occur within the planned time frame, the planned restart at the new location would not occur. It was important to monitor each step of the process to ensure that the planned time parameters were being met and that the final delivery of operational systems would happen on time. In these two cases, the emphasis shifted from process, in the first example, to control in the second.

It is important to know where to put the emphasis in the monitoring and control phases of any project. If no actions will be taken as a result of collecting information about project status, or if the knowledge of the real-world happenings cannot be applied to future projects, then the use of resources to monitor and evaluate project status may not be justified. Too often the nature of the project, or the politics surrounding it, preclude any change to a plan once it has been set. Measuring and evaluating change in a simple, small project will consume more time than may be required for the completion of the remaining project activities. The resources used for monitoring and evaluating project progress may be the same resources allocated to the project, thus diverting resources required for a timely completion of the project.

Not all projects require full-scale monitoring. Project managers should decide if monitoring is needed before the project starts. Small computer-systems development projects often suffered from overcontrol and over-monitoring. Using project skills to define application objectives and to identify key activities and their resource requirements may be all that is needed to ensure that an application-development project is brought quickly to completion. Knowing when it is enough to plan and schedule a project, and then to work the plan, is a learned skill based on experience. New project managers often become discouraged early in their careers by trying to use all of the components of major project-management systems for all of their projects. However, where the opportunity exists for changes to plans, schedule improvements, new resource allocations, or even revisions to the project objectives, monitoring and evaluation become key project-management components.

Other classic reasons to monitor project progress include:

- Contracts may require progress reports for payment.
- Major changes to project objectives may be necessary once the project is underway.

- The size and complexity of a project often demands that progress be tracked to ensure that major milestones and interfaces are met.
- Key resources, not activity progress, are the project driver.

Each of these reasons for monitoring and evaluating project progress calls for a different approach to the collection of information and to evaluation and action. Change is the one sure element in every project. Successful project managers are well prepared if they know what changes they want to measure, how they want to measure them, and what they will do with the results.

The Monitoring and Evaluation Process

The decision to monitor project progress is made early in the project life cycle. It is based on a determination that knowledge of progress can result in changes to any of the following:

- *Activity duration:* The length of time future activities will require and their impact on project completion
- *Resource allocation:* The way in which money, materials, equipment, and people are assigned to uncompleted tasks
- *Project logic:* Revisions to the sequence in which work is performed
- *Objectives:* Modification of the defined completion of the project and its deliverables

If none of these project components can be directly changed by evaluating actual progress, then monitoring may not be cost effective. Once it is determined that the results of project monitoring can result in project change, the monitoring process becomes very important.

The output from the process of monitoring progress is information that either confirms the original assumptions about the planning, scheduling, cost, and resource requirements or suggests that the original assumptions were not valid. Depending on the extent of the variances from original estimates, the original objectives and plans may be changed, slightly or significantly, at each point where progress is monitored.

THE VIRTUAL PLAN
One of the most difficult lessons for new project managers is that they will almost never begin with an accurate project plan. As quickly as decisions are made on the knowledge obtained from the project-monitoring cycle, actions are taking place in the project environment that further change the project plan. When this continually changing complex environment consisting of logic, time, cost, resources, and project politics is captured at a moment in time and evaluated, it is called a project update. However, while the project manager is struggling with these complex interactions and making decisions on the basis of observer changes, additional changes are continuing to take place. Dealing with change is a prime responsibility of a project manager. This

ability to deal with alterations is a measure of a good project manager and is one of the reasons they are often hard to find.

EXAMPLE. An experienced construction manager responsible for a major pharmaceutical-laboratory renovation project was having trouble dealing with the concepts of project management. At the same time, his young planner was trying to apply network-based planning to the project. Frustration was evident on the part of the construction manager when he was given a weekly update that showed a slight, but different, completion date for the project than the week before. After one particularly long and difficult meeting with subcontractors, the construction manager bellowed at his planner that if he kept changing the completion date he might get it right when the project was over. Here was a clear case where no action was resulting from monitoring and there was no appreciation of the virtual nature of a project plan. Sometimes the changing nature of a plan is understood by the customer and becomes the reason for rejection of monitoring processes and even for rejecting planning systems. Although heard less frequently, now than in the past, "Why should I plan, it will just change," was a classic reason to reject project-management processes.

Realization that project change is constant regardless of action, or lack of action, is the first major step to making appropriate use of the knowledge derived from progress monitoring. Equally important is acceptance that project updates are only snapshots of a moment in the project life cycle.

At each point of review, new estimates should be made on the basis of the ever-changing knowledge around the activities in question. If this new data is quickly included in the plan and its impact is evaluated appropriately, the importance of initial accuracy in the plan can be reduced. It is always better to have a best-guess estimate that is identified as a guess and that can be changed as the project progresses than to have no estimate because it could not be determined accurately.

THE IMPORTANCE OF MONITORING AND EVALUATION

Project-management systems offer many different types of information even before a project starts. They help identify, clarify, and communicate project objectives and scope. They provide methods for quick visualization of difficult concepts, help determine the practicality of ventures, and aid in the identification of time and resource requirements. However, once a project is under way and things are happening, it is the monitoring, evaluating, and response processes that become the project drivers. The processes for monitoring and evaluating the status of projects are as important to the project as the processes for developing schedules or building project teams. Often very large projects come with dictated project-control systems imposed by owners or large corporations on all of their projects. These systems are usually designed to ensure that preconceived milestones are met regardless of their meaning to the true management of the project. Monitoring and evaluation for the sake of reporting is of little value to those who are truly interested in bringing about change as a result of measuring the real world. Little in this chapter will be of further value if the project manager is not willing to plan the systems to manage the project with the same dedication that the project itself is planned. A measure of the commitment to nonmandated project monitoring is the extent of the commitment of resources (time, people, and money) to planning the monitoring and evaluation processes. If project managers are not willing to commit resources to the monitoring, evaluating, and reacting cycle, they are not serious about control.

WHAT TO MONITOR

The question is not what to monitor as much as where to place the emphasis. Project activities are completed through the application of resources to a defined task. The task progress is measured by determining the amount of each resource consumed over a defined period compared with the amount remaining to complete the task. One or more resources may be the key to activity completion. Other resources may be dependent on, or linked to, the key resource. This key resource determines activity progress. For example, the setting of poured concrete in a construction project is an activity almost completely dependent on the resource, *time*. Creation of a promotional brochure cover as part of an advertising project is much more dependent on the resource, *design*. In general, key resources are time, money, materials, and skills. Of course, a long list of very specialized resources may be required for any project. The list will differ even within a group of similar projects.

Knowledge of what is truly important to the owner or stakeholder is the best guide to knowing what must be monitored. So significant is this piece of information that it should be a part of the defined project objective. The objective for a systems-development project might look like the following example.

EXAMPLE.   "The objective of the 'Quick Connect' project is to design, develop, and implement a computer backbone capable of interfacing the administrative, engineering, and financial operations at the five major plants of X-Company. Quality and reliability of the system are the most important criteria. Although time and cost are significant factors, success will be measured in terms of the reliability of the installed system."

This statement leaves little about doubt that the monitoring and evaluation process should not permit the sacrifice of quality-assurance testing throughout the project to save time or money. Of course the statement of objectives could go on to include limits to the other major resources, including time and money. The point is that without knowing what is important to the owner or customer, it is not possible to design appropriate reactive processes to monitor the project.

Very similar projects can have significantly different objectives and therefore very different monitoring processes. In any industry where innovation is key to financial success, the definition of what to monitor on two development projects is quite different if one of the projects leads to an innovative new project in a highly competitive market versus a development project in a less competitive market. In the first case, time is likely to be the major objective, with cost the second objective. The development of products in less competitive markets may be allowed more time, if cost to completion can be reduced.

EXAMPLE.   The monitoring of progress against time was a prime objective in the contractor rebuilding of a fire-damaged section of I-195 near Philadelphia. The project contract had as its major objective the restoration of full use of the highway as soon as possible. To emphasis the importance of this objective, a $30,000 *per day* penalty/bonus related to project completion was part of the contract. Careful monitoring with emphasis on the management of the time resource was part of the project plan.

Know What Is Finished

The completion of activities, tasks, milestones, and subprojects are key events that are included in the monitoring process. Knowing when one of these events is completed is a significant piece of the monitoring the evaluation process.

It is very difficult to be just a little bit dead. However, some activities and even projects are a little bit finished for long periods of time. There is probably some reason for concern if an activity moves to 90 percent completion in ten weeks and requires thirty weeks to complete the last 10 percent. Progress cannot be monitored if completion of components is not recognizable. Project managers need to monitor the consumption of resources related to time, with emphasis on those resources that are key to meeting definable activity end points.

Just as a project has a definable start and end point, so must every one of the project components. If this very basic rule is violated in the planning process, monitoring progress is much more difficult than if activity definitions have been clearly set out and agreed upon.

Time as a Special Resource

Two key parts of the project-monitoring plan are the measures of resource consumption and the measure of work-unit completion. To measure work unit/activity completion, it becomes important to understand the very special properties of time. Time is often the sole measure of activity progress. Although it is a separate measure in the monitoring process, time is also a resource. Why not, then, be concerned only with the definition and measurement of resources, time included, rather than introduce a concept of activity progress/completion monitoring as a separate consideration? The answer is that time is a very special resource. There is no known way to increase or decrease the rate at which this resource is used. Where time is a limiting factor, no amount of money or application of other resources can buy more time. Time is also a limiting factor when exceeding the available time results in a consequence that is not tolerable to the project stakeholders. Another special property of time is that once a project starts, time is used at a constant rate. Although we can stop the consumption of other resources, time continues to be used, and past time cannot be recovered to be used again!

The term *buying more time* has little to do with time-limited projects. Time is not for sale in these cases. What is being bought is a delay in delivery of a project that was never time-dependent in the first place. This is a question of negotiating completion objectives rather than resource allocation. The penalty/bonus clause is the closest a project manager may ever come to buying or selling time. Penalty/bonus clauses are completion negation exercises up to the point that the penalty cannot be tolerated. At that point, time becomes a limiting factor—no more time can be "bought."

EXAMPLE.   People who manage events live every day with time as the key controller of their projects. Once a date has been set for a major convention, symposium, sporting event, or other fixed-time project, time becomes the controller. In the ever-changing business of international exhibit management, the one, and often only, factor that is certain is that the doors to the convention hall will open at the designated time. Late arrival of the exhibit can be fixed by using more people to assemble the exhibit. Loss of handout material can be rectified by purchasing more. Even a change in marketing direction can be dealt with by altering exhibit design and sale training. However, the one factor that is for sure on that day is when the doors will open. Project managers should know as much as possible about the true time constraints on a project. They need to decide whether time is really a limiting factor and be aware of the inflexibility of the time resource.

WHEN TO MONITOR

Because project plans are always changing, continual activity-monitoring is ideal. But the size of most projects is often the major reason to reject continual activity-monitoring as the template for most projects. The resources available to control projects have limits just like the resources used by the project being monitored. The factors contributing to the establishment of a monitoring plan include the following:

- Management information needs
- Acquisition of new activity information
- Changes in resource mix
- Occurrence of major events
- Passage of time

Each of these contributes to the determination of when and how often activity or work-unit completion and resource consumption should be measured. The criteria used to further determine when updating of project status should occur are easy to identify. Some are determined by factors that are not within the control of the project team. Other criteria are established by events happening in the real world that have a significant impact on project status. Another very important group of criteria leading to the determination of status reporting are those criteria completely at the discretion of the project manager and the project team. These criteria for monitoring are likely to be significant because they represent those things that the project team thinks are important. By looking at the criteria in light of the identifiable events, it is easy to see when to take that all-important snapshot of the project for evaluation and reaction.

Management Information Needs

Most companies and large projects have them. They are called by different names in different industries and in different professions. However, they are all mandated systems that attempt to give a small group of top-level people a clear, uncomplicated view of the status of major projects for which they ultimately have responsibility. Usually the information that is desired by these people or groups is extremely simple and straightforward. They want to know if their commitments to stakeholders, investors, partners, and customers will be delivered as defined, on time and at the projected level of resource (dollar) consumption. These people are project owners. Given positive assurance that the set of objectives to which they are committed are being met on a regular basis, they will leave the daily problems to the project team. If, on the other hand, this group thinks that the reliability of project completion is in jeopardy, they will be on the project team like bears to honey.

The project components that are of interest to the owner group may not be of logical importance to the work that follows or to the decisions about future resource allocation. They may only represent the completion of groups of work that are significant to an owner.

EXAMPLE.   Although completion of 85 percent of the construction of a strip mall in a small town may be of no significance to the construction-project manager, it might be a key event in the eyes of the owners in that it defines a point at which additional investors may be willing to join the project.

A key event is a milestone, and regardless of how they are defined, or for whom they have significance, they are events whose status should be captured. Many milestones in nonconstruction projects signal availability of information to other systems. They are established primarily as information-system links and trigger wide ranges of activity both within a project and in other projects. When one of these key items is completed, it is of interest to many different management levels because it indicates a new project phase, a shift of resource emphasis, or a critical decision point in the project. Where milestones have been defined in a project plan, activity should be measured and project status evaluated when they are reached.

Acquisition of New Activity Information

Way back in the planning phase of a project, the big problems were to define what activities were required to meet the project objectives, the resources that would be required, and how long these activities would take. Whereas others emphasize the accuracy of the activity definition, the reliability of resource allocation, and the precision of time estimating, the truly important issue was to develop a plan that best represented reality, as it was known at that point in time. In the planning phase it was important to use the best estimating skills available without being overcome by a demand for complete accuracy. Less than precise estimates can be tolerated for two reasons. First, no matter how good the estimates are, the real world will be different. For this reason, good project managers are always ready to deal with the reality of their projects as the days and weeks move forward. The performance of project managers is measured not by how good the estimates were, but by how well the project team can respond to the real environment. Second, the planning and control cycle continually offers the opportunity to change the elements of a project plan as the real situation changes. The capability to identify new information and incorporate it in the project plan is critical to managing a project.

The classic reason for creative people to resist the application of project-management systems to their work has always been that creative work "just happens." It cannot be managed because it cannot be planned with any degree of accuracy. Good project managers counter these arguments by explaining that it is not nearly as important to get the initial estimates right (within acceptable limits of reality and available resources) as it is to identify and report change as it occurs.

It is most important to identify when a point has been reached at which new information is available, and at which knowledge has increased so that including it in the project plan adds value. At this point it is critical that plans be updated with new information. It is more important to record change and react to new information as a project progresses than to be dead right in the planning phase.

Change in Resource Mix
It is very important to the successful completion of a project to be aware of the changing resource mix. Every activity in a project has a real or implied resource assignment. In some projects, resources are not assigned to activities. However, the type of activity may imply a particular resource assignment. Some tasks can only be accomplished by a crew of three; others may require two people plus special equipment. Every activity has an optimum, normal, and crash resource assignment. Any change in either the quantity or quality of resource assignments to activities can change the completion profile for the project. An obvious example of this type of change is the removal of a key person—say the lead market planner—on a strategic marketing-plan development project. The result can be either a change in the direction of the project, or an increase in duration, based on the quality and experience of the replacement.

Unlike changes in the time to accomplish an activity, or the change in logic, change in resource mix is often difficult to detect. Unless the resource is money and has been significantly cut or increased, processes must be in place to identify and monitor the changing resource mix.

Occurrence of Major Events
The completion of a major event is significant in the project life cycle and should be used as an opportunity to collect data about the project and review its status/progress.

Completion of an event can be either a positive or a negative occurrence as viewed by the project manager. If an event completes ahead of schedule, it offers the opportunity to improve time performance, reduce cost, or make other significant resource allocations. It may even offer the opportunity to modify project objectives or change project-completion logic. If completion is behind schedule, all of the opportunities become essential elements of a review aimed at returning the project to the scheduled completion.

Passage of Time

Although it is hard to imagine, there are a number of projects that do not have defined reporting points, changes in resource mix, occurrence of major events, or the discovery of new information occurring over reasonable time periods.

EXAMPLE.   The development of a trademark is a good example of this type of project. At the beginning of the project, there are many activities dealing with name definition, language conditions, name development, preliminary screening, focus groups, and name selection. Then comes a period after filing where very little happens for as much as eighteen months. Names are published and a response period for objections takes place. The question is, with no activity over an eighteen-month period, is any monitoring required? Even when nothing appears to be happening, project status should be monitored on some routine schedule to be sure that changes have not surfaced in the expected progress through a long period of inactivity. It is much better to know that a number of negative reactions are being received to a trademark filing as they occur than to learn of them when the period for objection expires.

The project manager may want to consider reviewing project status on the basis of the passage of time only (once a month) even if there is little or no activity.

WHO MONITORS PROJECT STATUS

Many projects require that progress be monitored by third-party teams. Although these groups can collect data, analyze it, and prepare reports, they are not usually able to take action to change project progress. Of course, they do make recommendations to project teams and owners.

The only group that truly can evaluate the impact of information collected in the monitoring process is the project team. Members of the project team must have responsibility to monitor their own activity, evaluate the information they collect, and recommend action to the team or project owner on the basis of their analysis.

Project team members are stakeholders in a project. They have participated in the definition of tasks and have identified the logic and resource requirements. The team has been a part of the definition of project objectives. They are best equipped to interpret what is really happening in the project and prepare appropriate responses. Where third-party monitoring is used, it often leads to unrealistic evaluations of status, inappropriate recommendations, and costly changes to project plans. Without a stake in the project, it is difficult to see and react to changes as they occur.

HOW TO MONITOR

It would seem to be quite easy to monitor project progress: One merely needs to go out and look at what is happening and compare actual progress to the plan. The problem is that just looking at what is happening is not as easy to do as it is to say. Monitoring is plagued by two major problems. First, there is always the question of the accuracy of the information collected. The second major problem is the way the information is presented. Understanding these two potential trouble spots will make the process of collecting and reporting project progress less difficult.

The purpose of monitoring a project is to learn as much as possible about what is happening in the project environment *now*. It is not about what would be nice to happen, what happened yesterday, or what may happen in the next few weeks. Monitoring is real, here, and now. By the time events start to happen in a project, the processes to capture the activity must be in place and the project team must be ready to act on the information.

Accuracy and Project Monitoring

The very best project team, with a well-defined project objective, adequate resources, and a sound logic plan, will fail without accurate information. Risks are taken in the planning phase of a project and it is acceptable to be unsure of the exact logic, time, or resource requirements as the plan develops. It is not acceptable to find that reporting of project status is not accurate. The decisions leading to successful and timely completion of a project are based on a cascade of snapshots, and the monitoring process must be the camera that captures reality.

EXAMPLE.   A number of years ago, when computers were big and had their own rooms, a major project was undertaken to build a billing and inventory system for a major department-store chain. The project was complicated by reliance on the development of an advanced computer hardware system to capture point-of-sale information. Two projects, one an owner-initiated software system and the other a vendor-supplied hardware system, were to progress in parallel. They were very interrelated projects and, at the time, few management processes were available to support monitoring. All went well for months. Regular status meetings showed that the projects were meeting the milestones and tracking nicely toward simultaneous completion.

As the two projects neared completion, it became evident that the accuracy of some of the reports was not very good. In fact, the hardware project lagged in both speed of development and expected quality of the emerging product. The situation became so bad that the whole project was aborted at significant loss to both participants. The key lesson is that, although accurate knowledge of the status of the project might not have changed the outcome, it might have contributed significantly to reduced loss.

A monitoring system must be able to identify the expected parameters, collect the data, check that the data is correct, review the data to see that it falls within expected limits, and check one more time to be sure. This process will ensure that the decisions made about future activity or resource allocation are based on reality. Those who monitor activity uncover the inevitable deviations from plans and schedules and must be relied upon to report what they observe, not what they would like to observe. Accurate observation and timely reporting are key to the most important step in project monitoring: reaction to change. If monitoring is not accurate, it can be more damaging to project control than no information at all.

Presentation of Information for Analysis
To simply collect information about the progress of a project by reporting completion and partial completion of activities is not enough to evaluate the status of a project. It does not present a meaningful snapshot. Even the careful evaluation of the type and rate of resource consumption is not enough for a full understanding of status. Monitoring is related to ensuring that the project will meet its objectives. Like all other aspects of a project, the objectives may change as the project progresses. To identify a set of activities leading to an objective and monitor progress toward that objective is only half the responsibility of the project team.

Monitoring includes the total project environment. The project team identifies changes in objectives themselves, the tool set available to meet the objectives, the mix, availability, the cost of resources, and the political climate in which the project is operating. The nonactivity, nonresource assigned elements can have as important an impact on the status and direction of a project as any of the planned components. Failure to consider the total project environment at any point in the monitoring process can eliminate opportunities to redefine a project to the advantage of owners and stakeholders. A checklist might be helpful to guide those monitoring progress to consider environmental issues. However, a specific list might serve to defeat the purpose. Monitoring should consider any factor that can influence the project.

EXAMPLE. A company was taking a risk and spending money to bring its toy dump truck to market ahead of the competition. As the team's project moved forward, it was critical to know that the competitor had gone out of business. This significant event would certainly have an impact on the way activities were to be scheduled and resources allocated for the remainder of the project. It was unlikely that the collapse of the competition was an activity whose progress was part of the monitoring plan. Competitive factors and a long list of other things that comprise the project environment can be as critical as any of the planned activities and must be included in the monitoring process.

HOW TO EVALUATE PROJECT STATUS
Three steps make up the project-status evaluation process:

1. Establish the evaluation parameters and the status window.
2. Evaluate time and resource consumption against planned activity.
3. Identify environmental factors and their impact.

Evaluation Parameters and Status Window

Even in a small project the parameters and status window are considered and endorsed at the start of every evaluation. It is important to confirm the relative importance of cost, time, logic, resources, and objectives at each update period. Without reconfirmation of the status parameters, it is possible for a project to drift away from the agreed emphasis discussed in the planning phase.

It also makes sense to define the *status window*. Although this concept is more critical to long and large projects, it should be considered. The status window is the time between monitoring and reporting dates. The length of this period is determined by the following:

- Amount of activity underway
- Occurrence of milestones or key events
- Criticality of resources to project objectives

The window is that next segment of the project that will be most influenced by the information collected in the monitoring process. Of course, it is possible that the analysis of the project status will call for changes to the project far in the future. However, it is most likely that near-term actions will be indicated more frequently. The window is the width of a project snapshot. It is not a fixed period and should change as the project demands. Why update every week if no activity is taking place?

Accuracy of all aspects of the project plan are related to their proximity to time now. In a very long project, it is not productive to make minor changes to logic, timing, and resource allocations to all the activities in the plan at every update. It is much more productive to concentrate the analysis on the next window or next few windows in the plan.

Evaluate Time and Resource Consumption

Here appropriate scheduling tools are used to produce a new plan and schedule based on an accurate analysis of the observed status of activities and resources. Comparison can now be made between the plan generated from the previous status review and the new plan and schedule. This mechanical/analytical process either confirms previous decisions or presents options to improve the project plan. The options and opportunities surfacing from the comparison of the plan to the actual situation is the basis for the decision-making steps that follow.

Identify Environmental Factors

The evaluation of the environment confirms that the playing field is still level or that it has shifted in one direction or another. Events that may alter every aspect of a project, including its basic objectives, can happen at any snapshot in the monitoring and control process. These events are so significant that they must be part of every project review. This step confirms that the assumptions about the factors influencing this project are the same as they were when the project was last evaluated. If not, their impact on the project must be considered.

Often the answers to these questions are very subjective and require careful consideration. They are also often critical to the decision process related to change. Change in the environment is often the cause of project failure. It is key to knowing the real status of any project. (See Chapters 15 and 16.)

Subjective measurement of changes in the environment may be as critical as late completion of an activity or change to project activity logic. Project managers need to evaluate the environment every time they measure project status.

Analysis of project status gives the project team an array of options and opportunities. It is not a device to measure performance of team members.

WHAT TO DO WITH STATUS RESULTS

With a clear picture of project status, the project team is in a position to act on their options and opportunities. Making actions responsive to observed actual situations requires a trip back in the planning process. Depending on what has actually happened, it may be necessary to reenter the planning process at any one or more of the key process flow points, as shown in Figure 23-2.

The information from the monitoring process may indicate that it is only necessary to enter the process at the *Allocate Resources* level. This indicates that the project definition and plan has not changed but better use of resources

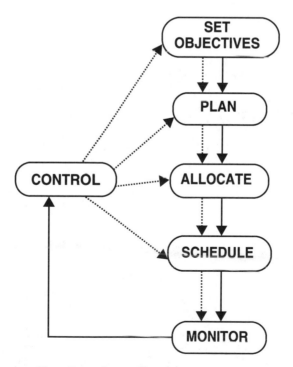

FIGURE 23-2   Process Flow-Reacting to Change

is indicated. Other data may show that it is necessary to reconsider how the remaining work should be performed. Replanning may be necessary. The monitoring process identifies changes to the basic project objectives. The opportunity to revise plans is often lost and results in an unexpected end point.

If actions require entry into the project-planning flow at any point, then all the points that follow in the process flow must be reconsidered. If replanning of project logic (*Plan*) is indicated, then it will be necessary to review the impact on the allocation of resources (*Allocate Resources*), and generate a new schedule (*Schedule*). It may be helpful to list the proposed actions resulting from monitoring status and identify the entry point in the process flow so that consideration of all the appropriate steps will be included in the revised plan. Changes in a project can require redefinition of objectives, replanning, reallocation of resources, and rescheduling. Key to what is required is where the process flow in Figure 23–2 for project monitoring is entered.

The end point of the whole monitoring and evaluation process is a new plan. As soon as that plan exists, the process begins again with the establishment of the next point in time or the next event that will activate the process.

BIBLIOGRAPHY

Ahuja, H. *Construction Performance Control by Network*. New York: John Wiley & Sons, Inc., 1976

Cleland, David I. *Project Management Strategic Design and Implementation*. Pennsylvania: TAB Professional and Reference Books, 1990

Martin, Charles C. *Project Management: How to Make It Work*. New York: Amacom, 1976

O'Brien, James J. *Scheduling Handbook*. New York: McGraw-Hill Book Company, 1969

Pinto, Jeffrey K. *Successful Information System Implementation: The Human Side*. Upper Darby, PA: Project Management Institute, 1994

Rosenau, Milton D., Jr. *Successful Project Management*. Lifetime Learning Publications, 1991

Stuckenbruck, Linn C. *The Implementation of Project Management*. Addison-Wesley Publishing Company, 1981

Willoughby, Norman. *Incredibly Easy Project Management*. London: NWM, 1994

What to Include in Project-Management Information Systems

Daniel F. Green

Biographical Sketch . . .

Daniel F. Green is a staff member of Carnegie Mellon University's Software Engineering Institute. His current focus is introducing software project-management process techniques and methods that support the software-engineering discipline. Mr. Green completed a U.S. Air Force military career in the administrative and information-systems areas, holds an M.B.A, and was previously a Research Fellow with MIT's Center for Information Systems Research. Mr. Green is affiliated with the Project Management Institute (PMI) as a member and as project leader for developing the Information Systems extension to PMI's Project Management Body of Knowledge.

A project-management information system (PMIS) is critical to a project because it is one of the primary delivery vehicles of project management. It is a means of building relationships and trust that lead to productivity and effectiveness. In building this communication link, the PMIS integrates and distills project data into a management description of a project's performance. Every project has the potential to produce large volumes and multiple varieties of data. This data is essential for managing the project but, in its raw form, is not useful for supporting management decisions. The role of the PMIS is to add value by selectively molding the project's data into information products for managing the project, reporting, and decision making. Automation usually supports a significant portion of the tasks associated with operating a PMIS. In practice, manually performed tasks may be found at various points along the PMIS information path.

Management Milestones

There are a few times during the project life cycle when all the divergent activities and processes related to a project converge at the same moment of the project's life cycle. These moments normally occur during management milestone decisions to initiate, plan, execute, or terminate the project. At these milestone decisions, there is a focus on providing a synthesis of information and a comprehensive snapshot of the project's profile. When a PMIS is designed to support milestone decisions, it is aligned with the decision makers through their leadership perspective and with every other element of the project involved in the milestone decision. Also, if the PMIS can provide the information needs for a milestone decision, it will usually provide the information necessary to manage the intermediate tasks leading to the milestone.

Define Requirements Before Planning the Project

A PMIS cannot effectively provide what isn't designed into its products. Before a project can be planned, the PMIS products for decision making and status reporting must be established both at the project level and with the project's stakeholders. For example, some U.S. government agencies specify project reporting content, format, and report frequency in requests for proposal, long before the government supplier begins project planning. If the requirements for PMIS products are not established before the project is planned, the information available from the project plan may not be sufficient to describe the project's baseline profile.

There can be heavy penalties for not establishing a project's PMIS products at the beginning of the project life cycle. The most significant risk is the potential for decisions based on inappropriate information. A second risk is friction between the project team members and stakeholders because of a mismatch of expectations for information. A third risk is the unanticipated cost of replanning or manually extrapolating data from the plan to correct deficiencies related to the stakeholders' information needs. It is unreasonable to expect the project-planning data to seren-dipitously match management and stakeholder needs. Without a PMIS, the information available for determining a project's status is typically incomplete and lacks a full ability to mitigate these risks in a comprehensive way.

The PMIS development path shown in Figure 24–1 depicts the sequence of first defining the PMIS requirements, then planning the project, and finally using the PMIS products. As shown, the PMIS requirements come from both internal and external stakeholders and from the information needed to support management decisions. The initial PMIS product is the baseline profile, which uses project-planning data to describe the project. The baseline project profile becomes the standard of comparison that actual project performance is measured against as the project progresses. The project's actual performance, represented by the current project profile, is the basis for predicting future project trends that include the project's cost at completion and the project's completion date.

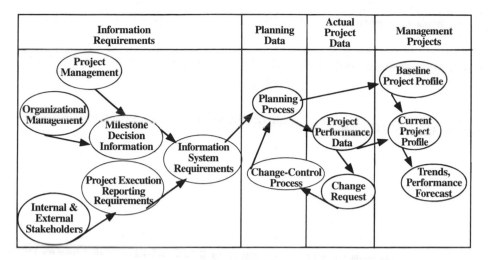

FIGURE 24-1   Project Management Information System Development Path

The Five Basic Elements of PMIS Products

Specifications for PMIS products are derived from answering the fundamental project-management questions in the following areas:

1. *Progress:*   What is the status of the project's accomplishments compared with its scheduled commitments?
2. *Cost:*   What is the status of actual costs compared with budgeted costs?
3. *Effort:*   What is the actual effort used by the project compared with the budgeted effort?
4. *Quality:*   What is the level of deficiencies compared with standards and previous projects?
5. *Stability:*   How many changes have been made to the project's requirements and to the processes used to develop the project's product? How does this level of change compare with the change levels anticipated by the project plan?

The information requirements for every project are a variant of these five basic questions of project management. The resulting management profile describes the current project status and points toward future trends. The information products developed from these five areas provide the intelligence essential to effectively and efficiently manage projects.

Tailoring the PMIS to a Specific Project

Tailoring PMIS products is important for matching the PMIS to both a specific project and to that project's organization. Before planning begins, there are three tailoring tasks that should be considered. These tasks are the following:

1. Defining data items to ensure an integrity of meaning
2. Establishing the level of detail needed for data items
3. Defining the time duration of work packages

Tailoring PMIS products in these three areas promotes a harmony where the data input to the PMIS is a natural consequence of performing project tasks or is derived from data already provided through existing organizational information systems, such as a financial tracking system.

DEFINING DATA TO ENSURE INTEGRITY OF MEANING
Defining the data items is essential to ensure an integrity of what data items mean to management and stakeholders. Defining the data items is also essential to ensure the integrity of the resulting project profile. For example, if an organizational financial system provides cost-tracking support for a project, it would be important for the project and the financial system to use the same definition for the data elements. The definition of costs associated with people's effort frequently includes more categories than salary and benefits. Also, people's overtime effort may not include additional vacation, retirement, or health-benefit costs. The practical test for data consistency is being able to produce PMIS management products by comparing apples to apples; that is, comparing baseline and actual project data that have a consistent definition.

ESTABLISHING THE LEVEL OF DETAIL FOR DATA ITEMS
The detail level of planned work packages should fit the project task being performed. There are two considerations. The first consideration is expense; detail is expensive to plan and expensive to maintain. However, a counterbalancing consideration is that detail can reduce the guesswork involved in analysis and problem solving. A rule of thumb for the level of detail is to use larger chunks to plan and track areas of the project that have a consistent performance history. A finer level of detail for planning and tracking is appropriate in areas of the project where data from previous comparable experiences is not available. The intent of the PMIS using lower levels of detail is to provide the data needed to analyze performance, establish confidence in estimates when they are made without a historical basis, and establish trends for future performance.

PLANNING THE TIME DURATION OF WORK PACKAGES
Establishing the time duration of data item units is an opportunity to align the project plan, other contributing information systems such as a financial system and the project reporting cycle.

A time duration alignment of data items improves the confidence of the project's status, which in turn contributes to confidence in management decisions. For example, if an organization requires its projects to report monthly, and the financial system reports monthly, then it would be useful for the project's work packages to be described in monthly increments or work packages that combine to end at the monthly reporting point. The target for the project would be to have few open work packages in progress at the time of the report to reduce the amount of estimating needed to report the status of the open work packages. However, it is important to avoid optimizing an alignment of work packages to the reporting cycle at the expense of accurately describing the project's tasks.

Developing the Baseline Project Profile

When the project plan is completed, it is possible to prepare the baseline project-management profile of the project. The baseline profile is a management description of the project that is useful for communicating the project's scope and preparing management and stakeholders for project reporting once the project begins. The baseline shows the planned profile of the project's schedule, cost, effort, quality, and an estimate of changes across the time period of the project's execution and closing. The major payoff from establishing a baseline comes when the project plan is being executed and project results can be viewed from the perspective of comparing the planned baseline with actual project data.

Reporting Progress

Figure 24–2 is an example of tracking progress using a Gantt-type chart. A quick look reveals that Task A started late and ended late but used approximately the same number of calendar days as originally planned. Task B started early and recently missed its scheduled completion date. Task C started early and is not yet completed. Task D started late. This is an example of project-management information pointing toward potential problems. Project-management information systems are reliable in defining the basic questions but don't always answer the questions. In this case, the project manager is prompted to explore the delay of Tasks B, C, and D, and the impact these delays will have on the project's other tasks.

Enhanced progress reporting could include the following:

1. *Extending the data and analysis.* The information could be extended to show the relationship and dependencies between the project's tasks. For example, if the start of Task D depended on the finish of Task A, the late finish of Task A affects Task D and may have implications for other tasks as well.

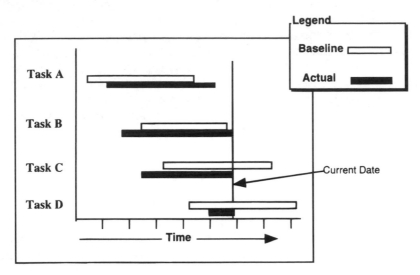

FIGURE 24–2   Tracking Progress (Project Execution Life Cycle Phase)

2. *Establishing performance thresholds.* These thresholds could describe how much the project can vary from the baseline schedule before higher levels of management become actively involved in managing the project. Critical or risky projects would probably have a narrow performance threshold. Routine projects, headed by a seasoned project manager, would probably have broader performance thresholds.

3. *Tracking potential improvement areas at a low level of detail.* This enables one to understand trends, relationships, and possible improvements. Low-level tracking information also provides a baseline to measure the effect of improvements as they are implemented.

EXAMPLE. The project manager, in reviewing Figure 24–2, immediately notes that only Task A is complete. Task B, which started early, has just missed the scheduled finish date. The project manager is a bit concerned about the late finish of Task B because of the dependencies between Task B and both Tasks C and D. The project manager knows the delays in finishing Task B jeopardize finishing the project as scheduled, because 75 percent of the scheduled time has been used and it would be extraordinary to get back on schedule even with extra project staff, funding, and equipment. The project manager assumes the project will be late. The task now is how to explain the project's status to upper management and why the project will end late and probably cost more than originally planned. The project manager is depending on the PMIS for supporting information that describes the current project status.

The first thing that went wrong was that the project started late (note Task A), but it wasn't the project manager's fault. The project plan was finished ahead of schedule and management had approved the plan ahead of schedule. The problem was getting the technical staff assigned by the matrix manager. The staffing for this project was planned to come from another project that finished late. That late finish made this project start late.

After the late start, the matrix manager flooded this project with a surplus of staff when another project was canceled. This additional staffing allowed Task B and Task C to begin early, but the results only looked good on paper because a majority of the surplus staff didn't have the right experience or skills. Having this surge of unqualified staff resulted in the fully capable project staff assuming a training mentor's role that was an extra task not budgeted in the original project plan.

In addition, a unique piece of equipment and its operator were needed to finish Task A. The same equipment and operator were also needed to start Task D. The late finish of Task A caused the late start of Task D.

Reporting on Cost

The comparison of planned and actual costs provides several valuable perspectives on the project. Figure 24–3 shows a project spending more money than budgeted—the *cost variance*—and less work is being performed than scheduled—the *schedule variance*. In this case, both the cost variance and the schedule variance are flagged for further review by the project manager.

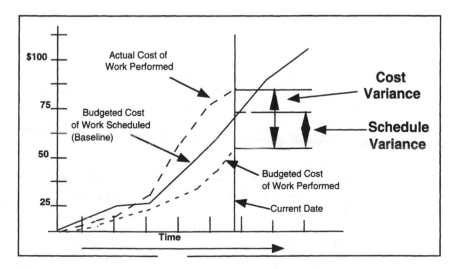

FIGURE 24–3   Tracking Cost (Project Execution Life Cycle Phase)

Enhanced cost reporting could include the following:

1. *Describing the relationship between cost and schedule.* This relationship supports prudent daily decision making by adding the cost value to changes in the schedule.
2. *Establishing a cost threshold counterpart to the progress thresholds.* The function would be the same as the progress threshold, which is to describe how much the project can vary from the baseline schedule before an increase in management participation occurs. The breadth of the cost threshold could indicate the confidence in the project manager or the critical nature of the project.
3. *Using cost as a primary indicator.* Costs could indicate the need for courses of action and determine where the greater benefit is obtained.

EXAMPLE. From Figure 24-3, the project manager observes that the costs were lower than planned at the beginning of the project execution phase, but the current status shows the project's costs significantly exceed the planned baseline. The project manager's quick calculation gives the following profile:

Baseline time schedule used: 72% of plan
Actual cost of work performed: 72% of plan
Budgeted cost of work scheduled: 65% of plan
Budgeted cost of work performed: 50% of plan

These indicators concern the project manager. From the cost report, the project manager sees that the project is 15 percent behind in completing scheduled work (schedule variance). The work that has been completed cost 22 percent more than was planned (cost variance). Both the schedule variance and the cost variance exceed the project-level threshold and require a senior management review. In this organization, cost information is the preferred basis for making decisions and other forms of measuring project performance lose significance unless tied to costs. From Figure 24–3, the project manager notes the following:

1. The beginning of the significant cost and schedule variance occurred shortly after the surplus staff were assigned.
2. Not only was the surplus staff assigned ahead of schedule, but the new staff members needed mentoring, a further negative impact on the cost and schedule variance.
3. The surplus staff's salary was higher than the original plan, which was another impact on cost variance.

These factors are the main reason for the rapid growth in cost and schedule variance. Having the surplus staff gradually become fully qualified accounts for the cost and schedule variance to run at parallel rates after their initial divergence from the plan. The surplus staff's higher-than-planned salary gives the project manager an opportunity to quantify a portion of the cost variance and to suggest that the organization fund the unplanned salary differential.

Reporting on Effort

Tracking the assignment of staff to a project relates strongly to progress and cost. In Figure 24–4, staffing lags the planned staffing rate at the beginning of the project and exceeds the planned staffing rate at the midpoint of the project's execution phase. Adding project staff late in the execution phase may compensate for the early delay in staffing. In some industries, such as the software industry, adding staff late in the project may be counter-productive, considering the amount of effort the original project staff must divert to bring the added staff to a fully effective level. (Please note that Figure 24–4 shows effort for the complete project life cycle. Figures 24–2, 24–3, and 24–5 only refer to the execution phase of the project life cycle.)

Enhanced effort tracking could include combining the effort tracking with the cost and schedule analysis. This can further validate the effort portion of the project's cost and schedule variance. The surge in staffing and the magnitude of the surge past anticipated project staffing shown in Figure 24–4, when combined with the cost schedule information, give a more complete understanding of all three sources of information.

In the example, the correlation between the schedule cost and the effort tracking validates the late assignment of unqualified staff as a cause of the project's cost and schedule shortfalls. The project manager knows the message of the late start and the impact of assigning surplus staff will be adequately conveyed to senior management through the PMIS products.

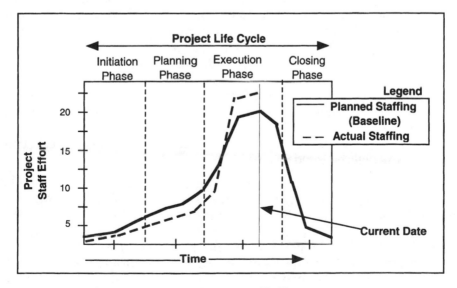

FIGURE 24–4   Planned and Actual Project Staff Effort

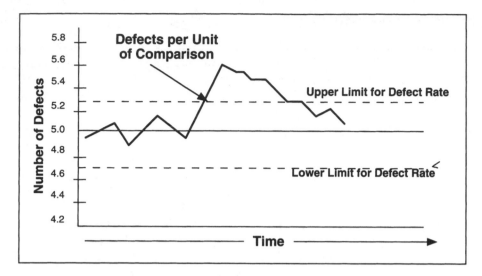

FIGURE 24–5   Tracking Quality (Project Execution Life Cycle Phase)

Reporting on Quality

The PMIS information applicable to quality refers to the amount of rework needed to bring products to a level fit for use. Baseline quality measures come from a standard or from the experience of previous projects. The quality baseline is established during project planning with the time, cost, and effort budgets adjusted accordingly. There is a strong relationship between quality measures and the project's cost and progress indicators. Exceeding the upper limit of anticipated defects as shown in Figure 24-5, and the resulting rework, would delay progress and increase the cost of completing planned tasks.

Enhanced quality tracking could include the following:

1. *Comparing data to historical averages.*   Management metrics could compare the number of open, closed, and pending trouble reports to historical averages.
2. *Analyzing defects.*   The cause of defects, and the effect of efforts to prevent defects, could be analyzed.

EXAMPLE.   The project manager finds the quality-tracking profile can be explained by the assignment of the surplus staff, which steadily improves as the surplus staff's skills begin to match the needs of the project. Actually, the project manager begins to see a positive side coming from the quality report. Using the quality perspective, an observation could be made that the largest drain on the project's productivity has occurred, the investment in the surplus staff has been made, and an accelerated project schedule could be possible.

Reporting on Stability

Stability refers to changes in the project's requirements or changes in the processes used for developing the project's product. The area of stability is industry specific. For stability to be a PMIS factor, the type of changes made must have an impact on progress, costs, quality, and effort. Different industries have different key measures. For example, the software industry frequently tracks requirement changes by the lines of code involved. Lines of code are frequently used as a common denominator for measuring many aspects of software development. A useful graphic display of stability information could be a format similar to Figure 24–5. Enhanced stability tracking could include an analysis that supports anticipating the impact that changes to requirements, processes, or equipment can have on the other PMIS areas of progress, cost, effort, or quality.

EXAMPLE.   The project hasn't been tracking the stability area and the organization does not have historical records that indicate the expected level of stability. In lieu of maintaining stability information, the organization provides each project manager a small reserve of funds for contingencies. Project managers have the latitude and responsibility to fund changes to requirements or improvements in work processes from this contingency fund. The project manager recalls an early decision to use a sizable portion of the contingency fund to improve the standard purchasing new process by equipment that performs on the leading technical edge of the industry's standard practice. For a time, the new equipment needed extraordinary effort by the operators to get even a modest product output. Now this improvement is beginning to pay handsome dividends and promises significant productivity increases in areas that were previously labor intensive. The project manager is encouraged for these reasons:

- The surplus staff is working at a productive and quality-effective level, which will decrease the schedule variance.
- Having a fully capable surplus staff releases the project staff previously used as training mentors to perform project work on a full-time basis as originally planned. This also will decrease the schedule variance.
- The new equipment has posted spectacular productive and quality results, and just keeps getting better. This will decrease both the schedule and the cost variance.
- The matrix manager, who originally overlooked the salary differential between the staff originally planned for the project and the surplus staff, has agreed to fund the salary difference. This will decrease the cost variance.

The project manager, supported by PMIS management products that answer the five project-management questions, takes the project's case to senior management. Senior management can see and track the reasons for the deviations from the baseline plan. They can also agree with the PMIS indicators that project performance has recently improved. With the improving trend in project performance, senior management asks the project manager to revise the project plan, proceed with the project, and document performance estimates for using the new equipment on future projects.

The conclusion of the project manager's report to management could have negatively affected the project manager's bonus or job without the project's performance documented by PMIS products. Without the PMIS products, a general unquantified understanding of the project's circumstances and causes could be described. With the PMIS products, the project's circumstances have a quantified boundary. They provide a basis for the resulting management actions to have a quantified boundary. The case study amplifies the following themes:

- The PMIS products don't always give answers, but usually point to the critical project-management questions.
- The individual areas of PMIS products addressed similar issues, but from different perspectives.
- The real issues, root causes, and ability to anticipate future trends frequently emerge by using PMIS products to compare the five areas.
- All five basic project-management questions can be valuable for identifying significant project-management issues. Project-management issues may not be recognized from reviewing a single area or several areas of the PMIS products. Significant project-management issues can seldom hide from all five of the basic PMIS product elements.

Summary

The role of a PMIS is to provide the information essential to effectively manage a project. The principal PMIS products are derived from describing the project's status in terms of progress, cost, effort, quality, and stability. The PMIS is critical to a project because it is one of the primary delivery vehicles of project management. A useful approach for establishing a PMIS is to focus on the management perspective of major decision points and to define the PMIS products before planning the project.

FURTHER READING
Cleland, David, I. *Project Management: Strategic Design and Implementation.* New York: McGraw-Hill, Inc., 1994

Frame, J. Davidson. *The New Project Management: Tools for an Age of Rapid Change, Corporate Reengineering, and Other Business Realities,* San Francisco: Jossey-Bass, 1994

Lewis, James P. *Project Planning, Scheduling & Control.* Chicago: Irwin, 1995

Lowery, Gwen. *Managing Projects with Microsoft Project 4.0.* New York: Van Nostrand Reinhold, 1994

Selecting and Using Project-Management Software

Harvey A. Levine

Biographical Sketch . . .   **Harvey A. Levine**, with thirty-five years of service to the project-management industry, is founder of The Project Knowledge Group, a consulting firm specializing in project-management training, project-management-software selection, evaluation, and implementation, and project management using microcomputers. He has implemented or enhanced the project-management capabilities of numerous firms, often combined with the selection or implementation of computerized project-management tools. Mr. Levine is the leading consultant to the project-management-software industry and is past president of the Project Management Institute.

The personal computer and user-friendly software are currently as prevalent in the modern project manager's toolbox as a screwdriver. Typically, project-management software can ease tasks such as identifying project work scope, planning and scheduling work, allocating or assigning resources, budgeting or managing costs, performing risk analyses, reporting project progress, and reporting or controlling resource usage. Failure to employ project-management software and allied products is analogous to using slide rules, rotary telephones, and coal-burning stoves. We need to be able to take advantage of the repeatability, speed, and precision that newer technology has to offer.

Classifications of Project-Management Software

Most, but not all, project-management software products provide traditional critical path scheduling. These can be placed into several groupings, based primarily on power and platform differences. There are also several specialty tools, under the general category of project-management software, that are designed to support specialized project-management functions. Here is a general description of the classifications of project-management software and some of the more popular providers within these groups.

MAINSTREAM

These are the popular, shrink-wrapped products, priced at under $1,000. Often, referred to, improperly, as "low-end," these products are clearly powerful and usable tools for many planners. Although they are generally grouped together, the characteristics of these products do differ and serve different needs. Software companies in this group include the following:

- Microsoft Corporation (Microsoft Project)
- Primavera Systems (SureTrak)
- Scitor Corporation (Project Scheduler 6 and Project Scheduler 7)
- Time Line Solutions (Time Line)
- Computer Associates (SuperProject)
- IMSI (Turbo Project)

POWER USERS

This group includes additional general-purpose project-management software, but at a higher level of capabilities. These may address such areas as more finite resource definition and assignment, higher capacities, advanced reporting and graphics, and stronger multiproject capabilities. Power user software companies include:

- Primavera Systems (Primavera Project Planner)
- Welcom Software Technology (Open Plan Professional)
- Artemis (ProjectView)
- Advanced Management Solutions (Schedule Publisher)
- SAS Institute (SAS OR Project Management)

CLIENT/SERVER PLATFORMS

There is an increasing demand for enterprise-wide project-management software solutions. These solutions will generally consist of connecting to corporate data, maintaining data in a common and secure area, and sharing computer facilities. *Client/server* is the common name given to these attributes, but they differ considerably among products. Companies offering this type of software include the following:

- ABT Corporation (Team Workbench and ABT Repository)
- Artemis (ProjectView)
- PSDI (PROJECT/2 Series/X)
- Digital Tools Inc. (AutoPLAN II)
- XPM Partners (XPM Enterprise Work Management)
- Mantix (Cascade)
- Primavera Systems (Primavera Scheduling Engine & Automation Server)
- Panorama Software (Panorama)

HIGH-END CONSOLIDATORS FOR LOW-END SOFTWARE

The increasing demand for enterprise-wide project management, coupled with the exponential growth in the use of Microsoft Project, has led to the emergence of an entirely new type of project-management software. This new classification of project-management products is aimed at consolidating multiple projects and enhancing workgroup communication. Most feature the consolidation of individual project data, from Microsoft Project, into a structured query language (SQL) database. Companies offering these products include the following:

- Information Management Services (Project Exchange-Distributed Project Management)
- Micro-Frame Technologies (Project Server and Time Server)
- Time Line Solutions (Project Updater)
- INNATE (Project Leader & MultiProject)
- Marin Research (Project Gateway)
- Advanced Management Solutions (AMS Timekeeper)
- Software Made Easy (Project Control)
- ABT Corp (Team Workbench and ABT Repository)

ADD-ONS

Another market that has evolved from the popularity of Microsoft Project (and some other general-purpose project-management software) is the add-on category. These products in this category cover all kinds of special needs, providing capabilities that are not found in the base product. These special needs may include advanced charting and graphics, risk analysis, project updating, and time capture. Companies offering add-ons include the following:

- American Netronic (Graneda): Gantt charts and network diagrams
- GTW (Project Partner): Plotted diagrams & graphics
- Jim Spiller & Associates (WBS for Project & XPERT): WBS (tree) charts, network charts
- Project Management Solutions (Risk+): Risk analysis
- Primavera Systems (Monte Carlo): Risk analysis
- adRem Technologies (Project Toolbox): Optimizing and fine tuning
- Parsifal Systems (BestSchedule): Optimized resource scheduling
- Experience in Software (Project Kickstart): Front end for organizing projects
- Timeslips (Time$heets Professional): Time capture
- HMS Software (Time Control): Time capture
- Artemis (TrackView): Time capture
- Marshall Technical Services (Time Wizard): Time capture
- CMR Publishing (Daily Log & Update Pro): Checklist and statusing

SPECIALIZED RESOURCE-MANAGEMENT SOFTWARE

A significant trend in the use of project-management software is the increasing emphasis on resource management (as part of planning and control). Almost any of the general-purpose products can be used effectively to plan and manage resource efforts. However, several products have been developed that provide special features in support of resource management.

- Artemis (ResourceView)
- Avantos (ManagePRO)
- Micro-Frame Technologies (Resource Server)
- XPM Partners (XPM Enterprise Work Management)
- The Allegro Group (Allegro)

MIS AND FINANCE APPLICATIONS

Information technology has become the fastest growing application area for project-management software. While these applications may be adequately served by general-purpose project-management software, there are a few particular capabilities that many information systems (IS) managers look for that are offered by packages directed specifically toward this discipline. Users also may prefer to work with a vendor that provides other products and services for IS applications. The following are examples of product marketed to the (MIS) application area:

- ABT Corporation (Project Workbench)
- ABT Corporation (ABT Repository & Team Workbench)
- Protellicess (Enterprise PM *{new Windows version of MicroMan II}*)
- Work Management Solutions (MultiTrak)
- Planview, Inc. (PlanView)

Selection

The specification, evaluation, and selection of project-management software should be an organized and orderly process. It should be treated just as you would treat any other project. Take a structured approach to this project. Resist the tendency to use whatever is lying around. Vise-Grips and screwdrivers are very handy tools, but how effective are they for driving nails?

Break this project into phases, starting with a thorough needs analysis. To determine your needs, define the kind of project work that will be done, and examine the methods for managing this work. This may be a good time to revise your practices (or to develop them if they are nonexistent).

THE NEEDS-ANALYSIS PHASE

The needs-analysis phase involves looking at project-management methods and your software needs as follows:

1. Determine your project-management methodology.

   - Identify project-management stakeholders.
   - Put together an evaluation team.
   - Identify system interfaces.

- Gather product information.
- Hold workshops and brainstorming sessions.
- Review project-management methodology.
- Assess the adequacy of current methods.
- Consider corporate culture and systems users.

2. Determine project-management software needs.

- Establish a framework for the selection criteria.
- Define selection-criteria items.
- Understand the available options.
- Make assumptions about the selection criteria.
- Rank criteria items.

From the needs analysis, project managers should build a selection specification. This can contain well over a hundred items. Therefore, you will want to prioritize them, noting those criteria items that are close to being essential. This may sound like a hedge, but it's not unusual to decide that a capability you thought was mandatory may be less important than some other item when you can't have both. This should be a team effort. Different stakeholders will have different needs and different priorities. The system coordinator should query them all and compile a composite specification.

THE SPECIFICATION PHASE
The specification phase involves development of the software specification and a vendor list as follows:

1. Develop the project-management software specification.

- Itemize specific project-management software needs.
- Assign weight factors.

2. Develop a list of candidate products.

- Identify available software.
- Obtain information about software.
- Develop a first-cut list, which will have more items on it than subsequent lists.
- Organize the product data.

To initiate the evaluation, start with just the must-have criteria. As you review products against this criteria, you will probably find that no single product fully supports all must-have items. You will have to make choices. You may find that you will reevaluate what is really important. Again, this should be a team effort.

THE EVALUATION PHASE
If you are considering a large group of products, it may be advantageous to divide the evaluation into two parts as follows:

1. Evaluate the preliminary alternative set.

    - Review products against must-have criteria.
    - Fill in data gaps.
    - Eliminate noncomplying products.
    - Identify the final alternative set.

2. Evaluate the final alternative set.

    - Review products against very-important criteria and against preferred criteria.
    - Fill in data gaps.
    - Assign scores for each product against each criteria item.
    - Compile weighted aggregate scores.
    - Consider getting the actual product.
    - Consider training before buying.

When you are down to the final two or three products, you will want to supplement the careful, weighted evaluation with additional judgmental research. Quite often the product that scores highest in a weighted review does not come out the best in actual use. If at all possible, try out the software before finalizing the decision.

THE SELECTION PHASE

The steps leading to the final selection and purchase include the following:

- Validate the data and assumptions.
- Evaluate the vendor, distributor, or dealer.
- Negotiate the purchase.
- Get people to buy into the decision.
- Determine life-cycle costs.
- Consider using consultants for coaching and startup.

Implementation

The implementation of a computer-based project-management process has the following five major phases.

THE METHODS PHASE

In the methods phase, the organization determine how it wants to manage projects. It thinks about what projects it wants to manage, what aspects of these projects are to be managed, and what level of detail is needed. The organization addresses issues such as how to organize to manage projects. Next, we can specifically address the issue: What practices should be put in place to support the firm's project-management objectives?

THE TOOL SELECTION PHASE

Once methods and practices are determined, we can get to the business of selecting and implementing tools for project management as discussed in the previous section. It is essential that the practice of project management be standardized. Computer-based tools make that standardization possible and make it more efficient.

THE TRAINING PHASE

Project management cannot be implemented without training. The organization should provide the following types of training: project-management training and project-management software training. This training should be provided on several levels. There should be in-depth training sessions for key project-management practitioners. These are the people responsible for developing plans and using the computer tools. There should be less detailed sessions for support people who have to provide information to the plans or progress data. They need to know what is needed from them and how the system uses their information. Another group to be trained is the people who get the information from the system, especially managers and decision makers. They need to know how the information got there and what it means. They need to know how to identify an out-of-tolerance condition, and how they are expected to respond. Everyone who has inputs to or gets outputs from the project-management system needs to have at least some rudimentary training in project management. Usually, a half-day overview session can provide the basics. In-depth training can run anywhere from a few days to about three weeks. The key is to determine who needs to know what and to provide that knowledge as needed.

Something that has gained significant popularity in the past few years is project-management certification. Many firms are recognizing (and sometimes sponsoring) certificate programs in project management. The Project Management Institute's project-management professional certification program has been recognized as the foremost program in project-management certification, and has enjoyed phenomenal growth in the 1990s. (See Chapter 22.)

THE IMPLEMENTATION PLAN

After defining project-management methodology, selected tools, and trained personnel, project managers must look at how the new process will be implemented. It is imperative to develop an implementation plan. The components of this plan include the following:

1. *Directive.* A directive from senior management must establish project management as a way of life and the firm must require support for project management as a condition of employment.
2. *Procedures.* A set of procedures should define the implementation process.

3. *Plan.*   An implementation plan should show the steps of implementation and a schedule for their accomplishment. It is not necessary to implement the full project-management process at once across the firm. It is best to select pilot projects for implementation. That gives people and the processes time to come up to speed. The practices can then be fine-tuned as people learn from our initial experiences.

4. *A kick-off program.*   Introduce the directive, the procedures, and the implementation plan with a formal program. You're looking for procedural and cultural change when you implement project management. You need to make a big deal out of it. You need to draw attention to the program and its importance. You need to make certain that people know that top management is serious about the program.

THE AUDIT PROCESS

You can't initiate a program and expect that things are just going to happen. There needs to be an audit process. So you need to develop a procedure for monitoring the implementation plan. The audit process ensures that the directive and procedures are clear and are being followed. Responsible managers are designated to conduct the audit on an ongoing basis. They will provide assistance in getting people up to speed, and, if necessary, call people to task for not supporting the program.

Figure 25–2 illustrates a typical project-management implementation plan. The timing is not as important as the phases and steps.

Using Project Management Software

Project managers should use project-management software to develop project plans, to optimize and balance the plans (establishing a baseline or target), and to track and control progress. Here is a description of each of the typical planning and control steps.

THE PLANNING PHASE

The following are steps for the planning phase:

Establish the Project Objectives

Resist the tendency to start scheduling the work until you define it. The initial computer-based effort should center on the work-scope definition. This should be as accurate as possible, because it will serve as the foundation for everything else that is done with these tools. Project managers should perform a strategic analysis of the project. Project objectives will serve as a guide for identifying the work to be performed. Timing and cost objectives and constraints will also serve as guides for scheduling and budgeting.

Project managers may want to start using their software to develop a project milestone schedule (see Figure 25–1). This example of a fast-track, turnkey power-plant project summarizes the major task groups for the

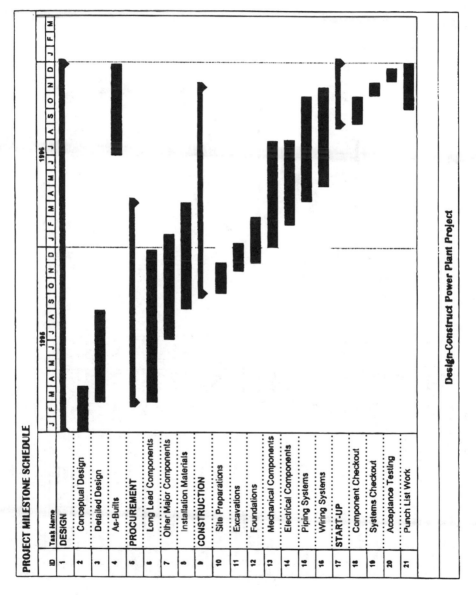

FIGURE 25–1   Project Milestone Schedule

335

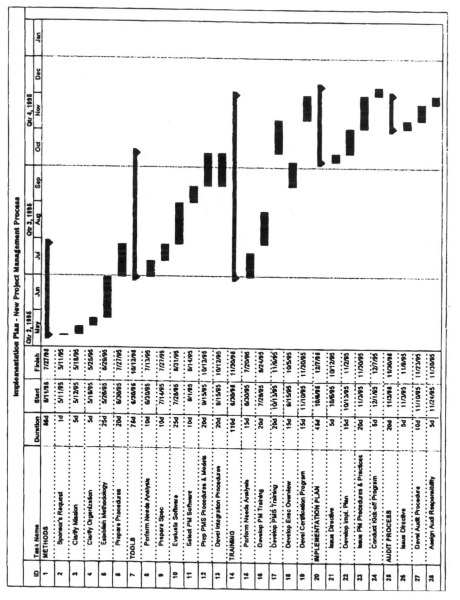

Implementation Plan - New Project Management Process

ID	Task Name	Duration	Start	Finish
1	METHODS	66d	6/1/95	7/27/95
2	Sponsor's Request	1d	5/1/95	5/11/95
3	Clarify Mission	5d	5/12/95	5/18/95
4	Clarify Organization	5d	5/18/95	5/25/95
5	Establish Methodology	25d	5/26/95	6/29/95
6	Prepare Procedures	20d	6/30/95	7/27/95
7	TOOLS	76d	6/30/95	10/12/95
8	Perform Needs Analysis	10d	6/30/95	7/13/95
9	Prepare Spec	10d	7/14/95	7/27/95
10	Evaluate Software	25d	7/28/95	8/31/95
11	Select PM Software	10d	9/1/95	9/14/95
12	Prep PMS Procedure & Models	20d	9/15/95	10/12/95
13	Devel Integration Procedure	20d	9/15/95	10/12/95
14	TRAINING	110d	6/30/95	11/30/95
15	Perform Needs Analysis	15d	6/30/95	7/20/95
16	Develop PM Training	20d	7/28/95	8/24/95
17	Develop PMS Training	20d	10/13/95	11/6/95
18	Develop Exec Overview	15d	9/15/95	10/5/95
19	Devel Certification Program	15d	11/1/95	11/30/95
20	IMPLEMENTATION PLAN	45d	10/6/95	12/7/95
21	Issue Directive	5d	10/6/95	10/12/95
22	Develop Impl. Plan	15d	10/13/95	11/2/95
23	Issue PM Procedures & Practices	20d	11/3/95	11/30/95
24	Conduct Kick-off Program	5d	12/1/95	12/7/95
25	AUDIT PROCESS	20d	11/3/95	11/30/95
26	Issue Directive	5d	11/3/95	11/9/95
27	Devel Audit Procedure	10d	11/10/95	11/23/95
28	Assign Aud Responsibility	5d	11/24/95	11/30/95

FIGURE 25–2   Typical Project-Management Implementation Plan

336

primary phases of the project and shows the target time periods for each. This serves as a guide for the detailed scheduling as well as a one-page communication vehicle for the client or top management.

Another step in using your project-management software is to set up various preferences, defaults, and project-level standards and forms. Calendars must be defined. Project managers need to establish the project start date (and target finish date, where available). There will be a default calendar, plus additional calendars for tasks, resources, and relationships. This varies from product to product. Most have a single project calendar and a calendar for each resource. More advanced products have both task and resource calendars. A few add calendars for the links between tasks (for lags and overlaps). Where the software supports it, set up the various code sets and/or work-breakdown structure (WBS) criteria during the planning phase. (For more on WBS, see Chapter 7.)

Define the Work

The work-scope definition is key to the project-management function. Without an accurate and complete definition of the work, there is no foundation for the management of time, resources, and cost. If you can't define the work, you can't load and evaluate resources and define a valid project budget. There are several techniques that have been recognized to aid in the process of work-scope definition. Best known is the WBS.

Project managers should use the WBS technique to break the project down into smaller, outlined segments until they get to work packages and tasks that specifically define the work to be done. The project-management software should support at least one WBS. It is practical to have multiple breakdown structures for tasks. The WBS and organizational breakdown structure (OBS) are traditional task-breakdown structures. It is also possible to have a hierarchical structure for resources. This is usually called a resource-breakdown structure (RBS). It is helpful if the software can easily organize the data by WBS and OBS. The software should support rollup (summarization) of data to various levels of the WBS and OBS.

Determine the Work Timing

The next step is developing the schedule. The project team should estimate task durations and define the links between tasks (precedence relationships). This is the place to use the computer. Critical path method (CPM) software can calculate a tentative schedule from the duration and link information.

The basic information required is a task description, a task duration, and a description of the relationships between tasks (predecessors/successors). Optional descriptive data may include task IDs, WBS numbers, other task codes, and textual comments. The CPM software will make a forward pass to calculate the earliest dates for each task. It will also (in most programs) make a backward pass from the project end date to determine the latest dates that any task can start and finish and still support that project end date. The system will also compare the early and late dates to calculate total float (also called slack). Tasks having the least float are said to be on the critical path.

There are also options to define factors that can further affect when a task will be scheduled. For instance, you may impose timing constraints, such as start-no-earlier-than (SNET), finish-no-later-than (FNLT), or must-start-on. These imposed dates will override the basic calculations when they are more limiting than the predecessor/successor constraints. But they will never (except in Microsoft Project) ignore a defined predecessor/successor relationship. You might use a SNET constraint to prevent work from starting earlier than the defined date. You could impose a FNLT date to place an early target date on an interim task. (This will force reduced float.)

Relationships can be conventional finish-to-start, or you can define lags and overlaps. You would use a lag to specify a delay in the start of a successor. For instance, strip and back-fill the foundation might follow pour the foundation with a three-day lag to allow for curing.

Use an overlap to show tasks in which some of the work can occur in parallel with a predecessor.

EXAMPLE.   A construction team is digging a 2,000-foot-long ditch, which will take 10 days. The workers can start placing pipe after the first 400 feet is dug. The task "place pipe" is a successor to "dig ditch" with a start-to-start relationship having a two-day lag, or a finish-to-start relationship, having an eight-day overlap.

Another advanced scheduling option is to bypass the fixed task duration and have the computer calculate the task duration from the specified resource assignment (e.g., the quantity of resources required). This is called resource-driven duration and will be discussed later.

Establish Resource Availability and Requirements

The first-cut schedule is probably not realistic because it assumes that there are unlimited resources available to do the work. The next steps will be to define resources expected to be available, and determine how many there are and when they will be available. Also, assign a cost rate to each resource so that the computer can generate a resource-driven cost estimate or budget for each task.

In advanced systems, you may have the option to define uneven resource availability and stepped cost rates. These options allow you to model real-world situations where the availability and rates may not be constant through the entire project.

Next, go back to the task list and schedule and assign resources to the tasks. You may want to designate some tasks as resource-driven. In this case, the computer will calculate the task duration on the basis of the specified effort (usually quantities and rate of use). There is another version of resource-dependent scheduling called effort-driven. Although sometimes confused with resource-driven, there is a significant difference. In the resource-driven mode, each resource assignment is unique and separate. The task duration will be determined by the most limited assignment on the task. In the effort-driven mode, the resources are considered to be interchangeable. The total resource requirement is defined for the task. As more resources are added, the time to perform the work is reduced.

If you are using fixed durations, you will have a choice of entering the total quantity of resource units to be assigned to the task, or the quantity per period. Essentially, they are three values to choose from: task duration, quantity per period, and total quantity. Enter any two of these and the system calculates the third. Advanced features, where available, allow you to specify assignments that are for less than the full duration of the task.

After the resources have been defined and assigned to tasks, the computer will provide an illustration (resource histogram or table) of the loads for each resource for each time period. This is called resource aggregation. If the histogram shows periods where the resource demand exceeds the defined availability, you have the choice of manually adjusting resource assignments or using the automatic resource-leveling features of the CPM software. Warning: Most automatic-resource-leveling routines are not very efficient, leaving periods of unassigned resources where there is work that can be done.

There are two types of resource leveling: Resource-constrained scheduling prevents work from being scheduled so as to require more resources than are available. Typically, this will extend the schedule. A variation, available in most products, is time-limited scheduling. This mode also attempts to avoid resource overloads by moving resource-conflicting tasks to other time periods. The resource-constrained mode never allows the resource limits to be violated, and the time-constrained mode protects the specified project end date. Resources are leveled and tasks delayed, but never beyond zero float. The result may show resources as being overloaded. This later method is also called smoothing in some programs. The result of a resource-adjusted schedule is the first-cut of the project-resource-loading plan or the resource baseline.

Establish the Cost Baseline

If you have established cost rates for your resources, they can develop a cost baseline or task budget. You may have to add fixed (nonresource) cost to some tasks. The computer will calculate the estimated cost for each task and roll it up to various levels of the WBS. Also, because the work is now scheduled, you will have a time-phased budget, usually called a cash-flow plan or project-expenditure plan. This will become a valuable baseline for tracking project performance later.

One advanced option, available in some products, is the ability to define cost accounts. These can serve as collector buckets, to accumulate the cost data in custom categories, separate from the WBS or RBS. The comptroller will love this.

There is very little that you have to do to obtain this cost data once you have things set up in the earlier stages. Anytime a change is made, whether to the schedule, assignment, cost rates, the cost rollups and the project-expenditure schedule will reflect this. That is what is so nice about using project-management software. From here on in there are tremendous benefits to be derived from the initial efforts to set up the program and define the work.

The process of establishing a baseline plan involves the following:

1. Evaluate the baseline plan.   At this time, you should have a baseline schedule, a baseline-resource-loading plan, and a baseline budget. What are the chances of this first pass meeting all of the project objectives and constraints? It will probably need to be tweaked a little.

You may want to save and copy the initial version and work on the duplicate until there is an approved target plan. You can do this as many times as one like and compare results.

At this point, you need to interrogate the data, and you need effective ways to access it. Look for software that allows you to see as much as possible on the screen (as opposed to requiring printed reports). This will allow you to interact with the data, to make on-the-run changes, and see the results. You'll want a 17-inch monitor with 800×600 resolution or better to get more information on the screen at a time.

Look for products that allow several ways of looking at the plans. Useful graphical views are Gantt charts (bar charts), PERT charts (network diagrams), tree diagrams (WBS charts), calendar views, resource spreadsheets, and resource histograms. The last two are usually added to schedule views as windows or split screens. You will also want to view the data in tabular form, either separately or in conjunction with the Gantt views. Look for a high level of user control and flexibility in these views; they are instrumental in making a product usable.

2. Optimize the baseline plan.   Now is the time to consider alternatives. If time is a problem, project managers should look at overlapping or expediting some of the tasks. This is where computers begin to pay dividends; they can easily do "what-ifs." The computers can point out the critical path. This is the series of tasks in the CPM schedule that will cause an extension to the project if there is a delay in any of these zero-float activities. This is where you will want to look for overlapping or expediting options.

If resource loading is a problem, you will want to consider such options as outsourcing or resource substitution. Time, resource, and cost-conflict resolution can also involve applying overtime, changing priorities, and even reducing scope.

3. Freeze the baseline plan.   Once you have developed an integrated plan, you can set the baseline (sometimes called *target*). This will allow you to measure schedule and cost performance during the execution of the project. Some products limit users to one baseline per project. There are times when multiple baselines are very useful. For instance, you may wish to have baseline 1 contain the original, approved target and have baseline 2 hold the most recent results just before doing an update. Then, each time you perform an update, you can compare the new schedule with either the original schedule or the previous schedule.

THE TRACKING PHASE

The tracking phase includes the following steps:

Change Control

During the tracking phase, we will oversee the work scope, the schedule, the resources, and the costs. The baseline that was recently established is like the abominable snowman. It is a myth, and it melts under pressure.

Scope change is a natural situation in projects. This is only a problem if it is not managed. Then it becomes scope creep, a really nasty situation. It is essential to establish a method of change control. When changes are introduced into the work scope, you must define the specific tasks that will be added, changed, or deleted and the effect on time, resources, and costs. One rule to follow is that the budget is always a task budget. The total project cost is the sum of the budgets for each task (plus contingency and margin). The task budget does not get adjusted unless there is a defined change in the task list.

To maintain full control over the work scope, make sure that all changes get into the official project plan. The computer-based project plan is the best ally in the quest to contain the project work scope and defeat scope creep. The software should allow you to make selected changes to the baseline. This way, you can modify the baseline to reflect the approved additions and changes without throwing away the rest of the original baseline.

One word of warning: Never change the baseline to reflect changes in effort or schedule because of poor performance. This negates using the baseline to measure performance. The modifications should only reflect changes to the approved work scope.

Track Work Progress

If you follow the defined process up to this point, you should derive significant benefits from the planning investment. From here on out, the process requires extreme diligence to continue the payoff. It is fair to say that there are those who will not want to make the commitment to track the work in detail or to track all of the project elements. For instance, one may want to track the work accomplished against the schedule (that's not too hard) and pass up detailed resource and cost tracking. Although complete project tracking and control involves the tracking of work, resources, and cost, there will be many situations in which this level of effort cannot be supported because of a lack of expertise or resources or because the tracking cannot be fully justified. This is a management decision that should be based on the particular situation. But here's what complete tracking and control involves.

Tracking the actual work consists of noting when a task has started and when it has been completed. Actual dates should be recorded. When a task has been started, but not completed (it is in progress), you need to note the percent completed and any adjustment to the remaining duration.

If you are going to do earned-value analysis (this will be covered in detail further on), you will need these measurements. The percent completed multiplied by the budget equals the earned value. This is also known as the budgeted cost of work performed (BCWP). You can compare the work accomplished (BCWP) with the planned work—budgeted cost of work scheduled (BCWS)—to calculate the schedule variance (SV). The SV is an excellent in dicator of project progress. It is much better than the popular (but perhaps overused) total float. Keep a trend curve of the schedule variance. If it starts out below target, look for improvement in future updates. The project manager who ignores an increasingly negative schedule variance gets what she or he deserves when the project comes in late.

Track Resource and Cost Actuals

This is the hard part. If resources and costs are tracked at a different level of detail than the project task plan, then it is almost impossible to match the tracking data to the plan data. If you are going to use time sheets and invoices, you will have to set up charging buckets to match the CPM tasks. This is easier said than done. However, it is easier to set up these charging buckets at the initiation of the planning process than in midstream.

There are two benefits to doing this tracking. The first is that you will be able to measure the actuals against the plan, evaluate performance, and facilitate replanning. The second is that you will be able to collect a project history. This is the only way you can eventually validate earlier estimates and improve upon them for future projects.

Compare with Baseline

SV measurements compare the amount of work accomplished with the amount of work that was scheduled to be done. One application for SV is in motivating subcontractors to intensify their project efforts when confronted with a downspiraling SV curve. There are many others.

If you're tracking cost actuals, you can also get a cost variance (CV). The actual cost of work performed (ACWP) is compared with the earned value or BCWP to compute the cost variance. How valuable are these simple measurements? Let's look at one situation that occurred a few years ago.

EXAMPLE.   A project was being monitored and had come to a point at which it was scheduled to be half done. The company comptroller noted that the project expenditures to date were only 45 percent of budget, and happily reported to management that the project was doing quite well. But the comptroller did not know the whole story. When the work was actually measured, the accomplishment value of the work (BCWP) was only 40 percent. Instead of good news, there were actually two bad results to report. The project was actually overspent (45 percent spent to do 40 percent of the effort) and it was considerably behind schedule. Only 40 percent of the effort had been accomplished when 50 percent was scheduled. The comptroller's erroneous report was misleading and had failed to sound the alarm. Earned-value performance measurements will provide better progress data and help to prevent this false performance assumption.

Evaluate Performance

Project managers should use their "actuals" measurements to track SV and CV and to analyze when progress does not support the plan. Using WBS frameworks, you can analyze the data at a higher level. Where an out-of-tolerance condition exists, you can drill down (expand) to the details to find the source of the anomaly.

The data can be analyzed in tabular or graphic formats. Figure 25–3 illustrates a formal cost/schedule status report. The data in the figure is summarized to the third level of the WBS. Work group A-1 is in progress and has fallen behind. Item A-1.1 is also running over budget.

Figure 25–4 compares BCWS, BCWP, and ACWP. Although this illustration was created in Microsoft Excel, many commercial project-management software packages can provide similar charts. The upper line (BCWS) shows the planned effort. Here the project is considerably behind the targeted effort, but money is being spent almost as fast as originally planned. Expenditures (ACWP) are way higher than the earned value (BCWP).

Figure 25–5 shows the cost performance index (CPI) and schedule performance index (SPI) trends. As noted earlier, this is an excellent way to illustrate the schedule and cost performance. You want to achieve performance values of 1 or greater. The curves in this illustration show that performance is getting increasingly worse. Work is being accomplished at about 69 percent of the planned effort and costs are exceeding the value of the effort.

Forecast, Analyze, and Recommend Corrective Action

There is no sense in collecting, analyzing, and evaluating all of these data unless you're going to do something about the results. These data can be used to forecast against key project milestones and to effect corrective action where needed. Project managers can establish interim milestones and trigger points. The latter are key events that occur (with adequate lead time) when there is still a window of opportunity to take corrective action or to adopt alternative strategies, because work is not going as planned.

Top management usually wants two key pieces of information: When is the project going to be completed? What is it going to cost? Using the computer-based ability to evaluate project performance and forecast these key items, you are in a position to provide a precise and intelligent management report. You can present the forecast schedule and costs, compared with the targets. You can include a trend curve and analysis and can focus in on trouble areas by using the drill-down capabilities. You can report on pending corrective action and the expected effect of these alternatives using what if analyses.

Illustration of Earned Value Reporting

COST/SCHEDULE STATUS REPORT			
CONTRACTOR:		SIGNATURE, TITLE, DATE FORM APPROVED	
LOCATION:	CONTRACT NO.	PROGRAM NAME	REPORT PERIOD	OMB# NUMBER
RDT&E__ PRODUCTION__		Prototype Engineering		2234327

Contract Data

ORIGINAL CONTRACT TARGET COST	NEGOTIATED CONTRACT CHANGES	CURRENT TARGET COST	ESTIMATED COST OF UNAUTHORIZED, UNPRICED WORK	CONTRACT BUDGET BASE

Performance Data

WORK BREAKDOWN STRUCTURE		CUMULATIVE TO DATE					AT COMPLETION		
		BUDGET COST		ACTUAL COST	VARIANCE		BUDGETED	LATEST REVISED EST.	VARIANCE
		WORK SCHED.	WORK PERF.	WORK PERF.	SCHEDULE	COST			
A	Radar Engineering	75046.15	64887.46	67799.04	-10158.70	-2911.58	272552.20	275418.35	-2888.15
A-1	Prototype Design	75046.15	64887.46	67799.04	-10158.70	-2911.58	134456.18	137384.19	-2928.01
A-1.t	Antenna Design	23613.72	16436.52	19347.10	-7179.20	-2911.58	47217.25	50128.40	-2911.14
A-1.2	Radar Interface Unit Design	23613.72	29820.72	29620.72	6207.00	0.00	49117.36	49117.09	0.27
A-1.3	Receiver Design	23613.72	18631.22	18631.22	-4982.50	0.00	33915.56	33916.31	0.25
A-1.4	Radome Design	4205.00	0.00	0.00	-4205.00	0.00	4205.00	4222.40	-17.40
A-1.5	Preliminary Design Review	0.00	0.00	0.00	0.00	0.00	0.00	0.00	0.00
A-1.6	Radar Design Complete	0.00	0.00	0.00	0.00	0.00	0.00	0.00	0.00
A-2	Prototype Manufacturing	0.00	0.00	0.00	0.00	0.00	138096.02	138034.16	51.88
A-2.1	Prototype Fabrication	0.00	0.00	0.00	0.00	0.00	61563.06	61818.54	-56.48
A-2.2	Prototype Procurement	0.00	0.00	0.00	0.00	0.00	46281.96	46332.72	-50.75
A-2.3	Prototype Assembly	0.00	0.00	0.00	0.00	0.00	19074.38	19071.40	2.99
A-2.4	Radar Integration	0.00	0.00	0.00	0.00	0.00	11176.51	11011.50	165.11
A-2.5	Ship Radar	0.00	0.00	0.00	0.00	0.00	0.00	0.00	0.00
SUBTOTAL		75048.15	64887.48	67799.04	-10158.70	-2911.58	272562.20	275418.35	-2666.15
GENERAL AND ADMINISTRATIVE									
UNDISTRIBUTED BUDGET		N/A	N/A	N/A	N/A	N/A			N/A
MANAGEMENT RESERVE		N/A	N/A	N/A	N/A	N/A			
TOTAL									

Earned Value Data - Rolled Up to 3rd Level

FIGURE 25–3   Cost/Schedule Status Report

Special-Purpose Tools

Traditional project-management software supports four primary functions: work definition, critical path scheduling, resource assignment, and costing. Project managers will often engage in additional project practices for which there are also computer-based tools available. It is highly recommended that

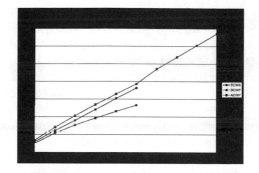

FIGURE 25–4   A Comparison of BCWS, BCWP, and ACWP

such tools be employed where appropriate. The tools can help with the following tasks.

RISK ANALYSIS

Project managers must manage risk, whether schedule risk, cost risk, or technical risk. Several techniques are available to support analysis and management of schedule and cost risk. These techniques are supported by various software products.

Schedule risk addresses uncertainty in task durations. One popular method is to employ a three-point time estimate (often called PERT

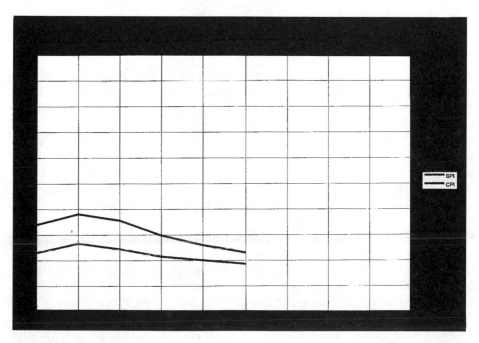

FIGURE 25–5   Performance Trend Chart

durations). For this, estimate the optimistic and pessimistic task durations, as well as the most likely duration. This not only reduces the bias or hedging in the time estimate, but also provides a range of durations for analysis. Using a mainstream project-management software package, such as Scitor's Project Scheduler 6, you can determine minimum and maximum project durations, as well as impose weight factors to skew the durations for either expedited targets or schedule contingency.

For further schedule-risk analysis, use a risk-analysis program, such as Primavera's Monte Carlo or Project Management Solutions' Risk+ for Project. These programs use Monte Carlo simulation of the possible task durations. The three-point estimates can be discrete, or they can be based on a plus/ minus formula. These programs will compute the range of possible project completion dates and calculate the probability of achieving each date. Figure 25–6 illustrates a project model, using Risk+ for Project. Here the twenty-day schedule is judged to have only a 10 percent chance of happening. The most likely project duration (50 percent) is twenty-three days, and it could take as long as thirty days.

These programs also calculate the potential of each task and path contributing to the project-schedule risk. Often, the highest risk path is not the same as the path with least float or slack. The path-risk computation considers merge bias: a condition in which the risk is increased when there are multiple critical tasks feeding a milestone or collector point. Monte Carlo also features such advanced risk-modeling features as conditional branching, probabilistic branching, and probabilistic calendars. Risk-analysis programs also calculate cost risks as well as schedule risks.

TIME CAPTURE
There is an increasing interest on the part of project-management-software users to integrate the collection of spent time data. Most organizations use time sheets to capture the time spent by accountable personnel. This function has traditionally been separate from the planning and control function, necessitating dual processing of time data when the control function wishes to capture actual time spent on project tasks. A few project-management- software products, especially those targeted at the information-systems disciplines, have built in a time capture capability. In these programs, such as ABT's Project Workbench, the task updating (actuals and estimate to complete) can be executed by the assigned resources in an automated, on- screen time-sheet form. The time data is held as "pending actuals," which the responsible manager can review and accept.

The market abounds with third-party programs that provide similar capabilities. These products, such as Time$heets Professional from Timeslips, provide connectivity to popular critical path software for downloading of resource plans and uploading of resource progress. All have various levels of security and management control. Many can also be integrated with the corporate-accounting-data repositories.

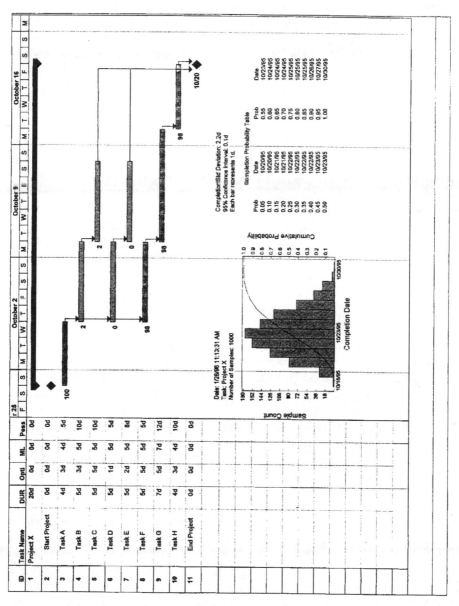

FIGURE 25–6   Risk Analysis Mode

The availability of such simple and powerful time-capture software ought to signal the replacement of traditional corporate time-accounting systems. However, this is not realistic. Until organizations can identify *all* accountable work in their project databases, and until they can develop a processing discipline equal to that in typical accounting functions, project managers will still require duplicate systems in most situations. There is one other factor to watch out for when attempting to capture actuals in the project database. There is a tendency to define work (the tasks) in greater detail than we are willing to record actual hours spent. Most programs will require a one-to-one relationship between the defined tasks and the charge items on the time sheet.

COST/SCHEDULE-CONTROL-SYSTEMS CRITERIA

Although the interest in time-capture programs is increasing, interest in cost/schedule-control-systems criteria (C/SCSC) applications is falling. C/SCSC protocols, usually required on major government contracts, are being requested less frequently. This is because there is a reduction in these megaprojects. However, if you get involved in a project with C/SCSC requirements, computer-based support is available from vendors such as Micro-Frame Technologies, Primavera Systems, Welcom Software Technology, and Artemis.

More Special-Purpose Tools

There has been a noticeable shift from a single-project focus to an environment in which we manage resources working on multiple projects. This has generated a shift in product emphasis from tools purely for project managers to those that also provide assistance to functional managers supporting multiple projects.

This assistance comes in many forms. Traditional project-management software now has more functional and resource-centric views and reports. Time-capture software aids functional managers. Another type of software— TeamFlow from CFM, Inc.—incorporates a responsibility matrix with the task list and flow diagram.

Allegro (Deltek) places the emphasis on resource assignment to tasks that have been defined and scheduled (non-CPM). ResourceView (Artemis) uses a two-module approach (Requestor & Allocator) to assign resources to work requests.

The need for comprehensive multiproject planning and control has led to the development of several products that consolidate individual project files into a single, SQL database, such as Oracle. Products, such as Business Engine, from MicroFrame Technologies consolidate project data from Microsoft Project (and sometimes other products). These consolidators allow enhanced communication and updating of project data outside of the CPM products. They emphasize workgroup communication, summarization, and drill-down capabilities. Other consolidators use Lotus Notes (Project Gateway from Marin Research) or Microsoft Access (Project Control from Software Made Easy)

If you require graphics capabilities greater than those supplied with the CPM package, auxiliary products, such as WBS for Project and XPERT (Jim Spiller & Associates), Project Partner (GTW), and Graneda (American Netronic) are available.

If you are not satisfied with the resource scheduling built into the software, you can try some of the resource-schedule optimizers available to work on top of Microsoft Project. Two such products are BestSchedule (Parsifal Systems) and Project Toolbox (adRem Technologies).

If you need some help in developing your projects, you can look into a front-end program, such as Project Kickstart (Experience in Software), or GuideLine (Time Line Solutions). Aiming at the information-technology sector, Primavera can link to project models developed in LBMS Process Engineer, and ABT offers Project Bridge Modeler as a link to Project Workbench or Microsoft Project.

Estimating is an important part of projects. Specialized software for estimating is available for construction and information-systems projects. Most of these can be connected to the popular CPM packages in those application areas. WinEst, Precision Estimator (Timberline), and G2 Estimator (G2, Inc.) are popular estimators for construction projects. Most of the specialized information-system providers can supply integrated estimating software.

Also, for construction applications, there are several integrated packages of project accounting, tracking, and documentation programs. These usually do not contain project-scheduling modules. COINS (Shaker Computer & Management Services) includes estimating, job status, accounts receivable, accounts payable, purchase order/inventory, payroll, billing, general ledger, human resources, and service management among their over one dozen modules. CFMS is a computer-based financial management system from Harper & Shuman.

Occasionally you might need to develop a very basic schedule presentation without using critical-path and resource-loading protocols. Basic bar-chart presentation packages are available for this, such as Milestones, Etc. (Kidasa Software) and Schedule Express (Foundation Microsystems).

Multiproject Issues

The project-management environment is shifting from the management of large, individual projects by dedicated project managers, to the management of smaller, multiple projects. Management of these smaller projects may be conducted by functional managers, cross-functional teams, and ad-hoc groups as well as more traditional project managers. This has dictated several changes in the tools used for project management. For instance, these products have been reconfigured to provide additional views and reports for functional and resource-type users. The most important improvements address the need to manage the information for multiple projects while maintaining individual project files and identity. If you have multiproject needs, you should be certain that your software fully supports these needs. The software should allow multiuser access to multiple projects while maintaining some access and data security.

In some instances, the entire paradigm for project-management software is changing to support this newer multiproject environment. We are beginning to see some of the project information processed outside of the self-contained critical-path software package. Instead, we might find people using other canned or custom applications to communicate with a scheduling engine, such as Primavera's Ra, or a consolidator, such as Information Management Services' Project Exchange. Many products are also now enabling exchange of project data via e-mail and web browsers.

Recently Microsoft introduced a new product, Team Manager 97, in an entirely new software category. Team Manager is not traditional project-management software. It shuns the conventional critical-path approach, opting instead for a priority and deadline basis for determining the best time to perform outstanding work (called Best-Fit). Team Manager emphasizes support for communication among work requesters, team members, and the team manager. It allows the consolidation of tasks across projects, departments, and teams, with various ways of viewing the data. It supports statusing across projects by teams and team members, including timesheet reporting.

Another issue arising out of the shifting environment is the trend to put project-management software in the hands of all potential users, rather than specialized, trained planning-and-control personnel. The effective use of project-management software requires a thorough understanding of project-management principles as well as the tool itself. There is a dangerous tendency to select these tools for the perceived ease of use so that they can be used by a wider group of less knowledgeable people. This could easily result in the selection of a tool that is too weak to support the true needs of the organization. It is also inefficient, because this wider use requires more copies of the product and forces nonessential personnel to take time away from their technical specialty area. In the end, there still tends to be a limited group of effective users.

Total Customer Satisfaction

Lewis R. Ireland

Biographical Sketch . . . **Dr. Lewis R. Ireland** is president of Project Technologies Corporation and specializes in project and quality management consulting and training. Consulting and training assignments have been in China, Russia, Saudi Arabia, United Arab Emirates, and the United States. Dr. Ireland has worked as a telecommunications project manager, a section manager supporting government international programs, a project planner, and a strategic planner. Dr. Ireland earned a doctorate from Columbia Pacific University, a master's degree from Florida Institute of Technology, and a bachelor's degree from Benedictine College. He is an active member and Fellow of the Project Management Institute.

T otal customer satisfaction is a vision adopted by many companies for their overall approach to achieving quality in products and services. Total customer satisfaction focuses on the buyer of the product and service and aligns the company's practices with satisfying those buyers.

For projects, contracts are signed with the best of intentions and with the expectation that the other party will fulfill every element of the requirements. Contracts, however, are often developed by the provider's sales department and the sales person is rewarded for closing the deal rather than for any major concerns over the feasibility of implementation. The project manager is the person who must deliver.

Project managers are often placed in an untenable situation when projects are sold without consideration for delivering the products or services. Project managers are torn between the parent company and customer satisfaction. The project manager's long-term interests are best served by the parent company, and many times the truth gets lost when dealing with the customer.

Some individuals see the quality movement as a fad that will soon pass. Skeptics may believe this when there have been many false starts on the road to improved quality and many workers have been frustrated through misguided efforts of managers. Some skeptics also see the quality movement as a jobs program for the quality-control people.

Champions of the quality movement, however, view the situation differently. Total customer satisfaction is seen as the only way to be competitive and to grow within their particular industries. These champions of quality believe that establishing a total quality program and practicing continuous improvement of products, services, and processes are vital to the survival of a business.

Although there is obvious controversy associated with the two extremes, there is little doubt about the need for quality improvements at all levels within private and public sectors. Consumers are demanding better products based on value rather than price alone. Terms such as *best value* are being used to evaluate proposals rather than *lowest price*.

What Is Total Customer Satisfaction?

Motorola Corporation uses the term *total customer satisfaction* to describe its quality program.[1] This title uses the concept of a customer focus to bring satisfaction to the customer through products manufactured by Motorola. The program also includes the concept that anything that has a negative impact on a customer is a defect that must be corrected.

Total customer satisfaction is defined as the vision for the business. Anything less than total customer satisfaction raises a concern about how to change products, services, or processes to bring about satisfaction. Rather than a single customer category such as the buyer, all categories of customers must be considered in the customer satisfaction equation. For example, there are internal and external customers who may be ranked in categories of primary, secondary, and tertiary customers for their distance from the provider.

Cost of Quality

Customer satisfaction has a price that must be included in the cost of quality. Cost of quality is most often added to a product cost as a direct result of the quality program. Typically, the cost of quality is included in the following categories.

- *Prevention costs:* costs associated with preventing defects in the product or service
- *Appraisal costs:* costs associated with inspection, evaluation, measurement, and tests performed to determine whether a defect exists

- *Failure costs:* costs associated with product failure, either prior to or after shipment to the client
- *Measurement and test:* costs associated with equipment, gauges, measuring devices, and other tools that support the appraisal process

Customer liaison and customer reviews would be included under prevention costs if the purpose is to identify requirements, work the requirements, and keep the customer informed about progress. On the other hand, customer liaison and reviews would be included in failure costs if the purpose is to repair the customer relationship after significant defects have been identified. The emphasis should be placed on the customer relationship that prevents the defect rather than on the attempt to repair an eroding relationship.

Any program that attempts to achieve total customer satisfaction must consider the costs associated with quality. This cost, however, is an investment and should have a return on the expenditure many times over. The investment may be a burden if not planned, budgeted, and managed.

Link Quality to Profits

During the 1980s, many companies started quality programs with the expectation that the cost of the program would be easily recovered during the first few years of implementation. In the early 1990s, some companies experienced a shock when the cost of the quality program exceeded the benefits (i.e., revenue generated). A quality program that focuses strictly on quality improvement without the accompanying financial benefits may have a serious affect on a company's existence.

EXAMPLE. Several companies in Europe had the experience of trying to perform all tasks to achieve customer satisfaction and found that total commitment to meeting all items caused chaos. There was always emphasis on continually improving the product and process. Some improvements were costly without the resultant return in sales or value added to the product or process.

To solve this problem, these companies adopted a rule of thumb that stated: "Any improvement must raise customer satisfaction by 30 percent and contribute to profit by 10 percent." Rather than having change for change's sake, the improvements were directly linked to customers and profit.

Principles

Quality programs must provide for the company's continued existence and growth as well as provide for a high degree of customer satisfaction. Principles associated with total customer satisfaction are the following:

- Satisfied customers make positive referrals for new business.
- It is easier and less expensive to obtain repeat sales from satisfied customers than to find new customers.

- Negotiating changes is easier with satisfied customers than with dissatisfied customers.
- Satisfied customers have confidence in the ability of the project manager and require less proof of progress.

Continuous Quality Improvements

Customers' expectations grow over time and they expect better and different products. Therefore, companies must constantly and continuously make improvements. Products may be improved with more features, longer durability, more reliability, and features that are easier to operate. Competitive offerings by other companies may cause sales to be lost when the customers' expectations are not met. Continuous quality improvement exists in two primary areas: product and service improvements and process improvements.

PRODUCT AND SERVICE IMPROVEMENTS

Product and service improvements add value in the eyes of the customers over a previously sold product or service. This added value is often provided the customer at little or no additional cost when the product or service is changed to more closely align with the customers' expectations.

The key to product and service improvement is through dialogues with customers to determine where improvements are needed. A few companies are requiring senior executives to visit customers specifically to discuss the customers' product-capability requirements. Many other companies are relying on surveys to collect information on customer satisfaction levels.

PROCESS IMPROVEMENTS

Product and service improvements may result from an improved process. Processes can be improved through such methods as instituting additional training for workers, simplifying the flow of the process, using materials that more closely match the manufacturing requirements, and purchasing machines to provide more uniform products than manual means. Process improvements will typically reduce cost, enhance the product grade, and shorten the time required to perform a given function.

EXAMPLE.   An example of a process improvement was demonstrated by the Roanoke, Virginia, Department of Public Safety when it was learned that a fire engine could not respond to a given location within five minutes, the standard for responding to reported fires.[2] The process was placed in a flow chart with a resultant eighteen serial nodes of activity. This process was refined to five nodes with two operating in parallel. A one-time cost of less than $300 for a printer in the firehouse to print the fire location was required. A five-node process reduced the response time by 29 percent.

Process improvements are within the authority of any company to analyze its functions to determine where changes can be made to simplify, correct, or replace the process. Process improvements can easily be conducted by in-house multidisciplinary teams with little training and without major expenses of contracting out the work. Flow charting, Pareto analysis, and frequency counts provide the means to determine where the changes may be made.

Customer Focus

Although some companies have direct contact with customers, others do not. Direct sales in a restaurant give the business an opportunity for contact with final customers, whereas a manufacturer of sheet metal may never have this direct contact.

Quality is customer-driven because all products and services are judged by customers, not by the manufacturer or other provider. Inspections by quality-control personnel and hyperbole by sales personnel do not provide customer satisfaction. Inspections only identify part of the total defects in a product. Sales personnel believe they add value to a product in customer's eyes. Initially, this may be true. However, in the long term, customers are satisfied only when the product or service delivers the desired level of performance.

Projects' charters are more frequently describing the relationship between the project manager and the customer. These descriptions will often specify the frequency of contact and information to be routinely provided to the customer. By doing this, the project manager becomes solely responsible for ensuring that customers' legitimate requirements are met within the context of an ongoing project.

Customer Identification

A customer is defined in ISO 9004[3] as the "ultimate consumer, user, client, beneficiary, or second party." This definition generically encompasses many different individuals. Companies may have other customers who are specific to their line of business and in categories other than the direct consumer or user. The following is a sample of customers and stakeholders in projects:

- Project's sponsor or financing organization
- Government regulatory agencies of the such as the Environmental Protection Agency
- Public interest groups
- Congress for federal agencies
- State and local governments for state and local agencies

When the definition of customer is expanded to include several stakeholders and anyone having an interest in the project, several more customers may be identified. The customer list may expand and contract for long-term projects. For example, once the decision is made to issue a construction permit, most issues should have been resolved to the satisfaction of all major stakeholders.

These individuals are no longer active customers to the project. Customer identification is critical to the process of achieving customer satisfaction.

There is a balance between meeting the requirements of a few senior managers and trying to meet the requirements of all project stakeholders. Meeting only the senior manager's requirements is following internal rewards and not necessarily satisfying the buying customer. On the other hand, one may view all participants as customers and try to satisfy each one's needs— which may be conflicting. There is a midpoint at which one should strive to meet customer needs and give those customers satisfaction.

Trust and Confidence

A trusting environment for customers and project managers can all too frequently change to one of open hostility. Changes from the mutual trust and confidence are not normally the result of one incident, but a series of incidents over time.

Some demonstrations of less than open and honest dealing with customers are the following:

1. Fast talk about schedule slippage.   A company was significantly behind schedule and stated that employees would work overtime to correct the schedule slippage. The company's program executive explained to the customer that the employees would work overtime fifty hours a week until the schedule slippage was corrected.[4] The manner in which the statement was made led the customer to believe that a total of fifty hours a week would be worked, when in fact the program executive explained this meaning several months later. The program executive stated that the correct interpretation should have been fifty hours a week overtime work, an impossible task. The customer lost confidence in the program executive because of the overtime issue and several other similar incidents. He was subsequently removed from the company. The project failed to achieve its technical goals and was canceled two years later.

2. Overly optimistic productivity projections.   A major provider of specialized software was developing a data-collection system for a telecommunications company. The project schedule continued to slip each week and the customer questioned the validity of the schedule. Each week the provider of software assumed an optimistic productivity rate in the future that was not being demonstrated in the past.[5] To achieve a show of progress, the provider redefined the work-in-process to indicate more progress than was actually accomplished. The redefinition and shading of the truth on the actual progress resulted in more questions from the customer. Customer inquiries about progress validity increased. Because of a less-than-honest approach to progress and providing the customer with invalid information, the customer could not plan to meet its commitments to consumers. The customer refused to make progress payments in excess of $1.5 million. The situation did not improve over an eight-month period and there is a high probability that the project will be canceled.

Trust between business associates is a must to ensure a smooth and open relationship for producing any product. It is commonly accepted that if a person lies once, that person's statements must always be checked prior to taking any action.[6]

EXAMPLE.   Will complained about his boss to a fellow worker: "Every time he opens his mouth, he lies, he lies, he lies!" Will, being a fair person, corrected his statement: "I take that back, I heard him tell the truth one time!" Will's colleague responded: "Well, that must have been an honest mistake!"

Trust is fragile and can be easily broken with one deviation from the truth. Project managers who bend the truth to fit immediate situations will lose out on credibility when it is truly needed. The following are four principles for good customer relationships.[7]

- Establish a good relationship and a sense of trust.
- Try to understand the problems of your counterpart.
- Learn to lose an occasional battle.
- Develop a general and highly visible ability to handle interpersonal relationships with the customer.

Attitude

Attitude is a vital part of achieving total customer satisfaction.[8] A positive attitude conveys to the customer important elements about the relationship and sets the climate for a cooperative partnership. A negative attitude, however, conveys to the customer a completely different picture about the relationship. One manager characterized the attitude of the project team as "ignorance emphasized by arrogance." The project-team leader refused to acknowledge that some minor errors had been made in the schedule and that these errors could be easily corrected. He would not admit that a minor error had been made because he felt any error would make him look foolish. His insistence that it was proper to execute and plan at the same time lowered his credibility with the customer.

Nine "Cs" of Quality

A concise list of items that encapsulates total customer satisfaction, as viewed by one company, is titled The Nine Cs of Quality.[9] These nine Cs reflect the general areas in which a project manager should concentrate to either build a total customer-satisfaction program or validate an existing quality program. The areas are as follows:

1. *Customer awareness.*   Project managers and team members should have an awareness of customers and their respective roles in making projects successful. This includes being aware of internal and external

customers as well as the different levels of customers. Different levels are the following:

- *Primary:* one who is the direct recipient of the benefits of the product or service being provided
- *Secondary:* one who is the indirect recipient of the product or services being provided, such as a manager of the primary customer
- *Tertiary:* one who has an interest in the product or service and possibly its use

2. *Communication.*   Communicating with the customer is essential to determine requirements and expectations as well as to set the customer's expectations for quality levels and delivery procedures. Communication is also important to maintain confidence with the customer about the progress of the project's schedule.

3. *Cost avoidance.*   Cost avoidance pertains to all actions taken to restrict expenditures for unnecessary work on the project. This includes all actions taken to avoid waste of time and materials. It does not imply or suggest that inferior materials should be purchased at lower cost than the proper grades.

4. *Contribution analysis.*   Contribution analysis is the comparison of contributions to the plan and the use of metrics to measure contributions.

5. *Controls.*   Controls are those necessary checks and balances to ensure that the project is progressing as planned, or that the work is being accomplished within the bounds of approved variances from the plan. Controls also identify those variances that require management actions.

6. *Coordination.*   Coordination is the element that ensures all affected participants are informed of future activities and these participants concur with the planned actions. Coordination also assures integration of efforts by all parties and prevents surprises.

7. *Competence and congruence.*   Competence is the physical and mental capacity to perform the work. Congruence is the consistency between what is written or stated and the work being performed.

8. *Commitment.*   Commitment is total dedication to performing all accepted tasks without excuses for not being able to do so. Commitment requires completion of the tasks to the level of required performance within the time frame. If it is determined that the task cannot be accomplished, team members should request relief from the person to whom the obligation was made.

9. *Cooperation.*   Cooperation is making every effort to work with others in an open and supportive manner. Cooperation includes assisting fellow workers, being receptive to the boss's instructions, and being friendly to others. Cooperation does not require an individual to compromise on ethics, values, or beliefs just to be one of the team. Honest disagreement over principles is acceptable behavior.

The Customer Is the Focal Point

Any company's quality program must have the customer as the focal point for all decisions. Identifying those customers, reviewing their needs, and meeting their expectations for products and services will more likely lead to greater customer satisfaction. Product and service quality is determined by the customer, and therefore the customer must always be the primary consideration in any quality program.

ENDNOTES

1 Motorola Corporation. Report on Malcolm Baldrige National Quality Award, 1990
2 Department of Public Safety Reprot to Quality Improvement Class. Roanoke, VA, 1992
3 ISO 9004. Quality Management and Quality System Elements: Guidelines, 1994
4 Personal observation during a project review. Toronto, Ontario, 1980
5 Personal observation during a project review. Chicago, 1995
6 Personal observation at work site. McLean, VA, 1985
7 Loweree, James H. The superior project manager in *Project Management: A Reference for Professionals.* Edited by Kimmons, Robert, 1988, p. 119
8 Adapted from a discussion with Mr. Jerry Lohfink, USDA National Finance Center, New Orleans, LA, April 1996
9 Adapted from a presentation given by Dr. E. Johnson at the Project Management Institute. Washington, D.C. Chapter, McLean, VA, 1991

BIBLIOGRAPHY

Company measures internal customer satisfaction. *Quality Progress,* 1994
Don't fall into these customer satisfaction traps. *Quality Progress,* 1993
Ireland, Lewis R. *Quality Management for Projects and Programs.* Upper Darby, PA: Project Management Institute, 1991
Ireland, Lewis R. Customer satisfaction: The project manager's role. *Journal of International Project Management,* 1992
Ireland, Lewis R. The customer's role in project success. Proceedings of the Annual Seminar/Symposium. Upper Darby, PA: Project Management Institute, 1993
ISO CD 10006 (draft). *Quality Management: Guidelines to Quality in Project Management.* Geneva, Switzerland: Organization for International Standardization, 1995
ISO 9000–9004. *Quality Management Standards.* Geneva, Switzerland: Organization for International Standardization, 1994
Joseph M. Juran. What Japan taught us about quality. *The Washington Post,* p. H1, August 15, 1993
Malcolm Baldrige National Quality Award Criteria, US Department of Commerce, Technology Administration, National Institute of Standards and Technology, Gaithersburg, Maryland, 1987–1996
Office of Personnel Management. *Federal Total Quality Management Handbook.* Washington, DC: Office of Personnel Management, 1990
Project Management Institute. *A Guide to the Project Management Body of Knowledge.* Upper Darby, PA: Project Management Institute, 1996
The bottom line on "People" issues. *The New York Times* p. F23, February 19, 1995

Chapter

27

Project Evaluation at Lucent Technologies

Dan Ono

T he strategic intent of the Lucent Technologies' project-management process was to create a competitive advantage by possessing a world-class group of professional project managers. the Project Evaluation Review Process is one component of this overall effort. This project-review process was developed to provide a means of continuous improvement for the project-management process used by the Lucent Technologies–Business Communications Systems. The Business Communications Systems' project-management process was created as a tactical tool for the long-term successful delivery of large communications infrastructure and PBX implementations.

Project-Management Organization

A group within the Lucent Technologies Strategic Business Unit is the National Strategic Opportunities Division. This division specializes in large telecommunications-related projects in the national and international environments. The group consists of a presale group, which includes presale strategic sales managers and presale strategic system designers as well as fully qualified presale senior project managers and a postsale group consisting of senior project managers, project coordinators, and systems administrators.

The majority of the AT&T/Lucent Technologies *Project Evaluation Review Process* was developed by the following AT&T/Lucent Technologies Project Managers: Tom Barnett, P.M.P., Randy Billman, P.M.P., Pat Pomponio, P.M.P., Dave Rogers, P.M.P., Frank Saladis, P.M.P., and A. J. (Hoppy) Thomas, P.M.P.
Subsequent amendments and updates for the Lucent Technologies projects were made by: Angel Barlow, P.M.P., Dave Emge, P.M.P., Kathy Marika, P.M.P., and Dan Ono, P.M.P.

The project-management organization preceded the creation of the presale group by four years and has been in existence for eleven years. Because an early requirement to enter the project-management group was the dedication of six years or the rest of a person's career, many of the senior project managers have close to eleven years in the organization and eleven continuous years of managing large telecommunications projects.

The reason for the unusually long commitment was the author's belief that you cannot build world-class competence in a short amount of time. This was going directly against the culture of the AT&T employee of the time. The AT&T job paradigm at the time of project-management group was created was one where employees changed positions every two or three years in a misguided belief that the more jobs they knew, the more valuable they were to the corporation. Unfortunately, this paradigm made the employees jacks of all trades and experts at none. This practice qualified these AT&T people for jobs in other Bell System companies, but for little else.

This project-management organization, however, has been able to stay intact for the last eleven years, while everything around them changed. With this unique opportunity, the project-management group has been able to build a process that has been classified as "best in class" by several benchmarking initiatives and is widely recognized as being a premier organization from inside and outside of Lucent Technologies.

Project Management Guidelines

The project review process known as the Project Evaluation Review Process (PERP) is part of the project-management process being used by the senior project managers in the organization. The documentation of the project-management process is called the Lucent Technologies–BCS Project Management Guidelines (PMG). The PMG consist of five (2-inch) volumes of process descriptions, examples, and operating instructions. These guidelines cover the recommended processes for each of the life-cycle phases involved in the communication projects. This chapter is abstracted from the full five-volume PMG.

Project Evaluation Review Process

OVERVIEW
The PERP was developed with several objectives in mind. They are as follows:

1. Benefits for current projects.   It was reasoned that if the review process were conducted at an early enough point in the project life cycle, benefits could be derived on the current project. Consequently, instead of the traditional postimplementation review, in which improved results are anticipated on some future project, one of the objectives of this particular review process was to deliver improved results and improved client satisfaction on the project being reviewed. Related to this objective was the complementary objective of maintaining the already established record of consistent delivery of projects that were high quality, on time, on budget, and that met the highest level of client satisfaction.

2. Correction of variances.   The second objective was derived to facilitate achieving the first objective. The project-review team is responsible for working with the project manager and the project team to correct any project-management variance discovered on the project. It was reasoned that, because the company was focusing some of the best and most knowledgeable project-management resources on the project, the company should be able to take advantage of this investment while this expertise was on the project site. If any variance was too large to resolve while these resources were on site, action items were created to resolve the variances. These action items identified the task required to resolve the variance, who was responsible for completion of the action item, and when the action item would be resolved. A follow-up process was incorporated to insure timely completion of the action items. This requirement was a change in philosophy from the traditional view, but was consistent with fundamental project-management objectives. The company wanted to head off any future problems on the project at hand rather than bring in the experts to identify what was done wrong after the ramifications of the errors had become visible in project results.

3. Quality measurement.   The third objective of this process was to provide a means of measuring the quality of the PMG implementation. The PMG provided the standard from which variance was measured. Consequently, the PERP was the means by which quality assurance of the project-management process was measured within the organization and on the specific project.

4. Project-manager training.   The fourth objective was to provide a training vehicle for the project managers to better learn the PMG. Learning was greatly enhanced through the use of on-site, one-on-one resources with PMG expertise because of the ability of the project managers to associate the application and implementation of the methodologies and principles included in the PMG on their own project. The company was highly successful in this area. One of the senior project managers was quoted as saying the review process was the best learning experience he had had in his AT&T career.

5. Continuous improvement.   The fifth objective was to provide a means of continuous improvement for the project-management process. The people doing the review were also the authors of the PMG. Whenever they found a poor result or a better method, their task was to include the improved method in the PMG. In addition, the people doing the review were in direct contact with the project manager. If the project manager related a lesson-learned experience to the review team, the review team was to develop and add the lesson learned to the PMG to permanently retain the process required to avoid the lesson-learned event in the future. The company's philosophy about lessons learned is that unless the lessons learned are integrated into the process description, in this case the PMG, they will not be properly documented for long-term benefit and retention. The company's philosophy is that the PMG serve as its corporate memory, which is why they are updated annually.

DESCRIPTION
The PERP provides a means to review the specific deliverables within any phase of the project's life cycle. A phase-identification process is used to determine the current phase (i.e., conceptual, planning, implementation, or close-out), and the extent to which that phase is completed. The targeted cycle for review will be determined by project complexity, project manager's experience, review-team availability, project health, and impact of the project on the organization. Most reviews will be conducted at the end of the planning phase, when the potential to influence project results is greatest.

Upon identification of the phase, the review process will focus directly on the status of the deliverables within that phase. Once the current status of the project is determined, the deliverables from the preceding phases that flow into the current phase will be reviewed for compliance with the PMG.

Upon completion of the review process, the project manager receives a written report documenting the results of the evaluation. The entire process will be managed as a positive, beneficial experience for the project manager and the project team. If the project review identifies specific areas for improvement, the project-review team, project manager, and appropriate project-team members develop plans and/or replan activities to correct the identified areas. A process will be established to monitor the implementation of the plan and the status of activities up to completion of the project objectives.

After completion and acceptance of the project by the client, the project manager conducts an internal project review with the project team and an external review with the client to document lessons learned throughout the duration of the project. These lessons learned will provide a basis for process improvement and continued development of Lucent Technologies PMGs.

SELECTION OF PROJECTS FOR EVALUATION
Initially, at least one PERP is conducted for each project manager during a calendar year. However, this process is reviewed each quarter in regard to a value analysis of the findings, district budget constraints, and resources available to conduct the reviews. In the selection process for projects, the following factors are considered:

- Identification of all current projects in the district
- Prioritization of high-risk projects
- Project financials such as budget and revenue
- New products or technology (controlled introductions)

- Project complexity (number of interfaces, project duration, and technical complexity)
- Geographic impact
- High exposure, political ramifications
- Client risk
- Project-manager experience
- Resources team availability
- Formal request for a review by a project manager or supervising manager

Evaluation Process

Once the review process is complete, the actual evaluation can take place.

TECHNIQUES

The project-evaluation team does the following:

- Ensures that each project-team member is properly introduced to the review team and that the purpose of the review is adequately explained.
- Informs the team that the reviewers will be documenting Qs and As to maintain accuracy.
- Is prepared to offer recommendations and suggestions to improve areas found to be in noncompliance with a standard or guideline.
- Identifies each area that may require improvement or modification. The project manager has the prerogative to not follow procedures in the PMG. If a variance is identified, it is important to understand why specific standards or guidelines are not being used for the project being reviewed.
- Emphasizes the strengths of using established standards and guidelines.
- Establishes a supportive atmosphere for the participants in the review.
- Displays and maintains a professional approach to the review process.
- Ensures that the participants are aware of the importance of the review process and the need to establish a method for benchmarking and continuous process improvement.
- Maintains a focus on factual information, not assumptions, rumors, or hearsay.

REVIEW-TEAM COMPOSITION

The project-review team normally consists of other unassigned senior project managers. Participation by supervising managers may be suggested for review feedback sessions. Actual evaluation teams are negotiated with the district manager and supervising managers.

The minimum size of the project-review team would be two. The review package contains lists of questions that allow for group or individual review of a specific phase by members of the review team.

PROJECT EVALUATION PROCESS

The project-evaluation process requires the review of specific deliverables as defined in the Lucent Technologies Project-Management Guidelines. These deliverables include:

- Contract and scope of work, project-assurance documentation, and hand-off materials
- Kickoff workshop documentation
- Work-breakdown structure (WBS)
- Master schedule
- Responsibility matrix
- Overall project network diagram and cutover network diagram (as applicable)
- Project plans such as quality, training, escalation, implementation, cutover, and so on.
- Monitor and control procedures, project escalation and jeopardy plans, and correspondence
- Monthly status reports, meeting agendas, and minutes
- Project budget tracking based on district guidelines

The documents are reviewed by members of the PERP team and compared with the Lucent Technologies PMG. Specific questions are asked to gain an understanding of how the project manager and project team are utilizing the deliverables to monitor and control the project activities. The interview questions are structured to generate conversation with the project manager. The intent is to establish a supportive environment that will allow the interviewing team and the project manager to discuss project details in a positive, educational manner. The data developed from this dialogue, coupled with the review of the deliverables, provides a basis for summarizing the results of the review.

The review team makes a determination about the health of the project and identifies strengths and areas that require replanning. These determinations often depend on the project phase and the professional experience of review-team members. The review team uses information from the PERP to work with the appropriate team member or project manager to develop plans for correcting areas that require improvement or replanning.

The findings regarding each deliverable are summarized in the project-review summary. The summary provides the project manager and the team with a detailed, objective document that can be used to improve the quality of project deliverables. The project-review summary also provides input for overall Lucent Technologies project-management-process improvement deliverables.

FEEDBACK

As the review progresses, the review team provides feedback that supports project strengths and identifies areas for improvements to the participants on specific findings. This encourages open dialogue with the participants and minimizes negotiation and conflict at the conclusion of the review.

A formal meeting is conducted at the completion of the review to provide a summary of all findings and recommendations to the project manager.

REVIEW REPORT DISTRIBUTION
A copy of the final review report with a developmental plan, if required, is distributed by the PERP team to the following persons:

- Lucent Technologies project-management district manager
- Lucent Technologies project-management district office (master file)
- Supervising manager
- Project manager and project-team members
- Other key individuals as deemed appropriate by the project manager

REVIEW SCHEDULING
Initially, identification of the specific phase of all projects that are currently in progress are used to develop a master schedule of projects for review for any given calendar year. The priority of the scheduling will be based on cutover schedules.

Evaluation Process Specification

PHASE IDENTIFICATION
Before the initiation of a project evaluation, it is necessary to determine the current phase of the project (conceptual, planning, implementation, or close-out) and the extent to which that phase is complete.

The phase identification will follow the project-management-process flow-chart recommendation. The following describes phase identification:

1. *The conceptual phase* ends with the completion of a signed contract, technical design review, project assurance, and documentation. The project is then handed off to the project manager.
2. *The planning phase* encompasses all kickoff workshop activities, committee formation, and draft-plan-preparation tasks.
3. *The implementation phase* starts when the functional organizations begin their tasks and concludes with completion of project objectives.
4. *The close-out phase* begins with client acceptance of the completed project. It also includes postcutover reviews or postproject reviews, the implementation of the operations, Administration and Maintenance Plan (OA&M), and final bill processing.

The phase identification is not meant to delineate all activities within the four major categories, but rather to define, in generalized terms, those basic activities associated with the transition between phases. In all project evaluations, the project scope, master schedule, and monthly status reports will be reviewed for assistance in this determination. Further, and most important, the individual project manager is consulted for input and agreement. The progress completion of any particular phase may be viewed in both real and ideal terms. That is, in real terms, what has actually been accomplished to date; and in ideal terms, what should have been accomplished at this stage based on the Lucent Technologies Standards and Guidelines.

By definition, a project is a unique undertaking, and time needed for each phase may differ from project to project; an implementation phase could be three months or three years in duration. However, all projects do have milestones that are identified and used in the project's progress determination. The following items will be used to identify progress:

1. Project scope. To maximize the benefits of a project evaluation, it is generally assumed that the evaluation is conducted during the early stages of the implementation phase. Projects in the implementation phase generally have detailed plans and control processes in place. Ideally, the review will occurs before completion of project deliverables. This provides sufficient time to prepare and implement required measures to affect project success positively. Review of the project scope, which is normally finalized in the planning phase, identifies the breadth of the project and the necessary components required to be addressed on a master schedule. This review is essential to obtain a complete overview of the project under evaluation.

2. Master schedule. The master schedule identifies activity durations, milestone dates, and planned and actual task-completion dates that will lead to project success. Therefore, the master schedule and detailed implementation schedule, if accurate and complete, will be a tool for the reviewers to use in determining the project-phase identification. It also provides the progress completion of a particular phase. It is assumed that the various scheduled activities are reflected in the PERT and Gantt charts and provide the necessary dependency relationships.

3. Monthly status report. The monthly status report should reflect the current status of the project through the previous month's reporting period. In addition, any critical issues associated with the project should be identified on the monthly status. Along with the master schedule, network diagram, and identified milestones, an accurate estimation of the real progress can be ascertained by the review team.

CONCEPTUAL PHASE CRITERIA

The conceptual-phase review focuses on activities that take place in the precontract environment.

This phase includes the project manager's involvement in the development of the Request For Proposal (RFP) response, the project manager's familiarity with the project-assurance binder, and adherence to the project-assurance standards.

The review will evaluate the following:

- Participation of the project manager in the preparation of the RFP response and contract determination, precontract scope development, and initial contract management.
- The project-assurance binder, which includes the custom contract, product agreements, and RFP, and compliance with project-assurance standards.

The performance-evaluation team will be selected based on availability, project-management experience, PERP evaluation training, and negotiation with the supervising manager or district manager. The candidates for interviews may include but are not limited to a project manager and project team. The project team includes a design specialist, a streamlined implementation project manager (SIPM), a site service manager, a dedicated switch-installation crew supervisor (DSIC), a data-technician organization supervisor, a technical-sales-support person, a network-design engineer, and other designated team members (based on project requirements).

Request For Proposal Response

The project manager's involvement in the RFP/project-request process determines the need for evaluation of this phase. During the RFP response, the project manager may be required to deliver detailed presentations to the project owner, the sales team, or client. Introductions of the project manager to the client and the sales team are usually conducted at these meetings. These presentations may include the following:

- The Lucent Technologies project-management process
- A preliminary implementation plan
- Key project participants
- Tools and techniques
- The project-request-worksheet process

Project Assurance Standards

Project-assurance standards and documentation provide a basis for the project manager to begin planning the project in detail. Project-assurance activities are the following:

- Project assurance documentation
- All agreements and elements of the project-assurance binder received and reviewed by the project manager and the project team, which include contracts, agreements, documents about scope, and notes
- Project-manager acceptance of the project and hand-off from the account team

When the project scope is understood and the design and project-assurance documentation is in order, the project manager accepts project responsibility from the account team.

PLANNING-PHASE CRITERIA

During the planning phase, the project team is formed, preliminary cost estimates are determined, initial project plans are developed, and the project team is prepares for implementation. The purpose of the PERP is to identify strengths and potential areas of concern in all phases. However, at this time, concentration is devoted to the planning phase. The review will assist in the development of corrective plans and contingencies that may improve the probability of project success.

Planning phase activities include project-team formation, budget preparation, project kickoff, and implementation planning.

These activities are reviewed and evaluated during the review process and compared with established standards described in this document.

The PERP objectives for the planning phase are to document, evaluate, and provide recommendations for improvement as required in the following areas:

- Project kickoff deliverables

  — Kickoff binder
  — WBS/responsibility matrix
  — Master schedule
  — Project scope
  — Project controls
  — Project administration
  — Meeting schedules
  — Reporting procedures
  — Documentation
  — Preliminary cost estimate
  — Finalized project budget

- Initial project plans

  — Implementation
  — Monitoring and control
  — Safety
  — Quality assurance
  — Change management
  — Escalation
  — Training
  — Test and acceptance
  — Cutover/rehome
  — Client acceptance
  — Operation, administration, and maintenance (OA&M)
  — Disconnect

- Use of PS7 project-management software

The planning-phase component of the project-management process will be used as a basis for the review process.

Team Formation

Project documentation should include a complete list of the project team assigned as well as second- and third-level supporting managers. A project-team-member information sheet should be included in the initial project (kickoff) binder.

Budget Preparation

The project manager is responsible for the preparation of a preliminary project-cost estimate and a finalized project budget. The finalized project budget includes the following: project-management overhead expenses, labor, and extraordinary expenses, such as rentals and miscellaneous equipment. The project manager is required to interview the functional managers and obtain all information relative to resource loading. Lucent Technologies' budget-preparation guidelines are included in the Lucent Technologies PMG. The project budget review is based on budget preparation, baseline, and resource management as presented in the Lucent Technologies project-management formal budget process training. After negotiation with the functional managers, the project manager finalizes the project budget and obtains approval from the project owner.

The Project-Kickoff Meeting

The project-kickoff meeting is essential to the planning process. The project manager is responsible for coordinating the planning session, internal kickoff workshop with Lucent Technologies' project-team members, and the external kickoff workshop, which adds the client. The project manager coordinates the preparation of the project binder and arranges for the final workshop deliverables. These are the deliverables:

- Kickoff binder deliverables

  — Project scope
  — Project team list
  — WBS/responsibility matrix
  — Master schedule
  — Project monitoring and control procedures

- Planning committees established at project kickoff

  — Implementation
  — Quality assurance
  — Change management
  — Safety (as required)
  — Cutover (as required)
  — Test and acceptance
  — Training
  — Operations, administration, and maintenance
  — Disconnect/close-out

Note: Some plans may not be required depending on the nature of the project. Where plans are not used, the project manager should be prepared to explain why the plans were not used.

Upon completion of the internal kickoff workshop, the project manager schedules a meeting with the customer/client to review the output of the internal kickoff meeting. Attendees at this meeting include the project manager, the account executive, the design specialist, and the client. The external kickoff meeting deliverables include the completed project binder for client review, and documentation of client acceptance of the initial project implementation plans as developed during the internal kickoff workshop.

Implementation Planning

During the planning phase, the project manager is responsible for the preparation of administrative guidelines. With the assistance of the project team members, the project manager develops the overall project plans. These initial plans are the basis for project control during the implementation phase. A network diagram, based on information gathered during the kickoff process, is developed for variance analysis. Project administration items in the project binder include the following:

- Status reporting procedures
- Meeting schedules
- Escalation and jeopardy procedures
- Interface agreements
- Recommended project plans to be utilized during project life cycle
- Project-management tools

  - Lucent Technologies PMP
  - Lucent Technologies PMG
  - Hardware/software platform

The Hardware/software platform includes the following:

- Project Scheduler 7
- Network/PERT Chart
- Gantt chart
- Ad-hoc reports format
- MS Word for Windows
- Project-status-report format
- Jeopardy format
- Minutes format
- ATTMail

IMPLEMENTATION PHASE CRITERIA

During the implementation phase, the project plans and procedures developed during the planning phase are actually applied to the project. The Lucent Technologies PMP and PMG can be used as a tool by the project manager to further develop plans and to assist the project team by identifying critical tasks that require attention. Primary activities within the implementation phase are the following:

- Contract/scope management
- Replanning
- Identifying and resolving problems
- Project monitoring and control
- Implementing the project and controlling change
- Managing cutover

The objectives of the review team during the implementation phase include a review of project documentation, interviews with the project manager and members of the project team, assessment of the use of project-management tools, and evaluation of overall project health. The process will assist the review team and the project manager by identifying the following:

- Areas in which implementation requires replanning
- Project successes
- Change-management effectiveness
- Effectiveness and use of project plans
- Project budget actuals versus planned expenses
- Project schedule performance
- Quality/process improvement opportunities
- Project-team effectiveness

The implementation-phase review concentrates on the activities listed in the section of the PERP called Implementation Phase Criteria and on the tasks identified in the project-management process. These activities are further defined as follows:

Contract/Scope Management
Project-assurance procedures include documentation of contract deliverables and custom contract requirements. The project-review team compares these documents with the actual work being performed during implementation. This assists the review team and the project manager in determining the degree of compliance with specifications. It also identifies areas in which additional work is required to meet specifications or in which unnecessary work is performed that may add expense to the project. Contract management includes terms and conditions that may involve subcontractors. An example of this may be a wire vendor's use of non-Lucent Technology suppliers for material and labor. Terms and conditions may include specific progress payments to subcontractors on identified dates.

Replanning
Identification of any changes in project cost and budgets, scope, resource, contract, schedule, or technical-performance standards may require the project manager and the team to replan certain aspects of the project. The replanning task requires the project manager and the functional managers to

revisit plans developed during the conceptual, planning, and implementation phases.

Identifying and Resolving Problems

During the course of a project, the project manager will be required to manage various types of problems that may affect project success. Constant monitoring and control of all aspects of the project will help identify these problems. Schedule conflicts, unexpected resource constraints, jeopardies, and budget overruns are examples of the types of problems that are common in a project life cycle.

Problems and challenges that are identified by the project manager and the project team must be evaluated to determine the impact on the project in terms of time, cost, and scope. After evaluating the impact of a problem on the project, the project manager and team members must determine what changes are required to minimize any negative impacts to the triple constraints. Recommendations for changes to the existing project plans may require approval from the customer, project owner, or other organizations that may be affected by the project-team recommendations.

Project Monitoring and Control

Lucent Technologies project managers are required to submit project-meeting minutes and status reports to the project team, supervising manager, district manager, client, and project owner with timely information about project progress. Project minutes are provided in a standard format as described in the kickoff-workshop training guides. Guidelines for product status have been established to maintain overall consistency in the delivery of these reports. Progress reports from team members may be provided through formal documentation or via status at project-team meetings. Project minutes can be used as a reference to verify assignment of tasks, action items, commitment statements, and to plan project activities. Status reports should address project progress in all areas of responsibility for each team member. These areas of responsibility include the following:

- Implementation progress (master schedule)
- Project costs (actual vs. planned)
- Current or potential jeopardies
- Critical issues (task dependencies)
- Resource issues (availability and cost)
- Subcontractor progress reports
- Project safety
- Project quality assurance
- Overall project health

Implementing the Project and Controlling Change

Managing project activities, events, and milestones requires the project manager to use the tools, reports, and quality reviews to ensure that the project meets the objectives of time, cost, and scope. As the project progresses through the implementation phase, the project manager must identify, evaluate, communicate, control, and coordinate all project changes. These changes may include the following:

- Project costs and budget changes
- Project scope changes
- Project resource changes
- Contract changes
- Schedule changes
- Technical performance or specification changes

The PERP provides the review team and the project manager with information that may be used to improve the Lucent Technologies project-management process. Frequency and similarity of changes identified in project reviews will assist in the further development of PMG's through process improvement. Changes in many cases result in increased project cost or delay project completion. Information gathered during a review may be used to modify procedures across organizations. Procedural changes may result in project cost reduction, reduced project duration, and increased customer satisfaction.

Managing Cutover

The term *cutover* is used to describe the event or action that takes place when the product, service, or project element contracted for by the client is placed in operation or turned over to the client. Cutover dates are negotiated by the project team and the client. Prior to actual cutover, the project team reviews the project's state of readiness. This is accomplished through a cutover-readiness review usually scheduled two to three weeks before the actual cutover. At this time the project team reviews the current status of the project and determines the probability of success. Cutover plans and contingency plans are reviewed and finalized. An OA&M plan is also reviewed and finalized. The OA&M plan addresses procedures and guidelines for use by the client after completion of the project, the resumption of normal day-to-day operations, and the departure of the project team.

The cutover-readiness review, conducted by the project manager, is designed to provide the client with a detailed evaluation of the project's current status and to gain approval from the client to proceed with the cutover plans.

CLOSEOUT PHASE

As the project nears completion, the project manager must begin the process of formal project closeout. This phase includes a number of activities that will evaluate the project in terms of time, cost, and scope:

- The provision of as-builts drawings
- Project closeout reviews

- Review of project deliverables
- Client satisfaction
- Effectiveness of the project-management process
- Quality reviews
- Customer billing
- Records retention

The project manager and the project team conduct a postcutover review to determine where specifications have not been met. A detailed list of items, known as a punch list, is created to identify noncompliance, quality-improvement areas, uncompleted tasks, and client concerns. The responsible project-team members are identified and assigned to correct any project deficiencies. Specific time frames for completion of these items may be included in the contract or may be agreed upon by the client and the project team during the postcutover review.

The project manager prepares a project budget report using PS6 software. This report will do the following:

- Identify actual project costs and compare them with baseline objectives
- Provide data for determining future product costs
- Provide information for process improvement in budget preparation and tracking
- Provide the project manager with additional training in project-budget development, if necessary

Project Closeout Reviews

Upon completion of all deliverables, the project manager schedules and conducts internal and external project reviews.

The internal review is attended by the members of the project team. This review is designed to provide an opportunity for the project team to identify project activities that were successful as well as areas that require improvement or change. The project manager prepares written documentation from this meeting, which is included in the project binder. A copy of this document is sent to the Lucent Technologies project-management district office for review and use in process-improvement activities.

The external review is scheduled and conducted by the project manager. At this review, the client provides the project manager and project-team members with an evaluation of the project team and the overall project-management process.

The client's feedback will provide the project team and the Lucent Technologies project-management district office with information that will enhance the project-management process and identify areas for improvement in customer satisfaction. Specific items for discussion include the following:

- Client satisfaction with the Lucent Technologies project-management process
- Project quality controls

- Adherence to project performance criteria such as specifications, schedules, and cost
- Overall project quality

Final Client Acceptance

The contract, addendums, and project documentation provide the basis for client acceptance. Specific details for acceptance are outlined in the cutover plan or in an acceptance plan prepared jointly by the project team and the client. Client acceptance is an extremely important part of the closeout process. It is an indication that the project was planned and implemented successfully. Final client acceptance will be achieved upon completion of all outstanding action items identified during the postcutover review and verified delivery of all contract specifications, or upon completion of negotiations with the client. Negotiations with the client and the account team may be required when additional work beyond the original scope is identified or where conditions exist that prevent completion of task items.

The review team evaluates project closeout documentation with the project manager and discuss the closeout process. This discussion provides the project manager and the review team with information that may be used for process improvement and customer satisfaction.

Project Billing

Upon completion of all project deliverables and client acceptance, the project team processes all remaining bills and invoices. The project manager's responsibility in the billing process is to ensure that the appropriate team members are assigned to process billing. Billing procedures are documented in the project binder and progress payments are tracked as a task on the network diagram if applicable. Billing procedures and documentation are included in the hand-back to the account team.

Project Termination:
The Good, the Bad, the Ugly

Carl L. Pritchard

Biographical Sketch . . . **Carl L. Pritchard** is the Curriculum Director for the Educational Services Institute (ESI) in Arlington, Virginia. He is responsible for developing and presenting project-management programs for ESI through The George Washington University School of Business and Professional Development. A certified Project Management Professional, he trains and consults in project management with emphasis on risk, communication, and strategic management.

P roject termination or closeout practices are as varied as the projects themselves, but project-termination models fall into three very general categories: positive, negative, and premature. There is, in some circles, a fourth type—antitermination—which is the failure to bring a project to closure. *Positive termination* occurs when the project comes to closure with a positive outcome and an upbeat relationship with the customer and stakeholders. *Negative termination* occurs when the project reaches closure at project completion, but with less-than-positive feelings between the project and client organizations. *Premature termination* occurs when a project is not near its planned closure, but a change in client needs, a lack of time, or a lack of funds force the early termination of the project. Although termination has some standard practices, each type of termination requires specific attention.

Positive Termination

Projects rarely terminate with fanfare. Project closure is normally a slow, quiet, unplanned process, rather than implementation of a clear exit strategy. That's unfortunate, because a well-considered exit strategy can be as critical as the project plan itself in terms of retaining customers and building stakeholder loyalty.

An exit strategy is a planned approach to administrative and customer closure that integrates the needs of team members, the needs of the organization, and the needs of the customers and stakeholders. The strategy should be a clearly stated mandate on how project-team members will guide the project *through* a successful conclusion, and the strategy should be supported by the project plan. This plan should include clear transitions of all parties and processes associated with the project. Exit strategies, however, are often antithetical to organizational reality. In many organizations, exit strategies are discounted as superfluous niceties, rather than essential aspects of the project plan. The only way to overcome that perception is to prove the value of effective closure—something only a handful of organizations have achieved.

An exit strategy should address the needs of all stakeholders who have been with the project since its inception. That includes, but is not limited to, the following:

- Team members
- Customers
- End users
- Subcontractors and vendors
- Management
- Project manager

Although these individuals had one set of needs during the project, at termination an entirely different set of needs may arise. If the project manager anticipates these needs, positive project termination can become a major growth opportunity for everyone involved.

IDENTIFYING AND PLANNING FOR STAKEHOLDER NEEDS

The most effective way to identify needs at termination is to ask the stakeholders to envision their perception of the ideal closeout. Team members may anticipate personal growth opportunities and organizational recognition. Customers may expect some formal ceremony or transition forum. End users may foresee nothing more than a smoother process or a new product. To develop these closeout forecasts, the project manager should interview all key participants well before the waning days of the effort. If the questions are delayed until the end of the project, many of the needs will be lost in the crush of activity that conventionally occurs at project closeout. After participants' needs have been established, those needs should be integrated into the project plan as clear elements in the overall exit strategy. They should be treated with the same level of attention and concern as all activities, and they should not be relegated to second-class status because they fall on the last days of the effort. It is crucial to evaluate stakeholder needs based on input from a variety of stakeholders, rather than a single source.

EXAMPLE.   A project manager with a Fortune 10 telecommunications firm tells the story of his delivery of final customer documentation. He mailed a bundle of copies of the product documentation in three-ring binders to the customer site, along with a brief handwritten note. After the delivery, relations with the customer cooled noticeably. He asked the customer if there was something wrong with the documentation, but the customer deferred the issue. Finally, several weeks later, at a postproject review, the customer excoriated the project manager for "shoddy documentation." After an extensive interview, the customer revealed that he had anticipated product documentation in a hardback binding. Even though the project manager felt the three-ring binder would allow for greater flexibility in dealing with updates and errata, the customer was unsatisfied. The documentation failed to meet expectations. Did the products and service work? Yes. Were the end users satisfied? Yes. But the customer with acceptance responsibility was disappointed. A few minutes of thoughtful discussion on expectations at closeout could have precluded a difficult experience for both the project manager and the customer.

For almost every project, there are some common needs at closeout that must be addressed. These often manifest themselves in organizational closeout forms and checklists, such as the ones prepared by the Educational Services Institute.[1]

1. External: Project
2. Internal: Project
3. External: Personnel
4. Internal: Personnel

The internal project issues include those related directly to the internal organization and the processes by which the team functions. The following is an internal project termination checklist.

- Are any deliverables outstanding?
- Have internal certifications and approvals been signed and received?
- Are there any outstanding internal commitments?
- Have project costs been charged to their appropriate accounts?
- Have all work packages been completed and closed out?
- Have any incomplete work packages been accounted for, rationalized, and documented?
- Has management been notified regarding the availability of project personnel?
- Has the project plan been updated through completion?
- Has excess project material been dealt with?

By addressing these issues, the project manager paves the way for full accountability on the project, the plan, and the overall status. Personnel issues are not among the first addressed, because they can best be dealt with after these questions are resolved.

The external project issues include those related directly to processes and organizations of the customer, end user, and outside vendors. The following checklist illustrates the need to focus on the full spectrum of stakeholders:

- Is the project owner satisfied with the deliverables?
- Have outstanding deliverables been accounted for and/or addressed?
- Have all certifications and authorizations been approved (and documented)?
- Have suppliers been notified regarding any outstanding commitments?
- Are all parties aware of pending termination?
- Have project facilities on-site been closed (or prepared for closure)?
- Have auditing and maintenance procedures been put in place and activated?

The focus in this list is purely on materials and organizations. By focusing on the mechanical issues with the customer first, project closure gains momentum. The customer answers a series of concrete, objective questions, all of which drive the project closer to closure. This allows the project manager to close out a significant number of project issues without delving into the personal needs and biases of the project stakeholders.

After some of the more clearcut and concrete details have been addressed, it is easier to make the migration into the realm of personnel topics. Managers' personal motivations, social pressures, and organizational pull (both internal and external) all work together to make it difficult to allow a project to close out naturally.[2] The project manager must work to overcome these emotional issues.

If the project manager hopes to resolve these issues for an outside organization, the issues must first be resolved internally. In reviewing the following checklist, one should consider the fundamental needs of the personnel involved and how these questions address those needs:

- Are all personnel aware of the exit strategy?
- Are they motivated to support that strategy?
- Have the project-team concerns regarding future employment been addressed?
- Is the project team dedicated to the remaining commitments?
- Are motivators and incentives still in place to encourage participants in the remaining tasks and obligations?
- Is a recognition and reward structure in place?

EXAMPLE.   A project manager based in the greater Washington, D.C., area was working on a nationwide installation project that kept her team members on the road for weeks at a time. In the course of a single year, most of the team members had spent only a matter of days at their homes and were grateful to see the project drawing to a close. The project manager wanted to do something to thank both the team members and their spouses for successfully weathering the project and seeing it through. She planned a gala weekend for all concerned, including fine dining and hotels and a celebration in New York City. To her chagrin, team members were universally unimpressed by the gesture. They just wanted to get home and stay there for a change. Although she went out of her way to get support for the team and to recognize their achievements, she failed to recognize some of their most basic needs—those of home and hearth. Had she considered the questions listed above, she would have recognized the need to include team members in the basic exit strategy decisions, including those related to reward and recognition.

The most challenging checklist in a positive closeout environment relates to the personal needs of personnel outside the project organization. Whether the customer is internal or external, the issues associated with this level of closeout remain the same.

- Are efforts in place to ensure that the project owner's interest remains high?
- Are efforts in place to ensure that the project owner's perceptions and attitudes regarding the project are positive and stable?
- Are transition issues (including personnel, material, and process) being addressed with the project owner?
- Are key personnel being apprised of project status?
- Is a communication structure in place to maintain owner-project manager relations?
- Have public relations opportunities been assessed and implemented?

The first four questions can be addressed through a comprehensive project plan and through day-to-day implementation. Most communication structures, however, evolve on an ad-hoc basis and don't take full advantage of communication methodologies already in place in both the customer and project organizations. Although organizations may have internal publications, broadcast e-mail structures, and other standard practices for disseminating information, project information is generally relegated to the informal networks (i.e., the grapevine). As team members (or project managers) are reassigned in either the project or customer organization, the channels for information can be cut short, and valuable opportunities to communicate may be lost.

MAXIMIZING POSITIVE CLOSEOUT

Although many organizations have large-scale public relations mechanisms in place, project managers have not historically taken full advantage of the opportunities they afford. In some organizations where public relations is left to the individual, the project manager may feel inadequate to be the PR representative for his or her organization.

Nevertheless, project managers should at least consider the public relations options available. Public relations is nothing more than the art or science of establishing and promoting a favorable relationship with the public.[3] To generate a favorable relationship, the project manager should consider what will make the project appear to be a success and what will make the customer appear more satisfied with the outcome. Both can be addressed through a simple technique that also magnifies the aura of closure associated with the end of the project. That technique is a formal transition. For years, the construction industry has mastered this art, and only now are other types of organizations seizing similar closeout practices.

Consider the completion of a shopping center, major highway, or Navy destroyer. They all have one element in common: ceremony. When a shopping center or highway is complete, a ribbon is cut. When a destroyer is finished, champagne is smashed upon its hull as it slides down the ways. Historically, when a software project is complete, documentation is transferred (either in a box or electronically), and team members walk quietly away. The latter doesn't have quite the same level of panache as the former. Thus, some developers of less tangible deliverables are looking for ways to adopt the ceremonial project closeout approaches of their peers in the heavy construction industries.

Some software developers have begun packaging a special copy of the software (or even a dummy disk or CD), framing it, and delivering it at a special customer meeting. Process developers can consider certificates, hardbound copies of their materials, or other high-visibility materials to help generate a sense of closure. The key is for ceremonial closure to make clear to all parties that the project is over and that transition is taking place. Even if a few lingering closeout issues remain, all participants share a common understanding that the project has been handed over to the customer.

Lessons Learned

Beyond clarity of transition, another key to maximizing positive closeout is the development and implementation of lessons learned. Some organizations perform this task extremely well, whereas others lose vast wells of corporate memory as project teams are disbanded at the end of each effort. Lessons learned are crucial to building corporate memory. Unfortunately, most organizations fail to build their lessons learned in such a way that the organization can take full advantage of the information gathered and generated through each project. Some organizations, like Malcolm Baldrige award-winner Eastman Chemical in Kingsport, Tennessee, build vast databases to retain lessons learned and improve customer relations through enhanced corporate memory. Whether the organization has such an advanced structure or not, lessons-learned exercises are invaluable in terms of enhancing individual and team project performance. Sadly, many organizations relegate lessons learned to a few lines on a project closeout sheet, rather than tapping them for the vast resource they can be. If the project manager hopes to enhance the lessons-learned experience for the entire project team, it's vital to have a comprehensive understanding of what a lesson learned should be. In reviewing project documentation, it is not surprising to see an entry that looks something like this:

Lessons Learned	Keep good documentation

Such lessons are virtually worthless. They provide no insight about what drove the project manager to the conclusion and provide no understanding beyond the thin veneer of the information provided. They are too shallow to be of any value. A high-quality lesson learned meets the following criteria:

- It is timely.
- It is detailed.
- It is relevant.
- It is in context.

Although other criteria may be applied, these will provide sufficient information to offer value to subsequent team members and project managers. Regarding being timely, it is vital that the project manager and team members develop lessons learned soon. The old adage "Time heals all wounds,"[4] certainly applies in the project environment. When a project is complete, it is very easy to overlook grievances that developed during implementation and to forget the day-to-day nuisances that degraded project performance. Thus, the more time is allowed to pass before lessons learned are developed, the lower the quality of the lessons learned.

In addition, detail is lost over time. It's very easy to forget the nuances of a customer relationship and the specifics of organizational practice, process, and policy in the days and weeks after a project is accepted. Detail is essential to high-quality lessons learned. Details about people, places, times, and issues become essential.

Details about individuals also become essential. Although the customer organization may, as a whole, be made up of qualified and talented personnel, there may be a handful of individuals whose approach to work may delay the project. Future project managers need to know who those individuals are in order to manage a project effectively.

Although relevance may seem somewhat subjective, the project manager should be able to ask (and answer positively) this question: Could this conceivably happen again to anyone else on a similar effort, and would they care? Relevance is crucial in determining whether a lesson learned is well constructed. Although most project managers tend to be brief, there are those who feel compelled to use lessons learned as an opportunity to build extensive histories of their achievements and accomplishments and their stellar relationships with everyone involved. In essence, they find that lessons learned afford them the opportunity to boast about their accomplishments in a forum that is socially acceptable. This is neither productive nor effective. If left unattended, this type of behavior can quickly relegate lessons learned to a position of organizational insignificance.

A high-quality lesson learned is presented in context. The environment in which an action or series of actions occurs is, in many cases, as crucial as the events themselves. Behaviors that in one context would be unacceptable and deplorable can go unchallenged in another.

Lessons learned are wonderful opportunities to develop information and to share personal and corporate tricks of the trade. They are not inherently negative and should not be treated as such. Lessons learned are an opportunity to share best practices, client information, and corporate insight. This is not to say that some projects do not end on a negative note.

Negative Termination

There are myriad projects throughout history that have ended on a less-than-positive note. Closeout is a high-stress time in the life of any project and can engender some extremely negative emotions. It is also a time when corrective action is expensive and time consuming. A study on project communication[5] indicates that although the number of problems reported is on the decline during the acceptance phase (normally closely associated with closeout), still, more than 10 percent of all project problems are reported during this phase. The same study reinforces the commonsense notion that problems encountered and addressed at closeout are among the most expensive to rectify. In fact, project costs may escalate at a much higher rate at project acceptance than at any other point in the project.

For the project manager in the field, there's a need to watch for the telltale signs associated with a potentially negative termination. These signs may have little to do with the quality of the project or the quality of the relationship between the project manager and the customer. They may, in fact, have more to do with the customer's internal problems.

No matter the cause, some measure of resolution (at least at a surface level) becomes the obligation of the project manager. If the customer cannot resolve these issues internally, the project manager, the team, and the project itself may suffer the brunt of the customer's wrath. The following are signs of a degrading potential for positive termination:

- Sudden, significant shifts in customer expectations
- Last-minute management changes in either the project or customer organization
- Hostility between personnel in the project organization and the customer organization

It could readily be argued that only the most insensitive of project managers could miss signs that are this obvious. However, project managers tend to operate with a very distinct frame of reference in their project and can easily be blinded to some of the impending crises swirling around them. Specifically, the approaching project closeout will sometimes drive project managers to believe that their projects are doing far better than the customer believes they are. The project manager may have a tendency to make "done" synonymous with "good."

When project closeout takes a negative turn, it becomes incumbent on the project manager to minimize the risks associated with customer and organizational negativity. At this juncture, not all the basic risk-mitigation strategies (avoidance, acceptance, and mitigation—including control and deflection[6]) can be applied. Avoidance is rarely an option at this late stage of the process; the customer relationship is established and few actions are available that allow the project manager simply to close the project and walk away without engendering stress on that relationship. Although acceptance remains a possibility, it can only be applied in organizations in which the customer relationship is not a high-value item. If the customer is truly valued and appreciated, accepting the risks associated with the negative termination will lead to long-term hostility and the potential abrogation of the relationship altogether. That leaves the project manager with control and deflection as the primary strategies to reverse a negative termination.

The steps outlined under positive termination afford a sound framework for projects in virtually any condition with the customer. In projects where the customer has an extremely negative attitude, however, additional effort must be applied. Some customers are already acutely aware that a negative attitude at termination works in their favor. For years, contracting officers have used acceptance as an opportunity to extract promises and guarantees from project managers that would otherwise be considered unacceptable or unworkable.

CREATIVE CONTROL STRATEGIES

Control is a key strategy in dealing with the risks associated in meeting supplemental customer requests. By minimizing the probability of their occurrence of their impact, the project manager can generate better value for the project and customer organizations. The challenge with control strategies is that they often require a high level of creativity. How can the project manager develop creative strategies that will still satisfy the customer? In some cases, the differences can be resolved by putting the project manager in the same position as the project manager attempting to close out a more successful (or more well-received) effort. The first step is to ensure that the project manager understands what the customer's vision of success is. In a negative termination, however, it can be assumed that there is a significant gap between the customer's vision and the current status of the project. In the field, the project manager may wish to bring in team members (or, later in the process, customer representatives) to answer the question of how to bridge the gap between the two sides.

ESTABLISHING AFFORDABILITY

At no time is the project manager being asked to commit the organization to anything outside the scope of the existing project. The project manager must, however, make accommodations for the differing perspective of the customer and must address the customer's valid concerns. The first issue of affordability is a challenging one at the end of the project. Correcting problems at close-out is twenty times more expensive than correcting the same problems during a project's initial design phase.[7] The project manager must select corrective actions carefully, opting for those that will do the most to influence the customer at the lowest reasonable cost. (Reasonableness is determined on an organization-by-organization basis.)

CHANGING CUSTOMER ATTITUDES

The second issue is one of customer satisfaction. Will the change actually influence the customer toward a more positive closeout? Team members who know the customer well may be able to accurately predict the level of customer satisfaction associated with a particular change, but the best answer to this question will ultimately come from the customer.

When addressing these issues with the customer, it is best to do so from the perspective of issues resolution, rather than presenting the option itself. "If I come up with widget enhancements, would that make a difference to you?" is actually a far different question from "If I put on widget process coolers, would that make a difference to you?" The first question allows for clarification of the issue at hand. It makes no promise to the customer and does not intimate that a specific solution is under consideration. The first question allows the project manager enormous latitude in resolving the problem. By merely introducing the second question, the project manager may establish an expectation in the customer's mind that the closeout issue is going to be resolved using one particular solution. If the solution is not the customer's ideal, the project manager is going to be taken to task, even if the solution would have worked. If the solution *is* the customer's ideal, but proves too expensive or unworkable, the project manager has been backed into a corner and may be accused of further failing to meet his or her obligations on the project.

KEEPING PROJECT PROMISES

The final issue in bridging the gap is one of customer entitlement. What does the customer deserve? The customer may have a far different perspective on this issue than the project manager. The customer deserves what the project organization (and the sales organization, in some cases) has promised. However, just because the organization has made a promise does not mean that the promise will be kept or kept well. The customer organization will look directly to the project manager to keep the project organization's promises, so the project manager must take on the perspective of the customer organization in reviewing requests related to termination. If they seem unreasonable, the project manager should not hesitate to let the customer organization know. But if the requests can readily be construed to be part of the original project objectives or requirements, the project manager should begin the resolution process, seeking ways to fill the satisfaction gap.

As these steps are implemented, the project manager must consider her or his attitude and that of the project team. The project manager who pushes for open communication heightens the probability that the team will continue to perform well over the long term (or at least through project termination).[8] This is not to imply that the project manager must take on the role of cheerleader. It is important, however, that the project manager recognize the importance of presenting the most positive face to the customer.

A project manager in the U.S. Department of the Interior once asked why some project managers in her organization were frequently perceived as successes, even though their projects had not achieved optimal results. After a lengthy discussion, it became apparent that their attitudes toward the projects were always positive and that they did not encourage or support any discussion (either in-house or at the internal customer's facility) that painted the project in a less-than-flattering light. Their projects were not ideal. They did not have all the best resources or all the best outcomes. The project managers did have a positive attitude about their efforts and shared that attitude with both the teams and the customer. Although attitude is not enough to overcome significant technical deficiency, it may be enough to hold sway over perceived deficiencies or over negative costumer attitudes. Customers select projects in hopes that the project will be successful. Toward that end, the more the project manager can do to envelop the project in an aura of success, the more effective the project manager will be in both negative and positive termination situations.

Most of the assumptions up to this point are based on the premise that the project will actually be taken to its logical conclusion. Some projects don't make it that far.

Premature Termination

As with conventional termination, premature termination can be either positive or negative. Most of the time, however, premature termination of a project is perceived as negative, because the project was not allowed to achieve its desired goals. That inability to achieve goals can be driven by a change in needs, a lack of funds, or a lack of time. Any or all of those three qualities can effectively shut down a project before it comes to fruition.

Most project managers will attempt to preclude premature termination as they work to perpetuate the efforts to which they've been assigned. The cultural drivers behind this persistence are strong.[9] Key figures throughout history are those who persevere and succeed. Rarely do we find historically powerful people who run away from a problem. Because of this tendency, project managers are not often the first to identify the need to prematurely terminate a project and are often the last to cling tenaciously to a sinking ship. Most premature terminations are driven by the customer organization.

For a customer to take the initiative to terminate a project, there must already be recognized shortcomings in the project's ability to meet the customer's needs. Once again, the project manager is driven to evaluate the customer's needs and how well those needs are being met. The two criteria that are easiest to evaluate are time and money.

If the customer is out of money, there is little the project manager can do to generate more funds for the customer organization. The project manager should examine the customer organization to identify areas in which the project could provide more extensive benefits to the customer organization. If such areas of benefit can be discerned, the customer organization may be willing to allocate supplemental funds to see the project through to completion. The project manager should also look internally to find ways to complete the project more cost effectively. A shift in resources or a change in the scope of the project may be sufficient to bring costs in line with customer expectations or capabilities.

If the customer is out of time, the project manager may consider how the project, in its existing form, can have value for the customer. In some cases, that's simply not possible. A software program with only half the code written has no salvage value and no practical use. In other cases, creativity may afford alternatives for the customer organization. A half-dug swimming pool, for example, could be converted for use as a decorative pond or a hydroponic garden. Although these may be far afield from the customer's original objectives, they afford the opportunity to snatch a small victory from the jaws of defeat.

FACING A POTENTIALLY HOSTILE ENVIRONMENT

The greatest challenges face a project manager when customers terminate a project because they feel that needs are not being met and satisfaction is not achievable. This often evolves in a hostile environment, where relations between the customer and project organizations are severely strained. In many cases, this environment begins not during the project's implementation phase, but in the very earliest stages of project development, because customer needs are either ignored or minimized.[10] Failure to establish the proper setting at project inception is a frequent cause of premature termination. The following three issues may influence an organization and cause premature termination:

- Professional and organizational needs
- Product and process needs
- Personal needs

Professional and Organizational Needs

Professional and organizational issues are difficult for the project manager to influence. Unless the project manager has influence within the upper echelons of the organization, it will be challenging to change organizational approaches and methodologies. Changes to organizational culture can be swift and devastating. In 1996, two Regional Bell Operating Companies (RBOCs), Bell Atlantic and NYNEX, announced a major merger. Project organizations in both firms immediately began reassessing their efforts and their objectives. Why? Because the potential merger could significantly influence which projects would be retained and which would be terminated. Project managers outside the RBOCs took a similar approach. They evaluated Bell Atlantic and NYNEX as customers and worked to determine how these changes would influence their contracts and their relationships. Not every project maintained by both organizations would survive a merger. Some would be phased out. Others would be altered to meet the objectives of a new, large organization. The project managers who succeed in a new environment are those who are best able to anticipate the new customers' needs and restructure the project approach into alignment with those specific needs.

Product and Process Needs

The deliverables for a project may also cause premature termination. In a prototyping environment, customers often get the opportunity to carefully examine deliverables before they are built on a large scale. As a result, customers may also find fault far earlier in the process than in an effort where deliverables are handed off at completion. Thus, in the early reviews, premature termination becomes a distinct possibility. In the early 1990s, a U.S. federal government agency committed to procurement of a network of 80286 computers. The procurement was based on the government's "minimum needs"[11] requirement, and the customer (the agency) didn't see a need for anything more powerful than an 80286. By the time the procurement was under way, the government recognized the need to consider the 80386 (or possibly even the prototype 80486) computers, which were then in production. Computer technology was changing so rapidly that before projects could be implemented, customer needs could change significantly. In this type of highly volatile environment, the project manager trying to avoid premature termination takes on the role of mentor and salesperson.

The project manager becomes responsible for customer education, enlightening the customer about how a change in product needs does not necessarily predicate a change in projects. For this approach to work, however, the project manager must be intimately familiar with the capabilities of the product or process being developed, and the project manager must have a sense of where the changes are heading.

Not all deliverable-oriented terminations are driven by changes in technology. Some are the result of customer intimacy. As a customer becomes familiar with the deliverable (whether it is a product or process), the customer may become aware that the deliverable is not what was expected and will not be able to fulfill the expectations of his or her organization.

Personal Needs

A fuzzy line exists between the concerns addressed as deliverable-oriented needs and personally oriented needs. The blur is generated by most customers' and project managers' unwillingness to acknowledge the influence of personalities on what is supposed to be a relatively sterile process. Personalities make a difference. Toward that end, project managers can take two approaches: maximize or minimize. The decision in a premature-termination environment to maximize or minimize personality issues will be largely based on whether a positive relationship has historically existed between the two parties. Table 28–1 examines specific steps a project manager may consider to preclude premature termination if personality is a major issue.

Both approaches are equally open and honest with the customer organization. Their orientations, however, are radically different. The maximized approach guides the customer toward a more personal rapport with the project organization, emphasizing areas of agreement, whereas the minimized approach guides the customer toward a technical analysis of the project organization. Even though the approach is technical, it still emphasizes areas of agreement. When there is any doubt regarding the quality of the customer-project organization relationship, project managers should strive to minimize personality issues.

Table 28–1. Dealing with Personality Issues and Premature Termination

Maximize	Minimize
Encourage one-on-one reviews of project successes to date and issues resolution in an informal environment.	Encourage team-on-team reviews of project successes and issues resolution in a formal environment.
Stress the familiarity of project team members with the organization, the personnel, and the culture.	Stress the familiarity of the project team members with the organization, its processes, and its technical approaches.
Emphasize the broad, open lines of communication between the organizations.	Stress the efficiency of the meticulously crafted communications network established between organizations.
Talk about the mutually shared vision of the future between the organizations.	Emphasize the clear support of the customer's vision of the future.

As a last resort, when personalities are a key issue that cannot be resolved, and the customer has no inclination to resolve them, the project manager should consider alternative personnel. Before going this route, however, the project manager should consult with the customer, asking the operative question: Will this make a difference? The customer may see premature termination as a foregone conclusion, regardless of the actions taken by the project organization. If that's the case, there's no need to drag in a second project team to suffer through the waning hours of a project gone bad.

CLOSING OUT IN A PREMATURE TERMINATION ENVIRONMENT
No matter the causes, the steps in the closeout process remain the same, whether the project is terminated in a timely fashion or prematurely. The differences with premature termination relate to the extra effort required of the project manager to ensure that all the steps are taken with the same level of commitment. Premature termination often leads project-support organizations to withdraw resources and reassign commitments before the project can be closed out properly. Even though a project is closed out before its scheduled termination, the same elements must be in place. Contracts must be signed off and accepted. Lessons learned are especially important. Customer inquiries and concerns must be resolved. Transition of materials and deliverables between organizations must still be completed. Even with premature projects, reward and recognition is vital.

In a premature closeout, reward and recognition are often difficult to achieve. Team members may feel their efforts were for naught because the customer was not able to see a finished product or process. Upper management may not feel inclined to provide any recognition, because the project is perceived as less than successful. Still, there are achievements to be recognized and milestones to be marked. To retain a sense of camaraderie (and to stand a chance of recruiting team members in the future), the project manager of a prematurely closed project must identify the successes of the effort and acknowledge the team accordingly. The project manager must also be acutely aware of the team's needs (as identified in Maslow's hierarchy). For team members suffering from low self-esteem, the project manager must mark the successes of the project. For those who fear the social loss at the end of the project, the project manager must establish communication networks to maintain team communication and build the corporate grapevine. For those who are concerned about personal safety and job retention, the project manager must secure, from upper management, specific commitments regarding assignments and responsibilities for members of the project team.

Antitermination

Antitermination is an utter failure to terminate the project and bring it to closure. For some project managers, project organizations, and customer organizations, this is the norm. Many organizations will keep a project alive indefinitively in the vain hope that the project will somehow turn around, generate profits, achieve goals, or restore processes simply by its weight and momentum.

Most projects that achieve this status are embedded in organizational cultures and have extensive support organizations. The scope shifts often enough to prevent any kind of blame from being ascribed for poor performance or failure to meet objectives. In some organizations, project managers will willingly participate in this environment ad infinitum, because they see it as a form of job security. What they may fail to recognize is that projects borne by this type of inertia are not generally perceived as opportunities for success or advancement. They are the placeholders of corporate culture.

For the project manager seeking to bring such an effort to closure, the final project objectives must be reevaluated, communicated, and approved. Those objectives should include a commitment from all parties that further modifications to the scope and approach will not be accepted. The exit strategy must be developed, and it should emphasize that commitment. After the stage has been set to migrate such an effort to closeout, the project manager must take on that effort with singleness of purpose (see Figure 28–1). Projects with a history of escalation and modification are not easy to eliminate.[12] But after a final objective has been established, standard termination practices (as outlined in this chapter) can be put in place.

The Wrap-Up

Regardless of the early successes in a project, customers, vendors, managers, and team members are most likely to remember the closeout far longer than

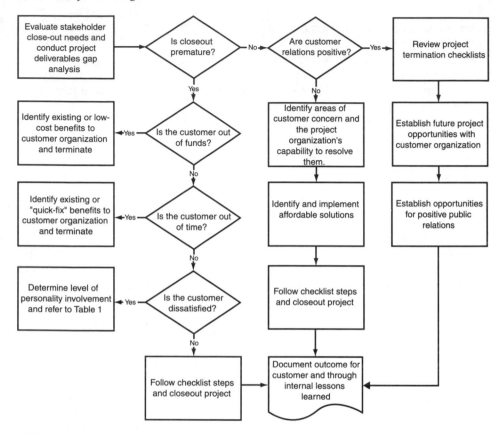

FIGURE 28–1   Closeout methodology

any other stage in the process. Toward that end, the project manager must ensure that the closeout is a positive experience in terms of the deliverables, the effects on the organizations involved, and the effects on the team members. By methodically evaluating needs and addressing those needs, the likelihood of positive closeout is significantly enhanced.

ENDNOTES

1 *Scheduling & Cost Control,* Arlington, VA: Educational Services Institute, 1993
2 Staw, Barry and Ross, Jerry. Knowing when to pull the plug. *Harvard Business Review* March-April 1987, Number 2, pp. 68–74
3 *The American Heritage Dictionary of the English Language,* Third Edition. New York: Houghton Mifflin Company, 1992
4 Terence. *The Lady of Andros.* ca. 160 B.C.
5 Maynard, David. *Bad News Is Good News; Good News Is Great.* AAI/SMI, PMI Symposium Papers, New Orleans, LA, October 16–18, 1995
6 Project Management Institute. *Guide to the Project Management Body of Knowledge.* Upper Darby, PA: Project Management Institute, 1996, p. 119
7 Maynard, p. 16

8 *Communications for High-Performing Project Teams*. King, Dennis and Synan, Joseph. PMI Symposium Papers, New Orleans, LA, October 16–18, 1995, pp. 103–104

9 Staw and Ross, p. 70

10 Maday, Brian. *How to Make Rapid Application Development Fail*. PMI Symposium Papers, New Orleans, LA, October 16–18, 1995, p. 312

11 Department of Defense. *Federal Acquisition Regulation*, 10.001. U.S. Government Printing Office, Washington, DC

12 Staw and Ross, p. 69

Team Management

Chapter

29

New Ways to Use Project Teams

David I. Cleland

Biographical Sketch . . .

David I. Cleland is currently the Ernest E. Roth Professor and Professor of Engineering Management in the School of Engineering at the University of Pittsburgh. He is the author/editor of twenty-six books in the fields of project management, engineering management, and manufacturing management. He has served as a consultant for both U.S. and foreign companies and has been honored for his original and continuing contributions to his disciplines.

The use of teams has expanded to meet many strategic and operational purposes in the enterprise.[1] Teams have been called the common denominator of organizational change because they are a medium for cross-functional and cross-organizational integration of resources to accomplish a specific purpose. For example, concurrent engineering teams may be composed of stakeholders from the original equipment manufacturers (OEMs), suppliers, unions, and community representatives. Many stakeholders, some of whom have business in the global marketplace, are linked operationally and strategically through teams. Different types of teams are listed in Table 29–1.

Corporations can use teams to respond to inevitable changes they face today. Research by Jerry Jasinowski and Robert Hamrin uncovered how U.S. industry regrouped in the mid-1980s and staged a remarkable rally. They describe the strategies of fifty real-life U.S. company success stories, and how people in these companies created success. "Teamwork is the single most prevalent characteristic found in our fifty success stories," according to Jasinowski and Hamrin.[2]

The basic paths to success are releasing the creativity and power of workers, pleasing customers, finding new markets, and focusing on continuous improvement. These are the elements that teamwork has to offer. Whenever teamwork is applied properly, the performance of the company improves, usually quickly and significantly.[3] A brief description of different types of teams follows.

Table 29–1. Classification of Teams*

Type	Output/Contribution	Time Frame
Reengineering Teams	Business process changes	Ad Hoc
Crisis Management Teams	Manage organizational crisis	Ad Hoc
Product/Process Development Teams	Concurrent product/process development	Ad Hoc
Self-Managed Production Teams	Manage & execute production work	Ongoing
Task Forces	Evaluate/resolve organizational problems/ opportunities	Ad Hoc
Benchmarking Teams	Evaluate competitors/ best in the industry performance	Ongoing
Facilities Construction Project Team**	Design/develop/construct facilities/equipment	Ad Hoc
Quality Teams	Develop/implement/ total quality initiatives	Ongoing
General Purpose Project Teams**	Develop/implement new initiatives in enterprise	Ad Hoc
Audit Teams	Evaluate organizational efficiency & effectiveness	Ad Hoc
Plural Executive Teams	Integrate senior level management decisions	Ongoing
New Business Development Teams	Development of new business ventures	Ad Hoc

*This classification is based on the one given in the article by David I. Cleland, "Leadership and the Project-Management Body of Knowledge," *International Journal of Project Management*, April 1995, pp. 83–88.

**These teams are often described as traditional project teams. *The Project Management Field Manual* describes the topic areas generally peculiar to these traditional teams. However, all teams can use the management techniques described in this field manual.

1. Reengineering teams.   These teams are used to bring about a fundamental rethinking and radical redesign of business processes to achieve extraordinary improvements in critical contemporary measures of performance such as cost, quality, service, and speed. Much attention is being given to the use of reengineering teams today—yet their ability to produce real results is sometimes questioned. The guru of the reengineering movement, Michael Hammer, openly admits that 70 percent of such efforts fail.[4] Nevertheless, such teams have produced impressive results.

EXAMPLE.   During one of the largest process-reengineering projects ever undertaken, GTE telephone operations management was stunned to find out that the administrative bureaucracy of the company was reducing productivity by as much as 50 percent. As part of its reengineering effort, GTE examined its own processes and compared them with processes used by eighty companies in a wide variety of industries. Reengineering teams then created new concepts, approaches, policies, and procedures for the new processes. The following specific goals were set for the reengineering teams:

1. Double revenues while cutting costs in half.
2. Cut cycle time in half.
3. Reduce product roll-out time by three quarters.
4. Cut systems development time in half.

These goals provided the motivation to make marked improvements in the company's process management. The findings from the reengineering were put into practice.

AT&T Global Business Communications Systems, which makes and installs private branch exchanges on the customer's premises, did the following in its two-year reengineering efforts:

1. Rewrote job descriptions for hundreds of people.
2. Developed new recognition and rewards systems.
3. Reconfigured its computer systems.
4. Initiated massive retraining programs.
5. Made extensive changes in financial reporting, proposal writing, and contracts.

The company also made major changes in its relationships with suppliers, its manufacturing processes, and its shipping, installation, and billing practices.[5] Reengineering teams are described in Chapter 30.

2. Crisis-management teams.   These teams are used to deal with any potential crisis that may arise in the organization's activities. Aircraft crashes, oil spills, fires, tornadoes, hostage situations, product-liability suits, loss of key personnel, and earthquakes are a few of the almost endless list of potential crises that can have an impact on an enterprise. When such crises emerge, the appointment of a team can serve to bring a focus to the use of resources, maintain damage control, and develop and implement remedial strategies.[6] When the crisis has a public relations context, how well the team deals with the public and the media is important.

3. Product and process-development teams.   These organizational units, often called concurrent or simultaneous-engineering teams, provide for concurrent design and development of organizational products, services, and processes. Processes may include manufacturing, marketing, purchasing, after-sales services, and engineering. The purposes of these teams are to develop products and services of higher quality with lower costs, earlier commercialization, greater profitability, and enhanced customer satisfaction. Chrysler used a concurrent-engineering team to design and develop the Neon, a small car that proved Detroit could bring forth a competitive small car. The Neon team mobilized 600 engineers, team members from other disciplines, 289 suppliers, and hundreds blue-collar workers to meet the goal of delivering the new model in a speedy 42 months, and for much less than any recent small car had cost at that time.[7] Concurrent engineering teams are discussed in Chapter 31.

4. Self-managed production teams (SMPTs).   SMPTs provide improved quality and productivity in manufacturing and production operations. These teams are unlike the traditional project teams, which are multidisciplinary and cut across many different organizational boundaries. SMPTs are made up of members from the same work area of the enterprise, and they typically have broad responsibilities and authority for planning, organizing, monitoring, and controlling the use of organizational resources to produce a product or service. Members of these teams, facilitated by a team leader, make and implement decisions in such matters as task assignments, work scheduling, work design, training, equipment selection, usage, maintenance, problem solving, and worker counseling and discipline. In some cases, these teams are given the authority to hire and fire members and assess merit evaluations, promotions, and pay raises.

At the Lord Corporation plant in Dayton, Ohio, self-managed work teams were the real power behind a corporate strategy to empower the people. In the old days, there were six layers of management for fifty-five people. After the initiation and maturity of self-directed teams in 1990, there were just the plant manager and seven self-managed work teams. Moreover, the plant's performance between 1986 and 1990 improved in the following ways:

- Productivity was up 30 percent and absenteeism was down 75 percent.
- Typical setup time was down more than 75 percent.
- No lost-time accidents occurred for six years.
- Scrap costs fell 85 percent.
- Manufacturing cycle time for one product was reduced from seventy-five days to seven days.
- Work in process was reduced by 75 percent.[8]

5. Task forces.   These are ad-hoc groups used to solve short-term organizational problems or exploit opportunities for the enterprise. Usually the solutions or approaches to problems or opportunities require cutting across organizational boundaries. For example, a major food processor used several task forces to study and recommend remedial strategies for improving the performance of the company in such areas as purchasing practices, overhead costs, corporate downsizing, and restructuring. Task forces have been used for ad-hoc work for many years. Today their use continues; they are easily formed and disbanded when the problem or opportunity for which they were appointed no longer exists.

EXAMPLE.   A procurement task force at H.J. Heinz Company was appointed to find and work out partnerships of the most efficient suppliers around the world and consolidate purchasing across all of the company's affiliates. So far, this team has saved Heinz $100 million on an annualized basis. The team's efforts with suppliers in value-engineering packaging and raw materials will provide additional opportunities for cost reductions in the years ahead. The pace of the task force was remarkable; it took less than four months from the time the task-force team was launched until the contracts with suppliers were signed. Traditionally, the company had negotiated purchasing agreements on an annual basis. The long-term contracts gave the suppliers security to work with the task-force team on value-engineering processes and generate savings for both sides of the relationship. The cost savings are due to reduced product costs in the suppliers' factories and in the Heinz production facilities.[9]

    6. Benchmarking teams.   Benchmarking is the ongoing strategy of measuring organizational products, services, and processes against the most formidable competitors and industry leaders. Benchmarking results in improved performance standards leading to improved capabilities.

EXAMPLE.   Union Carbide's Robert Kennedy used benchmarking to find successful businesses, determine what made them successful, and then translate their successful strategy to his own company. Reengineering strategies at Union Carbide were complemented by benchmaking teams to scrape $400 million out of its costs in just three years. The benchmarking team at Union Carbide looked to L.L. Bean for learning how it runs a global customer service operation out of one center in Maine. By copying L.L. Bean, Union Carbide teams were able to consolidate seven regional customer service offices, which handled shipping orders for solvents and coatings, into one center in Houston, Texas. By giving employees more responsibility and permitting them to redesign their work, 30 percent fewer employees were able to do the same work—including the analysis of processes to reduce paperwork to less than half. For lessons on global distribution, Union Carbide looked to Federal Express, and for tracking inventory via computer, Union Carbide borrowed from retailers such as Wal-Mart.[10] Benchmarking is discussed in Chapter 31.

    7. Quality teams.   Quality management is accomplished through the use of quality teams that use cross-functional organizational designs to integrate quality-improvement efforts. The use of quality teams to develop and implement total quality management (TQM) has gained considerable acceptance in contemporary organizations. Quality teams, properly organized and managed, provide meaningful opportunities for workers to get involved in improving organizational performance.

EXAMPLE.   The Allen-Bradley plant in Twinsburg, Ohio, makes circuit boards, programmable controllers, and other electronic devices. Employees had to cope with a pile of manuals, work orders, and memos, most written in "engineeringese." Frustrated with the blizzard of paperwork, workers resorted to their own methods of doing things—like taping up crude crib sheets on their work benches. The plant manager pulled seven assemblers off the floor, some for as long as seven months, and put them on teams with engineers and supervisors. Their task was to devise procedures comprehensible to everyone. Now paper and envelopes have been replaced by electronic mail, which delivers new instructions and purges the old ones.[11]

    Certainly part of the reason that such teams produce results is the interdisciplinary focus that they bring to the enterprise. There is considerable literature in the area of TQM to include how quality teams can be used to improve products, services, and processes.

EXAMPLE. The primary means that Motorola uses to meet its goal of Six-Sigma Quality (3.4 defects per million) is a dedication to employee empowerment that is focused on teamwork and extensive training and education. In developing and implementing a successful quality program at Motorola, several key observations have been noted: workers' knowledge and skills improved; workers learned how to function as teams; and the company learned how to be the best in the class of manufacturing and manufacturing technology.

8. Audit teams. These teams evaluate the competency of organizations, programs, projects, and functions to deliver quality products and processes. Projects in the public domain are usually audited to ascertain the prudency with which public funds have been used.

EXAMPLE. On a water-pollution-abatement project in a large city in the United States, a team was appointed to conduct an audit of the project prior to the initiation of detailed planning to turn the project results over to the user. This audit disclosed several sewage plant configuration changes that needed to be carried out. In addition, several contract amendments called for modifications that were unduly delayed. The late modifications could have had an adverse impact on the operational availability of the water-pollution-abatement system. By discovering the delay in these changes through the audit, the construction-project team was able to initiate remedial strategies to get the project back on schedule and meet its operational date.

9. Plural executive teams. These teams consist of senior level executives who work together to design and execute major strategies that will prepare the enterprise for its long-range future. The use of such teams provide for a top-level synergy in the strategic management of the enterprise. When the plural-executive-team members maintain surveillance over the operation of other teams in the company, considerable insight is available about how well the company is preparing for and dealing with the inevitable changes facing organizational products, services, processes, and resource utilization.

Various names are given to the plural-executive team in the United States, including Office of the President, Office of the Chairman, and Office of the Chief Executive. Many large corporations use the plural-executive team as a means of bringing together senior people to deal with key operational and strategic issues.

10. New-Business-Development Teams. These teams are used to explore the design and development of new business ventures for the enterprise. Such teams arise from the strategic planning effort that is carried out by the company. The work of these teams involves the assessment and development of new business areas, as contrasted with teams dedicated to a specific program or project within a new business area.

EXAMPLE.   At the Rubbermaid Company, a new product is introduced each day. Teams play a vital role in making the company a new-product-generating machine. Dozens of business teams, which are the key organizational units, work at developing new products. Every team, every year, is charged with reinventing what they have; everybody at every level is encouraged to innovate. The business teams are the basic business units and are the real drivers of innovation. Each product line has a business team that is managed by a core of representatives, one each from marketing, manufacturing, finance, and research and development.

New Approaches

New team models are coming forth and changing traditional roles of managers and supervisors. Project management has changed the way in which enterprise strategies are designed and executed and has brought forth new management and organizational philosophies—such as that of teamocracy.

TEAMOCRACY

We are entering the age of teamocracy, during which a change in the leadership and management of organizations will have a profound impact on how value is delivered to customers. The forces unleashed by teamocracy will have an impact on conceptualizing, designing, producing, marketing, and supporting product after-sales logistics. The move to teamocracy is nothing short of an intellectual revolution for which there is no precedent in the history of management.

I have coined the term *teamocracy* to describe the condition of organizations that are characterized by teams as the basic organizational design for bringing about a focus for cross-functional and cross-organizational work in the enterprise.[12] In a teamocracy, the team is the basic social unit based upon maximum empowerment, leading to acceptance of responsibility and accountability by the organizational members. Teamocracy is the result of converting the traditional bureaucratic hierarchy. Instead of the cumulative power of each organizational level rising through an organizational pyramid, a network of authority and responsibility is widespread and cuts through the length and breadth of the enterprise. In teamocracy, new power foci emerge, reflecting empowerment, dedication, trust, loyalty, and commitment embodied in a team organizational design in which the team leads and manages itself within the larger strategic management context of the enterprise.

The design of a teamocracy has the following five elements:

1. Strategic management of the organizational unit as if its future mattered
2. Operations that produce, in an efficient manner, current products and services
3. Decentralized units such as profit centers
4. Functional entities
5. Team members

Within these elements, decisions are shared, results are communal, and rewards are divided. Workplace communities in teamocracy accommodate self-managed teams as well as the more traditional configuration of the enterprise.

The hallmark of teamocracy is that customer value is created principally through the efforts of teams. Customer value is sustained by organizational infrastructures to provide operational and strategic guidance, resources, empowerment, and performance standards. The teamocracy is dynamic and responds to the need to bring about continuous improvement, and sometimes dramatic changes in products, services, and organizational processes. The characteristics of the teamocracy include the following:

- Everyone has the opportunity to be a leader and a manager.
- Trust, respect, loyalty, conviction, and commitment permeate the culture.
- Everyone knows what is going on because there is widespread sharing of information.
- All employees want to be responsible for quality work and to be proud of that work.
- Team members subordinate their egos and needs to meet the needs of the team.
- Team leadership is shared; management of the team's resources are also shared.
- Interpersonal networks strengthen both individual and team behavior.
- Assumption is widespread that every product, service, or organizational process can be continuously improved.
- Setbacks in efficiency and effectiveness provide new challenges for doing better and moving ahead through improvement strategies.
- Individual status and pride are enhanced through the sense of belonging and freedom that people feel when working together as equals rather than as subordinates.

Because leadership and managerial activities are widely dispersed in the teamocracy foresight and vision, two important responsibilities of leaders and managers are shared throughout the enterprise. Leadership comes less from an appointed position and more from the motivation that team members feel from within. Leadership is a fluid concept, and people exercise leadership at appropriate moments. Senior leaders and managers try less to extend their authority from the top and more to facilitate the cooperative effort of many people at many levels in the organization.

In the teamocracy, self-managed work teams choose their leaders, who function as facilitators. Team members negotiate their individual and collective roles and assign duties and responsibilities. Everyone has the opportunity to be a facilitator. Customers and suppliers become contributing members of the teams, and the teams work at spreading a clear perspective of what it takes to create value for customers. Barriers between team members are reduced, a greater interpersonal compatibility exists, individual and team objectives and goals are better understood, and the team by its own functioning helps to develop the individual and the team for enhanced productive performance.

Any bureaucracy has the potential to become a teamocracy if the leaders and managers are willing to change. In demonstrating that willingness to change, clear strategies need to be developed and executed throughout the enterprise, extending to key stakeholders such as customers and suppliers. People who do not change are becoming an endangered species.

Old Approaches

Traditional, authoritative managers and supervisors are endangered if they do not change their ways of working and their "I'm-in-charge" approaches to their duties. Team leaders and team members are performing many of the traditional duties of these former in-charge people. When empowerment is widely carried out by trained and competent people, both direct and indirect changes are seen. These changes have an impact on the role of traditional managers.

DIRECT CHANGES

Some of the direct changes include the following:

- Team members plan the work and assignment of the tasks by members of the team.
- Team members evaluate individual and team performance in doing the work.
- Team members play a role in developing strategies for individual and team awards.
- Peers counsel poor team performers.
- Team members participate in key decisions involving the work being carried out by the team.
- Members of the team organize their individual and collective roles.
- Teams assume responsibility for the quality of the work, team productivity, and efficiency in the use of resources.
- Teams develop initiatives to improve the quality and quantity of the output.
- Teams seek better ways of doing the work, and in so doing, discover creative and innovative means of preparing for the team's and the enterprise's future.

INDIRECT CHANGES

The indirect changes are subtle yet very real. For team members, these include the following:

- Team members have more interesting work.
- Team members have a greater sense of control over individual, team, and enterprise destiny.
- Team members have greater esprit de corps and pride.
- Greater financial rewards arise out of improved delivery of products and services to customers.

- Team members have a greater feeling of individual worth in being able to contribute to useful purposes that are realizable and measurable.
- Team members have more fun working.

The use of teams as instruments of enterprise strategy has helped change the theory and practice of management. The teams influence the culture and the culture influences the teams. Both the teams and the culture influence the thinking of everyone in the enterprise. In turn, the enterprise culture influences all of the people. Senior management needs to recognize these changes, understand them, and develop a strategy as to how the knowledge, skills, and attitudes of the people have to be adjusted as they perform their roles.

Role Changes

The transition from the traditional manager and supervisory roles to the facilitative, coaching, mentoring, and resource support roles found in the team-driven organizations is difficult. For those traditional managers and supervisors, the transition can be very threatening because of the following:

- The sense of loss of status or power—or even the job
- A fear of the unknown resulting from a lack of understanding of the reverberations set in motion by the use of self-directed teams
- Confusion because the role of the team leader is not defined and sometimes not understood
- Fear of personal obsolescence and changes resulting in the need to gain new knowledge, skills, and attitudes

Continued Growth

Teams will likely grow in use in the next decade because of the explosive growth in information, which enables employees to know so much more about the technical and managerial nature of their work than their managers could possibly understand. As highly educated, self-motivated, and self-directed specialists work together, their managers begin to know less of what the specialists are really doing. Managers become increasingly dependent on the specialized employees to make and implement decisions on the technical side of their work.

As more expensive, exotic equipment and other resources are used in the workplace, such as the computer and technical information systems, the costs are so high that people have to be able to work together and make real-time decisions and interventions on their own. The technology involved is so complex that only the specialists fully understand how to choose and use that technology to produce results that have value to the customers and other stakeholders. They must solve technical and organizational interfacing problems without having to "check with the boss."

Competitive pressures are causing enterprises to turn to teams to get the work done sooner and at lower cost because teams can reduce the need for traditional middle and first-level managers. A point often missed in considering the use of teams is how the leadership of the team is diffused among the team members. When such teams take on more of the functions of self-management, the manager and leadership functions do not disappear; rather, a moving leadership pattern emerges. Members of the team emerge as leaders as they are needed, when their particular technical work tasks are developed and integrated into the overall team effort.

Team Benefits

Experience has shown that the use of teams has helped to facilitate the introduction of new ideas in products, services, and organizational processes. People who previously worked alone can now gain new knowledge and learn new skills while serving as contributing members of a team. Working on the team tends to reinforce the workers' abilities, as well as provide an opportunity for synergistic thinking and action not usually available when the team members worked alone, out of the team environment. Communication ties are enhanced, and when technological challenges emerge, the entire team can deal with those challenges and develop team-based remedial strategies.

Participation on a team usually means that the team members learn additional skills through trade-off of job duties. By developing multiskilled capabilities, team members can perform many different types of duties while working on the teams and learn additional skills working on other teams. One important result of all this is to reduce the number of job classifications, thus simplifying the hiring and assignment of people in their work. The benefits produced by teams are many. Table 29–2 indicates some of the many results experienced by contemporary organizations.

In a team situation, employees feel that their opinions are valued and that they are trusted in having access to key information on the performance of the enterprise. People are treated as thinking adults. The cultural ambience of the enterprise encourages creativity and innovation—it's acceptable to make mistakes on the road to positive results. Everyone in the organization tends to have a clear and closer view of suppliers and customers. The special perks, such as reserved parking places and executive dining rooms, which were formerly provided to senior and special people, tend to be eliminated, thus adding to the culture of equality. Relationships among people in different specialties and at different organizational levels tend to improve as everyone recognizes that there is a high degree of interdependency among people.

When people work in teams, leaders can come from any place and from anyone in the organization as people make the correct choices in improving the use of resources in creative and innovative ways. The essence of strategic

Table 29–2. Team Results*

• Lower costs	• Improved production, efficiency, and effectiveness
• Higher quality	• Greater learning
• Manageable strategic initiatives	• More teamwork
• Interdisciplinary focus	• Leader and manager development
• Feeling of contribution	• Self-destiny
• Improved career development	• More skills
• More enjoyment	• Identification with organizational purposes
• More creativity, which leads to innovation	• Job enrichment
• Greater participation	• More fun
• Greater profitability	• Less parochialism
• Interpersonal empathy	• Better communication
• Fewer managers	• Greater sharing of information
• Changed role of managers	• Greater organizational synergy
• Less bureaucracy	• Enlightened adversary viewpoints
• Enhanced responsibility and accountability	• Empowerment
• Greater harmony of individual and organizational unit objectives and goals	• Improved culture
• Less command and control	• More consensus and consent
• Improved competition	• Improved organizational products and services
• Improved morale	• Improved organizational processes
• More association with winners	• More candid debate
• Cross-functional fertilization	• Systems thinking
• Self-management	• Greater pride
• Improved labor-management relationships	• Greater dissemination of organizational performance information
• Flatter hierarchy	• Shared interests

*David I. Cleland. *The Strategic Management of Teams.* New York: John Wiley & Sons, Inc., 1996, p. 131

thinking can be shared by all members of the enterprise. This is accomplished with ongoing questioning of the status quo, and a belief that thinking about and working with ideas for the future can help to influence that future according to what is best for the enterprise.

ENDNOTES

1 Portions of this chapter have been drawn from the book by David I. Cleland, *The Strategic Management of Teams.* New York: John Wiley & Sons, Inc., 1996

2 Jasinowski, Jerry and Hamrin, Robert. *Making It In America.* New York: Simon & Schuster, 1995 p. 33

3 Ibid., p. 35

4 Reported by Michael Rothschild, "Want to grow? Watch your language," *Forbes ASAP*, October 25, 1993, p. 19

5 Stewart, Thomas A. Reengineering—the hot new managing tool. *Fortune*, August 23, 1993, pp. 40–48

6 Swale, W. Stephen. Crisis project management. *PmNetwork*, January 1991, pp. 25–29

7 Woodruff, David and Miller, Karen Lower. Chrysler's Neon: Is this the small car Detroit couldn't build? *Business Week*, May 3, 1993, pp. 116–126

8 Stewart, p. 42

9 "The Power of Change," *The H.J. Heinz Company 1993 Annual Report*, p. 3, Pittsburgh, PA: H.J. Heinz Company, 1993

10 Sina Moukheiber. Learning from winners. *Forbes*, March 14, 1994, pp. 41–42

11 Ronald Henkoff. The hot new seal of QUALITY. *Fortune*, June 28, 1993, pp. 116–120.

12 Term coined October 25, 1994

BIBLIOGRAPHY

Camp, Robert C. *Benchmarking: The Search for Industry Best Practices That Lead to Superior Performance*. Milwaukee, WI: Quality Press, American Society for Quality Control, 1989

Cleland, David I. *The Strategic Management of Teams*. New York: John Wiley & Sons, Inc., 1996

Dumaine, Brian. How managers can succeed through speed. *Fortune*, February 13, 1994

Hammer, Michael and Champy, James. *Reengineering the Corporation: A Manifesto for Business Revolution*. New York: Harper Collins, 1994

Kamath, Rajan R. and Liker, Jeffrey K. A second look at Japanese product development. *Harvard Business Review* November–December 1994 pp 154–166

Kimball, Fisher. *Leading Self-Directed Work Teams*. New York: McGraw-Hill, 1993

Managing Reengineering Teams

Gwenn C. Carr,
Gary L. Englehardt, and
John Tuman, Jr.

Biographical Sketch . . .

Gwenn C. Carr is a project manager for PECO Energy Company. In 1995 she was the project manager for training services for PECO's Reengineering Into Service Excellence Project. Her experience includes twenty years in education, including serving as project manager of Middle States Assessment and Evaluation teams. Ms. Carr has published several technical papers and articles on information-systems education practices and trends.

Gary L. Englehardt is Manager of Integrated Network Policies and Practices for PECO Energy Company. He was instrumental in the development of the nuclear and corporate project-management programs at PECO and served as senior project manager of their Reengineering Into Service Excellence Project. Mr. Englehardt has extensive experience in planning and managing complex multiorganizational undertakings and in management of change in large-scale projects. He has been an instructor of project management for the Economic Development Unit of the World Bank and has presented papers at seminars of the Project Management Institute.

John Tuman, Jr., is President of Management Technologies Group, Inc., a U.S. consulting firm specializing in project management, organizational development, and information technology. Mr. Tuman provides consulting and training services to corporations in the United States and overseas and has given numerous presentations, seminars, and workshops on management issues and problems in the United States, England, Europe, Africa, Asia, and Russia. He is a contributing author to several textbooks on project management and has published numerous technical papers and articles on management methods, systems, and trends.

T here is an extensive body of knowledge on team building, reflecting to a large extent the increasing complexity of today's business environment and the need to more effectively harness an organization's diverse skills and abilities. The project-management environment has been an especially fertile laboratory and proving ground for team-building concepts and methodologies. The complexities of a modern project, which typically must be accomplished under stringent cost, schedule, technical, environmental, and legal constraints, require that teams function effectively and efficiently with minimum conflict. Otherwise, the project is doomed to failure.

Traditional Project Teams

In a traditional project, a team is assembled to accomplish a specific objective by a defined date for a specified amount of money. Typically, the project team accomplishes its objectives by using existing corporate processes, procedures, and systems that it understands and with which it is fairly comfortable. The team accomplishes tasks over a well-defined project life cycle; furthermore, the team operates, for the most part, within the boundaries of the prevailing organizational culture. In other words, team members know what is expected of them and how to interact with the rest of the organization to get things done in a manner that is acceptable to the organization. Normally, the team's project adds value to the corporation and helps to ensure its continued economic viability. Likewise, a successful project will help team members gain recognition, grow professionally, and ensure their continued economic viability. To a large extent, project success depends on how well the team interacts in dealing with the complexities of the project and the unexpected problems that develop. In many projects the issues around project team interaction and performance can be far more challenging than the actual tasks involved in the project itself. This is especially true in reengineering projects.

The Unique Demands of Reengineering

By definition, reengineering means substantial change. A reengineering team's mission is to do something entirely different—to change the way an organization does business. Typically, this means that a reengineering team must change the processes and procedures that everyone knows, the tools and techniques with which everyone is comfortable, and the standards and values that everyone has learned to accept. In many cases even the people who do the work must change. The end result of a reengineering project is an organization that functions more effectively and more efficiently by employing new business systems and technology—and probably fewer people.

The challenges for a reengineering team are far greater than those found in a traditional project. Because reengineering is relatively new, its methodologies are still developing and have a very limited experience base. To date, reengineering has produced few outstanding successes that can be used as how-to-do-it models. More significantly, reengineering involves changing the prevailing organizational culture. This type of change will be resisted. Additionally, reengineering engenders fear. Both those doing the reengineering and those affected by it constantly worry about their future. Anxiety brought about by the ambiguity of a reengineering project is extensive and can be destructive if not managed properly. In view of the complexity and demands of reengineering, how is a team organized and built so that it can accomplish its project goals constructively with minimum conflict and stress? Clearly, if reengineering is to be a success it requires a unique, creative, dedicated, hard-working team.

Team-Building Across the Reengineering Life Cycle

The traditional project life cycle as defined by the Project Management Institute (PMI) is a continuum of effort (in distinct phases) that starts by addressing a need or problem and culminates in a deliverable (see Figure 30–1). Resource expenditures tend to be low in the beginning but build up rapidly as the project enters the implementation or construction phase, eventually reach a peak, then drop off quickly as the project is phased out. In many projects there is continuity in team composition across the project life cycle and this helps to promote stability, learning, and trust among team members.

The reengineering life cycle also consists of a number of distinct phases of effort, but instead of a continuum, it consists of waves of intense work effort (see Figure 30–2). The resources expended in each phase can be extensive, depending on the issues involved in the total reengineering undertaking; and because reengineering can involve every facet of an enterprise's operation, a

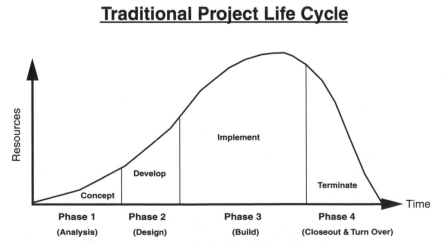

FIGURE 30–1   Traditional Project Life Cycle

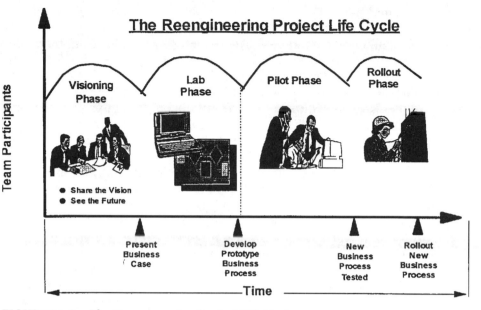

FIGURE 30–2   The Reengineering Project Life Cycle

diversity of project participants is needed to address a wide range of issues at different times in the project. Hence, there are usually more frequent changes in personnel than on a traditional project. The situation is further compounded by the fact that the mission, and even the management style of the project team, differs in each phase of the reengineering life cycle.

In determining how to organize and build an effective reengineering team, it is important to define the mission of the team, the style of management that is appropriate for that phase of effort, and the skills that are needed. The following sections offer the reader some insights on how to get the right team members, how to weld them into a productive, committed team, and how to avoid the pitfalls along the way.

PHASE 1: THE TEAM IN THE VISIONING PHASE

Activities in the visioning phase focus on what the company could be. This phase is characterized by abundant creativity and intense interactive communications. The reengineering team works purposefully to develop a vision of the future that is not constrained or hampered by the baggage of the past. Typically, the visioning phase results in a conceptual design and a business case that describes the improvements needed and the benefits to be achieved. If senior management accepts the business case, the project moves into the lab phase.

Clearly, the visioning phase of a reengineering project requires participants who are willing to challenge long-held paradigms and have the courage, wisdom, and creativity to conceive the way the organization will do its work in the future.

Senior management selects the key reengineering-project personnel and assigns them the task of determining the selection criteria and specific skills needed by all other team members. The selection criteria for team members should focus on the motivation of the candidates, the specific skills they bring to the team, and their willingness to take risks. The team should be made up of people who can conceptualize a new and better way of doing business and who have the drive and courage to make it happen. It is important that the team have the mettle to challenge the status quo. This will happen if the team has diversity; diversity generates constructive conflict where new ideas are thoroughly scrutinized and tested. The end result of the team's efforts will be sounder, stronger, and more durable. External consultants, specialists, and other support personnel should be identified and integrated into the reengineering team as needed.

Ideally, the best people in the organization should be selected for this phase of the project, but typically the best and brightest people are fully occupied carrying on the day-to-day business of their units. Usually their managers are reluctant to release them even for a temporary assignment. This situation may require the project sponsor to invoke executive power to get the needed resources. Another approach is to convince the managers involved that it is in their best interest to have their most capable people act as architects of their future. A number of individuals will see the reengineering undertaking as a career opportunity with substantial senior management exposure.

This is an important and difficult phase in the reengineering effort and it involves a considerable amount of learning for all the team members. The team has to learn how to envision the future and how to think and communicate in ways not constrained by their own experiences, values, and perceptions. This type of learning takes time and requires visible support from senior management, inventions by experienced team facilitators, and the proactive efforts of all team members. One of the keys is to provide enough time in the schedule to allow the team to develop through learning. In addition, the team needs a safe environment where it can experiment, make mistakes, try new approaches, learn by doing, and build synergy.

The team must face directly the issues of participating in an effort that can result in friends losing their jobs, or team nonsuccess contributing to company failure. Confronting and discussing these issues will allow the team to get past their fears and focus on the goals of the project.

The role of the project manager in this phase is that of philosopher. The job involves breaking ideological stalemates, exciting the team, encouraging varied contributions, and balancing passions without throttling creativity.

PHASE 2: THE TEAM IN THE LAB PHASE

During the lab phase the reengineering team details, tests, and solidifies various approaches to the new business process. Labs are at the heart of reengineering, with lab-team members bringing their experience, creativity, innovation, and energy to bear in the design of a new business process in the image of the vision. New approaches to doing work are structured, decomposed, mapped out, simulated, and evaluated. A multitude of ideas are proposed and tested, many to be discarded. The process is iterative, designed to foster creativity and innovation, and every avenue to accomplishing the breakthrough goals is pursued. The lab team considers all dimensions of a new business process, including the organization's culture and structure, the role of technology, job content and skill set requirements, and the interaction of activities that make up the business process. The lab phase is the most demanding, the most difficult to manage, and the greatest challenge to bring to closure. It is imperative to establish well-defined time boxes to give team members boundaries for the creative work involved in formulating a new business process.

The lab phase is completed when prototypes of the new business process are tested and validated to the point that the team is confident the process can accomplish the intended breakthrough goals. At that point the project is ready to test the new process in a small-scale, controlled, real-world environment, called a pilot.

The team in the lab phase will be larger than the team in the visioning phase. Team members in this phase need a wide range of skills that can address the technological, business, and human dimensions of inventing a new way of doing work. The team needs to be cross-functional, representing various components of the organization, and selected members of the original visioning team should be retained to assure consistency of the vision. Populating the lab team with diverse views is critical to this phase C, because this will stimulate creativity through conflict of opinion.

The challenge for the new members of the lab team is to see and accept the vision as conceptualized in the visioning phase. The vision must then be transitioned to the new team so that they can own it. The members of the new team must internalize the vision as a part of their value system and be energized by it.

Testing

One solution to the dilemma of changing the vision is to have the new team test it. For example, the lab team may question the constructability of the vision by asking the following questions: Can this system actually be built? Will it work? Can we do it? Should we do it? After a process of analysis, synthesis, and evaluation, the team should be able to develop answers to most of their concerns. The answers will either be confirming or conflicting. If the answer is conflicting, it is a flag that the information needs to be reexamined. If the answer is confirming, then the team members will be able to own the vision and move forward. Nevertheless, it must be recognized that the team's concerns will be intensified by the fact that the jobs of some team members and their peers and friends may be at risk if the new vision comes to fruition. It is in the lab phase that the stark realities of the vision truly become clear to the team members.

The lab phase presents the first opportunity to design and test a management-of-change strategy. Because lab members are from various parts of the organization, this test will simulate what will happen in the organization at large when the new systems are implemented.

This phase is also an opportunity to examine strongly held notions about how work can be done. The work history of the company will be challenged, and issues such as diversity, the value of cross-functional skill sets, and which tools and equipment are really required will be examined.

To ensure continuity, the lab team should contain key members from the visioning team; there is, however, a risk that every proposed change or compromise will be magnified and viewed by the original visioning-team members as a sellout of their innovative and creative plan. The original team members and the new members must develop a rapport so that the work produced in the lab phase can contain needed compromises without being labeled or viewed as a sellout of the vision.

Because of the nature of the work in the lab phase, it is difficult to develop quantitative performance indicators. The project manager must rely on qualitative indicators to measure success and accomplishments, as well as on the team's intuitive sense of how well they are progressing toward their goals. In the lab phase, the project manager must reconcile a diverse chemistry of interests, blending the team's mix of zealots, ideologues, front-line workers, and technical specialists wanting to transfuse the visions with their solid, but sometimes irrelevant, experience from the past. The role of the project manager in this phase is akin to that of an alchemist.

PHASE 3: THE TEAM IN THE PILOT PHASE

In the pilot phase, the project team attempts to validate, in a real-world setting, the anticipated improvements in the new process before massive investments in time and money are made. The team focuses on the tools, systems, techniques, and technologies that will enable the new process to work better, faster, and with greater payoff than the existing process. The team should expect problems and failures, but must concentrate on gathering objective data, making needed corrections, and evaluating the new process.

During this phase the news of failure or success spreads rapidly. The stress of meeting deadlines also raises anxiety levels. Intensity increases due to "opening day" jitters. The team's perceptions of success and failure should be identified and discussed as soon as possible to minimize concerns and the potential for bad decision making.

It is especially important in the pilot phase that undesired outcomes not be labeled as failures of the people involved, but as opportunities for learning and avoiding mistakes on a larger scale. These outcomes need to be seen as areas in which improvements can be made. Management and the stakeholders will critique problems; therefore, it is imperative that the team maintain a positive attitude and emphasize that the pilot phase is designed to discover shortcomings. If the team members look inward and believe that the "rest of the company is wrong," the result will be the perception that the team is arrogant. Because of its high sense of esprit de corps, the team needs to be wary about not insulating itself from the rest of the organization.

In the pilot phase, success indicators tend to be more quantitative and easier to measure than in the lab phase. Also, performance measurements move from a group effort to accountability of single individuals. If this phase is not managed successfully, the environment can move from "safe" to "cover up." This is when project management needs to ensure that a well-integrated plan is in place and that there is accountability for each item of work.

The end stage of pilot testing consists of proof testing and burn-in of the new business process, where major problems are fixed before total rollout. All of the issues concerning computer systems, software, networks, facilities, tools, equipment, people, and training must be addressed and resolved in this phase.

The role of the project manager in this phase is that of a test pilot, using skills, experience, and wisdom to guide the team in proving that the new process will perform as promised.

PHASE 4:   THE TEAM IN THE ROLLOUT PHASE

The final phase of the reengineering life cycle is rollout. This is a critical phase of work because existing systems must be phased out or shut down in concert with the rollout of the new systems, without adverse impact on operations. People must be trained, customers must be informed, and last-minute surprises and problems must be solved.

During the rollout phase, the new process becomes visible to the company at large and to the customer. Accountability and credibility of the individual rollout-team members are critical because the rollout of the process represents the culmination of the work of several teams. Project-review meetings must be held on a frequent basis and planning must continue, not decrease, as the project goal comes into focus.

Management sponsorship, clear communication, thorough planning, and effective management of change are essential to this phase. Rollout-team members are agents of the change and will be on the front lines as implementation of the new processes begin to have an impact on the lives of co-workers. Selection criteria for team members should focus on the individuals' belief in the necessity for the change, their understanding of the impact of the change, and strong change-management skills. Team members must have a desire to participate in the implementation of something different and new, while understanding that the new process may be seen negatively within the company and may not always work as expected. Enlisting candidates for this phase may be difficult and management assistance in recruiting the right people for the rollout team may be needed.

Rollout-team members must be able to clearly and persuasively articulate the business reasons for the new process and should agree with the process. There will be unanticipated problems to solve during implementation within the context of the new design. Recruits to the team need to understand the work done in designing the new process so that temporary "workarounds" will not conflict with the newly designed process. Because the recruits will not have the same training, experience, or exposure that the visioning, lab, or pilot-team members had, they must network with members of the earlier teams for feedback as the newly designed process is implemented. Members of the original teams may believe that the rollout team is tainting their newly designed process when there is news of workarounds. A smooth hand-off between the original teams and the rollout team requires clear communication on exactly what the new process is and feedback on how the process is being implemented.

Executive Sponsorship

Visible executive sponsorship is crucial in this phase. Ineffective or invisible sponsorship will signal to employees that the newly designed process is not important or that their part of the change will not make a difference. When the sponsor is not actively involved, employees may believe that they are being unfairly treated and will resist the change. Rollout-team members cannot be fully effective without visible sponsorship, and employees will view this effort as just another management fad.

As the old organization loses members to the new organization, there will be a feeling of being left behind by those who are maintaining operational capability. Those left in the old world may resent the use of acronyms used by those of the new world, and when technology glitches or performance failures occur, old-world employees may develop heightened fears about their crossover time to the new process. On the other hand, employees moving to the new organization may experience a feeling of disappointment when everything in the new world does not operate perfectly and they may begin to doubt those delivering messages about the new effort. Rollout-team members, while continuing the tasks of implementation, need to be sensitive to the feelings of the employees on both sides of the transition. The team needs to be aware of the grieving process that will occur as employees move into the new environment and should distance themselves from those who are cynics, victims, or bystanders of change. Similarly, when operating in the new environment, rollout-team members must be realistic about the new process changes, continuing to be open to suggestions and not becoming defensive when the new process is not a panacea to all problems.

The operational requirements of keeping the business running while employees are being trained in the new process is burdensome unless resources are used effectively. It may be necessary to train interim workers to take the place of those who are being trained in the new process. Training of the interim workers should be of high quality, because these workers represent the company during the transition period and can have a significant impact on operations.

Training personnel in a new process can be ineffective or slow as the employees work through the change issues, and rollout-team members need to be clear and consistent when communicating with those who are new to the change. Ineffective communication during this phase will provide fodder for the rumor mills. Clear communication by management will assist the employees in making informed decisions about what they need to do to be effective, and will help them to be more productive and to spend less time speculating on the change. Clear communications also allow the right questions to be asked as changes are rolled out to the organization and to the customers.

Reviews

During the rollout phase, the team must take time to review what has been learned. Specific lessons-learned sessions must be scheduled; otherwise this knowledge will be lost as the team concentrates on process implementation. This phase also requires reinforcement of positive behaviors as team members model the new values in the organization. Rollout-team members may need occasional reminders about the positive impacts of the change, for both the company and the customers, as they get caught up in the day-to-day implementation of the process.

The role of the project manager in this phase is that of construction manager. There will be pieces of the original design that will require modification to fit; there will be slowdowns, delays, and many fire drills; but the goal is to complete construction of a quality process on time, within budget, and as designed.

External Team Influences

Typically, reengineering-project-team assignments are performed on a full-time basis by a small number of employees sequestered in a remote location, or "skunk works." This is a proven approach to creating a hard-working, high-spirited, high-performing, breakthrough-oriented team. Unfortunately, this strategy also fosters an elitist attitude, isolates the team from contacts in their old departments, and fosters other dynamics that serve to insulate the project-team members. Unless the team works hard to overcome it, communications about team achievements, as well as reactions to objections and concerns from others, can take on a self-righteous tone that can polarize those who ultimately must support and execute the new process.

Key Lessons Learned

From experience in organizing and managing reengineering teams, we have been able to identify ten issues that invariably will plague the team and the project:

- Resistance to change
- Fear
- Hidden agendas
- Conflict
- Defectors
- Opportunists
- Poor performers
- Setbacks
- Periods of inertia
- Never enough communication

These issues must be dealt with effectively; otherwise, the project will be jeopardized.

THERE WILL BE RESISTANCE TO CHANGE

Experience and research show that change will be resisted regardless of the benefits or the compelling reasons for the change. Therefore, projects that involve significant change to the organization's culture, processes, procedures, or systems must implement a comprehensive change-management program. At minimum, the change-management program must provide training, consoling, mentoring, and support that helps everyone affected by the change make the choices necessary for the transition to the new organization.

THERE WILL BE FEAR

Change generates fear. Typically, the fear centers on the unknown. Participants in a reengineering project will fear loss of their jobs, positions, careers, or the security that comes from working in a structured environment. This fear is real and, if the unknowns are not addressed early in the project, will lead to overt or covert resistance, inertia, or defection. The fear issue has to be brought out into the open and addressed in a proactive manner by the reengineering team. One way of dealing with the fear issue is to make clear to all participants where they will fit in the new organization. Let people know up front if downsizing will be a consequence of the reengineering project and how this issue will be handled. Be honest and don't try to hide unpleasant news.

THERE WILL BE HIDDEN AGENDAS

Everyone involved in the reengineering effort will have a personal agenda. If the personal agendas are in conflict with the project objectives, the project will suffer. The key to dealing with this problem is to get individual wants, needs, and desires out on the table where they can be dealt with and to look for creative ways to meet individual concerns within the reengineering project agenda. For instance, if team members are concerned about job security, promotion, and recognition, project managers can point out how their needs can be addressed by broadening their experience and skills through participation in the reengineering undertaking. Project managers can emphasize the importance of individuals taking the initiative to reshape their personal paradigms to meet the needs of the new organization.

THERE WILL BE CONFLICT

Participation in a reengineering effort is demanding and stressful. Team members will be forced to deal with issues and problems that are new and complex. They will have to battle entrenched views and attitudes, and there will be substantial disagreement about the best way to approach a problem or deal with an issue. Team members must be trained to accept the fact that conflict is a part of the reengineering process and if managed properly can actually be an asset to creativity and problem solving.

THERE WILL BE DEFECTORS

No matter how well the reengineering team functions, or how exciting, rewarding, or forward thinking the program, team members will leave the project. Some will leave to seek security elsewhere, some will leverage their experience into promotions, and others will become discouraged or disillusioned. Regardless of the reasons, project managers need to be prepared to fill the voids with capable replacements. Always be on the lookout for viable candidates and build alliances with functional managers who can provide replacement resources; the best strategy, however, is to develop creative ways to reward participants and keep them from defecting from the project in the first place.

THERE WILL BE OPPORTUNISTS

No matter how careful the screening and selection process, a few team members will inevitably attempt to use the project to promote their pet project or particular philosophy. These individuals can cause a lot of harm if not spotted early, because they will attempt to increase or change the scope of the project, or even subvert project objectives. In most cases, their motivation is personal gain in some form or fashion. It is imperative that these individuals be identified early; and if their motivation and thinking cannot be aligned with the objectives of the project, they must be removed from the project at once.

THERE WILL BE POOR PERFORMERS

Some team members will not live up to expectations. They may lack the skills, experience, or motivation needed; but regardless of the problem, if their performance cannot be improved quickly, they should be removed from the project.

THERE WILL BE SETBACKS

As in any project, things will go wrong. Good ideas won't work out as expected, problems will develop, systems will fail, management will be unhappy, stakeholders will complain, and team members will become discouraged. It is particularly important that the project sponsors reassure everyone from the start that setbacks are to be expected in reengineering. Team members should accept setbacks as part of the learning process. Every setback provides valuable information and helps to toughen and mature the team. This idea has to be endorsed and communicated by senior management, the sponsor, the project manager, and all the team leaders.

THERE WILL BE PERIODS OF INERTIA

There will be periods when the project seems to lose momentum. This usually happens after a prolonged, intense effort that results in a major accomplishment, such as the successful installation of a new system or completion of a major milestone. There will be a psychological letdown in the team and it will be difficult to regain the intensity of effort and commitment. Project managers and team leaders must be prepared to deal with this situation or the project may stagnate and never regain the energy to accomplish its ultimate goal. Off-site training and team-building activities may be in order to help the team refocus and refresh their energies. It may be appropriate to bring in new team members to get a fresh perspective, or rotate team-member assignments to add some variety and excitement.

THERE WILL NEVER BE ENOUGH COMMUNICATION

No matter how elaborate the communication effort is in a reengineering project, stakeholders will always complain that they don't know what's going on and management is not keeping them informed. This problem is due in part to the fear that permeates a reengineering project and the resistance to change that everyone feels. Another part of the problem has to do with the development and implementation of a new way of doing business. It's hard to visualize and understand something that is in the process of being invented; hence, stakeholders feel that they are being kept in the dark. The solution to this is to never stop communicating. Senior management in particular must constantly articulate the goals and benefits of the project. Project managers must give timely progress reports, and team members must proactively communicate up and down and across the organization about matters within their realm of responsibility. The communication process must strive to assure that everyone is aware of the questions being asked and the answers being given.

Conclusion

Team building for a reengineering project presents many more challenges than are found in most traditional projects. The team must design and implement processes and systems that threaten the values and beliefs of the organization and potentially change the roles and responsibilities of everyone involved. In addition, the team has to perform its tasks with the knowledge that the end result may have dire consequences for the jobs and careers of friends and associates. The stress and anxiety that the team has to contend with are compounded by the ambiguity of the reengineering process itself. In order to build and successfully manage a reengineering team, project managers must formulate and implement a team-building program that continues through every phase of the project. In reengineering, team building is a continuous effort that is as important as the actual design and implementation of the new business processes.

BIBLIOGRAPHY

Champy, James. *Reengineering Management, The Mandate for New Leadership.* New York: Harper Business, 1995

Hall, G., Rosenthal, J., Wade, J. How to make reengineering really work. *Harvard Business Review* November–December 1993

Hammer, Michael and Champy, James. *Reengineering the Corporation: A Manifesto for Business Revolution.* New York: Harper Business, 1993

Hammer, Michael. *The Reengineering Revolution.* New York: Harper Business, 1995

Tuman, John, Jr. Project management as catalyst for strategic change: Restructuring the corporate environment for the 1990s; in *1989 Proceedings*. Upper Darby, PA: Project Management Institute

Tuman, John, Jr. and Englehardt, Gary. The triad for reengineering success: Communication dynamics, team diversity and project management, in *1995 Proceedings*. Upper Darby, PA: Project Management Institute, 1995

Tuman, John, Jr. and Evans, Celwyn. Creating a revolution in project management thinking, tools, and techniques to manage reengineering projects, in *1996 Proceedings*. Upper Darby, PA: Project Management Institute, 1996

Benchmark Tools for Operation Teams

Dale E. Knutson

Biographical Sketch . . .

Dale E. Knutson, PMP, is currently the Operations Manager for PNNL's Environmental Molecular Sciences Laboratory (EMSL). He has worked as a project manager during the past twelve years for Rockwell International and EG&G at the Rocky Flats nuclear site, and Battelle at Pacific Northwest National Laboratory. His recent projects include building the EMSL operating environment, implementing high-technology research equipment and computer requirements for EMSL, conducting environmental remediation of plutonium-contaminated facilities, and managing heavy-construction seismic-upgrade retrofits for nuclear facilities. This chapter's technical content benefited from the editorial and technical focus provided by Dr. Thom H. Dunning, Director, Environmental Molecular Sciences Laboratory at Pacific Northwest National Laboratory (PNNL); Dr. Douglas Ray, Senior Research Scientist, Environmental Molecular Sciences Laboratory, PNNL; and Col. (ret.) Duane E. Knutson, former Deputy Chief of Staff and Director of Engineering and Services for Air Force Space Command. Professional editing was provided by Jim Thielman and my wife Brigitte. The facts are clear because of their input; the conjecture and opinion belong to the author.

Only now are operations managers beginning to understand the benefits of applying project-management techniques to the operations environment. Benchmarks, the reference points for measuring quality, can help operations managers evaluate performance in an environment of incredible changes, and the resulting confusion, driven by advances in technology.

For many people the term *operations* conjures up a vision of the long-suffering manager struggling to keep the profit margin of his or her business process ahead of the finance cost curve. That vision can be pretty accurate. However, a transformation of the vision is occurring in business where technology demand is strong and the business environment changes rapidly.

Operational Functions

Operations can be defined as *intraoperational*. Facility and utility systems, maintenance, groundskeeping, and all of the factors associated with the care and feeding of the fundamental core of an operation are intraoperational functions. The intraoperational functions are typically delivered entirely within an operations department and the interactions are for the most part self-contained.

Conversely, the operational conduct of an enterprise is defined as *interoperational*. Policies, internal and external practices, external use of equipment, and all of the ways that operational objectives are defined and delivered are interoperational functions. The interoperational functions are typically delivered between departments, one of which is operations. Interoperational functions also include the ability to interact with intraoperational functions.

The performance or nonperformance of one segment of an operation affects performance in another, just like a project. It is the interdependencies between interoperational and intraoperational elements that create the need for change, and the pace of technological improvements that set the stage for application of project-management tools to operations.

Defining What Is Normal

In operations that use product-management tools, a definition of "normal" needs to be evaluated against understood objectives that support outcomes. In medicine, for instance, normal human performance is defined by measuring factors such as blood pressure or pulse rate. Each of these measures can be strongly influenced, both in positive and negative ways, by looking more deeply into what contributes to or is dependent on the measure. Today, definitions of "normal" that apply to operations are just as important. But thinking of operations in project terms takes getting used to.

Projects are defined as being:

- Finite in duration
- Quantifiable through measurable outcomes defined by clear scope statements and comparative cost, schedule, and technical baselines
- Capable of being described in terms of specific tasks that can be broken down into discrete deliverable products

An environment challenged by changing technology or rapidly evolving business conditions can quickly build definitions similar to those of the project and apply them to all elements of operations. Under these conditions, operations must do the following:

- *Understand the duration of a given technology, requirement, or application, and be prepared to adjust accordingly.* This corresponds to finite duration, which is a part of the definition of projects.
- *Measure the effectiveness of the operation in light of anticipated change.* As in the definition of a project, this requires clear scope statements with comparative cost and schedule baselines.
- *Understand the processes that implement operational objectives and how to improve them.* This requires specific tasks that can be broken into deliverable products as in the definition of projects.

It is exciting to see a world of change and know that the tools for building excellence in project management apply to the operational environment.

How Benchmark Tools Are Applied to Operations

The benchmark tools described in this chapter were used to create the operations environment for one of the U.S. Department of Energy's most modern state-of-the-art molecular science laboratories, Environment Molecular Sciences Laboratory (EMSL) at Pacific Northwest National Laboratory.

EMSL has operations spanning seven technical research directorates focused on various aspects of molecular science in eighty-four individual laboratories. Each directorate has its own programmatic objectives, as well as state-of-the-art facility and equipment requirements.

The aggressive combination of broadly based science and technology applications along with increased demands for a competitive approach to scientific funding led to the creation of this process. The approach is the result of three years of effort to define what is meant by state-of-the-art operations.

The process was created from a benchmark of IBM's Almaden research facility, DOW Corporation Research, Sandia National Laboratories Combustion Research Facility, The National Center for Atmospheric Research, Monsanto Corporate Research, and other laboratory research operations. These corporations and laboratories were selected based on their willingness to participate and the recognition of their operational approach as some of the best in the business of research. The benchmark process canvassed these operations to identify work processes or values that lead to coherent, efficient, well-defined elements of operation. The expressed purpose of this benchmark was to replicate the best practices in the operational conduct of EMSL.

Benchmarks have no ultimate formulas. However, it is important that operations teams use the tools described in this chapter to define their operations, then identify where benchmarks are appropriate.

Figure 31–1 shows the three-step operations alignment process developed for EMSL. These three steps are, by definition, interdependent paths that need to be regularly revisited in a changing environment. By monitoring the updates, and adjusting accordingly, the project becomes part of operations and helps to maintain the competitive focus of the organization.

This chapter will answer each question listed in Figure 31–1. Although it is desirable to look for answers to many of the questions in parallel, for the sake of clarity, the questions will be addressed in sequential order through the remainder of this chapter. The chapter headings correspond to the questions in Figure 31–1.

WHAT IS CRITICAL TO MY OPERATION?

For established operations, this is the question that builds the context and sets the stage for answers in all other steps, and it demands an integrated review of operations. In new start facilities, to the extent possible, this question is answered after the question, "What business am I in operationally?" There are many modern tools for correlating the work that is done by an organization with the factors that are critical to success. However, one simple tool for arriving at an answer to this question is the Taguchi method of brainstorming.[1] In practical terms it requires a one-day workshop commitment and follow-up over time from personnel representing each operations component. Each

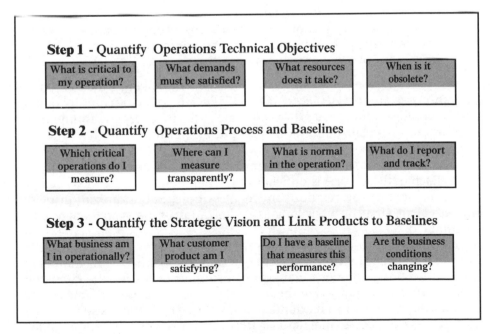

FIGURE 31–1   A Three-Step Operations Alignment Process

component of an operation, from administration, to executive, to production floor worker, should be represented.

Using a facilitator, the Taguchi method of brainstorming in this application suggests that each individual write down the factors that are critical to being able to do his or her job. Encouragement should be given to identifying factors that are taken for granted. Everything from pencils to licensed facilities and elements supporting the working area or office environment are fair game, with a focus on how work gets done. Project managers should group the outcome of this brainstorming into common elements. It is typical to find areas that reflect a critical need for factors such as:

- *A highly qualified staff.* This group of factors should contain elements of various technical and functional disciplines or craft skills.
- *A focus on customers' technical needs.* This group of factors should contain elements of market approach or a desire to work at a level that addresses pressing concerns of customers.
- *An open and available facility.* This group of factors should contain elements of access, capacity, minimum training, and a host of equipment, resource, and infrastructure needs.
- *A quality product.* This group of factors should contain elements of required peer review or independent verification of technical approach.
- *A safe and environmentally benign operation.* This group of factors should contain elements of expectations for permits, consistent laboratory bench-top practices, definitions of safe handling for hazardous or toxic materials, and waste-disposal practices.
- *Business practice and cost containment.* This group of factors should contain elements of competitive overheads, property management and inventory methods, reimbursement practices, petty-cash access, and capital-improvement investment practices.

These are but a few representative groupings, but they identify the elements of operation that are *critical success factors* (CSFs). There can be combinations of needs, or other groups, that are appropriate to the business environment and corporate culture surrounding the operation. But no matter how they are grouped, they articulate the areas of operation that must be delivered to be successful.[2] It is imperative to remember that this listing cannot be prioritized. Each of these areas is critical to the operation and they must be optimized in light of the relationship to the whole. Suboptimization of the individual area may occur as long as optimization of the overall operation is maintained.

For example, critical areas in operations may be compared to parts of the human body. One area may represent the head, another the heart, another the arms or legs. An operations manager can support or restrict the circulation and blood flow to a portion of the operations body for a limited time and the system will function. But an extended time without blood flow results in infection, disease, or stresses that damage the operational body. It is impossible to survive today's competitive business environment without all critical areas fully functional. A few of today's quality-improvement approaches look specifically at optimizing a single area of critical success. This decision is typically based on incremental cost. However, neglecting to look at the whole can easily result in loss or damage to an operational area.

An advantage of developing CSFs is that the project-management focus begins to emerge. The beginning of an operations work-breakdown structure (WBS) takes shape as each of these groupings is implemented by distinct work practices, which can be broken down further into discrete tasks and assigned individual, or at least departmental, responsibility. (See Chapter 7 for more on the Work Breakdown Structure.)

WHAT DEMANDS MUST BE SATISFIED?

As CSFs are identified, project managers and team members also begin to identify areas of operation that are not supporting one or more of the critical success areas. Some have called this the process of reengineering.[3] Project managers should not be surprised if the current organization chart is not aligned well with the CSFs, and project managers find active resistance on the part of participants who may feel threatened.[4] However, all operational groups represented in the brainstorming session should see themselves as owners of one of CSFs. This group must then define the work process that results in critical success being achieved.[5] The task of identifying the work practices that achieve critical success is one that can easily be subcontracted. If the work-process identification is performed internally, the work may require additional motivation. It is recommended, when using a subcontractor, that someone very familiar with the operation remain clearly focused on the definitions of critical success. Without that focus, an operation is likely to look like a consultant's vision of critical success, as opposed to the operation's vision.

As the work processes that support each critical success area are defined, whether by a subcontractor or by an internal reviewer, elements of perceived legitimate work will be identified that do not seem to support anything defined as critical. Certainly, the work process and elements that support critical success must be satisfied; one should not immediately dismiss this other work. The brainstorming exercise may not have fully identified critical tasks. Project managers must take a skeptical but honest look at why the remaining work in an operation is conducted. This work may very well be important, if not critical. If there are sufficient resources, both financial and human, additional tasks may be accommodated, but not at the expense of the critical tasks.

Once the activities are identified, the scope of operations has been defined. A WBS can then be created with updates scheduled on an annual basis or in support of periodic review cycles. A side benefit is that change control methods can be implemented.

Figure 31–2 shows how the CSFs are linked to work practices. These work practices are broken down into lower levels of functional work. This clarifies the definition of work-scope practices, their links to the operational practice, and their appropriate implementation level in the organization.

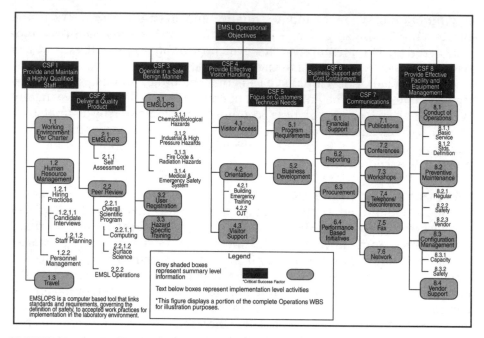

FIGURE 31–2   EMSL Operations Work Breakdown Structure

WHAT RESOURCES DOES IT TAKE?

As with any other resource estimate, each element of the work process defined must be clearly identified. In many cases, operations defines a level of service or response.[6] For some activities, this is represented by qualitative performance parameters such as the facility being safe, the floors being clean, the computer network not crashing. Quantitative parameters may include factors such as the shop acting on an order in two days, and a request for phone service being acted on the same day.

Each of these performance criteria reflects a level of customer expectation that must be balanced by the operations manager based on demand, acceptable levels of risk, or operational impact. If failure of a CSF has an impact on all other areas of performance, that CSF must be heavily supported with resources. Likewise, a CSF that has less of an impact should it fail, or that is more self-contained, can be less heavily supported. In the example of the human body, blood flow can be restricted in a way so that the appendage is not lost. Yet, an interesting event occurs, having made this evaluation. There are relatively clear minimum levels of performance that must be maintained or the operation, as currently defined, no longer functions. Finding this level has been historically an intuitive process; however, using project-management tools allows operations to define the scope of services as well as the costs to keep the operation functioning.

Every company has a method of defining or estimating resources that is unique to its corporate needs. The point to be made here is that operations should be estimated and balanced just like any other scope-driven task. The unique aspect of operations is that the balance changes over time as the operational focus shifts with technology, application, and business conditions. Having operational scope defined, with change-control mechanisms in place, allows a rational approach to managing operations that uses project-management techniques effectively.

WHEN IS IT OBSOLETE?
Operations age over time in the same way that any other business enterprise or biological system ages. The elements that support critical success wear out technically, or the environment surrounding the operation changes so that work processes or applications become inefficient or even irrelevant. Truly robust operational practices age well.' Other practices age quickly, sometimes quite dramatically, especially those based on technical innovations or quickly evolving applications such as computers and software. The answer to the question of obsolescence is important and it defines the finite duration of an operations process. There are at least two ways to answer the question using the techniques presented in this chapter.

First, the measurement tools described in the section headed Where Can I Measure Transparently? quantify normal for an element of operation. The easiest way to understand if an operational practice is obsolete is to determine that the process cannot achieve a normal rating due to limitations of technical or operational approach. Each of the CSFs defined by brainstorming needs to be evaluated in the light of a definition of normal. Obsolescence will typically involve a system that has achieved its design lifetime.[8] In some instances, a technical system supporting operations, such as secure network technology, other communications media, or software, will be surpassed by an alternative application that renders it obsolete. In this circumstance, a rational determination of obsolescence requires a strong core technical competency, or access to one, in the systems being used by operations. This is another area in which subcontracted expertise may be appropriate.

A second way of answering the question When is it obsolete? is to answer the questions Do I have a baseline that measures this performance? and Are the business conditions changing? These answers lead to an understanding of obsolescence based on evolution in the business environment that makes a work process obsolete. Obsolescence is difficult to determine, but the tools for achieving a successful resolution are contained in benchmark methods, total quality management (TQM) methods, and other methods that are already well-documented. Modern operations using project-management tools must maintain an active awareness of state-of-the-art practice. This operational awareness must facilitate an evaluation of maintaining output using existing practice versus costs for, and gains made by, internalizing the state-of-the-art. To do so requires a point of measurement as well as a baseline for comparison, which will be discussed later.

WHICH CRITICAL OUTCOMES DO I MEASURE?

The areas that require measurement are by definition the ones that contribute to achieving critical success. But that category is too broad to be useful, due to critical success depending on interoperational functions. As defined earlier, those functions span the entire operation, if not the whole company. Operationally, project managers need something a little closer to home that infers acceptable performance in many critical success areas, yet indicates weaknesses specifically.

There are many ways to measure performance that take advantage of existing business tools, such as staff performance review techniques and employee or customer satisfaction surveys. However, in this case, project managers need to focus on the processes that deliver specific operational objectives. Inherent in that statement is the fact that the measurement process must be adaptable to change as readily as the operational objectives. To that end, understanding the interdependencies of an organization holds great value. The places where multiple work activities converge into a single department, or even a single individual, give tremendous insight into which critical outcomes need to be measured.

For instance, in EMSL, a significant part of the work involves bringing external visitors to the facility to use research equipment. Each visitor brings a level of technical competence based on his or her experience. Visitors range in experience from summer students for whom this is the first exposure to the research laboratory environment, to leading scientists from around the world who may have invented the equipment or technique being used.

A CSF was to operate a collaborative research facility. This converged with another CSF, which was to maintain an open and available facility. The work practices of these two CSFs have the greatest overlap and operational impact in the area of training and qualification, which defines a need for operational safety. Measures of how long training takes, how it applies based on length of stay, and when it applies based on hazards, are very important and relevant, because so many interdependencies exist. Specifically for EMSL, these factors define the level of unrestricted access to an item of equipment or an individual laboratory for visitors. Conversely, these factors also define a level of dedicated technician time if training a visitor on an item of equipment is intellectually prohibitive. In some cases, it is more cost effective to dedicate a technician full-time to work on the equipment than to train a visitor to the required level of proficiency.

WHERE CAN I MEASURE TRANSPARENTLY?

It is important to remember that the act of measuring does not directly contribute to achieving operational objectives. Yet, without measurement, there is no way to describe the impact of change the or the necessity for improvement. To measure performance without adding work to the system, project managers must look for opportunities to measure transparently (i.e., no special reporting is necessary). The following are three examples of transparent measures.[9]

1. Operational capacity. Such measures look at how much of the operation is actually available to perform work. Entire volumes are available on reliability, availability, maintainability (RAM), and other physical-system measurements. Yet, the project-management approach indicates a need for an outcome measurement. For example, one could ask, How many hours are my main equipment capabilities not used between production or experimental activities? The answer could help turn a process around and adapt to change. This can be measured transparently by comparing maintenance logs and experimental or production-run logs. This does not add work to the process, but it does improve the quality of the information in the logs, as well as point out their value.

2. Cost containment. The operating cost of any level of service defines an infrastructure cost. In real terms, the operations manager needs to measure the intraoperational functions and costs to define the interoperational costs. It is easier and more transparent to measure intraoperational costs, such as the light bill and maintenance costs, than it is to measure the costs of computer security or other interoperational functions. This also allows a relative ratio of intraoperational to interoperational costs to be maintained as a definition of normal, which is discussed further in the next section.

Measures that address overall reductions in cost or external demand for services can be found by answering the following questions: What is the total equipment time made available for use by other (internal as well as external) departments or individuals? or How much does it cost to operate compared with other equipment in the business? The first is obviously a measure of use by others, but trends can also be a measure of customer satisfaction as well as cost reduction if an estimate of external use is prepared in the budget-development cycle as a baseline. In addition, budgeted cost of work performed and budgeted cost of work scheduled, compared with actual costs, is an appropriate set of measures for any of the service and maintenance activities in the operation. This useful information can be measured transparently by any number of accounting processes for direct billable hours, company-wide benchmarks for operation, or industry-available benchmark information.

3. Professional satisfaction or impact. Answering a question such as If we shut this process down, does any one care? is a true measure of the importance of the process. The answers to question such as how many publications reference the use of the organization's resources and capabilities out of the top ten journal publications, and whether that trend is increasing or decreasing, or what the level of return visits is by professionals or other customers wanting to use the organization's capability are gained by measuring transparently using independent peer review or other technical review processes.

These examples were chosen carefully because the information to generate the measurements is capable of being developed transparently with no special reporting necessary. Unfortunately, as the need to be more specific increases, so does the need for more intrusive measurements. Care should be taken here because this adds important but not critical work to the operation.

The operations manager, like the project manager, is ultimately responsible for the cost or value of the finished product, and measurement is required in balance with all other objectives. Each of these three examples leads to the natural definition of a baseline and to the question of measurement against what is normal for any given segment of the operation.

WHAT IS NORMAL IN THE OPERATION?

Stability in a world driven by change is extremely important for highly competent technical personnel, and for repeated achievement of critical success as well as effective use of project-management tools.[10] Being able to define normal in terms of capacity or level of service is very useful and allows stability to develop in spite of changing demands. Caution as well as good judgment is required to prevent stability from turning into stagnation with all of the resulting negative impact.

The definition of normal depends on the particular situation.[11] In a research facility, it may be normal for the maintenance staff to perform system maintenance during normal day-shift hours, because the research being conducted requires an empty building at midnight. Conversely, a production facility may never shut down to conduct maintenance, except during major holidays. Therefore, a definition needs to be based on the level of service that results in normal conditions.

For example, a piece of equipment demonstrates a run time of 600 hours per year with four major maintenance periods at 150 hours of operation per quarter. This is considered normal. Another example is the cumulative trend of a cost-performance index (CPI). This measures the budgeted cost of work performed divided by actual cost of work performed for maintenance activities. The result needs to stay between 0.95 and 1.05 on a cumulative basis to be normal. Each operation is different, but normal can be defined. When coupled to a baseline, what is considered normal provides real performance information for the organization. Linking the baseline to the CSF allows normal performance to achieve operational objectives. Iterating the definition of normal to reflect changing conditions is what allows improved long-term performance.

WHAT DO I REPORT AND TRACK?

The reporting function needs to be one that tracks the long-term, as well as intermediate, change in trends based on the impact to an operational objective. The long-term maintenance of a standard based on normal is the mechanism that helps to define obsolescence as well as the finite life of an operational practice. Many measures of performance reflect the trending of customer expectations.

A current reporting trend is the use of performance tolerancing that links a customer's, as well as a corporation's, expectations to a qualified measure of performance. PROMES, for one, uses qualitative probability distribution functions to assess subjective measures of performance such as excellent, satisfactory, or unsatisfactory.[12]

One capable method of defining normal using project-management tools is index comparison created from budgeted versus actual cost information. Other methods, which require history for comparison, are the maintenance of parametric values for operational capacity of individual equipment or production capabilities (e.g., this could measure how much the equipment is used).[13] Another is the definition of level of service based on technology hour. This latest measurement allows the operations manager to quantify normal in light of customer satisfaction and makes the tie to technology improvements (e.g., this measures what improvements are necessary to satisfy customers). Each of these is capable of being normalized to a standard of unity and evaluated as a deviation from normal. An example is provided in Figure 31–3. The (CPI) trend is based on an actual computer-network-and-information-distribution infrastructure development in EMSL. Definitions of normal can be reported in many standard project-management formats.

WHAT BUSINESS AM I IN OPERATIONALLY?

No matter what I say my business is, the things or work that I do, or that my operation is doing, is the business I am in operationally. That sentence is convoluted, but it is an absolute truth. It also brings to mind the story of the operations

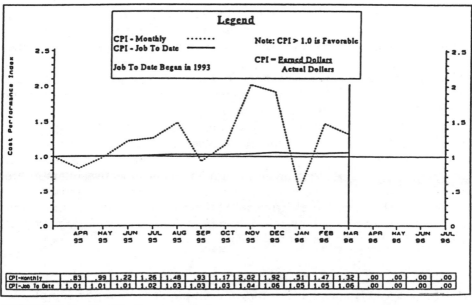

FIGURE 31–3   Cost Performance Index

manager for a logging company. The managers of this company were cutting trees furiously and making great progress; all the measures of performance were at the top peg of excellence. One day the operations manager climbed a tree to see where the crews were going and discovered the truth. They had been achieving tremendous production goals; unfortunately, they were in the wrong forest.

Making sure that the projects supported in the operations environment are conducted in the right forest is the purpose of this section. This requires the integration of vision statements, strategic planning, mission definition or chartering, objective definition, and operational alignment.[14] Basically it involves the hierarchical structuring of all the tools defined in this chapter to ensure that objectives support the mission so that the vision is implemented.

Operations managers, like project managers, typically have one common role. Some management roles are broader in context than others, but they all revolve around the verb *implement*. The role begins and ends with achieving the outcomes and expectations of the vision.[15] To do this requires CSFs that are supported by performance objectives that support mission objectives. The cynical reader may be pardoned for noting that it helps a lot when operational objectives are in alignment with the mission statement and corporate vision. The English language helps the operations manager in this regard. When used as a verb, the word *implement* has only three related terms: actualize, materialize, and realize.[16] Every time a vision or mission statement changes to reflect variations in market or customer demand, operations must rely on the word *implement* as a verb to define objectives. If the corporate vision statement or mission does not have an agreed-upon implementation activity, project managers should return to the negotiating table and negotiate their roles again.

EXAMPLE.   The operational objectives for the Environmental Molecular Sciences Laboratory are very direct. First, "To conduct molecular science using state-of-the-art methods, materials, and techniques focused on the customers' technical needs," and second, "To operate a national collaborative research facility."

Responsiveness in operations depends on known boundaries. The process of agreeing to what will be implemented as part of a coherent management approach defines those boundaries and actually enhances flexibility.

Further, boundaries should be described in terms of *what* to implement, not *how*. Each operation has a staff that knows more about how to implement an objective than any external expert. Facilitators can be very effective in bringing focus to a discussion on how to implement an objective; but there are too many customized work processes in real-world operations for an external expert to define how. More significantly, there is tremendous commitment and motivation to be gained by encouraging department participation in deciding how to implement an objective.

WHAT CUSTOMER OR PRODUCT AM I SATISFYING?

The answer to this question is intuitively simple but inherently complex in application. There are so many definitions of stakeholders and customers today that the lines between those merely interested and those that actually pay the bills are easily blurred. However, the operations manager needs to understand the customer set. The processes described in this chapter have broken down the operations environment into discrete products and linked the products through the CSFs to customer expectations. By correlating an employee's daily work activity with the CSFs, alignment is a natural outcome. The outcome is one of helping the individual understand how he or she fits into the big picture.

What typically happens, though, is that employees are spread across multiple tasks that require employees to prioritize their time among CSFs. When the competition leads to confusion over what customer is being satisfied or, worse yet, when it leads to making the employee choose which customer not to satisfy, the results are disastrous. The most successful organizations identify stimulating operational objectives *and* define a primary technical skill that an employee is responsible for maintaining.[17] The employee's focus, leadership, and primary tasks are directed at using that talent, which may span several areas of critical success. However, outside of the primary skill area, employees are encouraged to expand their expertise and participate through supportive, as opposed to leadership, roles.

DO I HAVE A BASELINE THAT MEASURES THIS PERFORMANCE?

Beyond the standard baseline measures and control processes used in project management, baseline measurement in this case takes on a new dimension. The process of identifying CSFs and optimizing the organization requires looking at which human resources are key to delivering operational objectives. Just as a project manager has to review the status of key technical personnel in the delivery of a project, the operations manager must look at key personnel in the delivery of critical success. There is no baseline more critical than understanding who it is in the organization that a majority of customers depend upon. If all, or a majority, of the CSFs depend on a single individual, the project-management tools of risk assessment need to be used to fully understand the implications of that individual being successful and promoted, being unsuccessful and leaving the department, or leaving the company because the operations manager burned up a key resource.[18]

ARE THE BUSINESS CONDITIONS CHANGING?

If the operations for which a manager is responsible is driven by rapidly changing technology, improved methods and applications, demands for faster return on investment and time to market, or any of the conditions discussed throughout this chapter, business conditions are clearly changing. Changing business conditions brings urgency to looking for areas in which obsolescence has set in or in which the work practice is not achieving the expected level of performance. It is especially useful to look at the tools described in this chapter as a stabilizing influence in a world where changes occur faster than companies have the ability to adapt. These tools represent a method to make rational decisions for or against change, based on information that actively accounts for the elements and work processes of an organization. One can look at these demands for change and understand that methods some take for granted in the field of project management have valuable application in the field of operations.

ENDNOTES

1 Kolarik, William J. *Creating Quality—Concepts, Systems, Strategies, and Tools.* New York: McGraw-Hill Inc., 1995, pp. 22–49

2 Ibid., pp. 90–109

3 Senge, Peter M., Kleiner, Art, Roberts, Charlotte, Ross, Richard, and Smith, Bryan. *The Fifth Discipline Fieldbook—Strategies and Tools for Building a Learning Organization.* New York: Bantam Doubleday Dell Publishing Group Inc., 1994, pp. 351–407

4 Jain, Ravinder K. and Triandis, Harry C. *Management of Research and Development Organizations—Managing the Unmanageable.* New York: John Wiley & Sons, Inc., 1990, pp. 135–156

5 Ibid., pp. 94–113

6 Grose, Vernon L. *Managing Risk—Systematic Loss Prevention for Executives.* Arlington, VA: Omega Systems Group, 1987, pp. 145–148

7 Collins, James C. and Porras, Jerry I. *Built to Last—Successful Habits of Visionary Companies.* New York: Harper Business, HarperCollins Publishers, 1994, pp. 1–42

8 Kolarik, William J., *Creating Quality—Concepts, Systems, Strategies, and Tools.* New York: McGraw-Hill Inc., 1995, pp. 173–197

9 Kolarik, pp. 215–240

10 Collins and Porras, pp. 80–91

11 Jain and Triandis, pp. 44–63

12 Pritchard, Robert D. *Measuring and Improving Organizational Productivity.* College Station, TX: Department of Psychology, Texas A & M University, Nov. 17, 1994

13 Kolarik, pp. 235–240

14 Cleland, David I. *Project Management—Strategic Design and Implementation.* Second Edition. New York: McGraw-Hill, Inc., 1994, pp. 235–264; Senge, Kleiner, Roberts, Ross, and Smith, pp. 397–346

15 Hitt, William D. *The Leader-Manager—Guidelines for Action.* Columbus, OH: Battelle Memorial Institute, Battelle Press, 1988, pp. 39–85 and 216–219

16 *The Merriam–Webster Thesaurus.* Springfield, MA: Merriam-Webster, Inc., Publishers, 1989

17 Collins and Porras, pp. 89–90

18 Grose, pp. 36–90

Chapter

32

Concurrent Engineering Teams

Preston G. Smith

Biographical Sketch . . .   **Preston G. Smith**, a Certified Management Consultant, heads New Product Dynamics, a Portland, Oregon, consulting firm that has helped managers in accelerating their new product development for over a decade. He often advises management in setting up development teams and trains and coaches these teams. He is coauthor of *Developing Products in Half the Time*, speaks frequently at conferences on development teams, and has taught product development and teaming techniques at several universities.

T oo many product-development teams fail to live up to expectations, actually performing more poorly than their members would have on their own. This chapter provides tools to aid the project manager in setting up an effective concurrent engineering team and avoiding the common pitfalls. Team staffing topics covered include selecting the team leader (who is usually also the project manager); recruiting team members; and dealing with the potential problem areas of part-time members, specialists, and suppliers on the team. The principal dilemma in team organization is that there are many organizational forms, but none is ideal in all circumstances. The trick is in knowing how to select the form that best supports the innovative needs of concurrent engineering—and in avoiding the pitfalls of some impotent forms. Because innovation demands a great deal of cross-functional communication, the emphasis must be on an arrangement that eases team communication.

The Scope of Concurrent Engineering

Although there are many definitions of concurrent engineering, the most common one comes from a military contractor's report:

Concurrent engineering is a systematic approach to the integrated, concurrent design of products and their related processes, including manufacture and support. This approach is intended to cause the developers, from the outset, to consider all elements of the product life cycle from conception through disposal, including quality, cost, schedule, and user requirements.[1]

Notice that this definition is far broader than just the design of the product and its manufacturing process. It encompasses the product's entire life cycle and includes several broad measures of success, such as cost, quality, time, and user satisfaction. Thus, concurrent engineering actually incorporates much more than just the engineering function in a company.

This definition is not limited to a particular type of product, and it does not specifically mention engineers. Thus, it applies to developing products in which there is little actual engineering. Concurrent engineering may apply to pharmaceuticals, paint, food, or sneakers. By extension, concurrent engineering could apply to developing services, such as insurance policies or trucking, although such applications will require some reinterpretation of the material presented here.

Concurrent engineering teams have the following three key attributes:

1. They must deal with the inherent uncertainties of innovation.
2. A broad range of professional skills is needed, including engineering, science, marketing, manufacturing, and finance.
3. Most of those involved are professional knowledge workers.

These attributes make concurrent engineering teams particularly challenging ones to set up and manage. This chapter focuses on topics that are particularly crucial for teams that develop new products and services.

The Earmarks of an Effective Team

Effective concurrent engineering teams typically have the following characteristics:

- They contain no more than ten members.
- Members choose to serve on the team.
- Members serve from the beginning to the end of the project.
- Members participate on the team full time.
- Members report solely to the team leader, and the leader reports to general management.
- Key functions—at least marketing, engineering, and manufacturing— are included on the team.
- Members are co-located within conversational distance of each other.

Few teams achieve all these characteristics; but teams that work well satisfy many of them and know where they fall short on the others so they can compensate.[2] Figure 32–1 illustrates an ineffective fragmented team having too many lightly involved members.

Dedication to project (%)

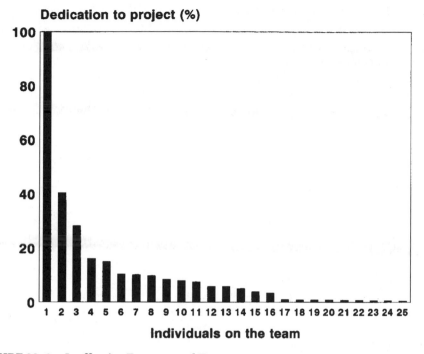

Individuals on the team

FIGURE 32–1   Ineffective Fragmented Team
Source: Smith and Reinertsen, Developing Products in Half the Time, Van Nostrand Reinhold, 1995

A small team (fewer than ten) strengthens commitment and eases communication. Not only is it difficult to communicate in a large group, but it is also hard to keep track of everyone's opinion and reach agreement. Note that the requirement for full-time membership naturally keeps the team small. If size is still a problem, the techniques of incremental innovation or product architecture can divide the work among smaller teams.[3] This is just what Boeing did when developing its 777 aircraft. The company divided the work among 238 design-build teams.

End-to-end continuity overcomes the communication and accountability gaps that follow from passing the project "over the wall" to the next group. Full-time involvement also clarifies accountability while simultaneously clearing people's slates so that they can concentrate heavily on this one project.

Reporting relationships are crucial, because to make fast cross-functional business decisions, the team must regard itself as an empowered business team, not just a group of functional representatives or a band of engineers.

Being co-located is another technique to greatly accelerate and raise the reliability of communication. This in turn improves problem solving and decision making, which are both core activities in product development. Because physical proximity of team members is a great asset to a team, it is worth the extra effort required to obtain it. Professor Thomas Allen of MIT provides the best analytical case for co-location. Figure 32–2 is a composite from several research and development labs investigated. It shows that people are far more likely to communicate when they are within conversational distance (closer than ten meters, or thirty feet).

However, the strongest case for co-location comes from teams that have tried it. There is no substitute for the way it enhances and speeds up commuiation. Those who have been on co-located teams would definitely choose it again if they had to get a new product to market quickly. Just as a real concurrent engineering team includes other functions, such as marketing and manufacturing, real co-location involves more than just the engineering members of the team.

As powerful as it is, co-location is not easy to accomplish in many organizations. Many development teams are dispersed among several sites, sometimes even on different continents. This makes co-locating difficult to impossible. Even for teams in the same metropolitan area, the obstacles include the following:

- Lack of sufficient floor space
- Concerns about distractions or lack of privacy
- Functional bosses worried about losing control of "their" people
- Perceived lack of status
- Lack of a permanent office home

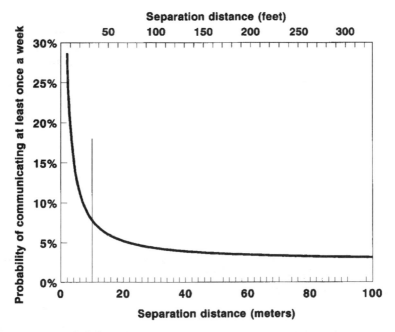

FIGURE 32–2   Probability of Communicating at Least Once a Week
Source: Allen, *Managing the Flow of Technology,* The MIT Press, 1977

Some people, especially in high-tech industries, claim that modern communications have superseded the need for co-location. But has voice mail (and phone tag) really made telephone communication any faster or more reliable that it was twenty years ago? E-mail allows one to broadcast messages more efficiently than before, but does that ensure that they are read, understood, or acted upon? Face-to-face communication remains by far the highest-quality medium for conveying many types of information and receiving accurate, fast responses. Thus, co-location is far from obsolete.

Each organization will have different difficulties in satisfying the characteristics that will make the team effective, but the biggest difficulties often provide the most opportunity for improvement. In highly hierarchical organizations, where the only general manager is the person at the top, it seems virtually impossible to have all development teams reporting to this CEO. Another company that has operations all over the globe may deal well with the general manager problem but have a great deal of difficulty with co-location. In companies that simply have too much on their agendas,[4] full-time involvement may be unthinkable.

TEAMS AND MEETINGS

Teams often get associated with meetings. Some teams form to solve problems or make decisions. For these teams, the team's work is done in meetings. However, a development team's job is to *do* things, things such as design, analysis, customer visits, prototype building, and testing. These tasks do not get done in meetings. So if team members think of their roles as holding meetings, little will get done, people will arrive at meetings unprepared, and progress will be slow. A development team should not define itself through its meetings, but rather as a group that completes the value-added tasks that breathe life into a new product.

Staffing a Team

Often, the team leader and the project manager are the same person. These two roles fit well together, and they provide some latitude in choosing a title that reflects the desired emphasis. The title should answer the following question: Are we looking for leadership or management? Is the object of this attention the project or the team?

It is when the project manager and the team leader are different people that difficulties can occur. If the project manager reports to the team leader and has little authority, this role can degrade into one of administrator. The project manager keeps the schedule and budget up to date but has little power to take action on the information he or she maintains. On the other hand, sometimes the team leader role is held by an executive who spends little time with the team. Then there is an ineffective absentee landlord situation.

The choice of team leader is the most important one management will make in the life of the project. A project to develop even a simple new product will have to overcome many obstacles because of the product's innovative nature. A weak leader will be unable to deal with the hurdles, so management will get drawn in, which simply is a slow way to run a project. Rapid progress depends on a readily available leader/manager with a can-do attitude who takes charge when difficulties arise. A part-time project manager or team leader is not sufficient. If management assigns anyone to the project full-time, it should be the leader.

The team leader should be considered first as a general manager, not a functional expert. The real skill needed is to integrate the marketing, engineering, manufacturing, and other departmental viewpoints into a solid business direction. If the leader is viewed as, say, primarily an engineer, then functional managers of marketing and other departments will feel obliged to get involved to protect their interests. This outside managerial involvement undermines the very advantage a cross-functional team can provide, which is fast, effective action on cross-functional issues.

TEAM-LEADER SKILLS

Two groups of essential skills underlie this general management capability: product-vision skills and people skills. A popular definition of leadership is the ability to transform vision into results. If this is the case, then to get a winning new product to market, the leader must have a broad, integrated, and focused vision of the product and be able to communicate this vision to others.

The need for people skills is probably obvious, but most of these skills stem from innate ability or long-term development; seldom can they be trained-in as needed. Such skills include the ability to do the following:

- Incorporate diverse views, especially from quieter people or on unpopular subjects.
- Resolve conflict.
- Develop members' skills and their confidence in them.
- Intrinsically motivate members.
- Move ahead with little or unclear authority.
- Obtain the human and other resources needed.
- Protect the team from outside distractions.
- Maintain a relaxed atmosphere under stressful conditions and employ humor effectively.

Clearly, the leader needs a working knowledge of the technologies and other professional disciplines involved in the project, but in-depth knowledge can get in the way by encouraging micromanagement. The team will also need conventional project-management skills, such as an ability to run effective meetings, schedule and monitor progress, draft and manage a budget, and comply with the corporate procedures on product development. Such skills are usually secondary in importance and can be learned on the job when necessary. The practice that many companies have of always selecting team leaders from a certain department, such as engineering, just places a misguided restriction on the search for a good leader. Engineers do not have a corner on the crucial vision or people skills.

TEAM MEMBERS

Effective team members have qualities remarkably like those of good leaders.[5] In particular, members should be self-starters who can work without supervision. Another essential attribute is a willingness to think independently and support contrary views when necessary. Groupthink is particularly destructive in a close-knit team whose job is to innovate.

In selecting members, the leader naturally makes sure to incorporate the key disciplines and professional skills—the so-called hard skills. However, there is another set of critical soft skills that is just as important to have available within the team. These skills include problem solving, idea generation, conflict resolution, and negotiation.

One earmark of successful teams is that members volunteer to serve on the teams. Given the hectic pace in industry today, it is unlikely that people will actually volunteer, but it is important that they are on the team because they want to be.

How does one recruit such volunteers? First, the team leader, who does the recruiting, identifies the people desired on the team. Then the leader goes to management and negotiates the availability of the desired individuals. In some cases, management can accommodate the leader, and in others the individual involved will be too critical to another project.

Then the leader discusses with the prospective member, in an honest and evenhanded way, the pros and cons of being on the team. The leader then watches and waits: Is the prospect excited about the possibility or does he or she raise objections? It will become apparent at this point whether the prospect chooses to be on the team. If not, the leader should look for someone else; this person is unlikely to put forth his or her best for this team.

HEAVY EARLY STAFFING

A common mistake made in staffing a team is not getting key players on board soon enough. Early staffing may be weak as new members finish prior commitments so that they can join the team. The team then gets off to a shaky and slow start, which puts it in a catch-up situation from the outset. When the late members do join, they are at a disadvantage, because they have not participated in the preparatory activities and early decisions. Quite simply, slow ramp-up sets the stage for failure.

Usually, when the objective is minimum cycle time, teams are understaffed throughout their lives.[6] Starting off understaffed just ratifies this unacceptable situation. Project launch is the time for the team leader or project manager to be most adamant about full staffing, because early shortfalls are likely to become the norm later.

For concurrent engineering, the late arrival of downstream players, such as those involved with manufacturing and field service, just perpetuates a situation in which products are not designed for manufacturability and serviceability. The only way to break this continuing stream of unmanufacturable products is to get the downstream functions involved at the outset.

THE POWER OF GENERALISTS

Ever since Frederick W. Taylor and Henry Ford, U.S. industry has encouraged labor specialization. In many cases, this is with good reason. Individuals feel good and can command better pay by doing something specific a bit better than others. In addition, organizational design is cleaner, because one can put people in definite pigeonholes and put precise labels on the organization chart.

Unfortunately, specialists create a host of problems on a product-development team. It is difficult to keep them gainfully occupied full-time on the project, so they come and go from the project as it needs their expertise. This creates scheduling, availability, and delay problems, which ultimately stretch the schedule. The specialists often feel little commitment to the project at hand. They are unlikely to understand well the project objectives, such as the product attributes the customer values most. Nor are they apt to comprehend how their work must fit with downstream activities, such as manufacturing, distribution, and promotion.

Thus, on balance, a development team can move faster and produce products that satisfy customers better by using a few generalists working full-time throughout the project. Clearly, there is a limit to how far one can go with generalists, because a company's competitive edge often depends on the distinct competencies that specialists provide. Yet, most firms would be much better served by shifting toward generalists on development teams. Ultimately, this requires favoring generalists through recruiting, compensation, training, recognition, and promotion.

Until these long-term measures create more generalists, team leaders should seek generalists—or those willing to try wearing different hats—when recruiting team members.

SUPPLIERS ON THE TEAM

Many companies, especially automobile manufacturers, are providing substantial roles for suppliers on their concurrent engineering teams. Supplier involvement is important in three situations. First is when the supplier's lead time is long or unpredictable, which can delay the whole project. Second is when the supplier's ability to manufacture the parts reliably and with high yields depends on the design that the team supplies. The third situation is when the supplier holds a special knowledge of a product technology that is critical to success.

In these cases a supplier should be a substantial member of the team. The critical item to manage here is getting the supplier involved early, when she or he can contribute to shaping the critical early decisions that will add value to the product. It is virtually impossible to get the supplier involved too early. Once the supplier is on board, project managers should keep in touch with that person on an ongoing basis (weekly), even when there are no important issues to discuss. This will keep the project manager up to date on the supplier's workload and thus the supplier's ability to respond when you needed by the team.

Substantial supplier involvement means that the supplier spends time on-site with the team, often co-located. Clearly, the supplier should receive equitable compensation for this, perhaps with upfront payments for his or her time, rather than having compensation amortized in the piece-part price later. This type of in-depth involvement carries its price, so project managers will want to select carefully the few suppliers whose contribution will warrant this special treatment.

TEAM TRAINING

Many teams succeed without training, but training of an intact team gets the team through its initial forming and storming stages quickly. This is especially true for a firm's pioneering concurrent engineering teams.

Two types of training are valuable. One relates to the soft team skills, such as defining roles and responsibilities, understanding the variety of personality types on the team and how they typically react, building trust, and resolving conflict. The other is the harder, more content-oriented skills, such as the techniques of rapid development, how to make customer visits, and how to use tools like quality function deployment effectively.[7]

The effectiveness of this type of training decays quickly, so it is best done exactly when the need occurs. Thus, advance planning and budgeting are essential to line up the training sources and have them available for timely insertion. Some types of training, such as conflict resolution, are more difficult to plan for. Consequently, having a trainer or facilitator on staff and accessible is of great value, especially for the softer skills.

MOTIVATING THE TEAM

This is a highly controversial subject with few clear answers. It is also an important subject, for it relates directly to individual and team effectiveness. The following are a few guidelines that apply especially to concurrent engineering teams.

Project managers should think beyond financial rewards. Although coffee mugs and T-shirts may have seen their day, there are many other options available to the creative team leader. For example, consider a photo of the team in the annual report, lunch with the executive sponsor, or a holiday weekend.

A preoccupation with financial motivation usually indicates something askew in the basic compensation system that patchwork rewards will not correct. People deserve fair compensation for the work done regardless of whether they are on a team.

Project managers should think carefully about the change in behavior they want, and plan motivation and rewards to encourage it. For example, recognizing individuals, just the team leader, or a core part of the team does not encourage teamwork.

Project managers should not depend heavily on rewards or other types of extrinsic motivation for obtaining results. There are just too many ways in which they can backfire. People will resist attempts to be controlled by rewards or money.[8]

Organizing a Team

Although there as many types of organizational structures as there are organizations, most of them fall somewhere on the spectrum from a functional organization (Figure 32–3) in which each person reports to a function manager to the stand-alone team (Figure 32–4), in which individuals involved in the project report directly to the team leader, who in turn reports to a general manager. Between these two ends lie a variety of options in which an individual reports simultaneously to a functional manager and a team leader. (See Chapter 14 for more information on matrix forms.)

Each of these forms has its strengths and weaknesses. The functional form is popular in industry because it has provided functional strength and expertise for years. However, in the functional form, communication and decision making tends to flow through the functional heads. This is simply not very effective for the heavy load of cross-functional communication entailed in product development. Decisions get made much better and faster with a more horizontal form.

Consequently, there is no one best form, and the one to use depends on the objectives of the particular project. Some projects developing highly innovative products can benefit greatly from the horizontal flow prevalent in the more autonomous forms. They are willing to tolerate the shortcomings of poorer functional coherence. For example, they may let designers on every project team select a different type of fastener, which ultimately causes factory complications. In contrast, for a more routine product upgrade project,

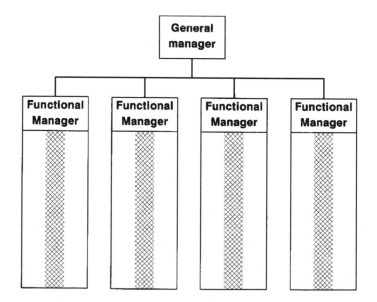

FIGURE 32–3   A Functional Organization
Source: Smith and Reinertsen, *Developing Products in Half the Time,* Van Nostrand Reinhold, 1995

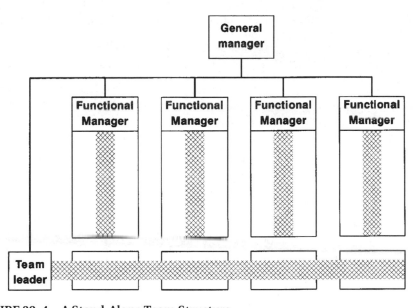

FIGURE 32–4   A Stand-Alone Team Structure
Source: Smith and Reinertsen, *Developing Products in Half the Time,* Van Nostrand Reinhold, 1995

the balance can be completely different, which suggests a different organizational form. The most effective teams design their organization to fit the job rather than just adopting the company standard.

Once the organizational form is selected, project managers should recognize its weaknesses and be sensitive to them. For example, if proliferation of fasteners is likely to be a problem, put some type of fastener standards or coordinating mechanism in place.

As companies remove layers from their hierarchies, they generally move toward more horizontal forms, which is generally in the right direction for development teams. However, this shift is not likely to be fast enough for the needs of an innovative development project. Thus, a concurrent engineering team may be in the position of pioneering new organizational forms in a company.

Just putting some people together or having a meeting, however, does not make a team. Real teams require real effort to set up and maintain, but they pay real dividends, too. The biggest mistake many project managers make is in assuming that a team will just happen.

ENDNOTES

1 Winner, Robert I., Pennel, James P., Bertrand, Harold E., and Slusarczuk, Marko M. G. *The Role of Concurrent Engineering in Weapons System Acquisition* (Report R-338). Alexandria, VA: Institute for Defense Analyses, 1988

2 Smith, Preston G. Your product development process demands ongoing improvement. *Research-Technology Management* 39(2):37–44, 1996

3 Smith, Preston G. and Reinertsen, Donald G. *Developing Products in Half the Time*. New York: Van Nostrand Reinhold, 1995
4 Ibid., Chapter 11
5 Kelley, Robert E. In praise of followers. *Harvard Business Review* 66(6):142–48, 1988
6 Smith and Reinertsen, Chapter 11
7 Hauser, John R. and Clausing, Don. The house of quality. *Harvard Business Review* 66(3):63–73, 1988
8 Kohn, Alfie. *Punished by Rewards*. Boston: Houghton Mifflin, 1993

Self-Managed Production Teams

Karen M. Bursic

Biographical Sketch . . . **Karen M. Bursic** is a research assistant professor in the Department of Industrial Engineering at the University of Pittsburgh. She received her B.S., M.S., and Ph.D. in industrial engineering from the University of Pittsburgh. Previously, she was a senior consultant at Ernst and Young (in Operations and Quality) and was a production supervisor and industrial engineer for General Motors Corporation. She is a registered professional engineer and a member of the Institute of Industrial Engineers, the American Society for Engineering Education, and the American Society for Quality Control.

Self-managed production teams (also known as semiautonomous, self-regulating, or self-directed work teams) replace the traditional, hierarchical manufacturing organizational structure. These teams are more firmly rooted in the organizational design and are a sophisticated, structured technique to facilitate employee involvement and empowerment in a manufacturing environment. Production teams are comprised of all workers from a particular work area or work cell that have broad responsibilities beyond those commonly given to other kinds of teams. Membership on the team is normally not voluntary—it is a requirement of the job. Production team members have a high degree of responsibility and authority to manage day-to-day activities, including task assignments, work scheduling, training, work methods, quality control, maintenance, problem solving, and even hiring or purchasing. In general, the employees are given most of the planning, organizing, motivating, directing, and controlling responsibilities formerly assigned to first-line supervisors or foremen. Team members may rotate job assignments, be paid for the various skills they master, and are often evaluated based on group rather than individual performance. This kind of organizational design allows for shared responsibility, authority, and accountability for decisions and results.

Self-managed production teams allow for a departure from the traditional, hierarchical organizational structure and movement toward a flatter organization with fewer management layers. Figure 33–1 displays this change in the organizational structure. In the traditional organization, individual employees work in the plant (perhaps on an assembly line or assigned to a particular work area) and report to a supervisor. There may

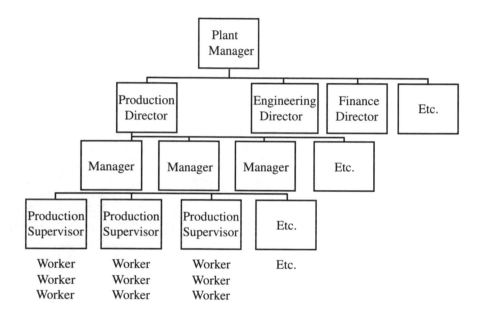

The Production Team Structure:

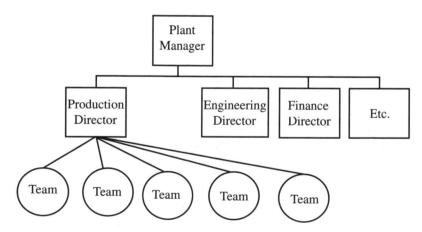

FIGURE 33–1   The Traditional Organizational Structure

exist separate supervisors for operators, maintenance personnel, and inspectors. The supervisor in turn reports to a superintendent or department manager and the chain of command continues up to the plant manager. In the production team structure, groups of individuals, which include machine operators, skilled tradesman, maintenance personnel, inspectors, and so forth, work together in teams to produce the needed products. The teams report directly to the head of production or other high-level position. This structure reduces the number of management layers, gives employees direct responsibility to produce a product, and therefore facilitates employee empowerment. These kinds of teams contribute to the trend in industry today to extend decision-making capability to non-management and lower-management employees.

Industrial Examples

Teams have been used in industry in many forms for a number of years. Operations research teams date back to the 1940s and project-management teams have been popular since the 1960s. But teamwork did not become a central issue for U.S. manufacturing until the introduction of Japanese-style quality circles in the 1970s. Since that time, the use of teams as a tool to solve problems has dramatically increased. Today, it is not a matter of whether teams are used, but how effective they are at improving performance in the organization. One survey found that over 50 percent of manufacturing organizations are using a team-based work system.[1] However, the effectiveness of these practices has come under fire.[2] A recent survey which included 1,500 workers in various industries, found that 87 percent of respondents claim they use a team approach, yet only 22 percent are satisfied with the results.[3]

Volvo Car Corporation has been using production teams since the 1970s. In its Kalmar, Sweden, plant, fifteen to twenty employees form teams and operate without the assembly line. Each team builds large sections of a car. Volvo went even further when it completely replaced the traditional assembly line with production teams in its Uddevalla plant in the 1980s. The teams manage themselves by handling scheduling, quality control, and hiring. Volvo has eliminated first-line supervisors at the plant and maintains only two tiers of managers. The teams are responsible for building four cars per shift in their own work area. Team members are trained to do all assembly jobs and rotate jobs every three hours on average. Morale is high at the plant and absenteeism has been dramatically reduced.[4] Volvo was an innovator in the use of production-team concepts and many companies have followed their lead.

Since its inception, New United Motors Manufacturing, Inc. (NUMMI), a joint venture between General Motors and Toyota located in Fremont, California, has employed production teams. Teams are made up of four to six people including a UAW team leader. Three to five teams form a group that is led by a nonunion leader having traditional supervisory responsibilities. The group and team leaders work together with team members to determine work loads and job allocations. Jobs are rotated to the extent possible (model and technology changes may require people to learn new skills). Work teams share meeting areas on the production floor where charts are kept that contain information on quality, job allocation, and so forth.[5] Operators have the authority and responsibility to stop the production process if it is out of control or if a problem occurs. Some are convinced that the plant is one of the most efficient automobile assembly plants in the United States.[6] Others disagree[7] and insist that the stress caused by working in such an environment is inhumane. Still, the plant continues to operate successfully using production teams.

The use of production teams is certainly not limited to automobile manufacturers or strictly assembly operations. Another U.S.–Japanese joint venture, the I/N TEK and I/N KOTE steel plants, located in South Bend, Indiana, also use production teams. This joint venture between Inland and Nippon, which began in 1990, is a highly automated continuous production operation. Teams of eighteen to twenty-five workers have high levels of autonomy to run the operations. Their responsibilities include allocating tasks, inputting into work planning and scheduling, and setting quality standards. Workers rotate jobs within their teams. They also have the ability to stop operations if necessary. Because the operation is a continuous production system, the team has more flexibility to schedule meetings and other activities.[8]

The use of production teams is also not limited to foreign companies or joint ventures. Digital Equipment Corporation has used production teams in some of its manufacturing operations. Its Enfield, Connecticut, plant was designed and built with a number of human resource and organizational development issues in mind—including production teams. The plant opened in 1981 with only two levels of management and work teams of twelve to eighteen people responsible for every aspect of producing its products. The plant had some initial problems, brought on, in part, because of a lack of understanding about the amount of training that would be needed. Eventually, this was a very successful venture for Digital.[9]

For six years, *Industry Week* magazine has profiled the winners of its Best Plants awards and has also drawn conclusions about the commonalities among these plants. *Industry Week* reported that all twenty-five winners and finalists in 1995 relied on empowerment practices and that 88 percent of those plants have launched self-directed work teams (production teams) to some extent.[10]

XEL Communications, an electronics manufacturer located in Aurora, Colorado, and one of the 1995 Best Plant winners, uses production teams in 100 percent of its workforce. Process-oriented teams oversee circuit-board manufacturing operations. Product manufacturing teams handle manual assembly tasks and take responsibility for getting customer orders shipped on time. Plant management insists that without the teams, quality would not be as good as it is. Teams are held accountable for assembly defects, and they set their own goals for on-time delivery, rework, productivity, cycle time, cost per component, and reducing defects. Some teams meet twice a day to maintain organization. The teams make quarterly presentations to management, discuss goals for the next quarter, and report progress on meeting current goals. Line-supervisor positions have been eliminated on the plant floor. Management believes that implementation of empowered work teams is difficult and that they've been successful because of their strong commitment to the concept.[11]

Another of the 1995 Best Plant winners, Super Sack, which makes bulk containers for the food, agricultural, and pharmaceutical industries, attributes much of its success to the use of production teams. Each team meets at the beginning of each shift to discuss the day's work and quality criteria. Workers perform every aspect of the sack production and are responsible for safety, quality, and housekeeping. Individual duties may change depending on the needs of the day. Team leaders rotate every three months so all team members are able to fulfill the leadership role. The teams are even responsible for their own hiring, firing, and disciplining of workers on their team. Super Sack wasn't always successful with production teams. Their first attempt to form a team failed because team members were not given all the information they required. Management didn't realize how important training in communication, goal setting, and team building would be to the success of the teams. Another barrier that Super Sack had to overcome was the lack of trust among team workers. Early into the change to production teams, workers were reluctant to speak out. Once team members learned to attack problems, not people, they were able to overcome this reluctance.[12]

At the Electrical Distribution and Control Division of General Electric Company located in Auburn, Maine, all plant production employees are involved in product- or process-oriented work teams. Employees are clearly empowered to make all decisions about both product and process tasks. All employees are cross-trained to perform any job in the facility. A computer system communicates the real-time priority and status of orders, workloads, material availability, and quality requirements. With this information, workers can make their own decisions about where to work. There are no supervisors on the plant floor. Unlike some of the plants described earlier, this plant was not started up using teams. The plant has been in operation since 1967, but has been using teams since 1988. Management notes that it took five years for workers to fully accept empowerment through teams.[13]

These plants and others like them have been successful for a variety of reasons. There are ten common strategies that organizations report as contributing to the success of their production teams. Certainly this list is not exhaustive and a team program will not necessarily succeed simply because all of these strategies are implemented. These ten strategies, however, are known to contribute to successful teams. The following descriptions have been customized to the use of production teams in particular, but can be adapted to other teams as well—including project-management teams.

1. Senior management support.   This factor is absolutely critical to the success of any kind of team, including production teams. It requires commitment of both financial and physical resources, as well as allowing employees time off from other responsibilities to participate in team meetings and presentations. (See Chapter 17.) It also means management must be willing to share vital organizational information that teams will require to make decisions. One way to demonstrate commitment is to assign each team a sponsor from senior management, someone who can help break down barriers for the team. This worked effectively for an insurance company using quality-improvement teams. If a team was having difficulty getting other people committed to implementing its solutions to problems, it sought out intervention from the top management sponsor. And while XEL Communications recognized that implementing production teams is difficult, it also understood that management commitment to the concept contributed to its program's success.

2. Interdisciplinary nature and diversity.   Interdisciplinary means that the team consists of members from two or more disciplines or functions of the organization. On a production team, this might include several types of skilled trades, quality inspectors, machine operators, supervisors (or team leaders), and other necessary personnel. The members should represent all organizational functions that are needed to solve problems or run the day-to-day operations. One team spent a significant amount of time clearing up a serious misconception because there was no team member representing the distribution function. The team also had difficulty in getting their solution accepted.[14] Rather than permanently increasing the size of a team, some team members might be used on an ad hoc basis. For example, an industrial engineer may be needed only if the team is developing new work methods.

Diversity in team members is also critical for coming up with creative solutions to problems.[15] A team is strengthened when it includes a member who is task-focused, a member who is focused on the goal, a member who is process-focused, and a member who questions the team's direction. At the same time, diversity may sometimes cause other difficulties for the team that a leader or facilitator will have to address through conflict resolution. Team members should have some training in group processes and consensus-based decision making to manage conflict.

3. Integration and continuity.   If teams are to be successful for the long-term, they must be fully integrated into the organizational design. Because teams are a departure from the traditional hierarchy, they require that everyone understand how they are embodied into the organizational structure. This will ensure their continuation even in times of management and/or employee turnover. Responsibilities that belonged to first-line supervisors, which are now being transferred to the teams, must be clearly defined.

4. Education and training.   A recent survey found that 92 percent of U.S. team members receive some type of training.[16] Training for production team members may include the following:

- Team dynamics and team building (e.g., teams skills, meeting skills, negotiating skills, and knowledge of the phases of a team's life cycle)
- Problem-solving tools (e.g., brainstorming, nominal group technique, process-flow diagrams, pareto charts, and statistical process control)
- Interpersonal skills
- Communication skills
- Job skills

Managers at Super Sack, the bulk container maker, admit their biggest mistake early in their production-team implementation was a failure to recognize the importance of education and training. Super Sack's team members now receive training in job skills as well as communication, goal-setting, and team-building skills.[17] It is important to recognize that all of this training can be overwhelming, especially if it is given all at once. Skills that are not used immediately will probably not be retained. One approach, termed *just-in time training*, provides training to employees in specific skills as team members need them. For example, training in communication skills may be provided as teams are preparing for management presentations.

5. Effective leadership.   The team leader's primary role is that of task management: making sure objectives and goals are met. The leader of a production team will undoubtedly handle some of the responsibilities that may formerly have been held by the first-line supervisor. Thus the leader must be someone who is highly motivated and committed to the team as well as someone who knows the production process well. (See Section III for more on leadership.)

6. Effective facilitation.   One of the roles that is vital to any kind of team is that of a facilitator. The facilitator's primary responsibility is to manage the team process. When faced with a problem to solve, the facilitator should keep the team focused on the problem and moving along each step of the problem-solving process. In addition, a good facilitator will ensure that everyone truly participates in the team process and contributes to the team's ability to function. The facilitator must be skilled in interpersonal relations and conflict resolution. The leader role clearly differs from the role of a facilitator, although some leaders are able to orchestrate both roles simultaneously.

7. Clear team mission, objectives, and goals.   By definition, a team must have a common purpose, otherwise one simply has a group of people who happen to work together (perhaps under the new label of "team"). The mission must be specific and clear. Telling a team to "fix the accounting system" is like telling it to "eliminate world hunger." Teams need a specific definition of the problem they are addressing.[18] Team members must understand why teams are being formed and introduced into the organizational design. The early communication process is critical to a team's start-up.

Production team members must buy into the mission and its supporting objectives and goals. A common reason cited for team failure is the lack of focus on a mission to which the team and management are committed.[19]

Although the mission itself may be defined before the team is formed, team members should be actively involved in developing objectives and goals to support the mission. If, for example, the mission is to produce high-quality products that satisfy customer requirements, team members should be involved in setting the goals that will meet these requirements and in determining strategies for obtaining the goals. These objectives and goals should help clarify the needs of the team's customers and stakeholders.

8. *Team chartering.*   A team chartering process is the process by which a number of these strategies are established. Chartering involves selecting team members, defining the team's mission, holding kickoff meetings, providing initial training, and selecting the team's leader and facilitator. All of these tasks must be completed before the team will begin to function effectively. It has been recommended that team members be provided with training as a group and thus begin working as a team immediately.[20] One of the characteristics of successful team programs is careful attention to the chartering process.

9. *Clear team roles and responsibilities.*   Although each individual has specific skills and knowledge that he or she contributes to the production process, objectives cannot be met without an interdisciplinary team approach. Team members should understand their roles, what tasks and responsibilities are theirs, and how they can make a contribution. Several high-performance teams outside the corporate world were recently profiled in *Fortune*.[21] In the profile, it was clear that, although members of teams such as the Dallas Cowboy's offensive line, the U.S. Navy SEALs, and the Massachusetts General Hospital Emergency-Trauma team may have large egos, they tend to check those egos at the door when working with their teams. Teamwork, not individual success, is the focus for these teams, even though each member has a clear role and particular responsibilities. The same holds for production and other industrial teams.

10. *Balance of authority, responsibility, and accountability.*   Again, by definition, teams and their members must be empowered to not only set objectives and goals and to solve problems, but also to make decisions about work methods, job assignments, and implementation of solutions to problems. One of the biggest mistakes management can make is to give teams responsibility and accountability for their tasks yet not give them the authority to act on their decisions. This balance of power is critical to the success of production teams.

The Benefits of the Use of Teams

Teams typically develop better solutions to problems than individuals. Because they include diversity in discipline and perspective, teams are better at generating a number of options and exploring the advantages and disadvantages of those options. This leads to improved decision making and implementation. Teams bring together the people who will have to implement new ideas and systems once these decisions are made. They will therefore be more committed to these decisions and will be less resistant to change.

Another benefit reported by companies using production teams is that of enhanced skill, agility, and flexibility in the workforce. Milwaukee Electric Tool reports that this benefit is not just a result of their use of teams, but of the introduction of a pay-for-knowledge program that offers financial incentive to workers who learn new skills.[22] Keithly Instruments reported a 90 percent increase in productivity and 75 percent reduction in absenteeism as a result of the use of production teams.[23] Volvo also saw its absenteeism reduced dramatically after its full implementation of production teams at its Uddevalla plant.[24] The Electrical Distribution and Control Division of General Electric has seen productivity and quality increase in recent years, in part because of the use of production teams.[25] XEL Communications and Super Sack report similar benefits. Increased job satisfaction and motivation, reduced absenteeism, improved productivity and quality, and increased organizational flexibility have all been reported as benefits of the use of production and other kinds of teams.[26]

Tips for Creating Successful Self-Managed Teams

Aside from the obvious need to pay attention to the ten strategies previously cited, a number of management tips are critical to obtaining the benefits of production teams. A study conducted by a cultural anthropologist and marketing researcher in 1993 and 1994 and sponsored by the American Society for Quality Control, Disney, General Motors, Kellogg's, and Kodak, revealed three important findings that play a role in why teams fail. These include employees' need to know what's in it for them, people's previous unpleasant experiences with teams, and the individualistic nature of American culture.[27]

When asked to participate on a team, employees will nearly always want to know what's in it for them. If this is not clear to team members, then the team will have commitment problems. Good facilitators and leaders can demonstrate what's in it for individuals by emphasizing a number of personal benefits that come from participating on teams.[28]

- *Job security.* Because teams are often aimed at improving customer satisfaction, they can also increase business. Increased business means more job security for everyone.
- *Learning opportunities.* Being a team member should mean that employees will receive training in areas such as problem-solving techniques, interpersonal skills, and job skills.
- *Improved communications.* Teams help to improve communications with fellow employees, something nearly everyone recognizes as a major issue in any business organization.
- *Career Advancement.* Participation on a team increases one's exposure to senior management and can lead to career advancement possibilities.

- *Employee empowerment.* Team participation increases an individual worker's opportunity to make significant contributions to the workplace. Increased authority, responsibility, and accountability is a defining characteristic of teams.
- *Pride and satisfaction in the workplace.* Many team members find that team opportunities increase their individual job satisfaction and motivation.

People's previous experiences with teams may have been negative; thus, they may naturally be apprehensive about or resistant to joining a team. For example, sports teams in grade school are usually a negative team experience for an individual with poor athletic skills. Many people have been on teams (or committees) that have simply not accomplished anything. One of the ways to deal with this issue is to ensure early success with small problems before dealing with larger ones. For example, a team may spend time solving the problem of paper towel shortages in the rest rooms. Although they may not be making a significant contribution to customer satisfaction, solving this problem could give the team early encouragement concerning their capabilities to solve problems, make decisions, and work together.

One of the major difficulties with teams in the United States is that American culture goes against certain attributes called for in teams. In particular, many Americans have a strong need for have individual success at something. Sacrificing for the good of the team is not something Americans are predisposed to do. They also don't like to be forced to join a team. This resistance must be overcome if a team is to be successful. One of the ways to deal with this issue is to ensure that individuals as well as the team are recognized for contributions. This can be done by allowing each team member to play a particular role and to make some type of contribution to problems that are solved and decisions that are made.

Another important team management tip is to build trust among team members. If teams are to succeed, the team members must trust each other as well as their leaders and facilitators. Commitments and responsibilities for action items must be kept; otherwise this trust will suffer. A good leader will follow up with team members to ensure their tasks are being completed. A facilitator who understand group dynamics should also be able to assist in building trust among team members. In addition to trusting each other, the team must have trust in senior management. Continuous senior management support (through sharing information and providing resources) contributes to employees' trust in management's commitment to the teams.

If production teams are to be implemented in an existing plant, management must find ways to overcome the inevitable resistance to change. One approach is to focus on the benefits to individual employees such as those in this chapter. In addition, management should provide real examples of the success of team structures at other organizations and should include employees and any labor unions in the design and implementation of the new organizational structure.

The Future of Teams

Teams are now becoming a permanent part of the way many organizations operate. Although teams have existed for some time, we haven't always understood why they succeed and why they fail. There is currently much information about when and how to effectively introduce teams into an organization. The benefits that many organizations have gained from the use of teams ensures that manufacturing organizations will continue to see an increase in the use of self-managed production teams.

ENDNOTES

1   Osterman, Paul. How common is workplace transformation and who adopts it? *Industrial and Labor Relations Review* 47: 2, January, 1994, pp. 173–188

2   Cutcher-Gershenfeld, Joel, Nitta Michio, Barrett Betty, Belhedi Nejib, et al. Japanese team-based work systems in North America: Explaining the diversity. *California Management Review* 37: 1, Fall, 1994, pp. 42–64

3   Many use a team approach; few are satisfied. *Quality Progress* 28: 12, December 1995, p. 18

4   Kapstein, Jonathan and Hoerr, John. Volvo's radical new plant: "The death of the assembly line"? *Business Week*, August 28, 1989, pp. 92–93

5   Cutcher-Gershenfeld, pp. 48–49

6   Branst, Lee and Dubberly, Agnes. Labor/management participation: The NUMMI experience. *Quality Progress* 24: 4, pp. 30–34, April 1991

7   Parker, Mike and Slaughter, Jane. Management by stress. *Technology Review* 91:36–44, 1988

8   Cutcher-Gershenfeld, p. 50

9   Galagan, Patricia. Work teams that work. *Training and Development Journal* 4: 11, November, 1986, pp. 33–35

10 Sheridan, John H. Lessons from the best. *Industry Week*, February 19, 1996, pp. 13–20

11 Sheridan, John H. XEL communications. *Industry Week*, October 16, 1995, pp. 61–62

12 Verespej, Michael. Super Sack. *Industry Week*, October 16, 1995, pp. 53–54

13 Miller, William H. General Electric, *Industry Week*, October 16, 1995, pp. 30–32

14 Lyman, Dilworth and Richter, Ken. QFD and personality type: The key to team energy and effectiveness. *Industrial Engineering* 27:57–61, 1995

15 Parker, Glenn M. *Team Players and Teamwork: The New Competitive Business Strategy*. San Francisco: Jossey-Bass Publishers, 1990

16 Team tidbits. *Quality Progress* 28: 6, June, 1995, p. 18

17 Sheridan, 1996, p. 54

18 Cupello, James M. The gentle art of chartering a team. *Quality Progress*, 28: 9, September, 1995, pp. 83–87

19 Beck, John D.W. and Yeager, Neil M. How to prevent teams from failing. *Quality Progress* 29:27–31, 1996

20 Winning team plays. *Supervisory Management* 40: 5, March, 1995: p. 10

21 Labich, Kenneth. Elite teams get the job done. *Fortune*, February 19, 1996, pp. 90–99

22 Sheridan, 1996, p. 44

23 Parker, 1990, p. 3

24 Kapstein and Hoerr, pp. 92–93
25 Miller, 1995, p. 30
26 Bursic, Karen M. *Factors Contributing to the Successful Use of Teams (and Benefits Gained from Their Use) in Manufacturing Organizations*. Ph.D. Dissertation, University of Pittsburgh, 1990
27 Bemowski, Karen. What makes American teams tick? *Quality Progress* 28: 1, January, 1995, pp. 39–43
28 Milas, Gene H. Guidelines for organizing employee TQM teams. *IIE Solutions* 28: 2, February, 1996, pp. 36–39

BIBLIOGRAPHY

Baker, Edward M. Managing human performance, in *Juran's Quality Control Handbook*, Fourth Edition. Edited by Juran, J.M and Gyrna, Frank M. New York: McGraw-Hill, 1988

Cleland, David I. and Bursic, Karen M. *Strategic Technology Management: Systems for Products and Processes*. New York: American Management Association, 1992

Jaycox, Michael. How to get nonbelievers to participate in teams. *Quality Progress* 29: 3, March, 1996, pp. 45–49

Kern, Jill Phelps. The chicken is involved, but the pig is committed. *Quality Progress* 28: 10, October, 1995, pp. 37–42

Klein, Stuart. Teams under stress: The effects of work pressures and management action. *IIE Solutions*, 27: 5, May, 1995, pp. 34–38

Longman-Czeropski, Sue. Follow the leader. *Quality Progress* 27: 12, December, 1994, pp. 47–49

Scholtes, Peter R. Teams in the age of systems. *Quality Progress* 28: 12, December, 1995, pp. 51–59

Teegarden, James W. Use technology to unleash the potential of your quality improvement teams. *Quality Progress* 28: 10, October, 1995, pp. 111–114

Temme, Jim. Calling a team a team doesn't mean that it is: Successful teamwork must be a way of life. *Plant Engineering* 49: 1, January, 1995, p. 112

Index

463